Jebel Dhahran
and the New Saudi Generation

DS
215
S96
1993

A Personal Encounter

LAMAR UNIVERSITY LIBRARY

By

WALTER S. SYMONDS, JR. AIA

Copyright© 1990 by Walter S. Symonds, Jr.
All rights reserved.

Library of Congress Cataloging in Publication Data
Jebel Dhahran and the New Saudi Generation – A Personal Encounter
Bibliography
Includes Index

1. Saudi Arabia – History / Development / Government
2. King Fahd University of Petroleum & Minerals (KFUPM) -Dhahran
3. Personal Encounter

93-072890 CIP

ISBN 0-9638758-0-9

Published 1993 by Brockton Publishing Company
8326 Southwest Freeway
Houston, Texas 77074
1-800-968-7065

Printed in the United States of America

To: The New Generations - Both East and West

"... and as for Ishmael, I have heard Thee: behold, I have blessed him, and will make him fruitful, and will multiply him exceedingly; and will make him a great nation."

> The Holy Bible
> Genesis 17: 20

"Lord, Thou has been our dwelling place in all generations."

> The Holy Bible
> Psalms 90: 1

"We believe in God, and the revelation given to us, and to Abraham, Ismail, Isaac, Jacob, and the tribes, and that given to Moses and Jesus, and that given to prophets from their Lord: We make no difference between one and another of them: and we bow to God."

> The Holy Koran
> Sura ii 136

"To God belong both east and west: He guideth whom He will to a way that is straight."

> The Holy Koran
> Sura ii 142

"The aim of this government is to do its best for the benefit of the people... We are still in the study, planning, and initiation stage. We are still newcomers to the world of efficient administration and scientific development. However, when comparing our progress, timewise, with other developing nations, we find that we have achieved a great deal comparatively speaking.

We are going ahead with extensive planning, guided by our Islamic laws and beliefs, for the progress of the nation and the good of the people.

We have chosen an economic system based on free enterprise, because it is our conviction that it fits perfectly with our Islamic laws and suits our country by granting every opportunity to the people, giving incentives to every individual and every group to work for the common good."

        His Majesty
        King Faisal ibn Abdul Aziz al-Saud, 1974

TABLE OF CONTENTS

Author's Note		i
Preface		v
Introduction		vii

I - Historical Background

1.	Jazirat al-Arab - "The Island of the Arabs" - to 1700's	3
2.	The House of Saud - 1700's to 1932	19
3.	The Tangible Resource - 1932 to 1963	27

II - Transition

4.	Kingdom's Developments - 1963 to Today	39
5.	The Royal Hand	47

III - The Intellectual Resource

6.	The Bonds Begin to Break	59
7.	Founding a University - 1963 "The Quest for Excellence"	73
8.	Building the University - 1963 to 1975	93
9.	"A Jewel in the Desert" - KFUPM Today	129

IV - University Assignment - 1975 to 1986

10.	Assignment - 1975	149
11.	Beirut	161
12.	CRS on Site	169
13.	Construction Administration Phase IV - 1975 to 1986	179
14.	The Agony of Implementation	215

V - Personal Encounter - 1975 to 1986

15.	Amenities	245
16.	Character, Culture, and Climate	269
17.	Anomalies	309
18.	Overtones - Religious and Political	317
19.	Visitors	325
20.	Extracurricular	337
21.	Arab Travels - In Kingdom and Out	361

VI - Epilogue

Epilogue		403
Postscript No. 1		409
Postscript No. 2		411
Appendix No. I	1938 Rice Institute Theme	413
Appendix No. II	Dr. Saleh A. Bakhrebah Letter	431
Appendix No. III	Mr. F.W. Ohliger Letter	432
Appendix No. IV	King Addul Aziz Monument Inscription	433
Appendix No. V	Student Yearbook 1968-69	434
Bibliography		463
Index		467

Author's Note

In some books, the acknowledgments exhaustively list people, books, interviews, etc. I think this is done sometimes (particularly when writing of the Arab world) so that no one can be blamed too much for what is said. Real names are often omitted. Others mention editors and researchers who helped in the compilation.

I did most of the research for this book. I have used actual names, feeling that nothing herein should harm anyone. And many unusually talented and courageous people deserve a great deal of credit for their roles at the King Fahd University of Petroleum and Minerals in Dhahran, Saudi Arabia. Without this book to acknowledge their efforts, the world might never know what they accomplished.

Unfortunately, many others (Arab and Western alike) could not be identified in this account. For them, it will have to be as T. E. Lawrence wrote in *Seven Pillars of Wisdom*: "We did what we set out to do, and have the satisfaction of that knowledge."

When one starts a project such as this, there is often considerable self-doubt to overcome. Abdullah K. Mufti, a very patriotic Saudi, gave me initial encouragement. He was interested in seeing something written that would show the Saudis in a different light than they are usually shown to Westerners. Many other writers focus on the negative rather than the good which is readily apparent if one is interested and willing to see it. Thus, Abdullah was taking a chance in encouraging me.

After the book was nearly together, I was grateful for the helpful comments of Dr. Saleh A. Bakhrebah, particularly in regard to Islamic and Saudi history. His keen intellect was also a help in spotting weaknesses in the organization of my material. However, I alone am responsible for the content. Any misrepresentations or inaccuracies are unintentional, but they are my own.

Author's Note

Others in Houston whom I told of the book project said, "It should be done." This included Tom Bullock and Bruce Wilkinson of CRS (Caudill, Rowlett and Scott) and personal friends such as Hugh Gragg, Lynn Ashby, Fred Paulus, John Tomfohrde, Bill Ballew, John W. Kennedy, Harold Calhoun, and others whom I regaled on the subject for five years. Of course, my family bore the brunt of this regaling — but they were always encouraging and patient. Our son Richard, an attorney, was helpful in pointing out certain legal considerations of which I would not otherwise have been aware.

I owe a special debt of gratitude to those who were willing to "stick their necks out" with interviews — Abdullah Mufti, Mrs. Margaret Hall, Amedeo Porro, Nadim Nasir, Charles Lawrence, Joe Thomas, Ed Finlay, and Don Wines. I feel that their "conversations" lend much credibility to the story. They were there.

Scott Pendleton, a young journalist from Houston, who had written many articles for the *Saudi Business* magazine and *Arab News* in Saudi Arabia while we were there, returned to Houston to continue writing for various publications, especially on the oil industry. I showed him the rough manuscript in 1990, and he agreed to give it a general editing job. He made a major contribution in helping me organize my various interviews and material on the founding of the university.

In 1991, when I was hesitating, Dr. George Rupp, President of Rice University, encouraged me to complete the book. Mansour al-Saber helped me to break the deadlock at that time and get the project moving.

His Royal Highness, Prince Abdul Aziz bin Salman bin Abdul Aziz al-Saud, who graduated with a Master's degree from the College of Industrial Management at KFUPM, was a source of much encouragement for me to complete the book.

I am grateful that our friend of many years in Washington, D.C., the Honorable Robert H. B. Wade, former United States

Author's Note

permanent representative to UNESCO, took the time to give the manuscript a scholarly review with a polishing touch on its way to the publisher.

Brockton Brown of Brockton Publishing Company was tireless in keeping up with the numerous revisions and the editing that was done.

The King Fahd University of Petroleum and Minerals is a unique accomplishment by the Saudis. I hope that *Jebel Dhahran and the New Saudi Generation* shows this.

Our eleven years in Saudi Arabia were a once-in-a-lifetime "Personal Encounter," which I shall always remember.

Walter S. Symonds, Jr.
Houston, Texas
May 1993

Preface

Imagine life in a barren desert. Rolling dunes of sand are all you see. The distant horizon is as far as your physical world extends. An occasional oasis of date palms with a well of water might be your good fortune. Your most useful possessions are a few camels and goats. A tent is your only protection from the glaring sun or sometimes violent winds.

Under these circumstances, it might be hard not to feel godforsaken. Yet you pray faithfully to a Supreme Being that provides all good.

Suddenly, you have wealth enough to buy anything — but in the desert, there is nothing to buy. However, the desert also demands intelligence, resourcefulness, and a code of living that does not admit defeat or revel in self-pity. You have the ambition to build. But where do you begin?

The above scenario describes Saudi Arabia fifty years ago. In 1963, the "new generation" of Saudis began developing and modernizing their country — an amazing achievement against considerable odds.

My wife and I were fortunate to witness, and to take part to some extent in, these events over an eleven-year period. I participated in a billion dollars' worth of construction at King Fahd University of Petroleum and Minerals (KFUPM) in Dhahran. My wife, Mildred, taught a thousand students at the Saudi Arabian International School (Dhahran Academy). Our work involved us extensively with people of some 48 foreign nationalities as well as young educated Saudis.

Multiply the building activity at the university by a factor of 200 or 300, and you have an idea of the scope of building in Saudi Arabia during the 1970's and '80's. I think that the establishment and building of KFUPM was a cornerstone, a key factor, in Saudi Arabia's successful effort to develop itself.

By 1986, our final year in the Kingdom, many major projects had been completed or nearly so. Touring the country before

Preface

we left reinforced in our minds the magnitude of what had been achieved by the Saudis while we lived there.

On departing Saudi Arabia for the last time in July 1986, we genuinely regretted that we would probably never again see most of our friends there, and that a happy and fruitful experience had ended.

Introduction

Before my wife and I left Saudi Arabia, I had talked a number of times with Saudi friends about writing a book about our experiences in their country. Nearly everyone has thought of writing a book at one time or another, including myself on a previous occasion.

In World War II, as a Navy ensign, absolutely green and inexperienced, I was assigned as skipper of LCI (L) 230, an ocean-going landing craft capable of carrying about 300 infantry for three days. This was after only sixty days training at Northwestern University in Chicago. There I roomed next to John F. Kennedy, also a "sixty-day wonder," who went on to command PT-109, with a much more dramatic experience than mine.

With a crew of three officers — Grant Fitts, Wendell Decker, and myself — and twenty-one equally inexperienced sailors, we set forth in January 1943 from Boston to New York to Norfolk. We then sailed to Panama, Bora Bora, Samoa, Fiji, New Caledonia, and finally Sydney, Australia. After arrival, we went to Port Stephens, north of Sydney to train hundreds of troops in amphibious warfare. I actually did write about this unique experience in letters to my father but never completed it as a book.

So what about our Saudi experience would justify writing a book?

Of the thousands of expatriates working in Saudi Arabia from 1975-1986, we stayed much longer than average. As a result, we saw the total picture.

We were working on a continuing project all the eleven years, and thus were in a position to observe closely the "New Generation of Saudis."

I think what the Kingdom has achieved in the last twenty-five years is unparalleled in the world's history. The ability to accomplish this shows a character in these people not generally recognized by the Western world.

Introduction

Other books have proved disappointing to me because they suggest that flaws in the Arab character are behind the occasional frustrations and irritations Westerners have in dealing with Arabs. Such stereotyping, of course, is arrogant and baseless, especially considering the short time most writers spend among the Arabs to observe them. The typical image of an Arab, whether a Saudi or other, is not necessarily according to fact.

Many Americans are confused as to what constitutes the Arab world (See map). I am going to be talking primarily about the Saudis, who inhabit the large peninsula between the Red Sea and the Persian Gulf, or as they call it, the Arabian Gulf.

My interest in the Saudis spans fifty years, going back to my freshman year in 1938 at Rice Institute in Houston, Texas. There I read regularly the magazine "Asia," a publication on the Middle East. For my year-end theme in English, I chose the subject of "The Arab Nationalist Movement." I struggled through the night before it was due to type it according to Professor Whiting's requirements.

I kept the original of this theme intact, producing it on occasion to show my family when Saudi Arabia and the Middle East were in the news. (I'm afraid it provoked a minimum of interest.)

The theme is reproduced herewith as Appendix I and serves as background information for today's events in Saudi Arabia.

In 1975 my 37-year-old college theme influenced my career when I gave copies to Wallie Scott, the CRS partner who was interviewing me for a job in Saudi Arabia, and to Dr. Saleh Bakhrebah, the dean of business of the university, who confirmed my appointment by CRS. A couple of months later Dr. Bakhrebah said of my 1938 college theme: "Why, that sounds contemporary." His comment emphasized the sad fact that the problems of the Middle East seem very little different from 1938 to 1975 to today.

I learned later that 1938 was also the year that Well Number 7 in Dhahran became the first Saudi well to produce oil. In 1939, King Abdul Aziz came to the Eastern Province with an

Introduction

entourage of 2,000 people and turned the spigot which opened the flow of Saudi oil to the world.

The site of the celebration, as recorded in documentaries by Aramco, is now the location of King Fahd University of Petroleum and Minerals. Floyd Ohliger, manager of Aramco in 1938, recalled that Aramco had prepared temporary housing, complete with utilities, for the King. But Abdul Aziz and his entourage preferred their tents, which they pitched, as near as I could determine, on the site now occupied by the Athletic Stadium at the university.

The wife of Max Steineke, the prime geologist of those early days for Aramco, with their two little daughters, watched 2000 Arabs praying towards Mecca with King Abdul Aziz leading them. They watched from Jebel Dhahran, the hill on which the university is now built.

The coincidence of all this and my own early interest have led me to believe that I can contribute to telling the fabulous story of Saudi Arabia.

In 1965, when CRS started working on the university, it was still eight years before the oil embargo that would quadruple oil prices and bring money flooding into the Saudi desert. Everything was still to be done: roads, communications, infrastructure of all kinds, as well as many amenities or basic comforts for the Saudi people. Truly, Saudi Arabia was then a desert kingdom.

King Faisal characterized the situation best when he made this statement in 1964, as he was dedicating the College of Petroleum and Minerals (later the University of Petroleum and Minerals, and then King Fahd University of Petroleum and Minerals), which was just beginning its first academic year of classes:

> "This institute was a dream to us a few years ago, for we used to look around us and find ourselves frozen in our position and bewildered — neither able to emulate nor to compete with other nations in their progress and

Introduction

their movement forward. God Almighty, however, has eased the path and erased the obstacles which blocked our way. It is not of importance that we build institutes and celebrate their inauguration. The important thing is that we exert all our efforts to benefit from such institutes. To realize what our nation expects from us."

In 1987 I finally decided to write this book with the following objectives:

1. To give a brief history of Saudi Arabia and its rise to a position of major influence on the world scene.
2. To summarize the extensive accomplishments of the Saudis from 1970 to 1987.
3. To relate my wife's and my experiences with the "new Saudi generation" for eleven years of the boom period in Saudi Arabia.
4. To look at the status of Saudi Arabia and the aspirations of the young educated Saudis for the future. To anticipate their role as a world power by the year 2000 A.D., almost four thousand years after Abraham's journey.
5. To anticipate the day when East meets West and the differences are diminished. To see the affinity between Judaism, Christianity, and Islam, the three great monotheistic religions of the world.

Once I began, the first thing I had to overcome in my thinking were comments like "Who's going to read it? Who cares?" Some said, "You've got to have sex, violence, and scandal." I'll admit this almost caused me to abort the project.

My rationale finally was, "I give the American people more credit than that." I believe they can be interested in a people who aspired to build a modern nation in the middle of the world's largest desert. If nothing else, I'll leave it for my grandchildren — "the Newest Generation." In fifty years, perhaps they will like to hear of the amazing things that happened in Saudi Arabia and on Jebel Dhahran in the years 1935-1985 A.D.

PART I

Historical Background

Chapter 1   Jazirat al-Arab —
              "The Island of the Arabs" — to 1700's

Chapter 2   The House of Saud — 1700's to 1932

Chapter 3   The Tangible Resource — 1932 to 1963

"*Sweet are the uses of adversity, which like the toad, ugly and venomous, wears yet a precious jewel in its head.*"

— William Shakespeare

Chapter 1

Jazirat al-Arab — "The Island of the Arabs" — To 1700's

Three factors focus the world's attention on the Middle East today:

Energy — For transportation, the most practical, efficient, and economical source of energy to date is crude oil, making it the world's most sought-after commodity. The Arabs of the Arabian Peninsula are custodians of the largest reserves.

Religion — From 1900 B.C. (when Abraham made his westward journey across the Arabian Peninsula) until 600 A.D. (when Mohammed established the faith of Islam), man's concept of a Supreme Being solidified around the acceptance of one God only. Thus, the Middle East gave rise to the world's three great monotheistic religions: Judaism, Christianity, and Islam. Judaism came through Abraham and Moses; Christianity through Jesus; and Islam through Mohammed. The precepts of Judaism are found in the Old Testament and the Talmud; those of Christianity in the Old and New Testaments, and those of Islam in the Koran (which strongly resembles the Old Testament in places).

Politics — This is an outgrowth of religion. The human tendency to group according to race, color, and religious beliefs leads inevitably to the desire to define certain territory as "ours." Boundaries then become the focal point of dispute, injustice, and bloodshed.

These factors combine in the Arab-Israeli conflict. The problem is not insurmountable, but overcoming it will require the willingness to take a broader view than just our own and to give

Jebel Dhahran and the New Saudi Generation

as well as take. We must practice the precepts of our religious beliefs, whether we subscribe to Judaism, Christianity, or Islam. In this atomic age we cannot live "to ourselves alone," however much we would like to do so.

At one million square miles, the Arabian Peninsula is the largest such land mass on earth. It is attached on the north to Asia Minor by Jordan, Syria, and Iraq. Otherwise it is bounded by water: the Red Sea on the west, the Gulf of Aden and the Arabian Sea on the south, and the Gulf of Oman and the Persian (Arabian) Gulf to the east.

The ice age in Europe caused the Arabian Peninsula's climate to be far wetter, and the land greener, than now. As the ice retreated 15,000 years ago, it no longer diverted moist Atlantic winds over the mountains of western Arabia, and the land turned to desert. Encompassing the heart of the peninsula, Saudi Arabia, today's most influential Arab country, has not a single river. However, three great rivers — the Nile, the Tigris, and the Euphrates — nurtured early, significant Arab civilizations outside the peninsula.

Archaeology indicates that the peninsula had inhabitants who were hunters, who used flint tools and hand axes during Paleolithic (Stone Age) times as early as 50,000 B.C. Neolithic and Bronze Age artifacts show that habitation continued beyond 3,500 B.C. Old Testament genealogies indicate that Hebrews, Arameans, and Arabs all descended from the eldest of Noah's three sons, Shem (SEM); hence the term "Semitic."

One theory holds that Arabia was the original home of all the Semites, and that evidences of ancient Semitic culture in the Fertile Crescent (the Euphrates Valley to Syria, Jerusalem, and beyond) indicate an overflow of nomadic people who chose to migrate and settle there. The Arabs, meanwhile, gave their name to the peninsula, calling it Jazirat al-Arab (Island of the Arabs).

The desert nomads of Arabia most likely descended from

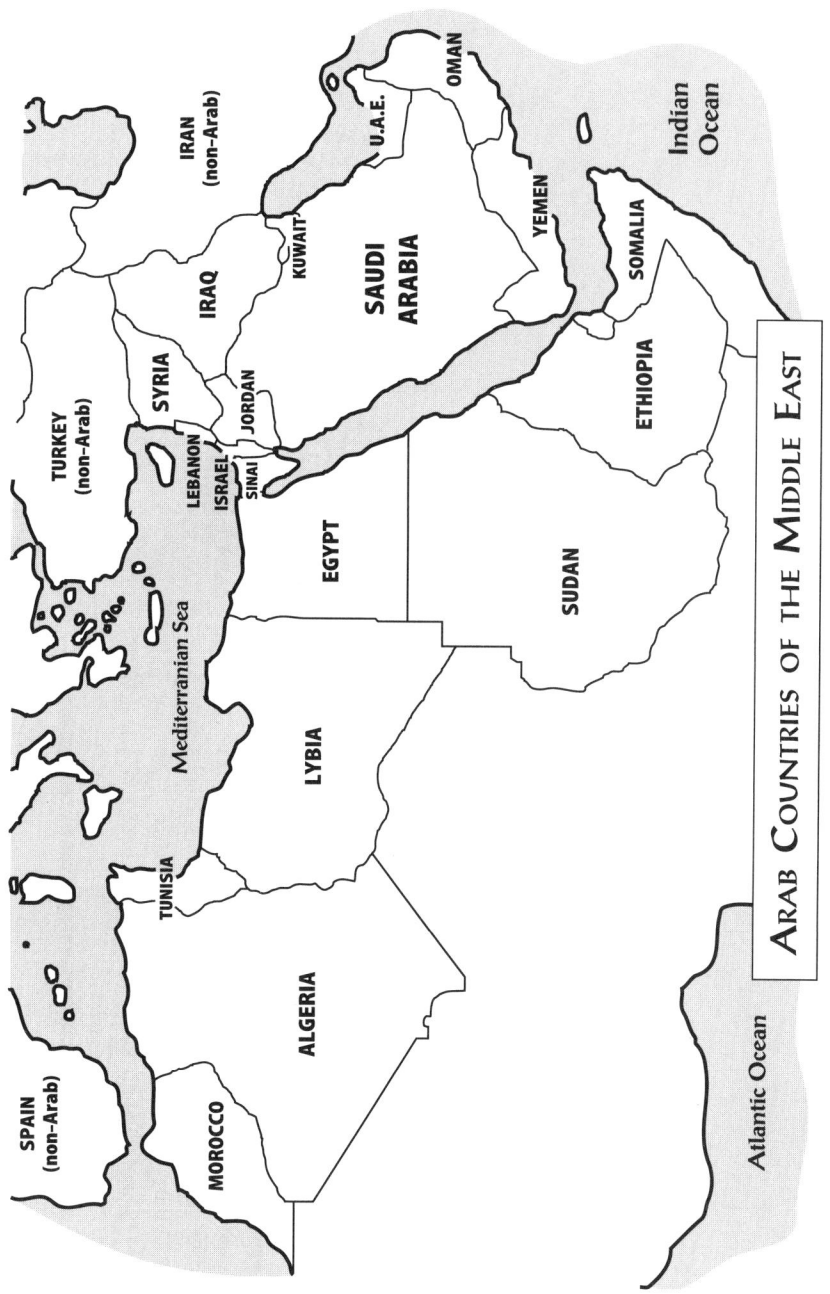

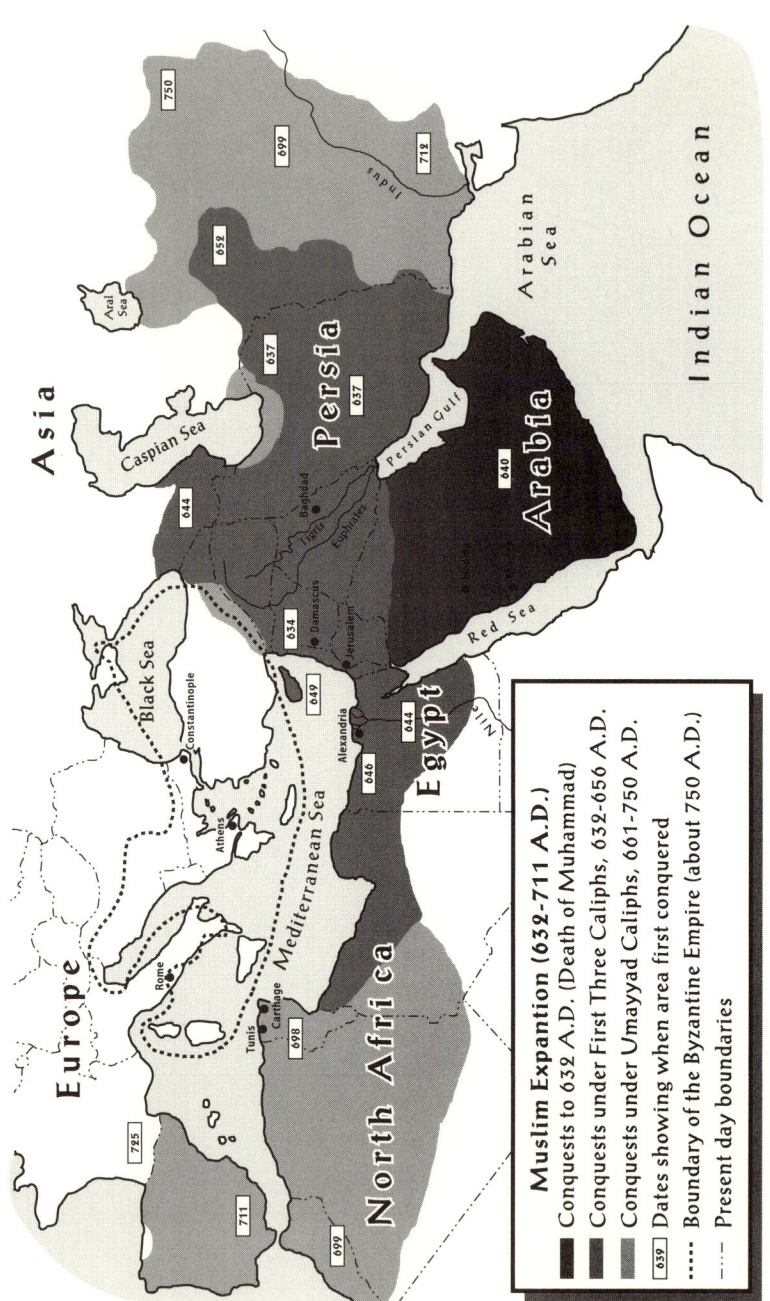

THE ARABIAN PENINSULA

Jebel Dhahran and the New Saudi Generation

two stocks, those from the southwest corner and those from the north. The northern group is reputed to be the descendants of Ishmael, the son of Abraham and the bond woman, Hagar. However, the civilizations of southern Arabia had notable similarities to the northern cultures, indicating a mutual Semitic origin.

The term "Middle East" accurately describes the Arab World. Lying athwart three continents — Europe, Africa, and Asia — its merchants were the middlemen for the passage of ideas as well as things. At the same time, though, formidable mountain ranges on three sides of the peninsula, as well as the harsh desert character of the interior, allowed the Arabian heartland to develop in isolation for long periods.

Several civilizations flourished in the period from 1,000 B.C. In present-day Yemen, the most notable was the Kingdom of Saba, land of the famous Queen of Sheba. The Arabs of the north were the "masters of the deserts." They developed a great network of caravan routes and the efficient use of the camel.

The main trade route from Yemen was along the west coast, through Mecca and Medina, then with branches to Mesopotamia, Syria, and Palestine and across Sinai into Egypt. Other branches went east and north from Najran in the southwest to Mesopotamia (now Iraq) and the Persian (Arabian) Gulf.

Sometime after 300 B.C. in what is now Jordan, the Nabateans, probably descendants of desert nomads, developed a civilization. Its centers were Palmyra, Petra, and farther to the south Madain Saleh, in what is now northwestern Saudi Arabia. Petra and Madain Saleh have remarkably similar tombs carved from sandstone cliffs. Egyptian, Greek, and Roman motifs indicate that the Nabateans had some contact with those cultures. In the 1st century A.D., Petra was absorbed into the Roman Empire as the province of Arabia Petrae. Madain Saleh, however, or any part of what is now Saudi Arabia, never came under the Roman sway.

Jazirat al-Arab — "The Island of the Arabs" — To 1700's

After the birth of Jesus in Bethlehem of Judea and his ministry, Christianity spread throughout the Roman Empire and beyond into Africa and into southern Arabia. Najran became a Christian center. There were churches in Aden, Sanaa, Hadhramaut, and on the island of Tarut near Qatif, in what is now the Eastern Province of Saudi Arabia. There were also Judaic influences in some of those areas.

Several trade centers developed on Arabia's west coast from the third to the sixth centuries, notably Tabuk, Khaybar, Medina, and Mecca. Mecca was destined to be the most important place in Arabian and Islamic history. It was built around the ancient shrine, the Kabah, which was built by Abraham and Ishmael, according to the Koran.

In 570, a child named Mohammed was born in the Quraysh tribe, the resident tribe of Mecca. After a normal upbringing by his grandfather and uncle (his father died before his birth and his mother died before he was six), including two years of the bedouin life of solitude, Mohammed married and had four daughters. He travelled widely as a merchant with trading caravans.

When in his forties, he began to spend time in seclusion in a cave on Mount Hira, outside of Mecca. There he received revelations enjoining him to proclaim the "Oneness of God" to all and to abolish the idolatry that prevailed at the Kabah. The revelations continued and were later incorporated in the Koran, the Scripture of Islam.

Mohammed's preaching antagonized idolatrous Meccans, who forced the Prophet to flee to Medina. However, his followers, known as Muslims, continued to increase and assumed a more militant character. In 629, he reentered Mecca without bloodshed, destroyed the idols in the Kabah, and ended pagan practices there.

Soon after this triumph, Mohammed died in 632.

Jebel Dhahran and the New Saudi Generation

Before his death, Mohammed appointed Abu Bakr to succeed him as the leader of the Muslims. Abu Bakr, who had accompanied Mohammed to Medina and stood by him for ten years, became the First Caliph (Successor).

Abu Bakr appointed Umar to be the Second Caliph. Within four years after Mohammed's death, the Muslim state had extended its influence over all of Syria and blunted the power of the Byzantines. This was followed by similar successes in Persia. Umar served as Caliph for about twenty years.

After Umar's death an advisory council, composed of six Companions of the Prophet who had been appointed by Umar, selected the Third Caliph, Uthman. His greatest accomplishment was the compilation of the text of the Koran as revealed to Mohammed. However, administrative weaknesses developed. Uthman was killed, causing a rift in the community of Islam that has never closed.

When Ali, cousin and son-in-law of the Prophet, was chosen to be the Fourth Caliph, the rift widened. Ali's election was not recognized by supporters of Uthman, who believed that he died at the hands of Ali's followers. This conflict eventually resulted in Islam's division into two major sects: the Sunnis and the Shiites (the partisans of Ali).

The difference is primarily political — the choice of the Caliph, or Successor, of Mohammed. They both observe the same basic rituals, but the Shiites have some additional rituals which the Sunnis do not accept.

The Shiites believe the Caliphate must remain in the family of the Prophet, with Ali as the first valid Caliph. The Sunnis believe that the Caliph (or Imam) is the Guardian of the "Sharia," or religious law, not necessarily succeeded by family.

In 661, Ali was murdered. His son Hasan was proclaimed Caliph, but soon deferred to Muawiyah, who was then recognized as Caliph in all the Muslim territories. This was the

Jazirat al-Arab — "The Island of the Arabs" — To 1700's

beginning of the **Umayyad Dynasty** which ruled for ninety years until 751.

The power center of the Umayyads was Damascus. With this shift and the end of the first four Caliphates, a change of attitude was apparent. Previously the extension of Islamic rule was primarily based on a desire to spread the Word of God. While the Muslims used force when they met with resistance, they did not compel their enemies to accept Islam. They permitted Christians and Jews to practice their own faith. However, with the Umayyads, secular concerns became more predominant, sometimes at the expense of religious concerns.

Under the Umayyads, Islamic power extended north toward Russia, east to India and the borders of China, west to North Africa, and in Europe as far as the Loire Valley in France by 713.

Lesser Umayyad Caliphs succeeded until groups from Khorasan and Mesopotamia proclaimed Abu al-Abbas Mansour to be Caliph. His ancestry traced to al-Abbas, an uncle of Mohammed. This ended the Umayyad Dynasty in the Middle East and began the *Abbasid Dynasty.*

However, one Umayyad prince, Abdul Rahman ibn Muawiyah al-Dakhil, fled to Spain. In 756 he set up a new Umayyad dynasty. He reigned in southern Spain (Andalusia) with wisdom and justice, treating Christians and Jews with tolerance. He improved trade and agriculture, patronized the arts, made valuable contributions to science, and established Cordoba as the most sophisticated city in Europe, along with Seville, Granada, and Alhambra.

During the centuries that the Umayyads were flourishing in Spain, the Abbasids gained control in the Middle East and transformed the Umayyad Arab empire into a multi-national Muslim empire. The capital moved from Syria to Iraq, where the fabulous city of Baghdad was built.

Jebel Dhahran and the New Saudi Generation

The Abbasids enjoyed a high caliber of Caliphs, notably Harun al-Rashid, who came to power in 786. Trade expanded to India, the Philippines, Malaysia, the East Indies, and China. This period has become known as the Golden Age of Islam, in science, technology, literature, history, linguistics, mathematics, astronomy, medicine, and chemistry. The advances that were made by the Abbasids during the eighth and ninth centuries provided much of the impetus for the European Renaissance.

Under subsequent Caliphs, however, things declined. Although the religious authority of the Abbasid Caliphate remained unchallenged, political power was dispersed among independent states for the next four centuries.

The *Fatamid Dynasty* founded in the ninth and tenth centuries, was a branch of the Shiites. Its followers began in North Africa in about 952 and expanded to Egypt. Their achievements were impressive. At their peak they controlled North Africa, the Red Sea coast, Yemen, Palestine, and parts of Syria. They survived to the second half of the twelfth century.

During the tenth and eleventh centuries, the coming of the *Seljuks* was the first penetration of Turkish elements into the Middle East. They were descended from a Turkish chief named Seljuk. Under their first three Sultans, they established a highly cohesive, well administered Sunni state under the nominal authority of the Abbasid Caliphs of Baghdad.

In the eleventh century began the period of Christian reconquest of Spain. The many rulers of Islamic Spain could not maintain their unity, and their kingdoms diminished. However, they continued until, in 1492, the Muslim kingdom was decisively defeated and annihilated by King Ferdinand and Queen Isabella. The remnant eventually emigrated mainly to North Africa.

By the early seventeenth century, few Arabs or Muslims remained in Spain. But the exquisite beauty of Alhambra, Seville, Granada, and Cordoba stand as a lasting memorial to that grand period of Islamic history and culture.

This was the status of the Muslim world at the end of the eleventh century as the Crusaders appeared on their first successful invasion:

1. The *Seljuks* in control of lands east of the Mediterranean and the Arabian Peninsula, including Oman and the Hijaz.
2. The *Fatamids* in control of Egypt and Sinai.
3. The remnant of the Byzantine Empire north of the Mediterranean.
4. The *Berber* nomads in control in Morocco.
5. The remnant of the *Umayyads* still in Spain.

The *First Crusade* began in 1095. It was an unbelievably ambitious mission against tremendous odds. The fervor and determination of the participants resulted in the successful capture of Jerusalem in 1099. The *Second Crusade* confronted Salah al-Din (Saladin). The Arab warrior eclipsed the Crusader attack in 1187, and recaptured Jerusalem. Further crusades were mounted over the next one hundred years, but never regained the initiative. Their final defeat was at the end of the thirteenth century by the Egyptian *Mamluks*. The crusades had a long-range effect on Western society, in terms of opening up the eastern Mediterranean to European trade and shipping.

Jebel Dhahran and the New Saudi Generation

In the thirteenth century, the ***Mongols***, led by Ghengis Khan, swept through the Muslim world to Baghdad by 1258, and put an end to the remnants of the once glorious "Abbasid Empire." In this disaster was lost much of the priceless cultural, scientific, and technological legacy that Muslim scholars had been enlarging for five centuries. What remained has been significant to mankind as a whole.

In the fourteenth century, Mongols drove Turkish tribes from their homeland in the steppes of Central Asia. The tribes embraced Islam and settled in Anatolia, where they formed the ***Ottoman Confederation***Under a chieftain named Othman, they had conquered much of present-day Greece and Turkey by the second half of the fourteenth century. In 1453 they finally conquered Constantinople.

The Ottomans had a special talent for administrative efficiency. Under the rule of Suleiman the Magnificent (1520-1566), they established an empire that at its height was comparable in size and splendor to that of the Romans.

In the sixteenth century three Muslim empires prospered:

1. The ***Ottomans*** under Suleiman.
2. ***Safavid Persia***under Shah Abbas the Great.
3. ***Mogul India*** under Akbar the Great.

In the Arabian Peninsula, Ottoman control extended to al-Hasa on the Arabian Gulf and to Yemen on the Red Sea. The Sharifs of Mecca and Medina, whose authority stemmed from being descendants of Mohammed, remained virtually independent. The Ottomans began a gradual decline in the middle of the sixteenth century to World War I. Under Mustafa Kemal Ataturk, the Sultanate was abolished, a republic was declared in Turkey, and in 1924 the Caliphate was also abolished.

Jazirat al-Arab — "The Island of the Arabs" — To 1700's
_____

In the latter part of the nineteenth century, the European powers began to dominate the Middle East, moving into the vacuum left by the long decay and decline of the last great Muslim empire, the Ottomans.

The invasion of Egypt by Napoleon in 1798 began more than 150 years of direct political intervention by the West, setting the stage for today's dilemma in the Middle East. In 1820, Great Britain imposed a pact on the Arab tribes in the Arabian Gulf region; in the 1830's France occupied Algeria; in 1839 Britain occupied Aden, at the entrance to the Red Sea; and in 1869 the French completed the Suez Canal. The French occupied Tunisia in 1881. Britain took control of Egypt in 1882, and Italy seized Libya in 1911.

In World War I, the Ottoman Empire sided with Germany. Great Britain encouraged and supported the Arabs in their revolt against the Turks. After the Arabs successfully pushed the Turks out of Arab lands, ending five hundred years of Turkish domination, France and Great Britain secretly agreed to partition the Arab provinces under mandates of the League of Nations:

1. Britain over Iraq, Palestine, and Transjordan.
2. France over Syria and Lebanon.

The mandates were contrary to British promises made to the Arabs and have been generally characterized as a "betrayal" that has generated, to a great extent, today's problems in the Middle East.

In 1896 Theodor Herzl published a pamphlet, "The Jewish State," which led to the formal development of *Zionism*, the quest to establish such a state. The Zionist claim to Palestine was based mainly on the historical fact that there had been periods of Hebrew rule in Canaan and the land west of the

Jebel Dhahran and the New Saudi Generation

Jordan River between 130 B.C. and 70 A.D.

The Arabs consider this claim invalid and point out that Palestine has been part of the Islamic world continually for twelve centuries — 636 to 1917.

The Balfour Declaration in 1917, issued by Arthur James Balfour, the British Foreign Secretary, promised British support for a "national home" for the people in Palestine, providing nothing was done to prejudice the civil and religious rights of existing non-Jewish communities, i.e., the Arabs, who were 93% of the population.

The Zionist leaders interpreted this to mean a sovereign Jewish state. However, Lord Balfour, Winston Churchill, and President Wilson's King-Crane Commission said publicly that the declaration did not necessarily imply a Jewish state.

During three decades of the British mandate, militant Zionists conducted continuous underground warfare against the British. Jewish immigration increased. Some recent leaders in Israel such as Menachim Begin and Yitzhak Shamir were leaders in this underground warfare against Great Britain. Finally, the British placed the problem in the hands of the United Nations, and in 1947 the United Nations voted to partition Palestine into Jewish and Arab states.

Neither Arabs nor Jews were satisfied. When Great Britain withdrew, the two sides went to war. The Jews prevailed, and the State of Israel was proclaimed in 1948. A state of war has existed between the Arab states (except for Egypt, which negotiated the Camp David Accords in 1979) and Israel to this day. Three to four million Palestinians, who fled homes in Israel, now exist as exiles.

Generally, in the Arab world since World War II, the last vestiges of political domination by Western nations has been eliminated. Arabs have assumed control of their own destinies. The major outside influences have been the United States and

Jazirat al-Arab — "The Island of the Arabs" — To 1700's
___

the now-defunct Soviet Union maneuvering for domination. In the Arab world, Saudi Arabia, the home of Islam, has a special prominence, because of its great wealth and petroleum resources.

Between the death of Mohammed and the rise of the **Wahhabi Reform Movement** in the eighteenth century, the history of much of the Arabian Peninsula was not well chronicled. The Islamic dynasties in Syria, Iraq, and Spain overshadowed the "Island of the Arabs," except for Mecca and Medina. The Sharif of Mecca, a descendent of the prophet and an ancestor of the present King Hussein of Jordan, was virtually an independent ruler. The annual pilgrimage to Mecca turned the holiest city in Islam into a prosperous center of trade as well. Islam spread to faraway kingdoms. The fabulous "Caravans to Mecca" continued to flourish.

During this period, the control of central Arabia was mainly in the hands of various tribal chiefs and Amirs. A few explorers from the West made incursions into these areas in the eighteenth and nineteenth centuries and wrote about their exploits. Otherwise, the "Island of the Arabs" remained relatively unknown, an enigma to the Western world.

During the first half of the twentieth century, Abdul Aziz ibn Abdul Rahman al-Faysal al-Saud was to change all that.

CHAPTER 2

THE HOUSE OF SAUD
— 1700'S TO 1932

In the early eighteenth century, Najd, the central region of the peninsula, saw events which would shape the future of what is now Saudi Arabia.

These began with the birth of Muhammad ibn Abdul Wahhab, the son of a religious judge versed in the Sharia law. Abdul Wahhab grew up in the village of al-Uyanyah, north of Riyadh, and studied in Mecca and Medina.

Abdul Wahhab observed that, over the years, superstition and cult devotion to local saints had arisen in Islam's birthplace, perhaps because of the great isolation of many areas. Disturbed by this trend of religious thought and the political and social problems of his time, Abdul Wahhab began to call for a return to the basic principles of Islam as contained in the Koran and Sunna, the teaching of "the absolute oneness of God."

As with most reformers, he ran into opposition. He was driven from al-Uyanyah and took refuge in nearby al-Diriyah. The ruler of that area, Muhammad ibn Saud, welcomed him and agreed to put his force of arms behind Abdul Wahhab's reform campaign. This relationship established by the two men binds their descendants to this day.

Abdul Wahhab's followers called themselves al-Muwahidun, "those who affirm the unity of God," or "Unitarians." After Muhammad ibn Saud died in 1765, his son, Abdul Aziz, continued to lend muscle to the Reformist Movement of Abdul Wahhab. In 1773, three years before the American Declaration of Independence, Abdul Aziz captured Riyadh and by 1788 controlled all of Najd.

Abdul Wahhab died in 1792, but the "Wahhabist" movement grew under the leadership of the House of Saud, which retained political control in Najd after the death of Abdul Aziz in 1803. By the early nineteenth century, the House of Saud controlled most of the Arabian Peninsula, including much of Oman, parts of Yemen, and the holy cities of Mecca and Medina.

The al-Saud incursions into what had been territories of the Ottoman Empire began to alarm the Ottoman Sultan in Constantinople (Istanbul). He ordered Muhammad Ali, governor of the Ottoman Province of Egypt, to undertake an expedition against the Saudis to reestablish Ottoman authority over the holy cities.

After several unsuccessful attempts, Muhammad Ali sent his son, Ibrihim Pasha, into Arabia at the head of a powerful army. In 1818 he arrived in Najd. He captured Diriyah from the Saudi ruler, Abdullah, and leveled the town. A year later, thinking he had destroyed the al-Sauds, Ibrihim returned to Egypt.

Another member of the Saud clan, Turki ibn Abdullah, had taken refuge, however, in a nearby town. In 1823 he mustered supporters and retook Diriyah and Riyadh without a fight. He then made Riyadh the capital of the new House of Saud, as it has remained to this day. Turki reigned for eleven years and restored most of the Saudi state, though he did not recover Mecca and Medina. He established a responsible government based on Islam and attempted to elevate the people to live according to its teachings.

Turki died in 1834 and was succeeded by his son Faysal ibn Turki. However, the Egyptians again gained control over Najd and in 1838 Faysal was imprisoned in Egypt. He escaped and returned to Najd in 1843, ruling until his death in 1865.

Following Faysal's death, rivalry over succession weakened Saudi unity. Taking advantage, the Ottomans in 1871 again occupied much of the peninsula's eastern seaboard.

In 1889, Abdul Rahman ibn Faysal emerged as ruler of the House of Saud. During the uncertainties of the Saud succession,

The House of Saud — 1700's to 1932

another family, the House of Rashid, had risen to power in the north central region of Hail. Attacks and counterattacks between the two dynasties continued until a Rashid victory on January 21, 1891. Abdul Rahman and his family took refuge in Qatar, Bahrain, and finally Kuwait, where they remained for ten years as guests of the al-Sabah family, the rulers there.

From the above, it can be seen that the family ties of the kingdoms of the Gulf States are strong and have existed for the most part for hundreds of years. The al-Sabah family still rules in Kuwait, the al-Thanis in Qatar, and the al-Khalifas in Bahrain. In the United Arab Emirates, which includes Dubai, Abu Dhabi, and Sharjah, as well as in Oman, the ruling families also have been in power for many generations. To the north and westward in Iraq, Syria, Lebanon, Jordan, and Egypt, political factions and partitioning have altered the sovereignties of the Arab states.

In 1901, at the age of twenty-one, Abdul Rahman's son Abdul Aziz ibn Abdul Rahman al-Faysal al-Saud (later know to the West as "Ibn Saud" and to his followers as "Abdul Aziz"), set off from Kuwait with forty men for Najd in an effort to reestablish the "House of Saud" as ruler of Central Arabia.

On January 16, 1902, after a legendary battle at the main gate to al-Musmak Fortress, the city of Riyadh was firmly in Saudi hands. However, Abdul Aziz faced a long, hard campaign to overcome completely the House of Rashid and its Turkish allies.

Abdul Aziz's strategy, in view of his enemies' greater strength, was to win the loyalties of tribesmen in regions where the control of the Rashids was tenuous. In 1902, Ibn Rashid was defeated by Abdul Aziz and forced to retreat to Hail. This victory strengthened Abdul Aziz's prestige with the people of Najd. After continuing battles, in 1904, Abdul Aziz became the undisputed master of Central Najd.

Jebel Dhahran and the New Saudi Generation

Ibn Rashid then enlisted the help of his Turkish allies and continued attacks in the Qasim area, but he was killed near Buraydah in April 1906. This ended the four-year contest between the Rashids and the Sauds.

About two years later, Abdul Aziz faced another adversary, Sharif Hussein ibn Ali. Hussein had been appointed Amir of Hijaz and the Holy Cities in 1908 by the Ottoman Government. He considered Hijaz as the kingdom of his family, the Hashemites. The Hijaz was tied to the Ottoman Empire by the newly completed railway, which the Turks built between Damascus and Medina.

Another weak spot in Abdul Aziz's rule was that the allegiance of the bedouin tribes was tenuous because of complex family relationships and tribal feuds. Abdul Aziz's strategy was to try to settle the bedouin in agricultural communities. He sent them teachers, who exhorted them to support a revival of pure Islam. Those who responded were known as Ikhwan, or "Brethren," and they grouped together in settlements with subsidies from Abdul Aziz. Soon there were many Ikhwan settlements throughout the Najd at strategic locations. The Ikhwan became the elite troops of Abdul Aziz.

After successfully consolidating the Najd, Abdul Aziz knew that his next target had to be the Turks, who still controlled eastern Arabia. With the Ikhwan, he overcame the Turkish forts at Hofuf, al-Uqayr, and Qatif. This completed the consolidation of al-Hasa.

The Turks continued to try to arm the House of Rashid, which was subdued by Ibn Saud but still hostile. To counter this, Abdul Aziz began discussions with the British, whom he had previously distrusted. This led to the Anglo-Saudi treaty of 1915, in which Britain recognized Ibn Saud as hereditary ruler of Najd, al-Hasa, Qatif, Jubail, and their dependencies in return for his support in World War I.

The House of Saud — 1700's to 1932

In 1914, Britain and the Ottoman Empire were the two powers in the Middle East. Britain controlled Egypt, the Suez Canal, Aden, and the Arabian (Persian) Gulf. The Turks exerted authority over Palestine, Syria, Mesopotamia (Iraq), and the Red Sea coast down to Yemen.

At the outbreak of World War I, Britain set out to take Mesopotamia from the Turks. It sought Abdul Aziz's help against the House of Rashid, the allies of the Ottomans. Britain also encouraged Sharif Hussein to drive the Turks from the Hijaz, on the west coast. This campaign immortalized T.E. Lawrence — "Lawrence of Arabia." Lawrence never fought alongside Ibn Saud, but as an ally of Ibn Saud's rival, Sharif Hussein.

To keep the Arabs as allies, the British secretly agreed with Hussein to support creation of an independent Arab state comprising most of the Arab lands east of Egypt. But after the war, the Allies recognized Hussein as king of only the Hijaz. Britain and France, by mandates, took over a large part of the territories that Hussein thought he had been promised — Palestine, Iraq, and Syria. These mandates constituted the famous "betrayal" of the Arabs.

This partitioning by Britain and France, along with the advent of the Zionist Movement, caused to a great extent today's turmoil in the Middle East.

The Rashids continued their persistent challenges to Abdul Aziz, who finally besieged their headquarters in Hail. After three months, Hail capitulated. The long rivalry between the two houses was at an end for all time.

From the end of World War I in 1918 until 1927, Abdul Aziz expanded his domain northward to al-Jawf and westward to Khaybar and Tayma. He took over Taif in September 1924. In October, Sharif Hussein left Jeddah for exile in Cyprus. His son,

Jebel Dhahran and the New Saudi Generation

Ali, assumed his throne as King of Hijaz; but Ali soon abandoned Mecca, and Abdul Aziz assumed control. Medina surrendered in December 1925. Two weeks later Jeddah capitulated. In January 1926, the citizens of Mecca acknowledged Abdul Aziz as King of Hijaz, including the holy cities.

Abdul Aziz's domain now extended from Iraq on the north to the Rub al-Khali on the south, and from the Arabian Gulf on the east to the Red Sea on the west. He convened an Islamic congress in Mecca in the summer of 1926 to reassure Muslims throughout the world of his recognition of the responsibilities which he now carried as Protector of the Holy Cities.

He then began the task of controlling the fiercely independent bedouin tribes. He made tribal chiefs individually responsible for maintaining law and order in their tribes. He would intervene only if they failed to do so. The tribes achieved a growing sense of unity, and rivalry between them diminished.

In January 1927, Abdul Aziz was officially proclaimed King of Hijaz, Sultan of Najd and its dependencies, with Riyadh and Mecca as his two capitals. In May of 1927, Great Britain in the treaty of Jeddah formally recognized the kingdom as a fully sovereign state.

On September 22, 1932, the country was renamed the Kingdom of Saudi Arabia. The Saud dynasty was now on track and heading for its great place in world history.

King Abdul Aziz (Ibn Saud) of Saudi Arabia (seated) with his son, Crown Prince Saud, who became king

The Saudi Dynasty

A.D.	A.H.*	
1726-65	1139-79	Mohammed Ibn Saud (39 years)
1765-1803	1179-1218	Abdul Aziz Ibn Mohammed (38 years)
1803-13	1218-29	Saud Ibn Abdul Aziz (10 years)
1813-17	1229-33	Abdullah Ibn Saud (4 years)
1817-19	1233-5	Period of occupation by the forces of Mohammed Ali and Ibn Muammar (2 years)
1819	1235	Mishari Ibn Saud (1 year)
1819-33	1235-49	Turki Ibn Abdullah Ibn Mohammed (14 years)
1834	1250	Mishari Ibn Abdul Rahman Ibn Mishari Ibn Saud (40 days)
1834-8	1250-4	Faisal Ibn Turki (1st time; 4 years)
1838-41	1254-7	Khalid Ibn Saud (3 years)
1841-3	1257-9	Abdullah Ibn Thunaian Ibn Saud (2 years)
1843-65	1259-82	Faisal Ibn Turki (2nd time; 22 yrs)
1865-9	1282-6	Abdullah Ibn Faisal (1st time; 4 yrs)
1869-74	1286-91	Saud Ibn Faisal (5 years)
1874-84	1291-1302	Abdullah Ibn Faisal (2nd time; 10 yrs)
1884-9	1302-7	Period of Al Rashid (5 years)
1889-91	1307-9	Abdul Rahman Al-Faisal (2 years)
1891-2	1309-10	Mohammed Ibn Faisal (1 year)
1892-1902	1310-19	Period of regime of Al Rashid (10 yrs)
1902-53	1319-73	King Abdul Aziz Ibn Saud (51 years)
1953-64	1373-84	King Saud (11 years)
1964-75	1384-95	King Faisal (11 years)
1975-82	1395-1402	King Khalid (7 years)
1982-	1402-	King Fahd

*Anno Hegirae, the Mohammedan era.

CHAPTER 3

THE TANGIBLE RESOURCE
— 1932 TO 1963

In 1932, when King Abdul Aziz proclaimed his Kingdom of Saudi Arabia to the world, Iran and Iraq were the only two oil-producing nations in the region. The economy of his own new nation was based primarily on agriculture, stock raising, and customs receipts from pilgrims visiting Mecca. The latter were dropping considerably because of the world-wide depression that prevailed. These revenues were insufficient to develop and manage a new country.

The presence of oil in Iran and Iraq and prospects in Bahrain naturally caused eyes to turn westward toward Saudi Arabia, which, being the only country in the Middle East outside the sphere of Western control, was scarcely known. One pair of eyes that turned in that direction were those of a congenial and energetic New Zealander, Major Frank Holmes.

After active service in World War I, he had appeared in Bahrain in 1922, where he made many British and Arab friends. A syndicate of London financiers, seeking profitable enterprises in the Arabian Gulf area, selected him as its agent in Bahrain.

In the summer of 1922, Holmes travelled to the east coast of Saudi Arabia. He visited with King Abdul Aziz in Riyadh and Hofuf. Sir Percy Cox, the British High Commissioner in Iraq, had advised the King that exploration of al-Hasa was premature, since it lacked the necessary elements of roads, communications, skilled labor, transport, and supply. Still, Holmes obtained a concession to explore for oil over 60,000 square miles of al-Hasa, the Eastern Province of Arabia.

After unsuccessful attempts to interest European and American oil companies, the syndicate let the concession lapse, thus giving up what would prove to be the world's largest oil reserves.

Jebel Dhahran and the New Saudi Generation

In November 1927, Holmes' syndicate sold its concession rights on Bahrain to Eastern Gulf Oil Company. Eastern, in turn, sold its Bahrain option to Standard Oil Company of California (SOCAL). Thus, the first wholly American-owned oil company entered the Middle East arena on August 1, 1930. It soon sent geologists, who concluded that Bahrain indeed had potential and should be drilled.

The American geologists then looked across the fifteen miles of blue-green water to the Arabian shore. Against the horizon the pale outline of "Jebel Dhahran" identified the area that within a decade would give access to quantities of oil that would satisfy the world's needs for at least the next century.

A SOCAL geologist, Fred A. Davies, tried unsuccessfully from May 1930 to get permission to visit King Abdul Aziz. He finally gave up and returned to San Francisco in September without getting to see the King or the Eastern Province, except the view of "Jebel Dhahran" that he had from Bahrain.

About the same time a conversation occurred in Jeddah, on the west coast of the Arabian Peninsula, between King Abdul Aziz and Harry St. John Philby, a British ex-civil servant, an Arabist, a recent convert to Islam, and a friend and adviser to King Abdul Aziz for over a decade. In light of the Kingdom's financial problems, Philby asserted, the King should continue the effort to develop the country's resources.

Not aware that Davies was trying to see the King, Philby recommended that Abdul Aziz invite Charles Crane, a wealthy American philanthropist who had established a reputation as a friend of the Middle East while serving on a commission appointed by President Woodrow Wilson. The King went along with Philby's idea, inviting Crane in 1931. During the visit, Crane offered the services of Karl Twitchell, a mining engineer with Middle East experience.

Twitchell prospected east and west, north and south. He scouted the Eastern Province that Davies had been unable to enter from Bahrain a year earlier. Encouraged by Twitchell's efforts and the drilling successes reported from Bahrain, King Abdul Aziz in 1932 authorized Twitchell to advise oil and mining companies in the United States that he was willing to discuss concessions again.

SOCAL got wind of the King's renewed interest and became fearful of being "shut out." The earlier Bahrain deal tied it to the London syndicate, which didn't want to act. SOCAL finally issued an ultimatum to the syndicate: If nothing was done by November 1st, it would consider itself free to negotiate independently with Ibn Saud. It tried to locate Philby to be its contact man, but he was somewhere in Europe. Unable to wait, SOCAL met Twitchell in Washington and signed him on instead.

Thus, the way was cleared for Lloyd Hamilton, SOCAL's chief negotiator, to land in Jeddah in February 1933.

The Saudi Minister of Finance was Sheikh Abdullah Sulaiman, a very capable and intelligent man — and a shrewd bargainer with that acute ability characteristic of the native traders of the Arabian Peninsula.

Lloyd Hamilton himself was an astute bargainer. After three and a half months of hard negotiations, they reached agreement. The deal was signed at Kazma Palace just outside of Jeddah on May 29, 1933. Amir Faisal, the Saudi Foreign Minister, signed for his father, the King. Amir Faisal would later be King of Saudi Arabia at the beginning of its historic period of economic development.

This was a day the world began to change. East and West were moving closer together. Also, America was becoming involved in the Middle East for the first time — though not yet politically.

The initial concession agreement was for 60 years and included everything in the eastern portion of Saudi Arabia, from Iraq on the north to the southern edge of the Rub al-Khali, and

Jebel Dhahran and the New Saudi Generation

from the Arabian Gulf on the east to the great red sands of the Dahna in Central Arabia — 320,000 square miles of desert. Areas west of the Dahna were covered by later agreements.

SOCAL created a subsidiary, California Arabian Standard Oil Company, or CASOC.

In a couple of months, work was underway by CASOC with a complement of ten men. In early October 1933, they were climbing around Jebel Dhahran, which was thirty years later to be the site of the prestigious King Fahd University of Petroleum and Minerals. Jebel Dhahran was what Fred Davies had earlier looked at longingly from Bahrain. The adjacent area was also to be eventually the world headquarters of Aramco, the Arabian American Oil Company.

At that time, CASOC set up headquarters in Jubail, where its representatives had first landed when crossing from Bahrain. Geological reconnaissance was now underway in the Eastern Province. Gradually the geologists began piecing together the puzzle of Saudi Arabia, which had now begun its emergence into the twentieth century. The early pioneers were blazing the trail.

In March 1934, an airplane was added to the exploration operations. Dick Kerr and Charley Rocheville landed their special Fairchild 71 in Jubail and were promptly arrested by the Amir of Jubail for landing without permission. He had received no direct instructions from his government. After several weeks that was cleared up, and the invaluable work of aerial photography and mapping was underway.

Additional crew members arrived in December 1934, including Floyd Ohliger, a petroleum engineer, who would later become general manager. A camp was established at the foot of Jebel Dhahran, and a pier was built at al-Khobar on the Gulf. Now there were drillers, rig-builders, carpenters, mechanics, a paymaster, and a Chinese cook. While the camp had some comforts, it was by any standards bleak, being treeless and vulnerable to the blinding sun, heat, and sandstorms.

Arabian American Oil Company - Dhahran

1936   Aramco Photo

1976   Aramco Photo

Jebel Dhahran and the New Saudi Generation

The CASOC team began rigging up Dammam Well No. 1. In April 1935, it was spudded in, and one year later, at 3200 feet, it was a disappointment, although the team was drilling below the deepest productive zone of Bahrain. The disappointments continued through Well Nos. 2-6.

Dammam Well No. 7 was spudded in on December 7, 1936. It was to be the first deep test hole. This was the crucial test. If it failed, the operations of CASOC would probably be over.

Through most of 1937, Well No. 7 progressed slowly. In early 1938, Max Steineke was recalled to San Francisco for consultations. The SOCAL management was becoming apprehensive about sinking more money into a "dry hole." Steineke persuaded the head office to continue.

In the meantime, Floyd Ohliger sent encouraging reports. Then on March 4, 1938, Well No. 7 tested at 1,585 barrels per day. Drilling was now being done at about 6,000 feet, over twice the depth of the wells in Bahrain.

The early optimism of the geologists thus proved to be justified, although no one yet realized the extent of their success and the long-range effect this would have on the politics and economy of the whole world.

In February 1939, the official name of the camp became Dhahran. The camp continued expanding, and work was begun on a major port facility at Ras Tanura forty miles to the north, with crude oil storage tanks tied by pipeline to the wells at Dhahran.

King Abdul Aziz decided to visit the site, and a celebration was scheduled for May 1, 1939. The King's caravan from Riyadh was made up of 500 cars and 2,000 people. They reached Dhahran on April 28 and made camp east of Jebel Dhahran. After two days they moved to Ras Tanura, and on May 1, 1939 the King turned the valve that started the flow of oil to the world.

The Tangible Resource — 1932 to 1963

Returning to Dhahran on May 10, Abdul Aziz hosted a banquet for all Americans. After the festivities, the King and his entourage returned to Riyadh.

On May 31, 1939 a final agreement was signed that gave the company operational rights, until 1999, to an area of 49,900 square miles in the north and 66,900 square miles in the south — from Iraq to Yemen — with preferential rights in the Central Najd, subject to further negotiations. This gave CASOC the greatest share of potential oil lands on the Arabian Peninsula, excluding the Qatar Peninsula and the coastal regions to the south that would become the United Arab Emirates.

The stage was now set for Saudi Arabia's transformation into a modern developing nation. But World War II began when Germany invaded Poland in September 1939. The destiny of "Jazirat al-Arab" and "Jebel Dhahran" was to be held in abeyance until 1945. Oil operations were curtailed, and the economy of the fledgling nation suffered, although production remained at 12,000 to 15,000 barrels per day, supporting the allied war effort and justifying the presence of the oil company.

In 1942 an American legation was opened in Dhahran, and in 1944 a Saudi legation was established in Washington. Near the end of World War II, King Abdul Aziz allowed the Americans to build an airfield at Dhahran for servicing Allied planes.

In 1944, the U.S. Government became interested in making greater use of Middle Eastern oil. Approval was given to construct a 50,000-bpd refinery at Ras Tanura. A rush of activity began. The small pioneering operation was soon to become a post-war colossus. The company name was changed on January 31, 1944 from CASOC to the Arabian American Oil Company, ARAMCO. The goal was 550,000 bpd, twenty-five times the existing production. One thousand Americans or more would be needed for the Ras Tanura refinery job. In February 1945, the

King Abdul Aziz hosts Americans - May 1939

President Roosevelt meets King Abdul Aziz - February 1945

wives and families who had left at the beginning of the war began to return. The fabulous post-war era had begun.

King Abdul Aziz met with President Roosevelt in February 1945 in Egypt. In March, Saudi Arabia officially joined the Allied cause in World War II.

In March 1945, Saudi Arabia joined Egypt, Iraq, Lebanon, Syria, Transjordan, and a representative of the Palestinian people in the formation of the Arab League.

In 1945, Prince Faisal headed a Saudi delegation at the founding of the United Nations in San Francisco.

In early 1953, King Abdul Aziz authorized the formation of a Council of Ministers with Crown Prince Saud to act as prime minister.

King Abdul Aziz died on November 9, 1953 after fifty-one years as leader and King of Saudi Arabia. The following appeared in *"Aramco And Its World"* magazine:

"Abdul Aziz's life, by any standards, was remarkable. In 1900, when he was twenty-three years old, the Arabian Peninsula was one of the least known and most isolated areas in the world; when he died on November 9, 1953, Saudi Arabia, because of his efforts, was well on the way to becoming a world power. His achievements indeed were almost unparalleled, and due, by common consent, to a powerful intelligence, unflagging courage, exceptional vision, and above all a profound faith in God."

Abdul Aziz was succeeded by his son, Crown Prince Saud. Although during King Saud's reign relations with neighboring Arab states improved and progress was made in education and social welfare, financial problems became acute. King Saud reigned until November 1964, when he abdicated in favor of Crown Prince Faisal.

Jebel Dhahran and the New Saudi Generation

Prince Faisal had held many important and influential posts as the Viceroy of King Abdul Aziz in Hijaz, Chairman of the Consultative Council, Minister of Foreign Affairs, and Representative to the United Nations Conference. He had traveled extensively and met many heads of state.

After becoming King, he made many progressive administrative changes. The government became more centralized. There are now fourteen administrative districts, five of which are provinces. Better communications facilities have allowed a more centralized form of government under the Council of Ministers.

The Sharia, or fundamental law of Islam, based firmly on the Koran and Sunna (Sayings of the Prophet) remains the essence of the legal system. Matters not expressly covered by the Sharia are regulated by the King through the Council of Ministers.

Part II

Transition

Chapter 4　　Kingdom's Developments — 1963 to Today

Chapter 5　　The Royal Hand

"...We used to look around us and find ourselves frozen in our position and bewildered — neither able to emulate nor to compete with other nations in their progress and their movement forward. God Almighty, however, has eased the path and erased the obstacles which blocked our way."

> — His Majesty
> King Faisal ibn Abdul Aziz al-Saud
>
> at Dedication of the
> College of Petroleum and Minerals
>
> December 1964

Chapter 4

Kingdom's Developments — 1963 to Today

The needs of the Kingdom of Saudi Arabia were mind-boggling in 1963, twenty-five years after Well No. 7 began producing oil in Dhahran.

What did the Kingdom need? Everything!
What did it want? Everything!
It wanted the most; it wanted the best; and it wanted it now!

Geography, climate, politics, religion, culture, logistics — everything would seem to argue that the Saudis could not do or have what they wanted. The priority needs were enormous for a young nation with so little material goods, but with such ambition and potential wealth — which started with nothing but desert, a will to achieve, and a profound faith in God.

The accomplishments in Saudi Arabia in the two decades from 1963 to 1985 were so extensive that it would be presumptuous to attempt to describe them in one chapter in this book. Hopefully, that will be done by others. This book focuses on one major accomplishment that was made during this period — a university. However, in order to acknowledge the extent of the other endeavors around the Kingdom, I shall summarize by categories those achievements as I know of them, leaving others to tell their story in detail.

In 1970, the *First Five-Year Plan* was initiated under the direction of the Minister of Planning, a young Saudi named Hisham Nazer, who had gone early to the United States for education at the University of California, Los Angeles (UCLA).

Following are some of the major categories which had to be addressed by the Saudis in 1963:

1. Education
2. Health Care and Welfare
3. Transportation (including land, sea, and air)
4. Communications
5. Agriculture
6. Electrical Power Systems
7. Water Desalination Plants
8. Commercial and Industrial Development
9. Housing
10. Banking Facilities
11. Military Facilities
12. Sports Facilities
13. Religious Facilities (including Haj Facilities)
14. Municipal Sanitary Systems
15. Governmental Offices — National and Municipal
16. Archaeological Pursuits
17. Tourism Development
18. Private Enterprise.

I shall briefly comment on some of these categories:

1. Education

The present King, Fahd bin Abdul Aziz, was appointed as the first Minister of Education in 1953, the year that King Abdul Aziz died and Fahd's half-brother, Saud, became King.

Fahd was instrumental in establishing the educational system of the Kingdom. He was well aware that without the education of its people, Saudi Arabia could not hope to assume its place in the world in a manner commensurate with the responsibilities thrust upon it as owners and custodians of the world's largest supply of its most vital resource, as well as the custodians of the most holy places of the Islamic religion.

Kingdom's Developments — 1963 to Today

King Saud cuts ribbon at offical opening of the Dammam Primary School - December 7, 1957

In 1953, the total number of students attending schools in Saudi Arabia was 35,000 (males) and there were no universities. In 1987, thirty-four years later, there were enrolled (male and female):

1. One and a half million children in elementary schools.
2. 630,000 children in intermediate and secondary schools.
3. 115,000 in seven universities in Saudi Arabia as well as in other countries.
4. 200,000 in some form of adult education.

Almost 25% of the total population, over two million persons were enrolled in educational classes of some kind!

Consider the impact in a generation or two!

The total number of schools, including institutions of higher education, increased from 3,107 in 1970 to 15,353 in 1987.

The number of boys' schools increased from 2,654 to 8,470 in the same time period and the number of girls' schools increased from 453 to 6,883.

Jebel Dhahran and the New Saudi Generation

There were about 9,719 enrolled in vocational and technical schools in 1987.

The seven major universities in Saudi Arabia are:

1. King Fahd University of Petroleum and Minerals in Dhahran
2. King Saud University in Riyadh
3. King Faisal University in Dammam
4. King Abdul Aziz University in Jeddah
5. Islamic University in Riyadh
6. Islamic University in Medina
7. Islamic University in Mecca

While statistics tend to be somewhat laborious and uninteresting, they are probably the best means of giving a brief overall picture of the incredible activities of expansion that occurred in Saudi Arabia in the period of 1970 to 1987.

Following is a summary of these figures in areas other than Education, already given above.

2. Health Care and Welfare	1970	1987
A. Hospitals	47	150
B. Health Care Centers	519	1,440
C. No. of Beds	7,165	24,644
D. No. of Physicians	789	10,845
E. No. of Nurses	2,253	24,801
F. Technicians	1,396	11,723

Many of the hospitals built in the period of 1970-87 are comparable to the best in the world — in quality of services, maintenance, food, management, and logistics. Many hospitals and clinics are specialized in maternal, dental, pediatrics, and chest and eye facilities.

Kingdom's Developments — 1963 to Today

		1970	1987
3.	**Transportation**		
	A. Kilometers of Earth-Surfaced Roads (Serving 8,000 villages)	3,500	61,500
	B. Kilometers Paved Roads	8,000	30,900
	C. Cumulative No. of Vehicles Registered	60,000	4,400,000
	D. Railroad Passenger Traffic	117,000	166,000
	E. Railroad Freight Traffic (ton/kilometers)	24,000,000	646,800,000
	F. Tons of Cargo Handled at Ports (Jeddah, Dammam, Jubail, Yenbo)	2,000,000	69,500,000
	G. Number of Passengers Handled at Airports (Arrivals and Departures)	1,600,000	20,900,000
	H. Tons of Cargo Handled At Airports (Arr. and Dep.)	15,900	315,100
	I. Number of Revenue Passengers Saudi Arabian Airlines	600,000	10,500,000
4.	**Communications**		
	A. Mail in and out (Pieces)	80,000,000	628,700,000
	B. Telegrams in and out (reduced rate due to growth of telephone and telex)	3,800,000	4,300,000
	C. Telephones	29,400	1,014,000
5.	**Agriculture**		
	A. Wheat (tons)	26,000	2,600,000

Jebel Dhahran and the New Saudi Generation

B.	Fruits and Vegetables (tons)	**1970**	**1987**
	1) Dates	240,000	484,000
	2) Grapes	24,000	100,000
	3) Tomatoes	100,000	346,000
C.	Poultry, Meat, and Eggs (tons)		
	1) Poultry and Meat	7,000	250,000
	2) Eggs	5,000	114,000
D.	Grain Silo Storage Cap.(tons)	40,000	1,580,000
E.	Flour Milling Cap. (tons/day)	270	5,400
F.	Loans to farmers (riyals)	16,600,000	1,000,000,000

6. **Electricity**
   A. Installed Capacity (MW)   344   14,909
   B. Subscribers   216,000   2,040,000

7. **Water Desalination Capacity (gal/day)**
   (13 PLANTS)   5,100,000   421,600,000

8. **Industrial Development**
   A. Chemical Fertilizers (tons)   24,400   950,000
   B. Cement (tons)   670,000   8,700,000
   C. Natural Gas   20.6 billion   32 billion
      (cubic meters) (48% utilization)
   D. Crude Oil Reserves   138.7 billion 169.6 billion
      (barrels)
   E. Crude Oil Production   3.8 million   4.2 million
      (barrels per day)
   F. Gross Domestic Product   17.4 billion   267.6 billion
      (Saudi Riyals)
   G. 1986 Value in-ground of Mineral Resources
      (Saudi Riyals)   not available   73.6 billion

Kingdom's Developments — 1963 to Today

Following are excerpts from the foreword to *Achievements of the Development Plans — 1390 to 1407 HIJRA (1970 to 1987)* by His Excellency Hisham Mohaddin Nazer, Planning Minister, from which the above statistics were compiled:

"Development is no longer questioned in Saudi Arabia as evidence of the country's intrinsic strength or the determination of its people. Indeed, the Kingdom of Saudi Arabia has achieved far more in seventeen years of development planning than many other nations have accomplished in as many decades.

"Throughout its *First and Second Development Plans (1970-1980)*, the Kingdom adopted a strategy with the objective of achieving balanced growth in all sectors. The Kingdom witnessed a remarkable expansion in all stages of education — particularly in girls' education. As a matter of fact, the Kingdom has progressed — in all essential respects — from the ranks of developing nations to those of advanced nations.

"The Kingdom is now covered with a vast network of highways; its shores are dotted with desalination plants; and all parts of the country are linked to the world by a most up-to-date telecommunication system. Loans for housing, agriculture, and industry have been granted; and vast sums have been spent on providing electricity and other utilities. These are only a few examples of the numerous achievements of the Kingdom to build an infrastructure as the basis for economic growth.

"But, all these material achievements notwithstanding, the Kingdom has never wavered in holding fast to its faith and protecting cultural values which are of particular importance in the lives of its citizens.

Jebel Dhahran and the New Saudi Generation

"The *Third Development Plan (1980-1985)* was characterized by the emphasis laid on initiating changes in the national economic structure by directing the greater part of capital and manpower towards productive sectors such as agriculture, industry, and mining. This was clearly reflected in the ever-increasing measure of self-sufficiency in food and agriculture products — and also in the increasing number of factories established.

"The *Fourth Development Plan (1985-1990)* was formulated to ensure continuity with the strategy of the Third Plan. Emphasis is put on efficient use of resources and development of producing sectors and human resources. It also emphasized diversification of the economy and encouraged the private sector's direct participation in the development process.

"The list of achievements is the basis for confidence in the future of the country and its capabilities and is a token of the resolution and faith of its people and their determination to remove all obstructions and overcome all difficulty that may stand in their way. It is also a clear indication of their resolve to triumph over all campaigns of doubt designed to impede the advance.

"The Kingdom has accomplished all these things in full assurance of faith and unbounded hope that God will crown with success the valiant efforts of its Leader, the Custodian of the Two Holy Mosques, King Fahd bin Abdul Aziz, in completing the course and in helping the Kingdom to attain its desired ends in the future as successfully as it has in the past."

Chapter 5

The Royal Hand

After a review of the history of Saudi Arabia, one would have to conclude that the amazing success of the Saudis in developing their country in the relatively brief space of twenty-five years has been to a great extent due to the quality of the leadership that they have enjoyed.

Without question, King Abdul Aziz had a sense of destiny and commitment in restoring his family to rulership of the greater portion of the Arabian Peninsula. As prolific a progeniture as he was, the impressive consequence was the quality of his offspring. The fact that so many of his sons and grandsons are intelligent men committed to the service of their country has made it possible to build a family power base with a control that few rulers have had.

The story of the Saud Family and the founding of the Kingdom of Saudi Arabia in 1932 by Abdul Aziz has been told in earlier chapters, as well as the transition from a desert kingdom of loosely related tribes to a unified modern nation with all the amenities of the twentieth century.

The Kingdom of Saudi Arabia is the only nation in the world named after the ruling family. The power of the King is constrained by the Sharia, the sacred law of Islam, which is based solidly on the teachings of the Holy Koran and Sunna, as revealed to the Prophet Mohammed. This is the primary source of legitimacy for the King. So, in that sense, it is not an absolute monarchy.

King Fahd has gone further and proclaimed that he should not be described as "His Majesty," but simply as "Custodian of the Two Holy Mosques." He has shed the customary cloak of royalty in assuming the duty of guardianship of the two holiest shrines of Islam. In so doing, he has indirectly proclaimed that the majesty accorded to God cannot be assumed by man.

Jebel Dhahran and the New Saudi Generation

The land that is now the Kingdom of Saudi Arabia, is once again in the role it was during the period after the Prophet Mohammed, when the Islamic state reached from China to the southern borders of France.

The Saudis do not distinguish between the state and Islam. The nation's flag shows only a sword and the Islamic creed in Arabic script: "There is no God but Allah, and Muhammad is the messenger of Allah." The Ulema, or religious scholars, are closely aligned with the Saudi royalty and are an effective and conservative force in maintaining traditional social and political values.

The economic modernization of the 1970s and 1980s has created some social and political strains, but the demonstrated stability of the political system is a fact. The present ruler, King Fahd, is the fourth son of Abdul Aziz to serve as king since the death of Abdul Aziz in 1953.

The ideological incompatibility of Islam with Marxism helped to counteract such proclivities in the Middle East. The biggest challenge to Saudi Arabia in recent years has come from the revolutionary Shiite regime in Iran, but this appears to be a manageable threat at this time.

The former rivalry between the United States and the Soviet Union tended to create an affinity between the United States and the Saudis. The Saudis were staunchly anti-communist, because of their fears about Soviet ambitions and oil needs, as well as the godless nature of the Marxist society.

The Arab-Israeli conflict, with the United States as the prime supporter of Israel, has created some strains in the relations with the U.S., although there seems to be an almost natural affinity with the Americans, stemming, no doubt, from the experiences of working together for the past half-century to develop the vital resource of oil.

*King Fahd ibn Abdul Aziz,
Custodian of the two holy mosques*

The Holy Mosque at Makkah

Jebel Dhahran and the New Saudi Generation

Shortly before his death in 1953, King Abdul Aziz formed the Council of Ministers. This was a most important step towards establishing modern institutions of government.

Under King Saud the Council grew, but was not effectively institutionalized until 1958, when Crown Prince Faisal became Prime Minister. In 1963, Faisal became Viceroy with all the authority of the King, and he was primarily responsible for the modernization of Saudi Arabia's apparatus of state. After Faisal became King, all ministerial policies were sanctioned directly by the King and local officials became responsible to the King. This ended the autonomy of the provincial Amirs that had existed previously, and the governmental functions became centralized with the King in the supreme role. This was made possible by the improvement in communications which took place at that time.

The first *Five-Year Development Plan* began in 1970, thus systematizing the allocation of governmental resources.

Saudi Arabia gained international stature under King Faisal, and the foreign policy machinery became more sophisticated.

The Ministry of Justice was created in 1970, ending centuries of Arabian tradition by which the judicial system was administered autonomously from the secular government by Muftis, or Islamic jurists.

With the expansion of the Council of Ministers from 14 to 20 in October 1975, under King Khaled, the government became the central power of the economy of the nation. The structure of the Saudi state has remained essentially the same to date.

The historical eighteenth century alliance between Muhammad ibn Saud and Muhammad ibn Abdul Wahhab, whose descendants are the al-Sheikh family, has continued into the twentieth century with many family members holding important religious and political posts in the Kingdom.

Although the de facto legitimacy of the rule of the House

The Royal Hand

of Saud has its foundations in the successful military campaigns of King Abdul Aziz, the main claim to legitimacy remains in the religion of Islam, in which the King is the upholder of the Sharia law and the defender and protector of the two holy shrines of Islam, Mecca and Medina. The twentieth century success of the al-Saud family in building its nation within the guidelines of the Sharia, as well as distributing its new-found wealth equitably among the broad spectrum of its citizenry, has further enhanced the position of the House of Saud.

The successful modernization of Saudi Arabia in the twentieth century, while at the same time preserving existing social and political values and traditions, has surprised many skeptics and social scientists in the Western world.

The final authority in almost every aspect of government abides with the King. All legislation is by royal decree or by ministerial decree, sanctioned by the King. The King appoints all ministers, senior government officers, governors of the Amirates (provinces) and military officers above the rank of lieutenant colonel. He appoints all ambassadors and envoys to other countries. Foreign diplomats from other countries must also be accredited by the King. The King is the final court of appeal and has the power of pardon.

The primary executive office of the King is the Royal Diwan, or Royal Court, from which much of the routine daily affairs are conducted. There the King also holds his regular "Majlis," where subjects can personally appeal to him for redress or assistance on almost any matter of grievance.

The present-day ministries include:
1. Foreign Affairs
2. Finance and National Economy
3. Defense and Aviation
4. Interior
5. Education
6. Higher Education

The present-day ministries (continued):
7. Health
8. Justice
9. Information
10. Petroleum and Mineral Resources
11. Pilgrimage Affairs and Religious Trusts
12. Planning
13. Municipal and Rural Affairs
14. Industry and Electricity
15. Commerce
16. Communications
17. Telegraph Post and Telephone
18. Agriculture and Water
19. Labor and Social Affairs
20. Public Works and Housing.

In the Council of Ministers in 1984, there were the twenty ministers plus the King, the Crown Prince, three royal advisers and several ministers of state. The majority of the council members were non-royal citizens with differing backgrounds, often persons with advanced degrees from universities in Great Britain and the United States. These men formed a sort of "technocratic elite," whose policy decisions were subject to the approval of the royal family.

In 1984, the Kingdom was divided into 14 Amirates:
1. Ar Riyadh
2. Al Qasim
3. Tabuk
4. Al Hudud Ash Shamaliyah (Northern Frontier)
5. Makkah
6. Al Madinah
7. Asir
8. Hail
9. Al Jawf
10. Al Qurayyat

The Royal Hand

11. Najran
12. Jizan
13. Eastern Province
14. Al Bahah

The governors and deputy governors of these areas are normally appointed from the royal family. The governors act as the King's representatives and as a liaison between the central government and the tribes. Each governor is assisted by a deputy governor and an administrative assistant.

The more populous Amirates are divided into districts and subdistricts (minor Amirates), whose leading officials are, in effect, "junior" governors, subordinate to the "senior" governors.

Appointed mayors are the chief officials in towns and villages.

Saudi decision-making has been guided by the principles of "shurra" (consultation) and "ijma" (consensus). The King's role is to guide consultations to reach a consensus on which decisions can be made.

Most petitions presented at the Majlises concern personal problems. However, any citizen is able to discuss almost any matter short of criticism of Islam or the royal family. This "one-to-one" style of rule is called "Arabian Democracy" by the Ministry of Information.

The traditional Majlis, however, is less effective in a modern society of fast-moving events and changing conditions. The "Majlis al- Shura" (Consultative Council), a representative body of local elders formed to advise the government, was considered by King Faisal but was never implemented by him.

In 1975, after Faisal's assassination, King Khaled appeared ready to act on this, but nothing was done until 1980. Crown Prince Fahd then appointed a nine-member committee to prepare a formula for the creation of such a council.

There is a Civil Service Bureau responsible to the Council of Ministers, which keeps records for employees of all ministries, government organizations, and autonomous agencies. This is the "watchdog" for the government to ensure that the various government agencies comply with the laws regarding the appointments and promotions of their employees. Then, there is a Civil Service Board currently chaired by the King. This board reviews the laws and regulations and any changes that are to be made, but does not exercise formal authority over the employees of the various ministries. Between 1972 and 1982, government employees increased from about 150,000 to nearly 400,000.

The autonomous agencies grew in number and include such organizations as the Saudi Monetary Agency (SAMA), the General Petroleum and Minerals Organization (Petromin), the General Audit Bureau, the Court of Grievances, the Investigative and Control Board, the Organization for Public Services and Discipline (of Public Officials and Government Employees), and the Organization for Social Insurance (GOSI).

Other semi-autonomous organizations include:
1. Universities
2. Port Authority
3. Royal Commissions for Jubail and Yenbo
4. Grain Silos
5. Electricity
6. Railroads

The House of Saud includes those who trace their patrilineal ancestry to Muhammad ibn Saud, the founder of the dynasty in the eighteenth century. While this would include many collateral branches of the family, the only such branches of significance are the al-Jiluwi, Saud al-Kabir, and al-Thunayyan families.

The main patrilineal branch of the al-Saud Family is known as al-Faisal, the paternal grandfather of Abdul Aziz. The males of this lineage, estimated to number between 2,000 and 5,000

The Royal Hand

in the early 1980s, are considered royalty and have the title of "Amir" or "Prince."

Since the death of Abdul Aziz in 1953, the main princes have been his sons (about 40 in number, dwindling to about 31 in 1983). Their ages range from 37 to 73. The sons of these princes, or grandsons of Abdul Aziz, are also of increasing significance.

Succession to the throne after Abdul Aziz's death in 1953, was through his sons rather than his brothers. He designated the eldest, Saud, to be his successor, with the next eldest, Faisal, as Crown Prince. Saud abdicated at the family's request in 1964. Faisal then became King.

Faisal was assassinated in 1975 and Khaled became King, his elder brother, Muhammad, having renounced any claim to the throne. Khaled died in 1982, and the present King Fahd succeeded to the throne, with Abdullah as Crown Prince, having been so designated by Fahd. All transitions have been smooth and unified within the family.

The order of succession after Abdullah is not certain. At some point in time, a major decision within the family will have to be made as to the "modus operandi" of succession.

Factions in the royal family are defined matrilineally, the 31 surviving sons of Abdul Aziz having 13 different mothers. The assumption is that full brothers have viewpoints that may differ from half-brothers. The most powerful of the family factions are the "Sudairi Seven," known thus because their mother was Hassa Bint Ahmad al-Sudairi. She was said to have been the favorite wife of Abdul Aziz. These seven sons include King Fahd, Princes Sultan, Abdul Rahman, Turki, Naif, Salman, and Ahmad.

The second most powerful faction centers on Abdullah, the present Crown Prince. He has no full brothers, but has cultivated close relationships with certain half brothers. He also gained strength from the fact that he heads the National Guard, an armed force of 30,000 men that functions as a loyal guard

Jebel Dhahran and the New Saudi Generation

to the royal family, originally organized by Abdul Aziz and composed of his Ikhwan warriors, who come from the various rural areas around the Kingdom, providing a broad base of loyalty.

The Sudairis are considered more as "modernists", favorably disposed to the United States. The Abdullah faction is composed largely of "traditionalists," with a foreign policy inclined toward non-alignment.

The third discernible faction would be the next generation of princes, the grandsons of Abdul Aziz. Some of these "junior" princes have assumed important positions and are beginning to distinguish themselves. They are generally characterized by a high level of education, often including graduate studies in Europe or the United States.

As might be expected, there have been some royal "black sheep" among the many princes, who have generally been disciplined for activities considered detrimental to the best interests of the royal family. The extreme wealth bestowed on the young princes has sometimes resulted in behavior that has presented a bad image to the Western world.

All-in-all, the royal family has shown a remarkable ability to achieve solidarity, assume its responsibilities, and discipline its members whose actions are not felt to be in the best interests of the family or the Kingdom.

Probably, the real strength of the regime and its best hope for survival are in the unity of the family and its dedication to the welfare of the Kingdom.

An important ingredient for future success will be the ability to curtail excessive royal privilege and the encouragement, recognition, and appropriate reward of the non-royal citizenry, fast becoming a highly educated group of people with abilities and ambitions that must be fulfilled.

PART III

THE INTELLECTUAL RESOURCE

Chapter 6   The Bonds Begin to Break

Chapter 7   Founding a University — 1963
              "The Quest for Excellence"

Chapter 8   Building the University — 1963 to 1975

Chapter 9   "A Jewel in the Desert" — KFUPM Today

"It is not of importance that we build institutes and celebrate their inauguration. The important thing is that we exert all our efforts to benefit from such institutes. To realize what our nation expects from us."

       — His Majesty
         King Faisal ibn Abdul Aziz al-Saud

         at Dedication of the
         College of Petroleum and Minerals
         Dhahran, Saudi Arabia

         December 1964

CHAPTER 6

THE BONDS BEGIN TO BREAK

The founding of what would become KFUPM was a sign that Saudi Arabia was outgrowing the rather loose relationship it had with Aramco from the awarding of the oil concession in 1933 through the reign of King Saud, which ended in 1964.

Whatever went on in the Kingdom was Aramco. The concession in the Eastern Province included everything. Nothing could be done without approval from Aramco. Up to this point, the Saudis were more or less blindfolded, taking what was given to them. The oil revenue was more money than the Saudis had ever had, but their share was still far less than they could have had. They didn't have the technical expertise or knowledge to realize that they were being taken advantage of.

Abdullah Mufti, an alumnus of the first class of the College of Petroleum and Minerals (CPM), recalled: "In 1959, I came to Dhahran to work for Aramco like many other young Saudis. We were put in barracks, and the experience was not a happy one. All Americans, regardless of what they did, were the 'boss' to any Saudi. So, resentment toward the Americans began to build up in the Eastern Province.

"As Saudis who were educated came along at Aramco, they were never given the post of manager or supervisor. They would always have an American over them. That was the way the Aramco management dealt with the Saudis."

During King Saud's reign, Abdullah Tariki was appointed Minister of Petroleum and Minerals. He was young, educated in the United States, and very intelligent. Until his appointment and for a while after, the full power of the economy of Saudi Arabia was in the hands of Aramco, or in other words, Americans.

Tariki, however, as he got into the job, became quite aggressive with Aramco. He perceived inequities in the relationship,

Jebel Dhahran and the New Saudi Generation

and he set about to correct them. As an example, for the pipeline that carried the oil from the Eastern Province to the east coast of the Mediterranean, Aramco paid substantial taxes to Syria, Jordan, and Lebanon to run this pipeline through those countries. However, nothing was paid to Saudi Arabia, although 90 percent of the line was in the Kingdom. Educated Saudis like Tariki began to question the equity of this situation.

Tariki confronted Aramco, which finally agreed that Saudi Arabia had a right to the tax, as the other countries did. So, that was a victory. Then Tariki questioned the twenty-odd years that had passed. He contended that Aramco should pay retroactive tax plus interest. Tariki held out for that, and Aramco did correct it, not wanting nationalization of the oil company as happened in Iran.

In 1962, a new cabinet was appointed by King Saud with Faisal as Prime Minister. Ahmed Zaki Yamani was appointed as the Minister of Petroleum and Minerals. (See Note 1, p. 91).

After Yamani became minister, he set about to implement an idea which he felt was very important to the Kingdom. This was the "College of Petroleum and Minerals" founded in 1963.

The name would be changed to the University of Petroleum and Minerals (UPM) in 1974. The institution received its final name, King Fahd University of Petroleum and Minerals (KFUPM), in 1986. Many of the people interviewed for this book say "UPM" regardless of the time period under discussion. Where quoted, that has been allowed to stand. Otherwise, the initials appropriate to the time period under discussion are used, as are the words "college" and "university."

The nominal purpose of the college was to serve as a technical training institute to ready young Saudis for low positions in the petroleum industry. But what the United States government and Aramco feared — and which Yamani wanted all along — was to turn CPM into a full-fledged university to train Saudis to be able to take over the oil industry from the Americans one day.

Riyadh University was not doing a very good job of attracting students at the time. The Ministry of Higher Education was only beginning to address the needs of a university, and many young Saudis were going abroad to study. Yamani would keep CPM under the Ministry of Petroleum for the time being.

"It had a special track that some of the institutions prior to that did not have," recalled CRS architect Ed Finlay. "Being under the Ministry of Petroleum and Minerals gave it a real shot in the arm."

Dr. Bakhrebah once philosophized, "UPM was an idea whose time had come. Tariki was the implementer, who happened to be there at that time. Later, Zaki Yamani did much more, although not just because he happened to be there. The right personality was there."

After CPM was established by royal decree, Yamani told Aramco, "You are obliged to support such educational projects, according to your contract with the government, so we want you to participate." Aramco, at that time, didn't want to pay any cash.

In 1964 Aramco gave CPM the "Saudi camp," consisting of 50 permanent buildings near Jebel Dhahran where Aramco had housed Saudi employees. CPM would use the buildings as dormitories.

This was what was called "reservation release." The contract between Aramco and the Saudi government provided that Aramco should have reservation over all the Eastern Province. Any land that was to be given to anyone for building or any purpose had to be released by Aramco and by the Ministry of Petroleum and Minerals. Nobody could buy or sell or dig without their permission.

Jebel Dhahran and the New Saudi Generation

When Aramco released the camp to CPM, it was told that CPM was to be only an institute to graduate technicians in the field of petroleum. Aramco agreed to that. But it eventually realized that Yamani and Saleh Ambah, the first dean of the college, had much bigger plans.

Once Ambah was unexpectedly called back from the United States by Yamani. Mufti, who talked to Ambah shortly afterwards, recounts what happened:

"Saleh," Yamani said, "come quickly to Dhahran because Aramco wants to negotiate a sale. It wants to purchase CPM from us." At a meeting with Aramco, Ambah said, "We are willing to sell. Let's go into the details of how much.'"

The president of Aramco said, "All right, how much do you want?"

"We want for the Saudi camp (that Aramco had donated to CPM just a year earlier) fifty million riyals."

The president answered in astonishment. "What are you talking about? The Saudi camp is ours."

Replied Ambah: "It was, but it is no longer. You gave it to us, remember? Now, if you want it back, we want to sell it to you."

"You can't do that to us," the president said.

"Oh, yes we can", Ambah replied. "We are free. You want to buy. We want to sell. This is the price. Take it or leave it."

"You are crazy. You are mad," Aramco's president said.

"Whatever you want to call me. That Saudi camp is fifty million. Now the buildings are something else. The furniture is something else."

So Aramco gave up on buying CPM. Ambah told Mufti: "We were planning to hit two hundred million."

Mufti asked Ambah, "Suppose they had agreed to pay you the money. Would you have sold it to them? How could you ever agree to sell it?"

Ambah admitted, "Of course we would have sold it. It was not worth ten million, and we were going to sell it for two

The Bonds Begin to Break

hundred million. We could go somewhere else to build a university with that much cash in our hands. Actually, Tarut Island was a site under consideration, and if the sale went through, we would go to Tarut and build a university there."

Looking back, Mufti offered this theory for why Aramco wanted to buy CPM: "The news had leaked to Aramco that it was no longer to be just a technical institute. It was, in fact, the nucleus of a large university. Something big was coming on."

This was especially evident from the design for a campus which CPM had requested from the Houston architecture firm CRS (now CRSS). It was clear that CPM contemplated "a masterpiece university" on the top of Jebel Dhahran. Aramco officials then realized things were getting out of control. They must stop it.

Mufti commented, "They always considered that the longer the Saudis remained ignorant and blindfolded, the longer they could squeeze out of this country the natural resources for their own benefit.

"If Tariki had not gotten an education, he would not have known enough to challenge Aramco on the inequity of the pipeline tax situation. They would certainly not have volunteered to pay.

"So, what about building a university and graduating four hundred engineers a year! That would be the end of them. And they really felt it. It was like any colonialism. The longer they keep the people of the colony ignorant or in subjection, the longer they can survive, the longer they can squeeze their resources and their wealth and take it home. America certainly knows that from experience. So, when the purchase of CPM didn't go through (and that was expected, of course, by Yamani and Ambah — theirs was just an act — to see how serious the Americans were about buying CPM), Aramco started getting very vigorous with CPM, very tough."

Jebel Dhahran and the New Saudi Generation

"I was one of those who helped to start this university," Mufti said. "I was so involved that I used to dream all the time about this place. I was afraid that Aramco would succeed in its opposition to it, and it would be closed down as an institution for higher education. That was really the big worry.

"They put communist leaflets in our rooms and told the secret police that we were distributing these among ourselves — that we were communists. That shows how much they were fighting us."

It was thought by some that the CIA was behind that opposition.

Charles "Tiny" Lawrence, an architect with CRS, recalls being approached by the CIA in Houston after the firm obtained the work of designing the university. "The CIA wanted to know if we would be willing to simply observe things when we were in and out of the Kingdom. This must have been a couple of years after we started working over there. Of course, the United States government knew that we were going in and out.

"This was before they were into the oil boom. They said, 'We just want you to observe things and talk to us about it after you come back.'

"I don't feel badly that they were asking us to do that. But our feeling was that we developed a certain trust with our clients, and we wouldn't do anything to jeopardize that trust. So, we just said, 'No, we're not interested'".

The Saudis may have viewed CRS as playing a more controversial role than CRS itself believed. As Mufti put it: "CRS was in a conflicting situation at the early stage. It needed to have a loyalty to itself as a company and its financial success and at the same time it should have a loyalty to its country. This was the irony. Although that university was built with support of an American organization, CRS, that support was in a sense working against the perceived interests of the U.S. government at that time."

The Bonds Begin to Break

But Lawrence saw it differently: "I personally didn't feel that we (CRS) had any direct loyalty to Aramco, just because it was primarily a United States company at that time. It was an American company (Exxon, Mobil, Chevron, and Texaco) that was doing well in partnership with the Saudis, and the college was an Arab institute that was interested in creating a fine college to help train Arab minds. We were working for the latter, and we saw no conflict there."

Americans who were Aramco's executives at the time say they didn't object to the creation of the university, only to its placement on land that adjoined the company's compound of offices, housing, and community facilities when so much empty land in every direction was available.

However, by that time the Saudis were beginning not to ask, but to tell Aramco how things were going to be. And Aramco was beginning to yield.

"On one of our first trips, at a meeting over at Aramco, there was a newspaper article with the first news that the Saudis were going to take over a larger percentage of ownership of Aramco," Lawrence said. "That was in 1965. I remember we kicked it around among ourselves. We wondered if this was the first move in the expanding process where the Saudis would eventually have the whole ownership. The mood was right because the Saudi nationals were saying, 'We want a bigger piece of the pie.'"

While Aramco may insist that it didn't work for or wish for the university's failure, it made no secret that it believed the university would fail. And while it cooperated with the university in many ways, Aramco also hindered it at times.

During the site selection process, "Aramco was helpful in providing people, information, and vehicles of all kinds. It was totally supportive," Lawrence said. Aramco even let a visiting team from CRS use a light plane to look over the potential sites.

Jebel Dhahran and the New Saudi Generation

Lawrence kept a diary of that initial visit to Saudi Arabia, Dec. 7-22, 1964.

On Wednesday, Dec. 9, he wrote: "Afternoon meeting with Harry Snyder and Frank Patterson of Aramco. Harry is in charge of special training; Frank is a planner. Both of these men ... have been thinking of sites for a Saudi Arabian technical school for years."

CRS reached its decision on Monday, Dec. 14. Lawrence wrote: "Ran through our first full analysis of all nine sites this morning, and the jebel we can see out our window shows the most strength...The jebel at Dhahran is now our definite choice. Meet in the morning with Aramco V.P. to discuss the site and its implications regarding the proximity to Dhahran (Aramco's compound)."

The next day: "Don (Wines), (Dr. Abdullah) Bakr and I get with Mr. Sullivan and Mr. Jones of Aramco to discuss our recommendation on site. Slightly sensitive since it is adjacent to the Dhahran-Aramco complex, but the meeting went well.

"Afterwards, we find out that the Minister of Petroleum and Minerals had announced to Aramco brass last Sunday that this adjacent jebel would be the site for the new college. We hadn't even decided at that time (caused chaos at Aramco)."

In a 1988 interview, Lawrence recalled: "We didn't think that they were negative. At least, that's the impression we got talking among ourselves. Harry Snyder, of course, was with Aramco at that time. Harry was a very objective man, and he was very dedicated to doing well for the Saudis. He was totally committed to helping the Saudis — their country and their people.

"There were some concerns at Aramco that if we built there, we would have to tie into their sanitary sewers and use their water and electrical plant. They wondered what that would do to them. Could they take the extra load? And I think there was a general concern about whether they really wanted that institution across the fence from their own camp, but there was no

The Bonds Begin to Break

outward display of hostility toward the idea," Lawrence said.

Joe Thomas, who did not come on that initial visit but later became the CRS project manager, remembered stronger opposition: "From all indications I got, Aramco did not want it to be built there. They wanted it to be anywhere else but there. It would be too close to Aramco. It would be up high and overlooking Aramco. They had all kinds of reasons and justifications in their mind of why they didn't want the college to be there.

"Of course, you can speculate on this, but I really think all along that Aramco thought that this idea was doomed to failure, that it was never going to happen," Thomas said. "They weren't tremendously worried about it. They thought, 'OK, so they have selected the Jebel. We don't want it there, but they are going to fail anyway.'"

Added Lawrence: "I think that was true. I guess it was based on the observation over the years that the Saudis had a hard time completing anything — getting anything going. So, they probably said, "We'll just let them talk."

Dr. Robert King Hall, an educator who had worked with Harry Snyder at Aramco and who had returned to assist CPM, once said that everybody at Aramco was looking over the fence skeptically, waiting for this ambitious project to fail. Aramco had predicted as much to the US State Department. But Dr. Hall was sure that the people in charge of this project would not fail — and they didn't.

Ed Finlay of CRS, who went on the 1964 visit to Dhahran, recalled that "Aramco people, especially, ... were very critical of us early on in trying to press for a quality level in design, construction technology, and long-range planning that would be required to carry out the design that we had tried to put up as a goal.

"I got the impression that Aramco mentality had always been somewhat like a military base that is both utilitarian and really kind of either temporary or at best semi-permanent," Finlay said. "They didn't think we should try to develop anything here that had such quality. One, it should be quick. Two, it should stay with existing traditional methods and not try to introduce new methods. They saw that as the reality. That was the way they built there. We should design that way."

Over the years, Thomas had several other run-ins with Aramco. One concerned "sewage, of all things. Aramco had a sewage disposal plant across the road from UPM. We got permission from them to tie into this plant for the 'Technical Institute' in Phase I. When it came to Phases II and III, we just did it without further consultation. One day, I received a call from the company representative."

The Aramco representative told Thomas that UPM couldn't tie into its sewer line for lack of capacity. That seemed strange to Thomas, who didn't think the plant was operating at half its capacity.

"The next day, I got another call from him. He said, 'Why don't you come over to my house tonight, and let's cook some hamburgers in the yard.'

"As we were cooking hamburgers on the patio, I looked out across his front yard," Thomas said. "It was about 50 yards to the fence, and beyond that was UPM property. I said, "That is a pretty view out there." He said, "Yes, my wife and I really enjoy that, looking out across the desert. We sit out here all the time in the evening."

So Thomas told him: "The next time you see me, I'm going to be constructing a sewage plant right across the fence in front of your house. I'm going to get a package sewage disposal plant with a leeching field and tanks. And that's a good place for it."

"Oh, you wouldn't do that, would you?" the Aramco executive said, horrified.

"You watch me," Thomas said.

Two days later, just before Thomas was scheduled to return to the US, the Aramco representative called. "I had our engi-

The Bonds Begin to Break

neers look at that disposal plant, and they think that we can handle your capacity for a year or two."

"That sure solves a lot of problems," Thomas said.

"I won't have to construct that sewage plant now."

"I didn't think you would," the Aramco representative said.

Looking back, Thomas commented: "So, there were these little shenanigans that went on. By the time we got into constructing Phases II and III, I think Aramco had realized that the university was going to be built. It was going to be built to a standard unheard of in the Kingdom. And come hell or high water, CRS was going to build it. So, from then on with Aramco it was really just a matter of negotiation."

Another item of contention concerned an Aramco soccer field below the jebel. "Every time that UPM scheduled a soccer game on that field, Aramco scheduled a practice for one of its teams," Thomas said. "Then UPM would have to reschedule its game and go through all kinds of trouble. It was a constant thorn in the side of UPM."

One day Thomas went calling on the Aramco representative. He was carrying a copy of the UPM master plan, which CRS and UPM had always refused to let Aramco see. After looking through it, the Aramco executive asked for a copy. Thomas agreed, but said: "I'll tell you what I want in return. I want that soccer field."

"You've got it" the Aramco representative said.

"Fine," Thomas said. "You keep the brochures, and I'll come by tomorrow and pick up a letter to me transferring that field to UPM." The next day Thomas told Dr. Bakr he had given a copy of the plan to Aramco. When Bakr asked why, Thomas handed him the letter transferring the soccer field to UPM. Dr. Bakr said, "I can't believe it. You got the Soccer Field for two copies of the master plan?"

Jebel Dhahran and the New Saudi Generation

It became increasingly apparent that the relationship between Aramco and the Kingdom of Saudi Arabia was changing. Although the relationship has continued on the basis of mutual respect and in the best of Western business traditions, no one could deny that the Kingdom of Saudi Arabia was now in the driver's seat. It was to be no nation's "tool."

Americans to this day underestimate the Saudis. They do not credit Saudis with the ability to grasp underlying realities and to shape events to their advantage. Also they have not recognized that given the opportunity, the Saudis would have the ambition and energy to continue to move forward. Testimony to this is the fact that today, more than fifty years after Dammam Well No. 7 began producing oil, Saudi Arabia is no longer a remote desert kingdom but a nation with all the amenities of twentieth-century technology. The president and chairman of the board of Aramco are no longer Americans but college-educated Saudis. And this condition happened by mutual consent of the Saudis and the American oil companies — not by arbitrary or military take-over.

As Bakhrebah put it: "There is a movement of history. Individuals add color. But, whether the course of history would have changed if this or that individual hadn't been there — no one can be sure. It is like a huge river — the movement of history. You can't dam it with one stone. But, by adding stone after stone, eventually you dam it — and you change the course of the river. History is the same. It is not just one individual."

In 1963, the bonds of pseudo-colonialism were, indeed, broken. A new era had dawned.

The course of the river had been changed.

The members of the board of directors of Saudi Aramco, who held their inaugural meeting yesterday in Dhahran, are, seated left to right: Dr. Abdallah E. al-Dabbagh, Ali I. Naimi, HE Hisham Nazer, Nassir M. Ajmi and Dr. Abdul Aziz al-Jarbu. Standing, left to right, are: Nabil I. al-Bassam, Harold J. Haynes, Dr. Abd al-Wahhab Attar, Clifton C. Garvin, Abdelaziz M. al-Hokail and Rodney B. Wagner.
New Saudi Aramco Board of Directors - (April 1989)

(Aramco Photo - Dobais)

CHAPTER 7

FOUNDING A UNIVERSITY — 1963
"THE QUEST FOR EXCELLENCE"

In 1963, when Yamani began to assemble the people who would found the university, a board of trustees was appointed with himself as chairman. There were other Saudis on the board, and also several Western people, well-known in the fields of education and petroleum. A charter was drawn up, and King Faisal approved it. Yet CPM was still an informal, embryonic thing.

Yamani asked Saleh Ambah to serve as the first dean of this new college. Dr. Ambah, then serving in the Ministry of Defense, was one of the first Saudis to study in the United States. He had received a B.S. in geology and chemistry from Cairo University, his M.S. and PhD in petroleum engineering from the University of Southern California.

Ambah recruited Bakr Abdullah bin Bakr, a field petroleum engineer at Aramco, to be his deputy. Bakr later left the university for a time in order to earn an MBA from Stanford University and a PhD from the University of Southern California.

One of the first employees of the college was Amedeo Porro, an Italian who grew up in Algeria and Tunisia (see Note 2, page 91). He had been hired by Aramco in 1955 to work for the railroad in Dammam and eventually became superintendent.

It happened that in 1963, Ambah was renting a house in the railroad organization compound, because none was available elsewhere. Ambah was a friend of the railroad general manager, Dr. Abdul Aziz al-Gureishi, who introduced him to Porro and offered him Porro's services. Porro remained on the railroad payroll but was put in charge of CPM's maintenance, food services, landscaping, housing, security, vehicle maintenance and almost anything else that needed to be done — which was considerable. Another railroad employee, a young Saudi named Abdul Mohsin al-Juraib, officially transferred to CPM, thereby

Jebel Dhahran and the New Saudi Generation

becoming its first staff employee. Porro remained with the university for 27 years, until his retirement in 1981.

"You had the feeling of being a pioneer with those young Saudis like Zaki Yamani, Saleh Ambah, Abdullah Bakr, Nasser Rashid, and Reda Nazer," Porro said in a 1990 interview. "You should have seen the enthusiasm of those young men. It was really fantastic."

In addition to being college-educated, "they were dedicated and hard-working. What impressed me more than anything was that they were very honest. Nobody could bribe them," Porro said. "If somebody tried, he was kicked out."

Yamani spent about half his time in Dhahran when the university was starting up, Porro recalled. He remembered the former oil minister as "an honest man. He was very patriotic about his country, like most Saudis. He was very intelligent."

The first need facing CPM's organizers was for a campus. Since CPM was operating under the Ministry of Petroleum, rather than the Ministry of Higher Education, the government gave to the college some land near Aramco and Jebel Dhahran, and a ministry branch building that was under construction. That structure is now referred to as "the Old Administration Building."

"The real job started around October 1963," Porro said. "They had already bought some portables from Aramco for the Ministry of Petroleum, and they were lying in place. We then bought more portables and installed them for housing."

"I had two Italians from the railroad who came after 4 o'clock in the afternoon to work there and finish them. Then we contracted with someone to complete the Old Administration Building. At that time, we bought three portables for laboratories — the English lab, the chemistry lab and the physics lab."

On his way to an OPEC meeting in Geneva in 1963, Zaki Yamani stopped in Dhahran to check on the progress. Late in the afternoon he went to the site where the new portables were being installed. As he approached, he heard voices and saw the

Amedeo Porro on Jebel Dhahran - 1967

San Francisco - 1990

Jebel Dhahran and the New Saudi Generation

legs of four people behind one portable: Ambah, Bakr, and two plumbers, trying to tie in the plumbing. Yamani was impressed with their spirit of dedication. He confidently informed the CPM board, "You will have a college next year."

It wouldn't be easy. "From November 1963 to October 1964, we were working every day of the week, sometimes ten hours a day, to build the North Compound, renovate the portables we were buying from Aramco, complete the construction of the Ministry of Petroleum building which had been given to us, and build and install the chemistry, physics and English language laboratories, etc.," Porro said.

But the task was accomplished. The college officially opened one year to the day after Faisal signed the CPM charter. "When the first faculty and students arrived in October 1964, everything was ready, including small trees, grass on the lawn, and completely furnished housing with food in the refrigerators," Porro said.

"The night before the first classes started, we were working with Mr. Bakr, who was then provost, rearranging the furniture in the classrooms. I had never seen so much hard work, cooperation, enthusiasm and goodwill. I think that it was because of this state of mind, which we transmitted every year to the newcomers, students and faculty alike, that King Fahd University of Petroleum and Minerals has become what it is now," Porro added.

Meanwhile, newspaper advertisements had announced that a college would be started in 1964. A committee traveled to Jeddah, Riyadh, and Dammam to interview applicants. The committee was quite selective, evaluating each student's personality, education, mastery of English (CPM's language of instruction), and his maturity. Entrance examinations covered math, science, and other subjects. The Saudis chose English as the language so their graduates could go on to England or the

Founding a University — 1963 "The Quest for Excellence"

United States to do graduate work.

Every student — Saudi or foreign, rich or poor — attended CPM on a scholarship. He also received free lodging, meals, and medical care. And he received a stipend: 600 riyals a month initially, later raised to 1,000.

Abdullah Mufti, one of the fifty-four Saudi students enrolled in CPM's first academic year, described the start of CPM in interviews in 1987 and 1988:

"Those were the best years — the first years. There was a lot of high morale among everybody — enthusiasm, anticipation, challenge. It was just burning with excitement, day and night. Just imagine a student attending his classes, then doing his homework, then taking up a guard position to guard his colleagues while they sleep. That was a fairly common routine. You must appreciate the morale we had in order to do that.

"Dean Ambah injected in every man, whether a student, a teacher, or even a waiter, a lot of confidence and love for this place, this project. Definitely the majority of the students and staff were willing to give their lives for that project. That is leadership."

As for the teachers, "Generally, they were very nice," Mufti said. "There was a Mr. Davis from North Carolina, who taught us mathematics.

"There was a Mr. Johnson from Texas, who taught us chemistry. He was a big name in the States. He had us make one hundred isotope projectors out of wood, metal, lenses, and spotlights.

"It was very difficult to understand him. First of all, he had a real Texas accent. Secondly, he used to talk with a cigarette in his mouth. We were young and very proud. He would come and put his feet up on the desk with his shoes in our faces. Of course, something like that was unacceptable to the Saudis. We considered it very impolite.

"I remember, I went to Mr. Bakr and told him I wanted to file a complaint against Mr. Johnson. Mr. Bakr was laughing and said, 'Well, you have to be patient. We are trying to give CPM a name and reputation by having him. So, see what you can do and just be patient.'

"I think that was probably the first time that I realized that a college professor is really the master, the god. Nobody can question him. Even the administration. They don't even come into the classroom to check on him. If he gives a mark, somebody deserves an 'A' and he gives them a 'C,' or vice versa, nobody can question him. It's as if it came from the sky.

"There was a Dr. Deever, a chemistry professor. He failed everybody but two for three semesters, consecutively. He did leave the University later, but they couldn't change his method, or anything, while he was there.

"The faculty lived in the North Compound. The dean lived in the large house at the end of the compound. On the left side were all the students and their cafeteria. On the right side were all the faculty and their families. We were all in the same compound, and it was like one big family. It was very nice.

"We used to visit our lecturers in their homes, especially Mr. Davis from North Carolina. His wife was a very nice person. She used to give us apple pie and coffee. We would sit and talk and visit with them on weekends. Then we would play football or something on the grass lawn in the middle of the compound.

"Mr. Dickenson taught English at CPM in 1965. At that time, when a new teacher arrived with his wife, we gave him a tea party. At the party, I said to Mr. Dickenson, 'What do you think of Saudi Arabia?'

"He replied, 'Oh, it's fantastic. It is great. You really have streets and buildings. I thought it was only a desert with sand dunes and tents.'"

Mufti asked Dickenson: "When you first made your contract with Dean Ambah, why did you accept to come and teach in a tent?"

Dickenson said, "Well, when they told me it was a college,

Founding a University — 1963 "The Quest for Excellence"

I thought maybe it was better than a tent, some sort of shack."

"I was really very upset to think that he was a teacher," Mufti recalled. "He was in education. He should read about history and geography. About two weeks later, it just happened that he was reading to us from the **Great American Short Stories** book. One of the stories was about the Red Indians. He started by saying that the Red Indians are the natives of America, the original inhabitants. So, I put up my hand and said, 'Excuse me, Mr. Dickenson, when you go back to the States, do you apply for a visa to get into America?'

"'What do you mean?' Dickenson asked.

"'Well, you just told us that the Red Indians are the native people of America. I know that if you go to another country, you have to apply for an entry visa to be able to get into the country.'

"Dickenson exclaimed with irritation, 'What are you talking about? How come you are a university student and you still don't know that we are the Americans who run the country and those Indians do not?'"

Mufti told him: "If I am a university student and I am ignorant about your country, you are a university teacher, and you are ignorant about my country. You said you thought we were living in tents."

"He got the point. The class was laughing and laughing.

"We were short of teachers, so that year the college arranged for the wives of some of the professors to teach us. Mrs. Hall taught us, and Mrs. Ambah taught us also. Mrs. Dickenson taught us English grammar. That arrangement lasted for a year and a half.

"They were happy to do it. We also had some ladies working as librarians at that time. Of course, that continued to be one of the jobs that the ladies could do."

Mrs. Hall recalled: "Mrs. Ambah was very full of life and wanted to do all these things. She was very helpful. She was willing to do anything to help push that institution."

Jebel Dhahran and the New Saudi Generation

For a while the college even had a Jesuit priest as a teacher. Father Sullivan was hired by Ambah with Yamani's knowledge to be head of the English Department. But he was asked to leave when students reported that he was saying mass in his home and at Aramco.

Nadim Nasir, a Palestinian with a PhD in physics from the University of Houston, joined the university in 1969 to establish a computer center.

Interviewed in 1988, Nasir recalled: "I received an offer from Dr. Saleh Ambah to come and work there. I looked at the offer, but he was not offering to pay me half of what I was making at Shell. So, I said, 'Well, I have two brothers in Saudi Arabia. Why don't I go visit and see the place? See what I would be going into.' Probably, in the history of the university, I was the only one that went to interview there, on location. I paid for my own round trip ticket.

"I checked around and it turned out that the university was offering me a fair market price relative to its employment. When I came back to Houston, I discussed the situation with my wife, Ghada, and she said, 'Why don't we try it?'

"When I went there all they gave me was four walls, a floor and a ceiling. They said, 'You have to create a computer center.' I asked, 'What is the budget?' They said, 'There is zero budget.' You have to remember that in those days, all the income from the oil revenues was not sufficient to build a highway to link the east and the west parts of the country.

"At that time they had one small IBM-1301. I understood that somebody told King Faisal that there was a computer at UPM. They really didn't have one, so to make the statement correct, they got a 1301. They were planning to install an IBM 360-50 system, which was exactly what Aramco had. We were going to run it on a commercial basis, whereby we charged computer time to all our clients and paid for the rental of it. By

Founding a University — 1963 "The Quest for Excellence"

December 1969, the IBM system was air-shipped from the States. We would then have a backup in case we had some commercial work and our computer was down. We could go to Aramco and say, 'OK, help us with this problem.' And vice versa. We told Aramco, 'In case your computer is down, you can come and use ours.' It was a sophisticated system for those days."

The UPM Computer Center won contracts with government ministries like petroleum and finance, and with the U.S. Geological Survey. "Philip Holzman was a big German contractor there, building an irrigation project, a huge project, using our computer. The Japanese had an oil concession there — the Arabian-Japanese Oil Company. They were using our facility, so we were able to pay the rental, but barely."

"I think UPM ranks along with the top 25 percent of the universities in the United States," said Nasir, who had returned to the University of Houston to teach. "The students there were better than the students I am teaching here by far."

"At the beginning of the university, there was a very strong motivation," Nasir said. "One thing was that if you were a freshman in the university and had a less than 2.0 average, which is a "C", you were put on probation. If the next semester, you did not get off probation by improving your grades, you were suspended for a semester or so. That motivated lots of students. No one likes to fail. But later on, I understand that suspension became very rare. They would say, 'You are on probation,' and you would stay on probation indefinitely until you graduated."

The first year's budget was 2.5 million riyals (less than a million dollars) from King Faisal. CPM used it up in six months. So Yamani had to ask the King for more. Faisal questioned how the money had been spent, and receiving satisfactory answers, ordered another substantial amount for CPM.

"Believe me, every student there, every waiter, every porter acted as if the money was his, as if it were given to him personally," Mufti said. "Everyone was so happy we got the money to keep the project going."

Some of the original 54 students are now employees of the university. Ibrahim al-Jalal is now the accounting department manager. Mohammad Abu al-Hammayel is director of the computer center. From the second class, Yousef al-Koheji became the director general of maintenance.

Besides Saudis, there were 15 Algerian students in the first CPM class. "In 1962, Algeria got its independence from France," Mufti explained. "King Faisal wanted to help the country, because at that time, all the Arabs there spoke French, not Arabic, after all the years as a French colony. After the independence, Algeria requested all the other Arab countries to help get the Arabic language and culture back into the country.

"This made the first class to be fifty-four Saudis and fifteen Algerians. Most of them stayed and completed their course, and then they were given scholarships to go to the United States at the expense of Saudi Arabia."

Since then the university has had students from Syria, Iraq, Bahrain, Lebanon, and other Arab countries.

During the first semester, the students were very nervous. CPM was keeping so quiet about its educational aspirations that even the students didn't know if they were going to receive a college degree or just a technical certificate.

The question came up one day at the morning briefing that Bakr routinely held with the students. Mufti said, "Excuse us, Mr. Bakr, but what is going to happen to us? What are you going to give us at the end? Are we going to study one year, two years, or five years? Is it a college or a technical institute? We keep hearing things that are not very nice, and we came here for a college, a university, to get a degree — not just a certificate or something like that."

Later, they saw why he could not be frank with them. The

Founding a University — 1963 "The Quest for Excellence"

administrators were working hard to establish a university, but they had to do it secretly to avoid opposition from Aramco and others. At the same time, they didn't want to say that the students were going to be only technicians, because that was not the intent.

Bakr told them, "Just be patient with us, bear with us, and you will get a degree. Don't worry." But the students were not very confident.

One student said, "Could you please give me a piece of paper with your signature on it to say that at the end I will get a degree?" Bakr replied, "Even if I give you this with my signature, so what? I'm telling you. You should believe me."

"In the second year, I think they accepted one hundred, so we were about one hundred fifty," Mufti said. "Some of the students from the first year left. Because they were scared, some students found it was a hard place to live. On the weekends, Thursday and Friday, I would walk through the barracks. I personally missed family life so much that I just wanted to hear a child crying. I wanted to hear more sounds of family life — like somebody doing dishes. It was so dry, so isolated, so quiet — no children, no families, no normal routine life, no market, no shops. It was just like the Army.

"We actually used to smuggle some tickets from Aramco to be able to see a movie. There was no television then. We used to get so fed up, so bored. Study, study, study, study. We were not used to that.

"One time I went to see Dr. Ambah during Ramadan together with two other students. One was Khaled Abu Saud, who was the first president of the student union. CPM had the Kingdom's first student union, a very strong organization with activities like photography, chemistry, gardening, excursions, and music.

"We wanted to establish a music club, and we didn't have any money," Mufti continued. "Dean Ambah was just like our father. We asked for 10,000 riyals. At that time, it was like

Jebel Dhahran and the New Saudi Generation

asking for 100,000 nowadays. He said, 'No, I'm sorry, I don't have it.'

"The same day, Zaki Yamani was coming to visit the college. He used to pay visits about once or twice a month. This was a project dear to his heart. He wanted to see that it was going along right. Whenever he came, we gave him a sort of party or celebration. We called him Uncle Ahmed, and he considered us like his pupils.

"The students explained their situation to Yamani. He said, 'Go ahead and buy what you want and ask the shop to send me the invoice.'"

"That would be out of his own pocket!" Mufti said.

"You know how we students were. We bought organs, guitars, amplifiers, loud speakers. We almost emptied the shop. And the bill was 25,000 riyals.

"When the invoice came to him he said, 'What have you done? You broke my back! Oh well, not to worry.' He paid it, you know.

"That was a big morale builder.

"Of course, what else do you want or expect from a leader — to support you, to be kind to you, to understand you, because he felt that we were the nucleus to build up a good reputable place. And I think he did succeed."

Margaret Hall, who spent 18 years at the university as the wife of Robert King Hall, the senior adviser, recalled in a 1988 interview another way that the administration looked after its students.

"Saleh Ambah realized when they had their first public presentation of any kind with these young men, that some of them came from homes where they could not possibly have bought a jacket for their son to wear," she said. "So Ambah had blazers made with the CPM insignia. The blazers were stored until a big occasion, when they were brought out for the stu-

Founding a University — 1963 "The Quest for Excellence"

dents to wear. They were there so that every one of those young men could be proud of himself and of his country."

Dr. Robert King Hall, is widely regarded as the most valuable non-Saudi that Ambah recruited. Shortly after being made dean of the college, Ambah sought advice from Harry Snyder on hiring an educator of international reputation to help CPM assemble a teaching staff (see Note 3, page 91). Snyder was a pro-Saudi educator at Aramco.

Snyder recommended Dr. Hall, an educational consultant to various governments around the world (see Note 4, page 92), to be senior adviser to the new college. The two had worked together at Aramco, developing a school system for the children of Western employees and others for the Saudis. Hall had also organized Aramco's Local Industrial Developments Department, which helped local Saudis to go into business as Aramco suppliers. Many became millionaires and developed into important merchant families.

By 1963 Hall had left Aramco and was doing consulting work in other countries.

"Bob was doing a study," Mrs. Hall recalled. "It lasted for over a year, just travelling from one country to another for the International Committee of the YMCA. We went all around South America. During that time, whatever major capital we arrived in, there would be a cable waiting for us there from Saleh Ambah saying, 'Please come help me.' So, we went back to Saudi Arabia."

"He was recruiting the faculty, writing the program of education, setting up the meetings then writing the minutes. They would simply say, 'Dr. Hall, we need this by such and such a date,' and he would do it. At that time, he was even typing all this himself. I really had to admire the man," Lawrence said.

Added Finlay: "Dr. Ambah had a lot of faith in Dr. Hall and realized the help he got from him. He and Dr. Hall had a very

Jebel Dhahran and the New Saudi Generation

close working relationship, I think".

Mrs. Hall remembered: "We would sometimes receive a call from Saleh Ambah. He might say, 'Margaret, I need to talk to Dr. Hall with you. This isn't office talk, so come on down to my house.' If I said, 'Saleh, we are in the middle of dinner,' he would say, 'Well, just leave it and come on down.' And we would. It got to be an old story after a while, but we had such an easy and relaxed relationship with him and with Zaki Yamani in those early days."

Dr. Hall's most amazing feat was getting 11 million riyals from Aramco. When he had worked for Aramco, he had written a proposal that the company give that amount of money to an educational institution. It was not intended to be a college or a university, but a technical school to train Saudis in some kind of management and engineering, and also in "hands-on" capability. However, though the proposal was approved, it had never been acted on. "It had gone into a drawer and been forgotten," Mrs. Hall said.

When he returned to Saudi Arabia to join CPM, Dr. Hall remembered the proposal. As CPM senior adviser, he went to Aramco and asked for the money that he had gotten authorized when he had worked at Aramco. "It took care of all the first construction," Mrs. Hall said. "No one else had any idea that the money was available."

"That was several years before the big oil money began coming in," Lawrence added.

"He had that combination of experience and skill that was needed there at that time," Mrs. Hall concluded.

However, Mrs. Hall says that her husband was just one of the men who had the talent, knowledge, and vision that CPM needed. "All the young men who were there and working with him had that too. It was a very rare thing to get four people (Yamani, Ambah, Bakr, and Hall) who could work so well together. I always believed that having Zaki Yamani as their head rather than the Department of Education was the thing that

Founding a University — 1963 "The Quest for Excellence"

helped get that project through. He had the broad picture, and he had vision. He saw what needed to be done and he did it."

"It was always on a friendly and constructive basis that they worked (to establish the university). It was extraordinary that everything about this was done in such a friendly way, and there was so much effort made to be helpful to a new generation of young men," Mrs. Hall said.

Porro remembered: "One thing about the Saudis. They have a very good perception of the people they know — like me. They knew that I liked them and I had been educated with the Arabs. They still call me and write to me. I don't think they did that for many other people."

Porro brought up a university employee named Keith Hester, who, as registrar, was the only Westerner on the administration staff. "One time I asked Dr. Hall why he thought Hester had done so well in such a responsible position for so long." Hall replied, "Because he is absolutely incorruptible. He wouldn't change a grade if his life depended on it."

Porro recalled, "I found that to be a very revealing comment about the values the Saudis placed on such things."

Porro remembers the day in 1967 that he received a call from a Saudi friend at Aramco. He told Porro: "There are a lot of people at Aramco who are going to the U.S. Consulate to make a demonstration. I know you have children at the school there. You probably will want to go and take care of them."

Porro drove to the consulate right away. "I thought that because I spoke Arabic maybe I could help if something happened. I went to the school and stayed there. I saw the whole thing — taking down the flag, burning the car, and so forth.

"You see, the demonstration didn't start with the college students. It started at Aramco, and most of them were Palestinians (protesting the shipment of oil from Ras Tanura to

Jebel Dhahran and the New Saudi Generation

Israel). They came down past the college and some of the students joined in, when they saw the crowds moving down the road. There was no thought of doing such a thing at CPM."

In 1969, the CRS project manager for the university, Joe Thomas, was sitting in the international lounge in the Beirut Airport, waiting for a Middle East Airlines flight to Dhahran. Suddenly the Saudi petroleum attache in Lebanon paged him on the intercom. He informed Thomas that he would no longer be going to Dhahran, but to Riyadh to meet Yamani.

In Riyadh, Thomas was taken to the Ministry of Petroleum and Minerals suite in the old Yamama International Hotel. "It was about 2 or 3 o'clock in the morning. They took me to a big room on the top floor of this hotel. There was no one there. All night long, I was wondering what the hell was going on," Thomas recalled.

The next morning, after a breakfast of goat cheese and Arab bread, Thomas was taken in a black Buick to Yamani's office. Yamani said, "Good morning, Mr. Thomas. I'm sorry to put you through all this, but I have something very important to discuss with you." Yamani then said, "We have just had a new assignment for the position of coordinator between the university and CRS."

The new coordinator was Nasser Rashid, a recent graduate from the University of Texas. He was young and inexperienced. Yamani said, "Your contact from now on will be with Dr. Rashid (rather than Dr. Ambah). He will represent me at the university. If you ever have a problem that you don't agree with Dr. Rashid on, you are free to call me and bring it to my attention. I hope there will be no disruption at the university, and the university will proceed normally, just as if Dr. Ambah were there."

Thomas answered: "Fine, I see no problem. We'll go on just as we have said." The whole meeting took about twenty minutes.

Founding a University — 1963 "The Quest for Excellence"

"So, I went right on with Nasser Rashid building the university," Thomas said.

The educational system in Saudi Arabia had advanced enough that the University of Petroleum and Minerals could be transferred from Yamani's ministry to that of the Ministry of Higher Education. Yamani and the original board began to phase out of the university. Yamani and Ambah had guided the university to the point where it was well-established and was turning out several hundred students every year with advanced degrees in engineering.

Today there are several thousand graduates of CPM/UPM/KFUPM. And they are making a positive impact on Saudi Arabia. They work at the Salt Water Conversion Commission, the Civil Aviation Department, and so on.

"It is good to see this," Mufti said. "Without a doubt, UPM has played a very important role in the development of Saudi Arabia. It is pure science and engineering. That is what is needed to build a country — engineering. It is the spine of development.

"I was talking to the SWCC general manager, Mr. Jamjoom, about a big project on which I was working. I told him, 'Your Excellency, I can see a lot of UPM graduates here that you have employed.' Jamjoom replied, 'You know something? When we interview students, for some reason, we can usually tell who is a UPM graduate.'"

"Oh, you are exaggerating, your excellency," Mufti said.

"But Jamjoom insisted, 'No, the UPM graduates have not only an excellent education, but also a personality. I don't know what they do with these students. They polish them, their character, their attitudes. It's not just in education or technical abilities — whether an engineer, a scientist or a mathematician — but also in personality.'"

Jebel Dhahran and the New Saudi Generation

By 1969, the "Tangible Resources" and the "Intellectual Resources" had both been tapped and were beginning to produce results. The years to come would show what "oil" and "education" can do for a nation if used in a constructive way.

As inscribed on the monument (see Chapter 20) which was built later at the site of King Abdul Aziz's 1939 encampment in Dhahran:

"The location chosen for the University of Petroleum and Minerals links the tangible resource of energy with permanent intellectual resources, and is a symbol of the continuation of the sunny present to a prosperous future, with the help of God."

Founding a University — 1963 "The Quest for Excellence"

Note 1
   Ahmed Zaki Yamani *was born in Mecca, Saudi Arabia on June 30, 1930. He graduated from King Fouad University in Cairo in May 1951 with a degree in law. In June 1955 he was awarded a master's degree in Comparative Jurisprudence from New York University, and in June 1956 he received a master's degree from Harvard Law School in Cambridge, Massachusetts.*
   In December 1957 he was appointed legal adviser to the Council of Ministers under Crown Prince Faisal. In December 1959 he became Minister of State Without Portfolio and a member of the cabinet of the Kingdom of Saudi Arabia.
   In March 1962 he was named Minister of Petroleum and Mineral Resources. He held this post during the first years of OPEC, which was organized in 1960.
   In March 25, 1975 King Faisal was assassinated in Riyadh with Yamani at his side. On October 29, 1986 Yamani was replaced as oil minister by Hisham Mohaddin Nazer and is now an international consultant on the petroleum industry.

Note 2
   Amedeo Porro *was born at the end of World War I in Milan, Italy. He grew up in North Africa (Algeria and Tunisia) with his father, who was in the mining business. He attended French schools in Tunisia and Rome, graduating from college in Tunisia.*
   In 1940, when Italy entered World War II, he was interned as a civilian prisoner-of-war in Tunisia by the French. After three months he was released and returned to Italy where he joined the Italian army and was sent to Libya. Eventually captured by the American army, he was sent to Scotland in August 1943 to a prisoner-of-war farm.
   At the end of the war in March 1946, he was repatriated and took a job as manager of a small hotel in Rome. In 1952, he married a Brazilian girl, Regina, in Rome. They had a daughter, Lalena, and a son, Marco.
   I recall a comment that Dr. Hall once made to me, "Amedeo Porro is always a gentleman, neat, tidy, and well-dressed."
   I also personally recall that his rebuke to the incompetent and lazy could be scathing — in English, Italian, French, Spanish, Arabic, or Portuguese. Mr. and Mrs. Porro now live in Sao Paulo, Brazil.

Note 3
   Harry Snyder *was a lieutenant colonel in the U.S. Air Force in North Africa in World War II. The Allied Forces were taking a beating from Rommel in the Libyan desert. It was thought by the High Command that it might be necessary to evacuate them.*
   One plan was to make the evacuation across Saudi Arabia to India. Harry Snyder was assigned to contact King Abdul Aziz and make arrangements to do this. The plan was to build an airfield just outside of Riyadh

Jebel Dhahran and the New Saudi Generation

for servicing Allied planes, etc. in this effort. In return for permission to build the airbase, the U.S. agreed to build a hospital in Riyadh. An agreement was finally reached to also build an airfield in Dhahran near Aramco.

In the meantime, the Allied situation in Africa improved and the evacuation was not necessary, so the airfield and hospital were not built. Near the end of the war, Harry Snyder was instrumental in arranging a meeting between King Abdul Aziz and President Roosevelt. At that meeting, the King said, "Where is my hospital?" He was told that since the evacuation from North Africa never took place, it was not built. The King insisted that the agreement was still in place, and it should be built. So it was.

Note 4
Dr. Robert King Hall earned his B.A. degree from Lake Forest College in Illinois in 1934, his M.A. from Harvard in 1935, and his MA. in education from the University of Chicago in 1936.

He then traveled extensively throughout South America. When he returned to the United States, he married Margaret Wheeler of Castine, Maine and they both began teaching careers. Mrs. Hall had graduated from Wheaton College in Norton, Massachusetts in 1931.

Dr. Hall then earned his doctorate in education at the University of Michigan. In 1951 he was awarded the degree of "Catedratico Honorario" from the University of San Marcos in Lima, Peru. Also in 1951 he received an honorary LLD from Lake Forest College as a Phi Beta Kappa.

The Halls had three children — Louise, Margaret, and Marshall.

Dr. Hall actually did his undergraduate work in mathematical physics. However after he saw the extent of poverty in South America, he decided to change his major and go into something where he could do more to help underprivileged people.

When World War II came along, he joined the U.S. Navy as an officer. He served with the occupation forces in Japan on General MacArthur's staff in charge of revising the educational system of Japan.

After the war, he returned to Castine, Maine (Mrs. Hall's 200-year-old ancestral home), where he wrote a book, "Education for the New Japan".

During that time, he was approached by Columbia University in New York to come as a professor and help to expand the Department of International Education, which he did until going to Saudi Arabia in 1953. His particular field of teaching was "Education for the Emerging Nations."

I don't know that I fully appreciated the stature of Dr. Hall for some time, but I did especially after reading his book on Japan. His experience in Japan was obviously a factor in his ability to accomplish what he did at the University of Petroleum and Minerals.

The prophetic nature of Dr. Hall's observations about Japan in his book, leaves one wishing that he had also written an epilogue to his work at the University of Petroleum and Minerals.

I can accept the conclusion that he saw there an Arab renaissance in embryo.

CHAPTER 8

BUILDING THE UNIVERSITY — 1963 TO 1975

In 1964 when the board of the new college authorized Dr. Hall to interview architects to design the campus, he went to New York and contacted the Ford Foundation's Educational Facilities Laboratory, with whom he had a working relationship. CRS founding partner Bill Caudill was well known by the EFL, having been active in education and its processes for years.

EFL recommended that Hall contact CRS as well as Perkins and Will of Chicago and several other firms. Hall arranged with Caudill to come to Houston to visit CRS. As it happened, Caudill was to be away when Hall came, so he asked Tom Bullock to play host to Hall. Bullock agreed and got Charles Lawrence to join in.

Hall was keenly interested in a junior college that CRS had designed in Rangeley, Colorado. It had been built on the edge of a plateau in a sort of arid, rocky country, similar to Jebel Dhahran. "Dr. Hall was very impressed with that particular college and saw in it, I think, the possibility of what might happen at UPM," Lawrence said.

Hall "left saying he was very favorably impressed. He said that CPM was under a very tight schedule. He asked that, if we were chosen, could we come over there to research and analyze the potential sites before the end of the year. Of course we said yes, as we say yes to any opportunity. We didn't hear anything. But we did begin preparing ourselves, because he indicated that we were a potential top runner," Lawrence said.

Later, when CRS was offered the opportunity in 1964 to go to this remote part of the world, there was considerable discussion and doubt among the CRS administration. Not many people at that time knew much about Saudi Arabia, not even where it was.

Jebel Dhahran and the New Saudi Generation

Aramco had been operating since before World War II. But the war interrupted the operation considerably. Following the war to about 1965, the company grew but the majority of people inside and outside of Saudi Arabia didn't know to what extent.

CRS was forward-looking, design-oriented and challenge-oriented, but the partners hesitated. Finally, John Rowlett and Herb Paseur tipped the scales and said, "Let's do it." This had to be one of the most fortunate decisions the CRS executive board ever made, beginning over twenty years of continuous association with the Kingdom of Saudi Arabia at the university.

Late in 1964 CRS heard it had been selected by CPM. Hall said that he hadn't got the contract signed yet, but he was authorized to tell CRS to come analyze the potential sites and make a recommendation. Then he would see about taking the next step.

The first team that went over for the task of site selection included Charles Lawrence, Don Wines, and Ed Finlay. "It happened so fast," recalled Wines. "We took shots not knowing whether our proposal would be accepted by Thanksgiving, as I recall. I think we were told that we had to do the site selection by the first of the year. In order to do this, we had to receive word by Thanksgiving. I left Houston on my way to Thanksgiving in Oklahoma. I stopped by Dallas. While there, I got a call from Houston saying, 'The trip to Saudi Arabia is on.'"

The CRS team left Houston on Dec. 7 and arrived in Dhahran the next night.

"What I remember about our first night there was an explosion in the Aramco compound, when somebody's alcohol still blew up. We wondered what the devil was going on," Ed Finlay recalled in a 1989 interview.

Charles Lawrence recalled: "It was very barren and beautifully primitive. I remember the color of light in early morning and late evening. The sunsets were very impressive. You would usually see the sun as a big fireball going down. The night sky was very clear when there wasn't a shamal blowing. You could see all of the stars. I remember thinking it was obvious why these people and their civilization were the first to start thinking about astronomy, what's happening up there and why. They had such a clear view.

"The people were gregarious and friendly. The Saudis that we were in contact with and were working with, we really enjoyed. They had a good sense of humor. They really seemed to feel that we were there to help, and they were there to help us do whatever we felt was proper in getting on with this thing," Lawrence said.

In his diary of the trip, Lawrence also wrote favorably of the dinner served at Dr. Ambah's house on Dec. 9: "Great sampling of Arab dishes. Ground meat and rice, wrapped in grape leaves — okra and ground meat, topped with a slice of tomato and onion. My favorite: ground spiced meat, wrapped in a multi-layered flaky pastry blanket (called sambousaks). A Mid-East meets West dessert — tapioca pudding with cream, orange chunks, and rind."

Dr. Hall knew in his mind where the best site would be, but he wasn't telling. He thought that if CRS came up with the same site, then he would know that the right architects had been chosen.

The CRS team narrowed the choices to three, doing a full analysis on each of them. They finally recommended building the university on the elongated Jebel Dhahran, only a few yards beyond the fence demarcating Aramco's compound, called Dhahran. This jebel (or hill) is a large outcrop of rock. It would be the most difficult place to build, but obviously the most impressive, like the Parthenon in Athens and many famous buildings around the world that have been built on hilltops or high points.

CRS site selection team - first visit on Jebel Dhahran - December 1964. Lawrence, Wines and Finlay (taking photo) with Nazer, Snyder and Hall

Thomas and Nye on campus - 1965

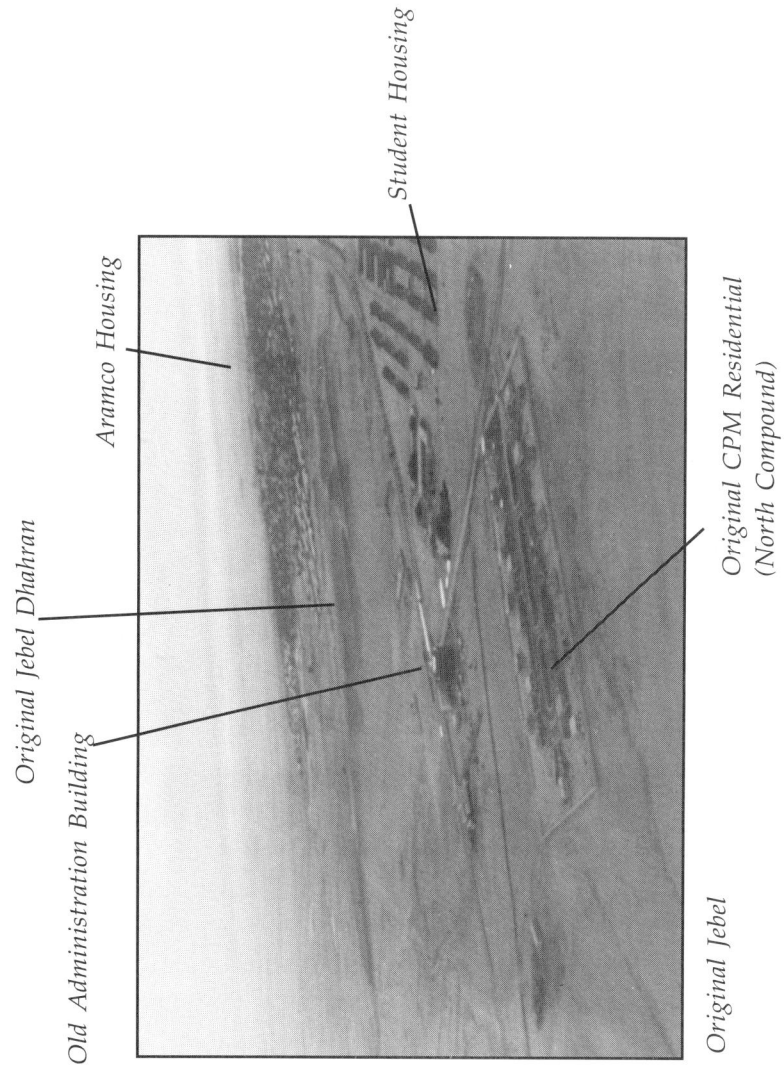

Jebel Dhahran and the New Saudi Generation

As Joe Thomas said: "That was the best (site) that CRS could find in the Eastern Province that would afford the most challenge and the best chance of producing an award-winning design for a college in Saudi Arabia."

Jebel Dhahran was also Dr. Hall's choice.

Mufti recalled:"Jebel Dhahran was an imposing site for the college. We used to run across the jebel on cross country runs as part of our physical education."

The CRS team returned in February 1965 to discuss the college master plan with the CPM board. The meeting took place in Riyadh on the top floor of the Ministry of Petroleum building in a large room with no draperies.

Recalled Wines: "We were making our presentation with an opaque projector, which requires a dark room. The light level was very high. We had some brown wrapping paper, which we vainly taped on the glass to try to get the place dark enough. The board had seven or eight members, including the chancellor of the University of Riyadh, who was myopic. He had very thick glasses. Here we were presenting a visual show, and this one member of the board couldn't see a thing, I'm sure."

"They were very responsive," Lawrence added. "By the end of this session in February, we had set all these design concepts. We spent a lot of time talking with Dean Ambah about Saudi character. We told him this was Saudi character in our interpretation." At Ambah's recommendation, the CRS team went to see the Alhambra in Spain, which Ambah considered to be the high mark of Moorish architecture.

"The biggest impact that it had on us, and we used it throughout the campus, was the use of waterways and fountains. At the Alhambra, you never walk anywhere that you don't see and hear water. Without that trip, I don't think we would have had nearly the waterways that we have now at UPM," Lawrence said.

Building the University — 1963 to 1975

"Everyone was so eager for us to be right, so helpful and so enthusiastic about the results of what we were doing. So, at that point, I had no doubt that it was going to be a great project, and it really was going to happen," Lawrence said.

The CRS team received more information about the number of students and began to scale the master plan accordingly.

Said Finlay: "What the university now has as a program is in no way what we had envisioned twenty-five years ago. Our role then was to develop a college that was to be a two-year college with a technical school. The understanding was that after two years the students would go and finish their work at major universities in Europe and the United States. It was never perceived initially as a four-year institution."

Added Lawrence: "We put together distinct groupings of education divisions, all strongly related to the scientific and technical needs of the industry in the Kingdom. Willie Pena was in charge of programming for CRS.

"We agreed that there would first be an orientation program and afterwards a technical institute with a three-year program — a program with industry that gets students to work out in the field. After that, a junior college offering mainly technical subjects and finally an engineering school. It seemed to me Dr. Hall was pushing that. He said, 'We want to keep in mind that we want to make this a real engineering college.'"

Finlay commented, "I don't think we ever dreamed that it would involve the millions of dollars that it did. The size and scope changed considerably from the original concept. However, I think that we always felt that it was going to be a little 'jewel in the desert', and really a showplace both of architecture and education for the Kingdom."

The CRS team developed the concepts for the arch and water tower during the second trip. It also came up with what Wines called the "train-wreck scheme" of long buildings laid out end to end along the rim of the jebel.

Jebel Dhahran and the New Saudi Generation

"It was definitely done to showcase the buildings," which would be visible from the busy Dhahran-Dammam highway. 'We opened them up with glass so that at night you could see into them.'

"Our concept with the oasis was to concentrate all the green in a traditional lush oasis, which is what we did. We wanted a well-defined area in which we would develop a lavish landscape of plants and water. Everything beyond that would be natural, and we would cultivate whatever natural grasses and things that grew in the desert. We saw at Aramco that if you start planting grass, where do you stop? It goes on forever."

Meanwhile, negotiations were underway with CPM over the fee for CRS. "I was designated partner-in-charge and given the responsibility for negotiating the contract for our services at UPM. That first trip (Dec. 1964) was covered by a letter of intent agreeing to pay for our trip to evaluate and recommend a site for the permanent campus. At the same time, I was consulting with our attorneys, Bracewell and Patterson, in Houston and meeting with Saleh Ambah in Dhahran working through the conditions and details of the contract. There was a lot of back and forth, and it got to the point where I was trying to be so careful and make sure, because we weren't familiar with Saudi law, or the way the Saudis would interpret the law. We were kind of second-guessing every sentence and phrase," Lawrence recalled.

Lawrence discussed the wording of the contract with Herb Paseur, who finally said, "Let's just get on with it and stop worrying."

One breakthrough on the fee structure came when Lawrence convinced Ambah that it would cost CRS more to work in Saudi Arabia than in the United States, beginning with travel costs and travel time.

But a bigger problem lay ahead.

Building the University — 1963 to 1975

Later that spring, the CRS team members returned. They took the schematic design and asked for approval to begin design development.

"We then asked for payment on that," Lawrence said. "I had written a letter to Dean Ambah trying to be very firm about what we needed for fee. I said that we couldn't do any more work until we had an agreement."

The letter greatly upset Ambah. On the team's fourth trip, when members presented a conceptual design for the first 26 faculty houses, a confrontation occurred.

Said Lawrence: "We had gotten into a bit of a hassle about the fee structure for the housing, because there was a lot of repetition. The university was taking the stand that it ought to be based on the design of one house with a small percentage for the repetition. We were agreeing that it shouldn't be just a straight fee, but we had a differing opinion of how much the repetition was worth."

"It was eyeball to eyeball," Wines remembered. "I was wondering if we were ever going to get our passports back. We said something about an Arab wouldn't see things the way we did, because of the cultural differences. Ambah came back saying that they understood just as we did, and there was no difference."

Added Lawrence: "The other comment he made was, 'I thought you were professionals, and you are acting just like contractors.' I said something like, 'You're making us feel like contractors.'"

"Ambah was so angry," Lawrence said, "that the pupils of his eyes turned white. I have never seen that in anyone. I have wanted to ask someone in the medical profession what causes this, because it just scared the hell out of me.

"I thought at that time, 'Well, this is it. Taking the project was a gamble, and we rolled the dice.' I said, 'Perhaps we had better just pack up our bags and head on home.' I stood up and walked out."

Jebel Dhahran and the New Saudi Generation

Joe Thomas had come along as the CRS team's project engineer. He told the CRS team and Ambah: "Hey, we've got to cool off. Let's just go back to the hotel and think about the situation, let UPM think about it, and then meet again tomorrow."

Recalled Thomas: "It came down to the fact that it didn't make any difference what the contract said. It was a conflict in interpretation. There were then two choices. The Saudis could fire us, and we could go home and that would be that, no matter what the contract said, or we could somehow arrive at a compromise solution."

If the conflict had happened sooner, no doubt CRS would have been fired and possibly the university would never have been built. But Ambah and the CPM board already had seen the schematics and design development drawings, and they liked what CRS had done.

Also, Dr. Hall, who had recommended CRS, stepped in to mediate the situation. He came to the CRS team and said, "I think that we can work this out," Lawrence recalled. Hall got Lawrence and Ambah to apologize to each other, and they reached a compromise on the fee structure.

It had been the intent of CRS on this trip to transfer the leadership of the CRS team from Charles Lawrence so that Lawrence could give more attention to projects in the United States. This seemed an appropriate time, so Joe Thomas then became project manager of the UPM project.

Thomas immediately set about to establish trust between CRS and CPM. "If that trust didn't exist, we were never going to pull this off, because there were too many problems between language, customs, and every thing else," Thomas said.

"One of the first things I learned about customs and traditions in Saudi Arabia was that if the man you are dealing with is sitting on one side of the table and you are sitting on the other side, you don't trust each other until you both get on the same side. I told Dr. Ambah, 'We will build you the finest university in the world. The only thing we will ask you to do is to pay us a fair price for our services, and pay us on time. All the contracts that we can draw up are not going to make these things happen.'

"After I said that at the early meeting, Ambah got up, pulled up a chair on his side of the desk and said, 'Now, you come around here and talk to me.' From that point on, I knew that Ambah and I were going to trust each other."

Added Finlay, "Ambah was very open and shared with us information we needed to know in order to do the right kind of job there for him. A lot of times, you don't see that kind of cooperation here in our own country."

Today, the Saudi government requires competitive bidding for all projects. CRS's work was all negotiated and continued thus until 1980, when the government insisted that some design work at UPM be put out for bids. CRS did all the masterplanning and design of all buildings on campus until 1981, when it did lose a housing contract to another American firm. Other than that, everything on the main campus went to CRS.

Of course, the idea of competitive bidding is to get the best price and quality, if possible, but it also opens the door to the possibility of lower quality. It was gratifying to hear Dr. Bakhrebah during 1985, the last year that I was there, say what good work they had gotten from CRS for a good price. Through the years the Saudis had seen many other construction projects on which, by the time the design was completed, insufficient money remained to build the buildings. Well, that wasn't so with CRS. The university did get a good deal, and it was good to hear it acknowledged.

CRS design teams began working in 1965. CRS is a very team-oriented company. There are no "prima donnas," as founding partner Bill Caudill would say. However, there has always been an inclination to give Charles Lawrence credit as

Jebel Dhahran and the New Saudi Generation

the chief designer and concept originator, because he was. It is amazing how close the final campus design follows his original master plan.

And there's a reason. While CRS was building the first project, the 26 faculty houses, it was designing Phases II and III. At the same time CRS was finishing the construction documents on Phase I and getting it ready for bidding.

At that point, Dr. Hall said, "I'm afraid that if we don't lock it in, Phases II and III will never be built in the concept that you have designed. How can we lock it in?"

Ed Nye, CRS chief structural engineer and Bram McClelland, geotechnical consultant, then recommended that all the excavation for Phases II and III be done along with construction of Phase I. The Water Tower was also built with Phase I. This "locked in" the design for Phases II and III.

In addition to being next to Aramco's compound, the CPM site was near the Dhahran International Airport, which doubled as a military airport. That fact nearly derailed the choice of Jebel Dhahran as CPM's site when the air base commander's office objected.

Recalled Thomas: "The general said that the jebel was strategically located for a missile site to defend the airport. Well, there were several other missile sites that were better in the Eastern Province. So, the whole thing sort of fizzled out from a military standpoint. Then he tried to lock in on the fact that the university on the jebel would interfere with the air traffic into the airport."

To make matters worse, George Noble who had been hired to be the CRS coordinator and "came to us highly recommended as to knowing what he was doing in Saudi Arabia," told Ambah that there was nothing to do but relocate CPM, Thomas recalled.

Thomas happened to be coming from Houston with a set of drawings "three feet thick" for Phases II and III of the campus construction. "Here I was sitting there with a set of construction

Building the University — 1963 to 1975

documents worth a million bucks that we hadn't been paid for, and my man-in-country had said we should move it, destroy it, and redo everything.

"I had made up my mind that, win or lose, we were going to go with what we had. We were going to put the university on that site. If we didn't, we'd have to go back to another site selection study and the whole damn thing would probably hit the trash can."

Thomas informed Ambah, who replied, "Well, that is not what Mr. Noble was telling me."

Thomas said: "I don't care what Noble said, I'm in charge of this project, and this is what we are going to do."

"OK, we'll take your advice," Ambah said.

Ambah had been a military man who maintained his rank for four or five years after the Ministry of Defense loaned him to the Ministry of Petroleum and Minerals. Later, it was decided that if he was going to continue as dean of the college, his files and papers might as well be transferred. So, he was released from the Ministry of Defense.

With that background, Ambah could see that the mountain was too close to the airbase for a radar system to give adequate early warning of attacking aircraft.

Based on this logic, the CPM board sought an independent opinion. Thomas recommended an expert on strategic military planning.

The college held the view that it was CRS's task to solve the problem. One Saudi who was there at the time said, "Joe Thomas always got the best ... people, the best man, the best this, and the best that. I give him credit for that."

As for the university's interfering with the airport traffic, Thomas sent a team of surveyors down to the airport to take some measurements. The surveyors returned with the answer he wanted.

They then submitted a very strong report to the Ministry of Defense. The facts about distances and directions were reviewed

Jebel Dhahran and the New Saudi Generation

in many meetings. Finally, CRS convinced the Ministry of Defense that, regardless of whether the university needed the mountain, it was unsuitable for their military purpose. Construction resumed.

Having overcome the military's objections, Thomas now had to collect from the CPM board for the design drawings he had brought over.

Thomas went to a meeting of the CPM board in Riyadh with Adnan Khayyal, the CPM comptroller. "Adnan was sitting next to me," Thomas recalled. "The meeting was in Arabic. He would always lean over and tell me what was going on. When it got down to the agenda with the construction on it, Adnan said, 'Now, they are getting ready to talk about the architectural engineering and design of the university.' I said, 'Great!' We had been sitting there for about an hour for all this preliminary stuff, and finally they had gotten to what I was interested in."

After a few minutes Adnan said to Thomas, "They just approved the construction of the university as designed by CRS on that site." In another few minutes he said, "They just approved to pay you."

"Great!" Thomas said.

Khayyal gave Thomas "the biggest check CRS had ever received," he recalled. Thomas flew back to Houston and went into the CRS office the following day. Waiting for him were Tom Bullock, Herb Paseur, Bill Caudill, and Bill Perry. They had all seen the communication from Noble about having to move the university, and were wondering if the job and even the whole company had been lost.

Bullock asked Thomas what had happened. "Well, it's a long story, Tom. But to soothe your fears a little bit, here's a check for a million dollars," Thomas said.

Bullock immediately called John Stanbaugh, a CRS business

consultant in Tulsa, Oklahoma. Bullock said, "John, Joe Thomas just walked into the office with a check for a million dollars, and Bill Perry fainted." Stanbaugh answered, "I just fainted, too."

CRS was paid for its work to date and received authority to proceed with designing and building the university.

With those unforeseen difficulties out of the way, CRS could now concentrate on the problem it had anticipated from the start. "The challenge here, in our minds, was to build a college or university in Saudi Arabia that would be as modern as anything in the world — in an area where modern construction techniques were non-existent.

"If the technology was not available in Saudi Arabia to do it, we were going to get the people that knew how, and we were going to bring them over there to show those people how to do it," Thomas recalled.

When the CRS team initially visited the Eastern Province, there were only two industries making construction materials: precast terrazzo and concrete blocks.

Many of Aramco's buildings were light, steel-framed, pre-fabricated buildings. The dominant style of construction in the Eastern Provice was of concrete, but it was very poorly done in those days. "I've seen them crack open bags of cement on the sand, pour some water and stir. That was concrete," Lawrence said. "We thought if we could just make them understand the importance of a proper recipe, the right mixture, and that if it's done properly, there was no reason why they couldn't have wonderful concrete.

"We also thought that we could develop a technically sound architectural concrete using Saudi limestone, sand, and cement. Then by sandblasting it, we would expose the raw aggregate," Lawrence said. "To take the method of building reinforced

Jebel Dhahran - untouched 1965

Jebel Dhahran with Water Tower - 1968

Aerial view of Jebel Dhahran - 1975

Jebel Dhahran and the New Saudi Generation

architectural concrete to where it could be used as a finish material was a big step forward."

On his first trip to Saudi Arabia, Jim Shilstone (CRS consultant for concrete) made test cylinders using sand from the water's edge at Half-Moon Bay (sharp and not round-edged), crushed limestone gravel from the "Dhahran rim", and cement that was currently in use. He tested them at Aramco's lab. Then he shipped large quantities of sand, gravel, cement, and water back to Shilstone labs in Houston for elaborate testing to determine the desired concrete mix. It was finally decided to build CPM out of poured-in-place concrete, with a sandblasted finish.

Construction of the permanent campus began in 1967. It proceeded in four major phases lasting until 1987. The result was classrooms, laboratories, athletic facilities, places of worship, administrative offices, a library, a cafeteria, an ampitheater, and all the other infrastructure and facilities of a modern, masterplanned university.

In addition to the phased construction, over 1,000 units of faculty housing and 1,500 units of dormitories, water treatment and storage plants, elementary schools for faculty children, a campus grocery store, a campus bank, and secondary physical education facilities were built from 1975 to 1987.

The first phase of the work (see table) was awarded to Taisei Construction Company of Tokyo. Work began in 1967 and was completed in 1970. As part of Phase I, Taisei excavated for the foundation of Phases II and III buildings. It took the top of the hill off at that time. It was an unusual sight to see the water tower sticking up on this hill with nothing around it.

The prices in 1965 certainly were lower than they would be later, but the risk was very high. In the end, Taisei apparently did lose a lot of money. However, in honorable Japanese fashion, it finished the project. Joe Thomas, Charles Lawrence, and

Building the University — 1963 to 1975

Terry Tengler then negotiated with Taisei in Tokyo for Phases II & III, but the price was too high. In later years, Taisei on at least one occasion checked out plans for bidding, but it never followed through.

Indeed, in the beginning CRS did have difficulty getting the contractors to mix the concrete in the right proportions. Recalled Thomas: "One night Jim Shilstone, our concrete consultant, and I were talking about it. Jim said, 'What we have to do is build a box with handles on it. We'll tell them to put in so many boxes of aggregate, so many boxes of sand, so many boxes of cement and so many buckets of water.' Jim designed the box and made a drawing of it. We then went to Taisei and said, 'You build this and tell your people out there to put exactly the number of boxes of aggregate, sand, cement, and water that we tell you to.' So, that's how we controlled the concrete."

Because large-scale equipment wasn't available in Saudi Arabia at that time, the contractors mixed the concrete in two-cubic-meter mixers — far too small for the job, but they made do with them.

Meanwhile, CRS's engineers asked for soil tests for the jebel. But the only soil-testers in the country worked for Aramco. Recalled Thomas: "We either had to go to Aramco, with hat in hand, and say, 'Can we use your soil-testers?' or we would have to go and get our own." CRS got its own.

The company hired McClelland Engineers in Houston. After McClelland's man had been in Dhahran three weeks, he cabled CRS in Houston. "At this rate, I'm going to be here about a year to get all these holes drilled that you want to test for the foundations. I need a certain drill bit that's out at Hughes Tool Co. on Katy Road in Houston. Here's the number of it. Please get it and ship it to me," the engineer said.

CRS did so, and that set a precedent. Anything that the university couldn't get, CRS would ship over and UPM would

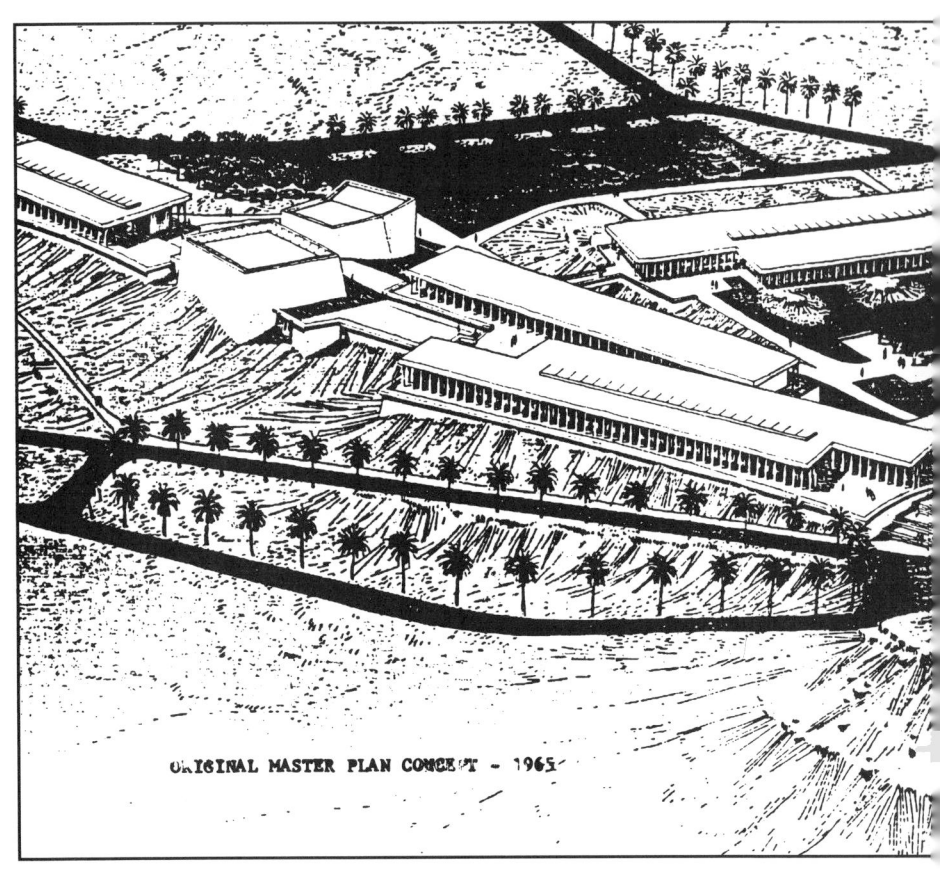
ORIGINAL MASTER PLAN CONCEPT - 1965

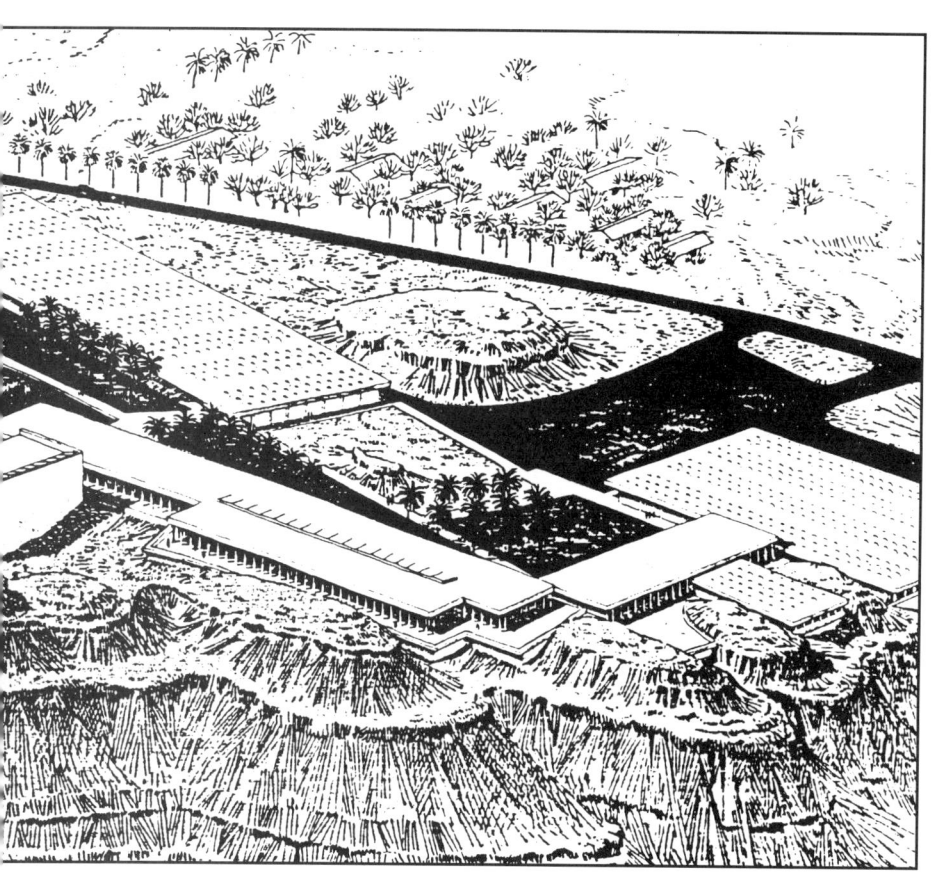
Original Master Plan Concept - 1965

Jebel Dhahran and the New Saudi Generation

reimburse CRS. The list of items even included graduation gowns.

About three weeks after the drill bit was sent, McClelland's man came back from Saudi Arabia. "What happened?" Thomas asked him. "Oh, I'm finished," the engineer told him. " That bit that you sent me just made everything happen. The bit that the well-driller had was completely worn out, and it took him forever to drill a hole."

By the time Phase IV was underway, during the height of the oil boom, numerous construction projects were underway in Saudi Arabia, and the most modern technology was readily available locally.

"The university was the granddaddy of all of it," Thomas said. "Without UPM, I don't think the things that are in Saudi Arabia today would have been built in the way that they have been built. It set a standard for the construction that followed during the great boom in Saudi Arabia. Everybody said, 'If they can do this at UPM, then the sky is the limit.'"

In May 1976, CRS founding partner Bill Caudill visited the university. He later wrote these thoughts:

"Neither Tiny Lawrence, Joe Thomas, Ed Finlay, Willie Pena, Don Wines, nor most certainly Bill Caudill was visionary enough to dream 12 years ago what's now on the top of that Jebel in Dhahran, Saudi Arabia. When the team first trekked up to the top of that protruding giant rock that hot day, it was beyond their imagination to visualize the current University of Petroleum and Minerals campus.

"It was a shock — a delightful one.

"During this last trip, my heart was singing with professional pride."

Charles Lawrence, the chief designer of UPM, remembered concerns he had early on: "What if we get over there, and

Building the University — 1963 to 1975

everything turns out to be awful?"

Then Lawrence thought, "Look, it's half way around the world from us, who is ever going to see it?.

"Boy, how wrong can you be?"

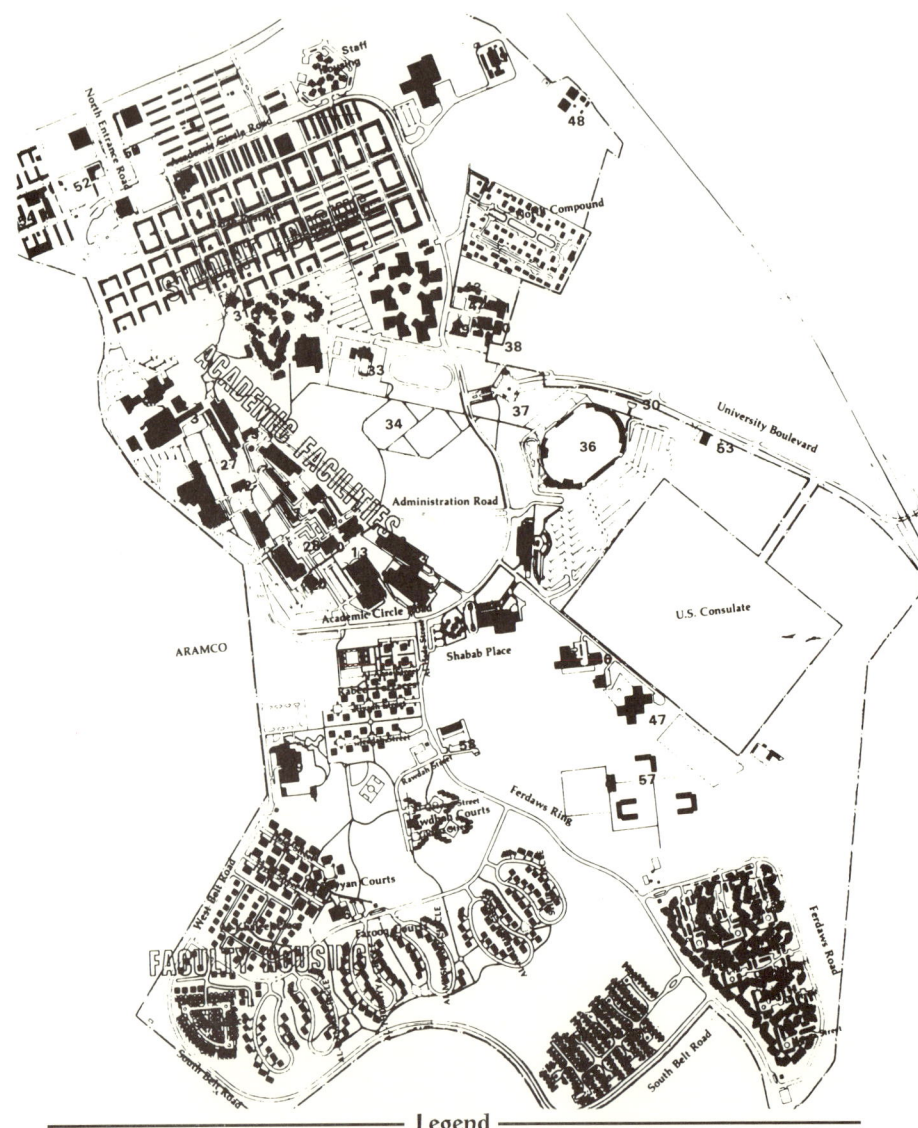

Legend

1. Building 1
2. Building 2
3. Building 3
4. Building 4
5. Building 5
6. Building 6
7. Building 7
8. Library
9. Faculty & Student Center
10. Auditorium
11. Gymnasium
12. Mosque
13. Amphitheater
14. Data Processing Center
15. Research Institute
16. Building 16
17. Student Affairs
18. Parking Garage
19. College of Environmental Design
20. Conference Center
21. Administration Building
22. Building 22
23. Parking Garage
24. College of Ind. Management
25. Parking Garage
26. Heavy Equip. Lab Building
27. Oasis
28. The Conference Center Medan
29. The Recreation Center
30. King Abdul Aziz Monument
31. Student Reception Center
32. Student Cafeteria
33. Physical Education, Lower Pool Complex
34. Soccer Practice Fields
35. Energy Research Lab
36. The Stadium
37. The Main Gate
38. Orientation Year Campus
39. Orientation Year Building
40. Computer Assisted Instruction Annex
41. Orientation Year Shop
42. Orientation Classroom, Bldg 1
43. Orientation Classroom, Bldg 2
44. Clinic
45. University Press
46. Telephone Exchange
47. South Water Plant
48. North Water Plant
49. Dangerous Chemical Storage
50. North Gate
51. Central Kitchen
52. Maint. Dept. Office
53. Bank
54. Store Houses
55. Dhahran Mosque
56. Al Farooq Mosque
57. UPM Schools
58. Coop Store

Reflecting Pool at Mosque

Research Institute

Photos p117-121 courtesy of CCC

Conference Center - Saudi Emblem

Bronze Doors made in Beirut

Research Institute - Lobby

Conference Center - Rotunda

Procession Hall

Entrance

Conference Center

Architecture Department

Research Institute

Medan Plaza

Main Entrance

Main Dining Hall

Student Dorms and Mosque

Oasis

Energy Lab

Building the University — 1963 to 1975

TABLE OF CONSTRUCTION AT KFUPM

Bldg. No.	Function	Completed	Contractor
Phase I			
0.	Water Tower	1970	Taisei
1.	Civil Engineering Lab and Powerhouse	1970	Taisei
2.	Computer Sciences (later: Petroleum Eng.)	1970 (1983)	Taisei (Beta)
3.	Classroom Building	1970	Taisei
Phases II and III			
4.	Classroom/Lab	1974	CCC
5.	Administration Bldg.	1974	CCC
6.	Classroom/Lab	1974	CCC
7.	Classroom/Lab	1974	CCC
8.	Library (later addition)	1974 (1977)	CCC (Redec Daelim)
9.	Faculty/Student Center & Dining Facilities	1974	CCC
10.	Auditorium	1974	CCC
11.	Gymnasium	1974	CCC
12.	Mosque	1974	CCC
13.	Ampitheater (outdoors)	1974	CCC

Jebel Dhahran and the New Saudi Generation

Phases IV, IV-A, IV-B

14.	Data Processing Center	1979	CCC
15.	Research Institute	1981	CCC
16.	Building 4 Addition — Faculty Offices	1980	Ballast Orient
17.	Building 9 Addition — Student Affairs	1981	al-Rashid Co.
18.	Parking Garage	981	CCC
19.	College of Env. Design	1981	CCC
20.	Conference Center	1981	CCC
21.	Administration Bldg.	1983	Redec Daelim
22/23.	Classroom, Garage & Computer Graphics	1984	Redec Daelim
24.	College of Industrial Management	1984	Redec Daelim
25.	Parking Garage	1984	Redec Daelim
26.	Heavy Equipment Laboratory	1985	Beta Company
27.	Oasis	1974	CCC
28.	Medan Plaza	1981	CCC
29.	Recreation Building Addition	1980	Redec Daelim
30.	King Abdul Aziz Monument	1980	CCC

Building the University — 1963 to 1975

31.	Student Reception Center	1980	Redec Daelim
32.	Student Cafeteria	1982	CCC
33.	Physical Education Lower Pool Complex		
34.	Soccer Practice Fields		
35.	Energy Research Laboratory	1986	Redec Daelim
36.	10,000-Seat Stadium	1982	CCC
37.	Main Gate	1982	CCC
38.	Orientation Year Campus		
39.	Orientation Year Building		
40.	Computer Assisted Instruction Annex		
41.	Orientation Year Shop		
42.	Orientation Classroom Bldg. 1		
43.	Orientation Classroom Bldg. 2		
44.	Clinic	1986	Redec Daelim
45.	University Press	1984	Yamama Establishment
46.	Telephone Exchange	1982	Redec Daelim
47.	South Water Plant		
48.	North Water Plant		
49.	Dangerous Chemical Storage	1982	CCC

50.	North Gate	1984	Redec Daelim
51.	Central Kitchen	1984	Fiafi
52.	Maintenance Dept. Office		
53.	Bank		
54.	Store Houses		
55.	Dhahran Mosque		
56.	Al Farooq Mosque	1984	al-Rashid Co.
57.	Elementary School	1985	Redec Daelim
58.	Co-op Store		

Chapter 9

"A Jewel in the Desert" — KFUPM Today

Jebel Dhahran —

The ancient traders from Persia and the Far East — the Turks who dominated the area for five hundred years — the bedouin travelling from the Nafud desert to intercept caravans carrying pilgrims laden with precious goods to trade in Mecca and the Hijaz area on the West coast — the intrepid geologists looking hopefully from Bahrain across fifteen miles of green-blue water of the Arabian Gulf.

None of these could have included in their wildest dreams a vision of the treasure that would one day lie on this geological outcropping overlooking the Arabian (Persian) Gulf.

This treasure of knowledge, now known as King Fahd University of Petroleum and Minerals, which sits atop Jebel Dhahran, was conceived initially to serve the petroleum industries and thus contribute to the Kingdom's economy and benefit its people.

In this chapter, I have drawn primarily from the King Fahd University of Petroleum and Minerals brochure entitled *Partners for Progress* published in September 1985.

The Royal Charter of the Institution provides that: "The university shall undertake all that is related to various petroleum and minerals studies and shall encourage scientific research in these fields. It shall endeavor to promote petroleum and minerals knowledge in the Kingdom and provide it with experts in the different branches of the petroleum and minerals industry."

Within these broad limits, the governing board of the university has built up over a twenty-five year period a body of principles and policies. The board's official statement of policy is: "The land, buildings, and facilities of the university are con-

Jebel Dhahran and the New Saudi Generation

sciously designed to contribute dignity and inspiration to the youth of the Kingdom entering the professions of engineering, science and management."

The policy on quality of program has the highest priority in the university's endeavor to serve precise professional needs. All academic programs are expected to meet the highest international standards of quality. To ensure that these standards are maintained, a visitation committee from the United States periodically conducts an evaluation process similar to the accreditation procedure of the Accreditation Board for Engineering and Technology (ABET).

The Consortium of American Universities involved until 1985 were: The University of Alabama, California Institute of Technology, Colorado School of Mines, Massachusetts Institute of Technology, The University of Michigan, Milwaukee School of Engineering, Princeton University, University of Rochester, and Wentworth Institute.

The American educational system of engineering schools has been adopted as the basic model, with appropriate adaptations for local needs.

The use of English as the language of instruction for all technical subjects is perhaps one of the most far-reaching and influential policies. This ensures access to the latest technical materials and prepares the graduate for effective communication with the managerial, technical, and scientific leadership of the major industries of the world.

The university is an indigenous Saudi institution. It was chartered by the Saudi government, is located in Saudi Arabia, serves the industry of the Kingdom and primarily enrolls Saudi students. It is financed exclusively with Saudi funding, is governed by a Saudi board, and is managed by a Saudi administration.

Although it is of national origin and constitution, it is in many aspects an international university. As many as three of the 12-member board in the past have been foreign members

"A Jewel in the Desert" — KFUPM Today

representing institutions of international eminence.

The university has a multi-national faculty derived from the major international sources of technology. The student body is international in composition, although primarily comprised of Saudi citizens. Preference is given to Muslims and Arabs in the admission of foreign applicants.

The university is a residential institution. All students reside on campus. The faculty and higher-level administration also reside on campus in facilities provided by the university. The student dormitories provide extensive intramural sports and extracurricular activities. Teamwork and cooperation skills are developed to emphasize the university's national character rather than local, tribal, or class loyalties.

An excellent program of physical education is provided, designed to develop physical stamina and good habits of health and recreation.

Part-time employment on campus and a required summer employment program provide the student with practical work experience and discipline.

The methods, techniques, and procedures used in all programs and management are consciously chosen to exemplify the most advanced methods currently used in international organizations. For example, when the first IBM 1130 computer was installed in 1967, it was considered by many outside the university to be a hopeless extravagance at that stage of development. Within three years, the data processing center had revolutionized teaching and research in the university.

The King Fahd University of Petroleum and Minerals (KFUPM) is a semi-autonomous government institution of higher education established to support the petroleum and minerals industry. It is operated under an independent board of the university and, like all other universities in Saudi Arabia, it is administratively attached to the Ministry of Higher Education.

Jebel Dhahran and the New Saudi Generation

Although begun as an undergraduate technical college twenty-five years ago, it is today one of the leading technical institutions in the Middle East.

The university was established by a royal decree on September 23, 1963 with the name of "College of Petroleum and Minerals." It opened its doors to students one year later.

The first chief executive officer, Dr. Saleh Ambah, then called the dean of the college, equivalent to the president of an American university or the vice-chancellor of a British university, was appointed by a Council of Minister's decision on September 29, 1963.

The first land, a plot about the size of a football field, consisting of unimproved desert, was transferred to the college on October 28, 1963, and the first budget was approved (approximately $444,000) on December 23, 1963.

Classes began one year later on September 23, 1964, and included 52 Saudis and 15 Algerian students, who were admitted on fellowships.

The first faculty consisted of fourteen instructors, lecturers and professors recruited from various parts of the world in the previous two months.

The academic program was initially limited to courses in English, mathematics, physics and chemistry. The curriculum expanded upward through the lower division of undergraduate studies to its present-day status.

This has been a pioneering effort in the classical sense and was marked by an unbelievably high morale and a determination to strive for excellence in everything that the university undertook. From these modest beginnings, the university has within two decades developed from a college into a full-fledged professional institution of university level.

The second chief executive officer, Dr. Bakr Abdullah bin Bakr, was appointed on May 23, 1971, and he became rector of the university, as it was officially designated, on January 17, 1975.

"A Jewel in the Desert" — KFUPM Today

The enrollment in 1985 was 3,500 undergraduate and 290 graduate students. They came from fifty countries in addition to those from Saudi Arabia. At the end of the first semester of 1985, the university had awarded a cumulative total of 2,956 B.S. and 188 M.S. degrees in science and engineering as well as 88 MBA degrees.

The full-time instructional faculty on campus in 1985 totalled 535, of which 396 were foreign-contract and 139 Saudis. The foreign-contract faculty was drawn from 29 nationalities:

- 94 American
- 77 British
- 27 Canadian
- 48 European
- 150 Middle Eastern, African, Asian, with Egyptian and Pakistanis representing the two largest nationalities.

Of the total faculty, 321 held PhD degrees. Of the 139 Saudi full-time faculty, 92 held PhDs in technical subjects from American or European universities.

The university occupies 909 acres (3,680,000 square meters) of land as its central campus and an additional 6,283,000 square meters of beach property at Half Moon Bay on the Arabian Gulf.

As of March 31, 1984, the capital assets of the university were SR 224,515,040 (US $62 million). The operating expense budget for 1985-86 totalled SR 520,550,000 (US $144 million). The capital expense budget for the same period totalled SR 166,600,000 (US $46 million). All budgets are financed by Saudi Arabian government appropriations.

Since its establishment, the university has received a total of 35 million U.S. dollars from non-government sources, principally oil companies.

As stated in the KFUPM publication *Partners For Progress:*

Jebel Dhahran and the New Saudi Generation

"The university is determined to evaluate its performance primarily by comparison with international leaders in its particular fields of technology. Government, industry, and the international academic world will provide the ultimate test of the university's achievement. Success can only come by achieving this goal of excellence in its third decade."

The university is currently divided into eight academic units principally concerned with instruction and research:

1. Preparatory Year Program
2. Six Undergraduate Colleges
   a. College of Applied Engineering
   b. College of Engineering Science
   c. College of Science
   d. College of Industrial Management
   e. College of Environmental Design
   f. College of Computer Science and Engineering
3. College of Graduate Studies

Programs of study leading to the Bachelor of Science degree are currently offered in:

1. Chemistry
2. Geology
3. Geophysics
4. Industrial Chemistry
5. Mathematics
6. Physics
7. Computer Science
8. Civil Engineering
9. Chemical Engineering
10. Electrical Engineering
11. Mechanical Engineering

12. Mining Engineering
13. Petroleum Engineering
14. Systems Engineering
15. Applied Civil Engineering
16. Applied Chemical Engineering
17. Applied Electrical Engineering
18. Applied Mechanical Engineering
19. Architectural Engineering
20. Architectural Design
21. City Planning
22. Industrial Management

Master of Science degrees are currently awarded in many of the above programs. Doctoral programs are currently offered by the Departments of:

1. Chemical Engineering
2. Electrical Engineering
3. Civil Engineering
4. Chemistry
5. Petroleum Engineering

There are several support services for the main academic programs.

The Library, with 7,000 square meters of floor space includes a multi-media collection of materials, audio-visual aids, and various equipment study aids. Its book collection numbers 222,340 volumes with about 75 percent in science and engineering and 25 percent in humanities and social sciences. About 18,500 volumes are in Arabic and the rest primarily in English. In addition the library has about 476,237 technical reports on microfiche as well as numerous 16 mm. films, cassettes, and other non-print materials.

The library collections are constantly updated and enriched through acquisitions, ensuring a continuous flow of books as soon as they are published. Obsolete and outdated materials are constantly being withdrawn and distributed to interested organizations in the Kingdom and abroad.

The KFUPM Library has spearheaded the interlibrary cooperation movement among academic and research institutions in Saudi Arabia and their counterparts in the Arabian Gulf region. It is a pioneer in the area with the use of on-line researching and an integrated library automation system.

On-line retrieval of information is one of the major services the library offers to the KFUPM academic community. The library has access to the two major services in North America — Systems Development Corporation's ORBIT and Lockheed's DIALOG, each located in California.

The Data Processing Center at KFUPM is one of the major data processing facilities in the Middle East. Besides its services to the university community, it also provides services to external government and industrial agencies.

The center includes the latest IBM and Kodak equipment and also provides graphical capabilities to both academic and business applications. The center supports administrative data processing for the university (payrolls, budget, student records system, library, storehouse, inventory, etc.); academic computer services for faculty, students, staff, and the Research Institute, and external computer services for the outside community, particular government agencies.

Other academic supporting services include the *Central Research Workshop* the *English Language Center*, the *Physical Education Department* and the *Cooperative Work/Study Program*.

The 12-member board of the university, originally having the Minister of Petroleum and Minerals as its chairman, is now headed by the Minister of Higher Education, with eight government officials as ex-officio members and three other appointed members.

"A Jewel in the Desert" — KFUPM Today

For the first fourteen years, the appointed positions were held by representatives of distinguished foreign technical institutions. Now, they are filled by the Minister of Municipality and Rural Affairs, the Minister of Pilgrimage and Endowments and a prominent Saudi engineer.

For more than six years, the former dean of the Graduate School of the Massachusetts Institute of Technology (MIT) served on the board until his retirement. Two presidents of the American University of Beirut (AUB) served for a total of twelve years. The director of the Institut Français du Petrol (IFP) of Paris, France served on the board for twenty years.

The Saudi Minister of Foreign Affairs, the Minister of Planning, four Ministers of State, the president of the Islamic Development Bank, the Saudi representative to the International Atomic Energy Commission in Vienna, several deputy ministers and others high in the Government of Saudi Arabia have served on the board.

THE BOARD OF THE UNIVERSITY in 1985 consisted of:

H.E. Sheikh Hassan bin Abdullah al-Shaikh (chairman)
    Minister of Higher Education
Dr. Bakr Abdullah bin Bakr
    Rector of King Fahd University of Petroleum and Minerals
Sheikh Abdulwahab Abdul Wasie
    Minister of Pilgrimage and Endowments
Sheikh Ibrahim al-Angari
    Minister of Rural and Municipal Affairs
Dr. Abdul Madi Taher
    Governor of Petromin
Dr. Mansour al-Turki
    Rector of King Saud University
Dr. Saud al-Jammaz
    Deputy Minister of Education for Technical Affairs
    Ministry of Education

Dr. Saleh al-Omair
   Deputy Minister of Finance for Budget Administration
   Ministry of Finance & National Economy
Dr. Nasser al-Rashid
   Businessman
Dr. Abdul Rahman al-Shubaili
   Deputy Minister for Technical Affairs
   Ministry of Higher Education
Mr. Abdul Aziz al-Shunaiber
   Deputy Minister for Administrative Affairs
   Ministry of Petroleum & Mineral Resources
Mr. Ghazi Sultan
   Deputy Minister for Mineral Resources
   Ministry of Petroleum & Mineral Resources

THE ADMINISTRATION OF THE UNIVERSITY — 1985
THE COUNCIL OF DEANS

Dr. Bakr Abdullah bin Bakr
   Rector of the University
Dr. Fahd M. Dakhil
   Vice Rector for Graduate Studies and Research
Dr. Youssef O. al-Rashid
   Vice Rector for Academic Affairs
Dr. Saleh A. Bakhrebah
   Secretary General
(To be appointed)
   Dean of Faculty and Personnel Affairs
Dr. Ruwaid A. Akkad
   Dean of Student Affairs
Dr. Abdullah E. Dabbagh
   Director of the Research Institute
Dr. Mansour Nazer
   Dean of Engineering
Dr. Fahd A. al-Husseini
   Dean of Sciences

Dr. Abdulrahman al-Jafary
    Dean of Industrial Management
Dr. Zamil A. R. al-Mokrin
    Dean of Environmental Design
Dr. Abdullah al-Zakri
    Dean of the College of Graduate Studies
Dr. Saleh J. Ashoor
    Dean of Library Affairs
Dr. Mohammed Ghazali Khayat
    Faculty Member, College of Engineering Sciences
Dr. Mohammed Maqsood Khan
    Faculty Member, College of Applied Engineering
Dr. Hassan al-Tayyem
    Faculty Member, College of Sciences
Dr. Ghazi Mahmoud Habib
    Faculty Member, College of Industrial Management
(To be appointed)
    Faculty Member, College of Environmental Design

SUPPORTING SERVICES

Dr. Abdulrahman al-Ageel
    Acting Assistant Comptroller
Mr. Norman Keith Hester
    Registrar
Dr. Mohammed A. Abul Hamayel
    Director, Data Processing Center
Dr. Yousif el-Dukair
    Director, Medical Department

CHAIRMEN OF THE ACADEMIC DEPARTMENTS

Dr. Mohammed A. Hasanian
  Chemical Engineering
Dr. Islam A. Basunbul
  Civil Engineering
Dr. Mohammed al-Suwaiyel
  Computer Science and Engineering
Dr. Farid M. Zedan
  Electrical Engineering
Dr. Jasim al-Ansari
  Mechanical Engineering
Dr. Mohammed Ali-al-Marhoun
  Petroleum Engineering
Dr. Ala H. al-Rabeh
  Systems Engineering
Dr. Ahmed M. Bukhari
  Chemistry
Dr. Abdulmalek Kadi
  Islamic and Arabic Studies
Dr. Abdul Rauf Jado
  Earth Sciences
Dr. Bakr Hassan
  Mathematical Sciences
Dr. Osama B. Dabbousi
  Physics
Dr. Abdulrahim Ali al-Gattan
  MBA Program, College of Industrial Management
Dr. Mohammed al-Mubarak
  Undergraduate Program, College of Industrial Management
Dr. Mohammed A. Buraey
  Management Development Program,
  College of Industrial Management

Dr. Ibrahim M. Shukri
  City Planning
Dr. Abdulmohsin al-Hammad
  Architectural Engineering Program
Mr. Orhan Ozguner
  Architecture
Dr. Saadi A. Assaf
  Construction Engineering and Management
Dr. Mohammed Amin Mulla
  Director, Preparatory Year Program
  and English Language Center
Dr. Ali Abu Saleh
  Director, Physical Education

The Rector of the University is assisted by two Vice Rectors (One for Academic Affairs and one for Graduate Studies and Research); the Secretary General; the Council of Deans (composed of the two Vice-Rectors, the Secretary General, eight Deans, the Director of the Research Institute and one faculty member from each Undergraduate College); and several advisory Standing Committees.

The two Vice Rectors are appointed for three-year terms (renewable once). Academic Department Chairmen are appointed annually for one year.

The Secretary General is assisted by six Directors General and several Directors of the Administrative Units, who are appointed for indefinite terms. These positions are reserved for Saudis.

The Research Institute, established in 1975, is an integral part of the University, but has its own permanent, independent, full-time research and support staff adequate to maintain a sustained level of research capacity in six functional areas.

Jebel Dhahran and the New Saudi Generation

These include:
1. Petroleum and Gas Technology
2. Geology and Minerals
3. Water Resources and Environment
4. Energy Resources
5. Metrology, Standards, and Materials
6. Business Studies.

The Research Institute conducts research programs of three types:
1. Departmental Research
2. University-Sponsored Research
3. Contract (or Project) Research.

The Research Institute depends on the available support services of the university for generalized support but maintains an independent staff for its specialized needs.

An important stimulus for research, with the capability of providing appropriate levels of funding, is the King Abdul Aziz City for Science and Technology (KACST), a government agency entrusted with the responsibility for promoting and encouraging applied scientific research. A number of KFUPM faculty members are currently conducting applied research at the university under KACST financial grants.

As the university approaches the end of its third decade, it can truly be said that the motivations and goals of its original founders remain unchanged and the long-range impact and benefits from this "treasure on Jebel Dhahran" are beyond calculation at this point in time.

The following quote from the brochure, *Partners for Progress,* probably describes best the quality of the people who have made the university what it is today and of those young Saudis of the "New Generation," who will go forth to create the Saudi Arabia of tomorrow:

Crown Prince Fahd visits - 1980

National Guard Band

Graduation

Dr. Bakhrebah leads procession.

Dr. Bakr awards the diplomas.

"A Jewel in the Desert" — KFUPM Today

"The faculty who come, the Saudis and the foreign contract men who join the university, will be a different kind. Some may be misled with the image of easy professional advancement, high salaries, and the excitement of effortlessly riding the booming economy to personal wealth.

"These are false goals, and men so motivated will not last. The men who come to stay and to succeed will be men who bring the same professional ethics, the same insistence on excellence, and the same commitment to teach and to learn that have created great universities in other times and other places.

"The King Fahd University of Petroleum and Minerals today seeks individuals who long for a new frontier, one of the intellect and of the discovery of the unknown. It does not seek those who are frustrated by difficulties, but rather those who would surmount them. It wants men whose security comes from professional competence and not the rules of bureaucracy. It wants individuals who create, not merely repeat.

"For those who want to share in the educational development of young men in a new and different society, and who want to contribute something of great value to positive creative efforts for world peace and understanding, the opportunity to serve on the faculty or research staff of the university is probably unmatched anywhere else today. It is an opportunity for men of strength, wisdom and character — and for those who expect to find, and to contribute to this university's 'QUEST FOR EXCELLENCE.'"

PART IV

UNIVERSITY ASSIGNMENT — 1975 TO 1986

Chapter 10   Assignment — 1975

Chapter 11   Beirut

Chapter 12   CRS on Site

Chapter 13   Construction Administration Phase IV — 1975 to 1986

Chapter 14   The Agony of Implementation

"*Give help in whichever country you are and do not say 'I am a stranger.'*"

Ubaid ibn al-Abbas
Arab Poet

CHAPTER 10

ASSIGNMENT — 1975

In December of 1974, King Faisal dedicated the first three phases of the campus master plan for the University of Petroleum and Minerals in Dhahran. This was quite a ceremony. I don't know that it was written up in the American press. At that time, I was working in Houston and don't recall seeing anything about it. Meanwhile, the oil embargo had taken place starting in September 1973, so there was quite an anti-Arab feeling among most Americans, as lines at the filling stations became long and the ability to get all the gas we wanted all the time disappeared.

Then, three months after the dedication came the startling news that King Faisal had been assassinated by a deranged nephew. That did make headlines. King Faisal's picture was on the cover of Time magazine.

On the personal side, I was not satisfied with my work and was looking for something else to do. About May, I read that the architecture firm CRS (Caudill, Rowlett, and Scott) was working in the Middle East. Through the American Institute of Architects in Houston, I knew the principals of CRS — Bill Caudill, John Rowlett, and Wallie Scott — and also Herb Paseur, who was president then, and Tom Bullock, the chairman. However, I had never had any business dealings with them.

The article in the paper sparked my interest, so one day I picked up the phone, called Herb Paseur and said, "Herb, I'm looking for an interesting job."

He replied, "Well, we're doing some pretty big projects in Saudi Arabia."

My thought was not going to Saudi Arabia, but possibly just working on those projects in the Houston office.

Herb said, "You know Wallie Scott. Why don't you come to see him tomorrow?"

Jebel Dhahran and the New Saudi Generation

Wallie confirmed that CRS had been working in Saudi Arabia for ten years. As a matter of fact, a large new phase of their project was just starting.

Wallie said, "Why don't you turn in your resume to the personnel director?"

I did, and included a copy of my Rice Institute theme. Wallie was quite surprised to see it. He was amazed that I had written it in 1938, when few people knew or cared that Saudi Arabia existed.

I didn't hear anything from CRS for several weeks, so I began to look elsewhere. Then one day I got a message that a Joe Thomas from CRS had called.

"How would you like to go to Saudi Arabia?" he asked when I called him back.

I said, "Well, that's a big question. I don't think I can answer that right off. I'll have to talk to my family." We'd never been anywhere together but Mexico.

That night I explained the offer to my wife, Mildred, and our three college-age children — Dick, Becky, and Cheryl. Far from opposing it, they all thought it was a great idea.

The next day, I interviewed all day at the CRS office with Joe Thomas and others. At one point Joe posed what was supposed to be a hypothetical question. I later found out this related to a real problem at the UPM project.

He asked, "What would you do if a contractor was not performing according to the contract?"

I said I would sit down with him and try to determine the reason. Then, if it continued, I would threaten to withhold payment.

I must have given him the right answer, because at the end of the day he said, "We're ready to offer you the job."

I said, "I'm ready to take it."

From then on things really accelerated. Mildred and I needed passports, visas, shots, etc. She had to arrange to terminate her

Assignment — 1975

teaching work at St. John's School. We decided to sell our house and store our furniture. CRS wanted me to start coming to the office right away to familiarize myself with the job.

One day in July, Joe Thomas asked me to go to Austin with him. I already had plans to visit my mother in San Antonio, since I wouldn't see her for a while once we moved to Saudi Arabia. We agreed that I would drive up to Austin after my visit.

That morning in Austin, I met my first Saudi. Dr. Nasser al-Rashid was the CRS Saudi partner in Saudi Arabia. He was a University of Texas graduate, and had taught there as a graduate assistant. He would later become a big entrepreneur in Saudi Arabia — very influential and close to the King. He had just resigned as dean of engineering at UPM and had established his own engineering firm. Joe gave him my resume to take back to the university for approval.

I was then told that a new dean of business, Dr. Saleh A. Bakhrebah, was taking over the responsibilities of supervising university projects. Dr. Bakhrebah interviewed me in Houston a few days later. I sat in on all his meetings with CRS on the new projects under design.

On the second or third day, we were sitting in a conference room with a glass wall that looked onto a concrete patio. Suddenly, the sky broke loose. Rain began filling up the patio. Soon the lights went out. Everything was in disarray. Everyone disappeared. Dr. Bakhrebah and I watched the water rise, not knowing what to do. Conrad Neal was frantically trying to unstop the drain on the patio. CRS finally sent everyone home. I mention this because it became somewhat prophetic of my first days in Saudi Arabia.

Once I had received everyone's approval, the next thing was to get there. Getting a visa is something that can take quite a while sometimes. Dr. Bakhrebah said, "I'll give you three letters. One letter is inviting you and your wife to enter the Kingdom for ninety days. The second one will be for sixty days, and the

Jebel Dhahran and the New Saudi Generation

third one will be for thirty days. You'll go to Beirut, make your visa application there, and take the longest visa they will give you. That will save time, rather than waiting for it here."

Before we left Houston, Mildred packed in her suitcase a compass and a United States flag. She had no intention of getting "lost in the desert", and she wanted it known that she was an American.

Joe Thomas prepared a travel schedule. We arranged to stop in London to visit our daughter Becky, who was living in England at the time. After several days in London, we caught a Middle East Airlines flight for Beirut. There, we got our visas, visited the CRS office, caught our Saudi Airlines flight and arrived on schedule in Dhahran at midnight on August 15, 1975. We were beginning to see an environment and culture unlike any we had seen before.

A fine young Saudi, Abdullah K. Mufti, met us at the airport, and our Saudi Arabian days and nights began — 4,001 of them.

It was obvious when CRS offered me the job that there was an urgency to our arrival. From the time I was offered the job to the time we were ready to leave Houston a little over a month had elapsed. CRS would like it to have been less. In the meantime, CRS had been sending people over for a month at a time. I saw Alex Brailas in the Houston office before I left, and he was there in Saudi Arabia when I arrived. He stayed for two weeks and returned to Houston.

From the project correspondence I saw in Houston and conversations with Joe Thomas, I had learned that the urgency concerned a housing project. An error in the survey had led to a site-fill discrepancy.

It was, however, really more than that. Six months earlier, CRS had thought its work at UPM was more or less finished. It had completed Phases I, II, and III and demobilized the onsite

Keith Brandie and Don Chambers - British Tennis

J.C. Kim, Don Chambers, Bob Cook - Library Addition

Jebel Dhahran and the New Saudi Generation

staff. Everybody, including Don Chambers, (the project engineer at that time) went to the new CRS office in Beirut.

Don said that he was looking for other jobs, perhaps in Africa or Australia. A Houston architect-engineer named Bob Hendrickson had been in charge for Phases II and III for about three years. He, too, had gone to Beirut.

Then CRS decided that it needed somebody back in Dhahran when it won new design work at UPM, the 189 Faculty Houses project. Don volunteered for the job of resident architect-engineer. Bob Hendrickson, who had been his boss before, did not want the job.

Hendrickson then went to work as vice president of operations for the Lebanese contractor who was going to build the houses. I'm sure the contractor thought Hendrickson's experience with CRS and UPM would be good for the company. Instead, a personal relations problem developed between Hendrickson and his former subordinate, Don Chambers.

Don was a British mechanical engineer who had lived for fifteen years in the Middle East — Iran, Kuwait, and Saudi Arabia. Two of Don and Pat's children, daughter Jill and son Laurie, had been born in Iran. Michael, the youngest, was born in England. Don might be called the typical British expatriate. After observing the British for eleven years, I concluded that an innate quality common to them all makes them good at international work. In fact, at one time it made them colonial masters of the world, with the greatest empire that ever existed.

I had a chance to "settle in" to Dhahran before I met Don, who was on vacation in England for two weeks after we arrived. Physically, Don wasn't imposing —fortyish, medium height and build, a rather quiet, unassuming demeanor.

The problem with Hendrickson was something Don didn't like to talk about. It seemed to "pain" him somewhat. He said he had always thought of Bob as his friend. He didn't know

Assignment — 1975

what had happened.

Many attitudes and relationships in the Middle East do indeed seem to defy explanation. It became apparent to me that Don's character and personality could not be defined accurately by physical standards alone, although he was a champion tennis player and loved British football (American soccer). His true make-up was really in the mental realm. I learned this after some time. His mind was like a "computer." He observed everything in detail, and it was all plugged into the "computer." It was then available for assimilation and recall at any time.

He was totally unemotional. He would stare you straight in the eye while you were talking and without betraying his thoughts or reaction. Although he had a very engineering-type mind, there was, oddly enough, an underlying artistic quality. He would draw elaborate, very artistic "doodles" while in a conference.

Don was, as they say, "unflappable." He was an untiring and unflinching competitor — in sports or in an argument. He was not personally sensitive or inflexible, however — but could change course or position if he felt he was wrong or saw a better way to go.

I would not say he was compassionate, but he was a devoted husband and father.

I felt that Don was skeptical of my abilities the first six months I was there, but after seeing me survive several crises, I felt that I gained his confidence and respect. Apparently our qualities complemented each other, because we worked successfully together as a team for seven years. Then for four years I was in charge in Dhahran and he was my boss in Houston. Beneath his implacable exterior, I discovered a constant underlying sense of humor, sometimes hardly perceptible.

I don't say that all that he did was the way I would have done it, but he was a very safe administrator for CRS. He was always looking out for the company, to the point of stretching the facts in its favor. That is the ideal person for a company to

Jebel Dhahran and the New Saudi Generation

have in a position like that. By the time he left, seven years later, and I took over his job for four years, I had learned enough from him to feel that I could carry on.

We landed in Dhahran after midnight. We couldn't see much on the drive from the airport except the magnificent water tower which CRS designed on top of Jebel Dhahran, brilliantly lit at night. It was quite spectacular. Our house was a bit of a shock to Mildred at first, because it was just a small prefab, one of a hundred that were in one compound of the university, which were obtained from Aramco.

As a matter of fact, the main problem at the university at that time was a housing shortage. It had these hundred, which were in the best setting of all and were in an area that had grown up like Aramco with trees and grass. It was very pleasant from that standpoint. But the houses were below expectations for most people, who came from better than that back in the States —certainly we did. In addition, there were about a hundred houses of better quality that CRS had designed in the past five years. However, assignment to these was more or less prioritized by faculty seniority.

The next day, Mildred was still overcoming jet lag. She stayed home in bed. One of the CRS men, Paul Roy, picked me up and I reported to the CRS office. The office staff was not at full force, since the only work at that time was warranty work on Phases II and III.

From then on, day by day, we began to get the feel of things. We went to town to shop the second night we were there. Alex Brailas, who had been there several times, took us to the main street of al-Khobar. We went to a small grocery store there and did our first grocery shopping. Mildred never batted an eye at anything. I heard Alex behind us say, "Well, she passed the first test."

Assignment — 1975

As for going to town and shopping, quite a change took place in the eleven years that we were there. The number of stores downtown multiplied. By the time we left, there was a large Safeway store, which was as well stocked and managed as any in the United States. Other supermarkets opened. At first, we often went shopping at the open souq (market) in Dammam on Thursdays. The last few years, we rarely did. In some ways, the early days were interesting, because you were more into the old native atmosphere.

Six months after we arrived in Dhahran, I came close to bringing our stay to an early end. Through the school where she worked, Mildred had the opportunity to attend an educational conference in Isfahan, Iran, in April. I had applied for exit visas, which expatriates must have for any trip out of Saudi Arabia, but somehow mine hadn't come through. I was not going to let her go to Isfahan without me. The day before the visa was required, the passport department advised that it wasn't there and it didn't know when it was going to be. I really blew up. I marched into Dr. Bakhrebah's office. Mrs. Kirkwood, who was visiting at the time, was there with Don Chambers. I sputtered that if I didn't get the visa the next day, I was leaving. Dr. Bakhrebah was quite taken aback and said, "You mean for good?" I replied, "Yes."

The next day I had the visa. I don't recall many instances when I blew up like that. Being so new on the scene, I didn't understand the way things worked, and I guess I was under some kind of cultural pressure at that time. I later went in to see Dr. Bakhrebah and apologized. I said, "I hope you can find it in your heart to forgive me." Forgiveness, according to Western perception, is not an Arab characteristic. Dr. Bakhrebah, however, didn't seem to mind, but did say, "We don't like to operate under threats."

Jebel Dhahran and the New Saudi Generation

Although I initially had a little difficulty with Dr. Bakhrebah, I soon established a good relationship with him. He was inclined to play cat and mouse with you. He must have respected me, however, because from then on I think he tolerated a lot of things from me. He was definitely forgiving.

The Saudis who were running the university, and for that matter a lot of the development in the country, were quite young. It reminded me of the early days of America, when many men in responsible positions were in their late twenties or early thirties. It is hard to realize the responsibility they were taking. Dr. Bakhrebah was around thirty years old when we went there. Abdullah Mufti and Mansour al-Saber were also about thirty as were many others. Dr. Bakr, the rector of the university was only thirty-eight.

These young men were making decisions on millions of dollars of work with completely new concepts. And these people worked. Dr. Bakr, Dr. Bakhrebah, Mansour al-Saber, Abdullah Mufti, Yousef al-Koheji, Ibrahim al-Jalal, Abdul Rahman al-Ageel, Abdul Aziz Bulaihid, Abdul Aziz al-Dukhayil, Abdul Rahman al-Zamil — all these young Saudis at the university got where they were by their own efforts.

I've heard expatriate workers say that the Saudis don't want to work. Maybe they don't want to do a lot of manual labor - but who does? I have never seen anyone work harder than Dr. Bakr, Dr. Bakhrebah, Mansour al-Saber, and other administrators at the university. Really, they were a rare breed. Today, they are in their forties or early fifties.

A new generation is coming along. The critical thing will be the quality of those coming along in the next twenty-five years, with many more becoming educated. Will their sons have the same qualities and vision? Perhaps they have had too much handed to them on a silver platter. I hope not.

Mansour told me he gave a lot of credit for his desire to be educated to his mother. He was raised in Mecca. He talked

Assignment — 1975

about sitting on the floor and reading by candlelight. I asked him, "How did you happen to come to the university?" He replied that he just heard that it was a possibility and that there were opportunities. He became a civil engineer because that is what was offered.

I heard similar remarks while having lunch with some people from the Saudi air force base; the vice-rector of the university, Dr. Abdul Aziz Gwaiz; a prince who was a jet pilot; and the base commander. I asked the prince why he became a pilot. "That is what was available," he replied. "Then, you didn't have many choices. You took what presented itself. First of all, you had to have the ambition to do something more."

"Now," he said, "my son will have a choice, if he wants to be a pilot, or a teacher or something else."

The author of a new book about Saudi Arabia emphasizes having practiced underground reporting, writing articles for newspapers clandestinely from within this "closed" country. There is a little drama and appealing mystique to that. You feel, "Here I am on the 'inside' now, and I can let the 'outside' world know what is going on."

My wife and I successfully concluded eleven years on a definite basis of friendship with the Saudis. We came under no pretenses. We never tried to be something we weren't, and they respected that. The Saudis were open with us, and on a one-to-one basis there was never any deception or feeling of spying or any such thing as that.

I recall reading that the reason the early Americans at Aramco did well, wasn't because of the U.S. government, since those relations were not anything to speak of in the early thirties. The oil roughnecks that went over were a straightforward, hard-living bunch of guys, but they were basically honest, and the Saudis respected that. People talk about the Saudis being somewhat devious and that sort of thing, but they could make a contract on a handshake basis just like the oil operators did in the Esperson Drug Store in Houston in the old days, and they had complete faith in each other.

An incident comes to mind that occurred after we had been there awhile. All contracts had to be approved by what was known as the Bids and Tenders Committee, chaired by Dr. Bakhrebah. We were presenting our recommendation for awarding the contract to build the newest dormitories to the Korean firm, Redec Daelim. Some new young members of the committee were somewhat contentious and maybe a little anti-CRS. One of my faults is a tendency to over-analyze people and things. I felt they (and this is a committee of twelve) were getting off on a tangent, and I was assuming this and that about what they were thinking.

Dr. Bakhrebah was very pragmatic and knew how to handle them better than I did, of course. He knew how he wanted it to go, but he diplomatically wanted everybody to have his say. (Incidentally, Dr. Hall once told me that in dealing with the Saudis, one of the worst things you can do is to cut them off in conversation.) I made some comment to Dr. Bakhrebah that I was afraid they were misinterpreting something.

He was very patient, but finally said, "Walter, will you please stop trying to figure us out and just do what we say."

It was good natured. So, I stopped trying to "figure them out."

Chapter 11

Beirut

My fascination with Arabs actually began in my senior year of high school. It was shared by many teen-age boys at that time with a yearning for adventure. Lowell Thomas' book on Lawrence of Arabia, and Richard Halliburton with his somewhat exaggerated tales of adventures around the world were common reading material. Another book, a gift from my uncle, further whetted my appetite for adventure and travel. This was *"Personal History*" by Vincent Sheean, a journalist who had travelled extensively in Africa, the Middle East, and the Far East, always seeming to be in the right place and at the right time to observe history being made.

I was reassured that destiny was on track, on our first night in the beautiful new Holiday Inn in Beirut, when I saw and purchased a new book entitled, *"Faisal, the King and His Kingdom"* by Vincent Sheean. In 1960, he had spent six months as Crown Prince Faisal's guest in Riyadh.

That was August 12, 1975. Four months before, in April, the civil war in Lebanon had begun to erupt. There was a lull in the fighting between April and August. We saw evidences of the military around, but there was no actual fighting going on at the time. The war accelerated after we were there in August.

What we didn't know then was that the beautiful revolving restaurant atop the Holiday Inn overlooking the Mediterranean (where we had the first of many exotic dinners in the Middle East, complete with tuxedoed French-speaking waiters) would become within the year a command post for one of the rival factions of the newly erupted civil war in Lebanon and would be completely destroyed. The demise of Beirut, as the Paris of the Middle East, is perhaps one of the saddest by-products of the Middle East turmoil.

Upon our arrival in Beirut, a CRS Lebanese driver met us

Jebel Dhahran and the New Saudi Generation

at the airport and took us to the Excelsior Hotel. The next day he took us to the Saudi Embassy, and promptly left us on our own. There we were in what seemed like a movie setting of Arabs, Egyptians with red fezzes, and nobody speaking English. Miraculously, we were able to make our application all right. We had about two days to wait. So, we toured Baalbek in the Beka valley, the site of some magnificent Roman ruins. We were glad that we did this, because it is not possible to go there now. It is presently the headquarters of the Shiite Fundamentalist Movement.

We also visited the CRS office in Beirut. While sitting in the reception room, we were surprised when Frank Lawyer, one of the CRS chief designers from Houston, "popped in," said "hello," attended to some business, and promptly departed. This was to be routine experience for many CRSers in the Middle East during the next ten years.

Construction was just beginning at UPM on the 189 Faculty Houses project. The construction company, which was running into trouble over the site-fill problem, was called Express Contracting. It was owned by Jack Seikaly, a Lebanese-American from Syracuse, New York, and Beirut. The business was a family one with four brothers, headquartered in Beirut. One brother, Richard, came to Dhahran within a month after we did to oversee the project along with a cousin, Bob Abdo, also from Syracuse. Richard was a personable fellow who had been in charge of Carrier Corporation's operation in the Middle East.

The construction company that they had put together for Saudi Arabia was new. The family was already into printing, insurance, and transportation. Another enterprise that Jack Seikaly had in Beirut was a nightclub, "Jack's Hideaway," adjacent to the Commodore Hotel. During the latter days of the civil war in 1982-83, you would read that all the news correspondents assembled at the Commodore Hotel.

Beirut

Jack Seikaly knew people on both sides of the war. One thing about the Lebanese (Jack himself told me later) is that they will adjust, they will go with the people in power. There are many political factions, but the Lebanese businessmen will go the way the wind blows. Jack would go to Beirut, and somebody from the military would come to pick him up at the airport. He was a Christian, but I think he lived in West Beirut. At that time, West Beirut was predominantly Muslim, but not exclusively.

After our arrival in Dhahran in September, we received the startling news that Jack Seikaly had been shot and wounded in Beirut.

Jack had been driving one night from East to West Beirut, and one of the irregular private militias that maintain checkpoints in the streets called upon him to stop his Cadillac. He didn't do it, so they opened fire on him as he was crossing a bridge, and he was hit. The car went over the edge and hung there. He was not able to move. When both sides found out who he was, a personnel carrier was sent out to rescue him. He went back to Syracuse for hospitalization. I then heard stories in Dhahran about what an energetic and likable person he was.

About six months later, he came back to Dhahran, and I met him for the first time. He had recovered somewhat. However, he was slightly paralyzed on one side and walked with a cane. One of the bullets had grazed the back of his head. He was intent on taking charge of his business again.

From then on, for ten years, I saw and worked with Jack off and on. He never totally recovered. I remember after the heaviest bombing of Beirut in 1982, I saw him in the Dhahran airport one night and I said, "Where have you been?" He replied, "I've been in Beirut." I said, "How in the world could anyone live in Beirut, the way we saw the bombing on television?" He shrugged his shoulders.

He had a fine apartment there with some beautiful furnishings. One day he left the apartment and went somewhere else.

Jebel Dhahran and the New Saudi Generation

The next day, the apartment caught an incendiary bomb, which destroyed everything. He felt it was time to leave. I said, "How did you get out?" He said he took a boat to Cyprus, and the next thing you know, he's in Dhahran. He then moved his office to Athens. Most of the Lebanese companies that operated out of Beirut moved their offices to Athens, when the going got too tough. Many of them are still there. Jack continued to come and go. As soon as the fighting would die down, he'd be back in Beirut again.

I was surprised in February 1987, after I had returned to Houston, when I read in the Houston Post that a Lebanese-American businessman, Jack Seikaly, had been taken hostage in Beirut. It turned out later that it wasn't an American political hostage deal, but rather a Lebanese gangster-type situation. Someone was trying to extort money from the family. The money was paid and he was released.

Going back and forth to Beirut was typical. The workers on the jobs did it all the time. For the entire eleven years we were there, no matter what you read in the newspapers, the Middle East Airlines would fly into Dhahran loaded with people from Beirut.

In March 1977, when we were flying to Rhodes for Mildred's NESA Conference, we flew directly over Beirut at a high altitude. Looking down, we could see many fires testifying to the fighting that was going on.

I went to Beirut one time in January of 1981 to inspect the bronze doors for the beautiful Conference Center at the university, which were being made in Beirut by an Armenian craftsman who had a shop there. He was about eighty years old and had been in Beirut about sixty years, since the Turks drove him from Armenia. I went with Sabah el Mareb, a young Lebanese architect with the contractor, CCC. We worked closely together building this new Conference Center which CRS had designed.

Beirut

The university had given CRS "carte blanche" to design something that would be elegant in every way. Putting it together was quite a challenging job.

Sabah's home was in Tripoli, north of Beirut. As soon as we arrived at the airport, he left immediately for Tripoli. I was picked up by the son of the contractor, Gabis Dantziguian, and he took me to the Royal Gardens Hotel in West Beirut. The next day, we were to visit his father's shop in East Beirut.

The day before I left Dhahran, I visited with the rector, Dr. Bakr, and he was concerned about my going to Beirut, because Americans were not all that welcome there at that time. However, I really never felt any concern about it. I don't know if it was because I was going with Sabah or not, because that really didn't make any difference.

When we were driving down Hamra Street, I heard "popping" going on all around, and I asked Gabis, "Is there fighting here?" "Oh no," he replied, "just bombs." All night long this "rat a tat tat" continued. You couldn't imagine it going on all the time. What were they shooting at? I told a Palestinian friend about it later. He had been in Beirut at that time. I said, "They told me it was just a celebration." He said, "Don't worry, it wasn't a celebration."

In addition to the sounds of guns popping, there was evidence all around of Beirut as a dying city. One sight that was very visible was the obvious scavenging of electricity. You could see everywhere the power lines with hundreds of visible taps like tentacles sucking the electricity illegally from the main lines. It is almost unfathomable how the various city services were kept in operation at all.

Speaking of the constant "popping" of guns, surely one of the most difficult things in the future will be overcoming the psychological effect that this environment will have had on this generation of Lebanese and Palestinian boys, who are growing up to think that guns, shooting, and killing are "normal." When you watch television, it's almost as though the participants

Jebel Dhahran and the New Saudi Generation

were playing "cops and robbers" or "cowboys and Indians." To a certain extent, I think that is what it has become to them. Only the ammunition is real, and the results are too often final.

Perhaps it was unwarranted concern but, as an American, I felt that I might be under surveillance from the time I collected my bags at the airport. At the Royal Gardens Hotel, a short while after I was settled in my room, there was a knock on my door. When I opened it, I was greeted by, "Sorry old chap, I must have the wrong room." I then conjectured that the British fellow was checking me out for the British, the Lebanese, the Americans, the Israelis, or someone else. Or, he had been arranged for by the rector of the university to look after me.

Relating this later to Mildred, she was certain I had read too many spy novels.

Expecting that my room might be entered while I was out, I placed my briefcase standing just inside the door, so that anyone entering would inadvertently knock it over and never get it back in the same place, giving me notice that someone had been there. I didn't think that "Smiley" could have been more clever. But when I returned, the briefcase was intact in its location. Whether or not the concern was real or imagined, nevertheless, the exercise made the game more fun.

This "Sorry old chap, I must have the wrong room" routine, I began to feel was a commonly used technique. Four years later at the Oriental Hotel in Bangkok after our female greeter at the airport unsuccessfully tried to pressure us into a tour of the city immediately after checking into the hotel, I answered the phone to hear the same routine, — "Sorry old chap—". Con artists abound in that part of the world. Also having arrived from Saudi Arabia, many drivers, clerks, porters, etc. assumed that you were loaded with money or valuables. And no doubt many times this was true.

Beirut

I drove all over Beirut with Mr. Dantziguian and his sons. One night they wanted to take me to dinner. I agreed, so we went to L'Orangerie, a fine French restaurant. They were happy for the occasion and excuse to go out with their wives for dinner. We had a pleasant evening and a very good meal. I mentioned that my brother's wife, Priscilla Pointer (stage name), was an actress and was a regular on the TV show, "Dallas." They got all excited about it, and said that they watched it all the time. They said they had friends in Ankara, Turkey, who watched it regularly. They said one night the electrical power went off in Ankara and they couldn't get anyone to do anything, because everybody had been at home watching "Dallas."

It is astounding how the people in Beirut carried on. Now, this was a year and a half before the invasion by Israel and the merciless bombing of Beirut, which we saw on television. I remember that I read in the paper the day I left Beirut in January 1981, that Yasser Arafat made the statement that Israel was going to invade Beirut. That was a year and a half before it happened.

Beirut struggled on. It's hard to see how it can recover anytime soon. We drove across the "Green Line" several times. We saw the little children coming from school in their neat little uniforms, as if everything were normal.

The Lebanese are an amazingly resilient people —and so are children.

Chapter 12

CRS ON SITE

After arriving in Dhahran in August 1975, I recall, my initial impression was the deadness, the slowness, the inability to make things move. No salesmen came into the office to offer you products. If you tried to make a phone call, it might take several days to actually make the connection, even on local calls. There was a real temptation to just throw up your hands.

Don Chambers was successful, because he never acknowledged those problems as insurmountable. He always operated as if it should happen, it should go through, and there was never any justification for a contractor or anyone else to use that as an excuse. This was a very good attitude, because it was the only way that you could ever get anything going.

The amazing thing was, that when we finally left in 1986, it was almost like America in some respects. We had salesmen coming into the office every day with products of all kinds. The telephone system and communications had become superb. We could dial direct from our house to anywhere in the world with no delay at all. The first few years, proper billing was a problem. It was all hand done, usually in Arabic. The last few years, we had automatic billing from the computerized phone system. We talked to our children nearly every week. In fact, it became quite a temptation, because we ran up a pretty hefty phone bill — but it was worth it.

The CRS representative on site at the beginning of Phase I in 1965 was an engineer named George Noble, who was there by himself. Then there was an Italian-American named Victor Lasprogato, who was followed by Bob Bruce. According to Don Chambers, Lasprogato was quite a flamboyant character. An interesting anecdote that Don related proved that no matter whom you are dealing with, you should always treat him as if

Jebel Dhahran and the New Saudi Generation

he might later be your boss. The university provided Lasprogato with a young Saudi student to help him test concrete. Apparently, Lasprogato treated him quite badly. Years later, Lasprogato wanted to come back to the university. By that time, his former Saudi assistant was in a position to approve or disapprove his appointment. Needless to say, Lasprogato didn't come back.

Don Chambers came there in 1968 to perform mechanical and electrical engineering duties for CRS at UPM on Phase I. He had been with a British mechanical and electrical contractor, Haden International, in Kuwait. He met Joe Thomas in Beirut while representing this contractor.

Various additions were made to our staff. In 1976 Bob Cook, a structural engineer, arrived with his British wife, Glynis, son John, and daughter Leslie. His bouncy, buoyant, sometimes cocky spirit helped to lift us above the "down-drag" that sometimes seemed to take over. Bob had been a lieutenant colonel in the U.S. Air Force and had spent a good bit of time in Thailand building airfields. Glynis' father was captain of a famous but ill-fated British dirigible. Bob and Don and I then carried it for two years.

At the end of 1977, Phase IV was inaugurated by King Khaled. Obviously, the CRS staff was going to have to be beefed up. So, two more architects were authorized. The first was a Britisher named Trevor Dodgson. He was a competent architect, and he did a good job for a couple of years. Then he moved on. He became dissatisfied with his pay situation.

Harry Tooker came in January 1978, and from then on we had a number of rather flamboyant characters, Harry being the most flamboyant. Two engineers came, mechanical and electrical. They were men with overseas experience, but they were never really happy. They stayed only one year. I think Joe Thomas had given them the idea that we were a big company like Northrup that had a personnel manager to take care of all their personal problems, and they just had to do their job. When they arrived, we told them, "You are on your own. You get your own visas and do everything you have to do. There is nobody taking care of you. We're not that big." They didn't really like that, and after about a year they were unhappy and left.

Two more engineers came, Howard Von Weiss, an American electrical engineer and a World War II fighter pilot, and Keith Babb, a mechanical engineer, a British fellow that Don recruited in England. Don was a mechanical engineer, so CRS had been reluctant to hire another one. It was thought that Don could do that work in addition to running the office, but it was too much. Finally, Don asked if the company would let him recruit another engineer. He went to London, advertised, and hired Keith. Keith was of an international background, his father having been on the famous police force of Hong Kong. He had been in the Navy and had a mechanical engineering degree. At that time he was about thirty-five years old, a rather quiet, staid Britisher. It was his underlying sense of humor that I always liked. He worked out very well and took over the office when I left in 1986.

Harry Cretin came in 1979, replacing as structural engineer Bob Cook, whom I was sorry to see leave. Bob had decided to go to work for a local Saudi contractor. Many men tried this kind of thing without success. Bob succeeded for about six or seven years, making more money than he would have with CRS. Harry was an ex-marine and also flamboyant. With Howard Von Weiss, Harry Tooker, and Harry Cretin we really had some rugged individuals. I mean the fast-talking, cigar-smoking, poker-playing, tall-tale guys. All good engineers and all good at the overseas type of work. It was good to have those types of qualities there. They were aggressive and confident. That was the CRS staff for the greater part of the CCC contract in Phase IV.

Then in 1982, CRS became very economy-minded. We didn't feel that CRS at home really recognized what we had to do there. The company had a number of other jobs in the Middle

Jebel Dhahran and the New Saudi Generation

East, but even Don never felt that it really understood that being right on campus under the client's nose 24 hours a day, we had a demand on us that was different from anywhere else. Besides, we didn't administer just one contract. At one time we had as many as fifteen different contracts. Most of the other projects around the Kingdom involved only one contract, and the owner was not occupying the site.

But CRS was cutting costs, so in March 1982, Joe Thomas paid us a visit and as Harry Cretin said, "Joe Thomas came and waved his hand and half of us disappeared." Don was assigned to the Houston office. I was offered Don's job. Keith took on the electrical work in addition to the mechanical. Howard Von Weiss and John Schoenberger took jobs with other companies in Saudi Arabia.

John had come on board in 1980. He was a young architect from Chicago who was quite competent. He was given a delay to stay on for six months to finish what he was doing. But he was somewhat offended by the whole thing. He ultimately went to work for a Saudi contractor who went bad later. This was an unwise move. He was a young fellow with a lot of confidence and ability, but I don't think he was perceptive enough to see what he was getting himself into. In this particular contract, the American project manager for the Saudi was put in jail on unsubstantiated charges and remained there for about a year. I think anyone who worked for this contractor had a good chance of ending up the same.

That now left Harry Cretin, Keith Babb, and myself on the job until I left in 1986.

The relationship that I had developed with Mansour al-Saber and the university administration, Dr. Bakr and Dr. Bakhrebah, really stood me in good stead. I always felt that they were trying to help me succeed. Although we had lots of problems the next four years, I never felt anything but cooperation from them.

CRS on Site

The CRS office, when we first arrived, was in the original building that the government had given to the university. It was built by the Ministry of Petroleum and Minerals and housed the first college. We were there for three years, 1975-77, at the foot of "Jebel Dhahran," a few hundred yards from where King Abdul Aziz camped thirty-five years before. Later in 1980, the Koreans started another big project, and they built another building for us. We were able to design this building as we liked.

We were provided secretaries by the university. When I arrived in 1975, there was a Cuban lady, an American lady, and later a Ukrainian lady. It was up to us to find these people from the group of professors' wives. We got two more British ladies. We had one Pakistani man, Maqbool Ahmed, furnished to us by the university. Normally, the secretaries on the campus were men, either Pakistani or Indian. The university let us have this one fellow, and he actually got along fine with the ladies. He was a very good secretary. He made a point of the fact that in Pakistan, he wasn't just a secretary. He was more like a cabinet member's assistant.

We were fortunate to have Maqbool because he was a Muslim, and he had a "feel" for the Saudi attitudes and reactions. On several occasions, he probably saved me from negative reactions. I might write a letter with a certain paragraph in it. He would come to me and say, "Do you think that sounds right? Is that a good idea?" I would reread it, give it more thought and see what he was talking about. It might have an implication that I had not thought of. I would revise it, and he probably saved me from a problem. Because many of these secretaries and other executive workers were Pakistani, there existed a sort of Pakistani "sub-culture" on campus. Also, their language was not understood by many, so they had a degree of confidentiality that others did not enjoy.

Maqbool was somewhat of a leader in the Pakistani community at UPM with many of them coming to him for advice and

Jebel Dhahran and the New Saudi Generation

help on various matters. There was an apparent "class" distinction, however, between those Pakistanis who worked for the administration and those who worked for those in lesser capacities. Most secretaries for the top administrators were Saudis.

Strictly speaking, female secretaries such as our ladies were not allowed according to the "religious police." However, the university not only was aware of ours but paid their salaries. Our main secretaries were Britishers June Brandie, Jacqui Flint, June McCarthy, Connie Hafseth, Pat Parker, Ukranian Slawa Olesniesky and Cuban Maria Scott.

One day, someone came into our office to report excitedly that the police were next door in CCC's office checking to see that everyone had work permits. The fear was that they might next come into our office where they would run head on into our lady secretaries. Considering that wisdom was, indeed the better part of valor, we sent our three ladies "packing" out the back door and across the sand to their houses and averted a potential problem. In a few minutes, the police came in and found only Maqbool hard at work.

Reporting this to Mansour later, he said with genuine concern, "Were the ladies all right?" Mansour al-Saber and Dr. Bakhrebah were always looking out for us under these conditions as a sort of extension of their activity.

Don had set up a very good filing system and paper movement procedure. The amount of paper that moved through our office for the construction of these buildings was surprising. In the four years after I took over from Don, I could truthfully say that if I ever left the "in basket" for more than four hours unattended, it would be at least a foot to eighteen inches high. It had to move out that day, or soon I had an unmanageable stack. We had a very efficient system and considering the amount of work that we did, I think it worked very well. Don got it started right.

The secretary who was the "backbone" for over twelve years was June Brandie, a British lady. She and her husband, Keith, were career international people. He was a professor of mechanical engineering. They had been in Hong Kong for eight or ten years, and had been at the university for almost ten years. They were champion tennis players, as many of the British were. Most of the British invested in houses back in England. They were preparing for the day when they moved back. Real estate was one of the best investments they could make. They also had an advantage in that they had no taxes at all. The British government, through their many years of experience, realized the importance to it economically of the people working overseas, so it rewarded them accordingly with tax benefits. The U.S. struggled long and hard to arrive at that realization, but it finally did.

Office boys, who cleaned and served tea or coffee, were furnished to the CRS office by the contractors. When CCC was in dominance, it was a Pakistani fellow named Faisal, a big lumbering guy who wasn't too bright really, but good-natured and he tried hard. Faisal once returned from vacation in Pakistan with a porcelain tea set for Mildred and me. It was not an expensive set, but it was something he was proud to do. You really felt for these people. He finally was sent back to Pakistan by CCC. Some time later he returned. CCC had rehired him and was sending him on to Riyadh. When he came by the office, it was very sad. He said his wife and child had died at childbirth.

One of the very important fringe benefits for Muslim workers like Faisal was that their company allowed them to take time off at least once during their contract as workers to make the Pilgrimage to Mecca, known in Arabic as "the Haj." Faisal took advantage of this opportunity to fulfill his obligation towards the "Five Pillars of Islam."

After Faisal left, a boy from Bangladesh was supplied by the Koreans. Of all the places that I have read about, Bangladesh seems to be the most barren and desolate. There seems to be nothing but floods, famines, or disasters. He was a bright young

Jebel Dhahran and the New Saudi Generation

boy named Islam. He had a minimum education, but our British secretaries could see that he had some innate intelligence, so they started teaching him about filing and soon he took over a lot of it. He could do it. He was just supposed to be an office boy, but soon he started learning to type. Redec Daelim's main secretary, Zia al-Haq, was also Bengali, and Islam aspired to be like him. If he hadn't been an office boy he would have had to be a laborer out on the job site, so naturally he wanted to keep the job with us. None of the office boys wanted to leave us when the time came.

Islam went home to get married. We gave him a party and a gift. He was able to stay in Bangladesh about six weeks because he had accumulated leave. He returned from Bangladesh after being with his bride for only a short time. Some months later, he was quite "down in the dumps," because he hadn't heard from her in many weeks. He didn't get to go home but once every two years, and anything could happen in that time. It was a hard life for some. On the other hand, they made more money than they ever would at home. Our Pakistani secretary, Maqbool Ahmed, had his family with him. He had a college degree. He eventually went back to Pakistan, bought a house, and started a business. What those people were paid would seem very little to us, but it was a lot of money back in Bangladesh, Pakistan, or India.

Harry Cretin, our very robust and vociferous structural engineer, established a good relationship with Islam. He would knock him around a bit verbally, but Islam apparently liked the treatment. Harry would come into the office in the morning and in a kidding manner he'd holler out, "Islam, Islam, where's my coffee?" Then he'd say, "You can do it, Islam, You can do it." Harry bought him a bicycle once, and he loved that. It made him a little special among his peers.

The payments from the university to CRS were something that I never had to get involved in until I took over from Don. In the early days, I don't even think Don got too much involved.

CRS on Site

It was all handled directly from Houston. But in the last four years I was there, the billings came directly to us from Houston. It was up to us to get them submitted properly with Arabic cover letters and also to correct them, if there were things wrong. Then we had to follow up on them for payment, and that became a problem.

The last three years, it got quite sticky. The university was owing CRS quite a bit of money. CRS in Houston couldn't understand why I couldn't get the money. But it was awfully hard to go to the people you work with every day, dun them for money, and still keep good feelings. That was what I was supposed to do.

I finally wrote to CRS saying that I had heard the U.S. ambassador talk at the American Businessmen's Association. This was at a time when the Saudis were beginning to have problems financially in 1985-86, and many American companies were having problems with late payments. The ambassador said that there was hardly a company there that didn't have a payment problem; and he could understand how the local project managers were having a difficult time with their boards and executive officers back home.

The ambassador said the Saudi attitude was that companies (especially like CRS) who had been there a long time and made a lot of money, should now be tolerant with the Saudis in their difficult times. He thought the best policy in the long term was patience. So, CRS was patient, although there were letters from Houston, which I had to pass on to the university. It was a bill-collecting situation and was difficult, because I had to work everyday with Mansour and Dr. Bakhrebah.

The last year CRS required me to send a telex report back to Houston every Monday detailing what the status was, whom I had talked to, what I had done, if someone was going to Riyadh to collect the money, etc. All our telexes were sent through the university machine, which was not private. So I sent these rather sensitive telexes every Monday night through

Jebel Dhahran and the New Saudi Generation

the International Hotel, which probably wasn't private either. It was really quite awkward.

I did feel like Dr. Bakhrebah and Mansour al-Saber were sympathetic and were trying to get it all together. By the time I left, we had collected most of the old bills. As Don said, "You'll go out in a blaze of glory." If I had left without collecting the money and Keith later had collected it, it really wouldn't have looked too good for me in Houston. I was grateful to Dr. Bakhrebah and Mansour al-Saber that they got that taken care of.

CHAPTER 13

CONSTRUCTION ADMINISTRATION PHASE IV — 1975 TO 1986

Soon after arrival at the university, I had reported to Dr. Saleh Abdullah Bakhrebah, who at that time was dean of business and technical affairs.

Dr. Bakhrebah was born in the Hadhramaut, an area of Yemen. His father died when he was a young boy, and he was raised by friends of his father in Jeddah, Saudi Arabia. It soon became apparent that he was very intelligent, and he was admitted to the Madras Thagher School, which accepted only students with the highest grades. He was definitely keen on reading and writing from early childhood. Zaki Yamani, whom he knew in Jeddah, seeing what a bright lad he was, helped him to proceed with his education through college, and to earn a B.Sc. degree in civil engineering from the University of Colorado and a PhD from the University of Illinois.

I quickly developed a great respect for this young Saudi, twenty-five years my junior, who became my boss. The only difficulty that I had was in always feeling that he was smarter than I was.

Mildred went with me to the university administration building when I reported to Dr. Bakhrebah. She had had dinner with him, Mohammed al-Owaid, Joe Thomas, Conrad Neal, and their wives at Brennan's in Houston before we left. I commented on the fact that she was intruding in the "men's domain." He replied that although it wasn't often done, it was certainly all right with him. We developed a very friendly relationship with Dr. Bakhrebah, his wife, Afaf, and their children.

Dr. Bakhrebah's assistant was the young Saudi who met us at the airport, Abdullah K. Mufti.

The rector of the university, whom we met a little later, was Dr. Bakr Abdullah bin Bakr. Dr. Bakr was a man of outstanding administrative ability. He was at that time about thirty-eight years old. He had worked at Aramco and received his education at the University of Texas, Stanford University, and the University of Southern California, earning degrees in petroleum engineering and MBA and PhD degrees in business administration.

At the time of our arrival, Dr. Bakr had been rector for about five years. The university was one of the smoothest operations in the Kingdom, I'm sure. I think that he should get much of the credit for it. I used to think with some awe, "Here is a man who has entertained the King of Saudi Arabia, the Queen of England and Prince Philip, the King and Queen of Malaysia, the Queen of Denmark, the King and Queen of Spain, and many others. This is a man who has associated with the top ruling people of the world." Dr. Bakr had a very commanding presence with a deep resonant voice. He obviously was a man who could make difficult decisions and stand by them. I know he had the final word on everything.

When CRS was designing the Energy Lab in 1982, one of the last projects CRS did, the design team was there making its presentation. Frank Lawyer was in charge of the design team. He had taken over from Charles Lawrence, who had retired. Frank designed two buildings, the Energy Lab and the Clinic. Suthipan Smittipong, a talented young designer from Thailand, designed the last dormitories under Frank's supervision. Frank then retired from CRS and came to the university as a professor of architecture for seven years.

The plan was to locate the Energy Lab over by the Central Kitchen, which was really on the fringes of the academic campus. It was felt that it was of somewhat the same functional character as the buildings in that area. Yet it was actually an academic building and was part of the Research Institute.

At one point in the presentation, Dr. Bakr said, "Why can't we locate it over here in such and such a place on the academic

Construction Administration Phase IV — 1975 to 1986

side?" Dr. Bakhrebah began giving him the reasons for locating it as planned. Dr. Bakr wasn't going to accept it. It was a surprise to everyone. Finally, Dr. Bakr said, "No, I want it over here. Dr. Bakhrebah always wins, but this time I'm going to win." It was said good-naturedly, of course. The building was relocated, and it proved to be the better location. I think probably the fact that it was energy-related and had some radiation aspects was what had concerned everybody. However, the protective devices were thoroughly studied by CRS, and there was really no danger.

Dr. Bakr made many other decisions that affected the direction of the university. At one time, he wanted to bring in other schools, like a medical school and a women's school. He felt that the university was eminently qualified to build and operate them. However, authorities outside the university were in opposition to this idea, and it was never done. There was talk of his becoming a minister, but he is still rector and has been for over twenty years.

Two weeks after we arrived in August 1975, CRS in Houston received a telex from the university authorizing CRS to proceed with design work for Phase IV, approximately $600 million worth of construction work. The university wanted the design in six months, ready to go out for bids. It was a tremendous order. Immediately, things became very active. In addition to the houses we were building, which had the site-fill problem, CRS began sending over programming and design teams for the new work. We were never without a touch from home base for several years.

CRS finished all the Phase IV drawings in the spring of 1976. It was an amazing effort. Then, as is often the case, nothing happened. They were held up in negotiations with the Lebanese contractor, Consolidated Construction Company (CCC), for almost a year. Finally, a contract was awarded in the fall of 1977,

Lawyer, Bullock, Kobs - 1984

Kollaer, Neal, Brailas - 1976

Bob Cook with Express Workers - 189 Houses

Lawrence and Symonds

Jebel Dhahran and the New Saudi Generation

and construction started.

In the summer of 1977, an addition to the Library was put out for bids. A Korean contractor, Redec Daelim, was the low bidder. It was awarded the contract, which began a long relationship of that company with the university.

The various contractors that we worked with over eleven years were Lebanese, Korean, Turkish, Dutch and several Saudi. The Saudi contractors usually had staffs of Filipinos or Asians of some kind, and their managers would often be British.

I listed all the nationalities of workers that I had worked with, and there were about thirty-five. We got varying degrees of performance, of course. The Koreans were one of the best. You gave them a job, and you knew it was going to get done. They were very accommodating and bent over backwards, to their own detriment sometimes, to do what you wanted them to do. We developed a very good relationship with the Koreans.

If a person is reasonably cooperative and fair, he is going to have good relations with the Koreans. We got things done overnight with the Koreans sometimes, because they wanted to do it. It was a tremendous help to have a contractor like that around. It took a lot of burden off us.

An example of the Korean's helpful attitude occurred when Queen Elizabeth and Prince Philip visited. We were given the itinerary of their tour of the campus. They were going to be coming out of the library and walking up towards the administration building. Just outside the library were two large reflecting pools with fountains. The university was considering eliminating these because they had not been functioning properly. The water had been drained and the fountains removed. With the mob of followers that would be coming out of the library with the Queen, these two areas constituted a distinct eyesore and considerable hazard. Overnight, the Koreans filled in these areas with concrete and made their appearance acceptable, so the Queen and company walked out of the library and didn't know it hadn't always been that way.

Phase IV Inauguration - 1977

King Khaled and Entourage

Dr. Hall and Dr. Pickering

Jebel Dhahran and the New Saudi Generation

One bit of humor that went around was that in England, the Queen thought that everything was freshly painted and in Saudi Arabia, the King thought that the entire Kingdom was carpeted with oriental rugs. When they arrived on the scene that's the way it always appeared to them.

In the fall of 1977, the contract for Phase IV was finally negotiated with CCC, and the word came that King Khaled was coming to the university to inaugurate it.

Along with King Khaled came Crown Prince Fahd, all the major princes, ministers, and many others. This was, no doubt, one of the largest collection of royalty and VIPs that had ever been at the university at one time, and it was a successful occasion. This kicked off (two years after we arrived) what was to be just under a billion dollars' worth of work in the next nine years. The activity was intense from then on — but stimulating and unique, to say the least.

All the major planning and design work for the university was done by CRS in the Houston office. CRS would send out teams of programmers and designers to meet with the university administration, which meetings Don and I would usually attend. Then the final construction documents were sent to us ready to be put out for bids.

From then on it was our baby. The university would advertise for bidders. All kinds of contractors would submit requests to be pre-qualified. This was a long process and on many occasions there would be 100 to 125 companies bidding. We had to review every one of these and sift them out to determine which ones appeared to be qualified.

We would then come up with a list of about forty that we would submit to the university with the recommendation that they be pre-qualified to bid. The university then sent invitations

Stadium - Ladies above

Prayer before graduation

10,000-seat Stadium

CCC Workers

Construction Administration Phase IV — 1975 to 1986

to about 25 or 30 of those to submit bids. Out of that list, there might be 15 or 20 that would pick up plans. They had to buy the plans without refund. Those that were serious would submit bids. This might be 10 or 15 per project.

When the bids were in, we would have a process of evaluation similar to what we might have here in the States. As is true here, the low bidder is not necessarily the best bidder. To award a contract strictly on the basis of the lowest price would not always be doing the best service to the university, and in several instances when this was done, there was trouble.

As a result, Dr. Bakhrebah developed a two-tier system of pre-qualification. After the bids were in and we had a list of bidders, there was a second stage of pre-qualification. This was explained to the contractors before they submitted their original bid. The university would appoint a committee, including CRS. The committee would visit the previous work of the several lowest bidders to determine what quality of work they had done. If the low bidder still appeared to be qualified from observation of his work, fine. But, if not, the second lowest bidder might be favorably considered and awarded the contract. Even this sometimes presented a difficulty in getting a contractor without potential problems.

Part of the Phase IV contract with CCC was a *10,000-seat Stadium,* expandable to 20,000. The Saudis are very strong on sports facilities. Many stadiums were built around the Kingdom. The one we built at the university was as good as any of them for its size. The field was covered with "Superturf," which was made by Chevron. The stadium was used primarily for soccer and track. An annual Gulf States tournament was held there in 1986.

Building No. 11, the Gymnasium, was built in Phases II and III. It had very good facilities for basketball, racquetball, squash, and swimming, an Olympic-size pool. The Saudis were intent

Jebel Dhahran and the New Saudi Generation

on making their young men "fit" and also teaching them to compete in athletics such as judo, track, soccer, and tennis. The athletic department generally was run by the British, who were good athletes and teachers. They did a good job. The Saudis had a soccer team that went to the 1984 Olympics, and they were quite proud. I think in years to come, if they keep at it, we will find that there will be some Saudi front-runners. You have to admire them for another one of those many areas that they are trying to promote and are working hard at it.

Another part of this phase was the Dormitories. These were the first new dormitories to be built and were to be more or less a prototype. After they were built by CCC, they were redesigned, and Redec Daelim built some more. The university will now continue to build more to the revised design, as money becomes available.

In Phase IV there was a *Student Reception Center* and a *Building for Highly Volatile Chemicals*. There were modifications to the existing buildings and to the site in general. A bus system was to be established on campus. Four or five bus stops were built, some by CCC and some by Redec Daelim. This was one of the ideas that sounded good on paper, but actually didn't work out as planned. Nobody used the air-conditioned bus stops. They would stand outside in the heat and wait. Ultimately, these were put to other uses or weren't used at all.

The question of awarding contracts to Saudi contractors was sometimes a problem. In 1982 we were going to begin construction of a new *Press Building*. This would probably be the best-equipped press facility in the Eastern Province. It wasn't an especially large project, but it was highly technical and a quality project. It was put out for the usual bidding process of advertising and then selecting a list of bidders. The Saudi contractors were qualified by the government according to the size of the project that it was felt they could handle. Being a smaller

Construction Administration Phase IV — 1975 to 1986

project, this would naturally attract smaller contractors. When the bids came in, the low bid was from a small Saudi contractor, Yamama Establishment. He had done some good work. Going through the process of visiting his projects and finally interviewing him was interesting. Naturally, Dr. Bakhrebah and Mansour al-Saber were interested in helping a Saudi, but their first priority was to get the university a good job. If at the same time they could give it to a Saudi — well and good.

In this case, the selection finally came down to this one Saudi, so we looked at his previous work. It was not the best, but it was not bad. Then we interviewed him, personally. He was a typical self-made Saudi. I don't know how well-educated he was. He was literate, whereas some Saudis, even successful ones, were not. He had built his business mainly with Filipino staff. When we interviewed him the conversation got into Arabic with Dr. Bakhrebah. He was an older man, old enough to be Dr. Bakhrebah's father. He talked animatedly in Arabic. After he had finished and left, Dr. Bakhrebah said, "He's an old fox." There was something about him that he admired. Probably, his cleverness. They do admire that quality.

The contract was finally awarded to him. He had two sons, and the eldest was due to take over the business. This son had been in the United States quite a bit, so he was very Western-aware, and he was quite gregarious and outgoing. The job went along reasonably well. About six months before the end of the project, the father died, and the eldest son took over. He had confidence that he could do it, and I think that he did well.

As Phase IV went along, the university administration came up with new ideas, which were called *Phase IV-B Revisions* The administration was thus able to put this work in as modifications to the projects already going, although it was entirely new work. It was this kind of creative administration that kept UPM expanding and progressing.

Jebel Dhahran and the New Saudi Generation

Phase IV-B Revisions included the beautiful *Conference Center*, and established a new focal point for the campus, the *Medan Plaza*.

Another part of Phase IV-B Revisions was built by the Koreans — two large Academic *Buildings with Parking Garages* and a new *Administration Building* The academic buildings included extensive computer facilities. The administration building was a beautiful building with a high atrium in the middle going up eight stories. It was completed in 1983 and was a very successful building. The function was very smooth. It had a beautiful glass wall at one end, eight stories high, looking out over the Gulf from Jebel Dhahran. The glass was furnished by Pilkington Company of England, which told us that it was the tallest installation of this kind of suspended glazing in the world.

Although the largest portion of Phase IV was negotiated with CCC, a considerable amount was put out for competitive bidding.

The largest part of this work was awarded to a Korean contractor, Redec Daelim. This was the large Korean firm, Daelim, from Seoul with its Saudi partner, Redec, a company owned by the Saudi entrepreneur, Gaith Pharoan. Pharoan's father was a long-time physician to King Abdul Aziz and adviser to his sons until his death during King Fahd's reign.

Phase IV-B Revisions included *454 Housing Units*. These were apartment-type units, one, two, and three bedrooms, designed more or less in Arabic style, looking almost like an Arabic village. They were really designed to be support staff housing, which would have been primarily for people from the Middle East, Pakistan, India, etc. They were more suitable to them than they would be to Western people, because they had smaller living areas. They are used to living in closer quarters, although it was still much better housing than they would have had in Pakistan or India. But, as was the case with some of the

Dining with Redec Daelim

Keith Babb, Howard Von Weiss, Symondses, Elaina and Harry Cretin

J.S. Kim, Howard Von Weiss, and Symondses

Dining with Redec Daelim

Mildred with Sean Cretin, T.P. Lee, J.K. Choi

Three CRS Ladies and Three Korean Ladies

Construction Administration Phase IV — 1975 to 1986

housing that was designed, the original intent didn't become the final usage. When these were completed, the urgent need was for faculty housing, not for staff. So, the faculty members were assigned to these. There was quite a bit of grumbling by the faculty, and a few resignations resulted.

We lived in one of these units for eight years after our third year. We were neither faculty nor staff. The CRS employees were the only consultants housed on the campus by the university. We had an 800-square-foot unit on the second floor with balconies on either end. We could look out over the Arabian Gulf. We had a large living area, a fairly large bedroom, and an adequate kitchen and bath. We actually enjoyed it. Of course, no matter what you provided, some people would complain.

Initially the university was unique in that it was able to award design contracts to CRS by negotiation. But in 1982, the government decreed that all design work also had to be put out for competitive bidding. As a result, the next group of Faculty Housing, Student Dormitories, a Clinic, and an Energy Laboratory, were put out for design bids. CRS got the design contracts for the Energy Lab, the Clinic, and Dormitories. However, it was not low bidder on the additional Faculty Housing, which was about a hundred units or so. This contract went to the first major architectural consultants other than CRS to be on the campus.

The construction contracts for the Clinic, Energy Lab, and additional Dormitories were awarded to Redec Daelim. Those were the last three projects that were built while I was there. They were completed at the end of 1986, about six months after I left. They were all very well received and functioned well.

I think the university would have a hard time finding any other firms that could have done the job that CRS did. The university could call CRS in Houston and within a few weeks (as soon as visas could be obtained), CRS would send over a

Student Housing 1986

Clinic 1986

team of programmers to determine what was wanted and then proceed on a very short schedule. The last dormitory group was a good example, one of the smoothest projects I had seen. All the dormitories that had previously been built, provided a good criteria source, so there was input from everyone — students, faculty, and administration.

CRS has a system of design and programming which it calls "squatters." When it gets a new project, it sends a team of programmers to the site for an intensive two weeks of conferences with the owner to determine what he wants and needs. The team then returns to Houston and prepares a program. No design work is done at those first conferences. The team just determines the needs. After the program is completed, it is submitted again to the university for approval. Then the designers take it. From the program, they work out the first schematic designs, or concepts.

After approval of the schematic design, they proceed with design development drawings, which are quite thorough. The building is pretty much together by that time. They then go into final construction documents. These were sent to us at the site for bidding and implementation.

The last project that we completed, the Energy Lab, was unique. The young Saudi scientists, who had been trained in the States and other parts of the world, came back with all kinds of ideas. Early when we were there, Dr. Osama Daboussi was head of the physics department. He had received a small neutron generator in one of the earlier contract packages, but it was never installed for use. There was never a place for it. Because of his efforts, however, the idea of an Energy Research Laboratory developed.

In 1983, CRS received authorization to proceed with the design of such a laboratory facility. Originally, it was to house a neutron generator and a tandetron machine. Then, during the

al-Juraib (left), and al-Saber (right front) at the celebration on completing new Administration Building - 1983

Symonds, Babb, Koheji

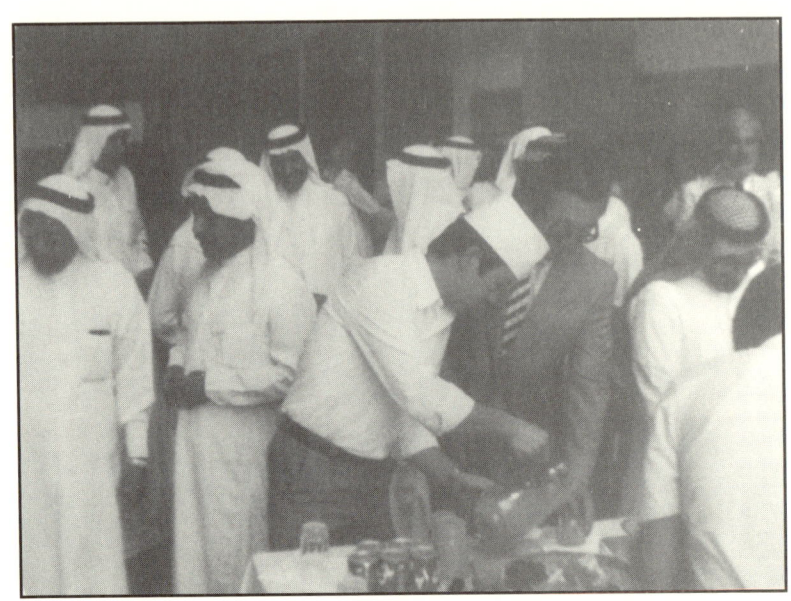
Celebration on completing new Administration Building - 1983

Sourani, al-Harbi, Koheji and Symonds

Construction Administration Phase IV — 1975 to 1986

middle of the construction, the university decided to introduce on the second floor, a *Laser Laboratory* It wanted to be involved in all the latest research — nuclear, laser, etc. There were rumors that there would be also a nuclear reactor, but this was not true. This was, however, the beginning of energy research at UPM.

Near the end of construction of the Energy Lab, Dr. Daboussi and the physics department lost control of the project, and it was decided that it should go under the Research Institute label. So, Dr. Daboussi's project became a reality, but he was no longer involved to the original extent.

In 1983 Dr. Hashim Yamani, a very bright young Saudi, who graduated from MIT in Cambridge, became Director of the Energy Lab. Under his leadership it has grown to be one of the most advanced facilities in the Middle East. Others who have contributed to the advancement of the Energy Lab are Dr. Fida F. al-Adel (laser research), Dr. Auni B. Hallak, and Dr. Ehsan Ellahi Khawaja.

The *Energy Lab* was completed in 1986 and should contribute greatly to developing the understanding of the various energy sources by the Saudi students. When the Israelis bombed the Iraqi nuclear plant seven or eight years ago, I thought Prince Saud al-Faisal, the Saudi Foreign Minister, made an interesting comment. He said, "If you accept the legitimacy of such a preemptive strike, then you could expect the Israelis to bomb a university in Saudi Arabia, because it might be training a scientist who would know enough someday to be able to make an atomic bomb." In other words, if you follow that logic through, it has no end.

With the completion of the *Energy Lab,* there really are no more urgently required academic or research facilities. The need now is to finish the 150 houses that remain fifty percent complete. That is expected in the near future. Then there will be no

Jebel Dhahran and the New Saudi Generation

need for further staff housing. There have been a lot of ideas broached in the past, and one of them was for a *Planetarium* Someday, the university might build one, but generally there is no more need for additional academic facilities. Additional dormitories are the outstanding need, along with some additional student facilities related to them.

The enrollment at the university in 1986 was about 3,500. The ancillary facilities are designed to accommodate about 4,000. Although the university has talked in terms of 6,000, that will require the increase of many related facilities, food service, housing, etc.

It was interesting to see, in the time that we were there, the changes that took place in facilities or in general infrastructure. When we arrived, the main road to Aramco from al-Khobar separated the student housing from the main campus. It provided a fairly direct route to Aramco, although it was not good because students had to cross this major thoroughfare to get from the dormitories to the main campus, and there were a number of fatalities.

In 1978-79, a lot of highway work was begun, interchanges and cloverleafs between Aramco and UPM. In 1980-81, a new highway to Aramco by-passed the university.

There was a lot of grumbling at first by Aramco, but it obviously was a good thing. The road through the campus was blocked, and we built a new main entrance to the university. We then built a loop road around the university, which tied it all together and made the traffic control good. This allowed the physical unification of the campus, integration of undergraduate dormitories with the main academic campus, and coordinated all circulation systems, support services, and buildings.

View from U.S Consulate

CCC's British Len Terry and Iraqi Victor Tumeira

Jebel Dhahran and the New Saudi Generation

The original land for the university was granted by royal decree of King Faisal, and it extended almost down to the air base. From 1975 to 1980, there was a running battle between the university and the air base for the bottom part of the property. The university intended to use this for additional housing. Finally, that part did go to the air base. This cut off a good portion of the land granted to UPM by royal decree.

The relations between the university and Aramco improved, although there was a good bit of "stand-offishness." Dr. Hall said that Aramco looked with considerable skepticism at the establishment of this institution of higher education. As it developed, however, it became a factor that Aramco could not ignore in almost any of its planning, such as water supply, irrigation, and sewage disposal.

Well No. 7, Aramco's first real producing well, was located high atop a jebel northwest of the university. There were oil wells scattered all over. On the campus, there were four producing wells that I can recall. These required a narrow strip of easement corridor across the campus on which nothing could be built. It was directly controlled by Aramco. After a well was drilled and producing, it was unobtrusive, with only a small valve structure above the ground. Pumps, as usually seen in west Texas, were not required, inasmuch as the pressure below ground was sufficient for the oil to flow without pumping.

There were seven water wells on campus. We built a one million gallon water storage tank. Originally, the water stored in the water tower was provided from there by gravity flow, but later when we built the water storage tank, it was pumped. There was a large water desalination plant built in al-Khobar, and there was interest in selling water. We attended a number of meetings with Aramco, government water authorities, and the university. By the time we left in 1986, UPM was still using the well water, although the water level in the ground was receding, because of the excessive demand, and I would assume that someday the desalinated water from the Gulf will be used.

Construction Administration Phase IV — 1975 to 1986

The organizational aspects of the university improved as each year went by. In some ways, this was a little more complicated for us, in that we couldn't freewheel as much as before. The university established the office of the Director General of Technical Affairs, which was responsible for overseeing all the projects of the university. The first person to fill this position was Mansour al-Saber. Prior to that time, we pretty much ran it ourselves with copies of everything to the university. I might hasten to add, of course, everything was always under the watchful eye of Dr. Bakhrebah, who was very meticulous, and didn't miss much.

When the university developed this office and had six or seven engineers working under Mansour al-Saber, all decisions were participated in by them, so it did make it more complicated for us, more bureaucratic. At the same time, we could understand why it was being done. The Saudis were learning, and they wanted to be able to do it. It always seemed to me that there was a certain amount of humility there. They admitted that they didn't know all these things. They had hired us to come and do a job, but they wanted to learn so they could take it over. That was what was known as "technology transfer." And they did learn.

At the university, the maintenance department, the technical affairs department, and all departments were constantly moving ahead and learning how they could best operate. When Dr. Hall was there, he had a vital part in everything. He was the senior adviser to the rector. The last few years his role was obviously being diminished. We always had thought that when he was gone, the Saudis just wouldn't be able to get along. He passed away in 1981 and things continued on in good order. The Saudis took our advice as long as they wanted it, but when they didn't need it anymore, they got along better than one thought they would.

After the award of the contract for Phase IV to Consolidated

Jebel Dhahran and the New Saudi Generation

Construction Company of Beirut (CCC) in the fall of 1977, the work accelerated rapidly. CCC was very competent, with lots of experience in industrial and civil work. The company assigned good people to the project. They were well organized, and overall they did a good job.

This phase of the university's development included many buildings, but the largest and perhaps the most outstanding was the **Research Institute** This had as many square meters of floor space as all the other academic buildings combined up to that time.

This would be the first research institute of its kind, certainly in Saudi Arabia and perhaps in the Middle East. Dr. Hall was determined to get someone of prestige to head it. He finally succeeded in recruiting Dr. William Pickering, who had just retired as director of the Jet Propulsion Laboratory in Pasadena, California. He had headed up JPL for about thirty years during the period when it launched the first "Surveyors" to the moon and many other space shots. He was a big "catch," you might say.

Dr. Pickering was involved in the operational planning for the Research Institute. He wrote the operational plan. Dr. Bakhrebah recalled, "Dr. Bakr gave me a copy. I read it on the plane coming to Houston. I was so enthusiastic about it. I wanted to have it translated into Arabic and present it to the board because it was so impressive. I found out that Dr. Bakr had already done that. Dr. Pickering was a great man."

Dr. Pickering was at UPM about four years. Mildred and I got to know him and his wife, Muriel, quite well. He was a very fine person, a New Zealander, and an outstanding administrator and scientist, having guided JPL during its major growth period. In 1979, Dr. Pickering developed a physical problem and was in the hospital at Aramco for some time. He went back to the States for an operation, which was successful, and then returned to UPM until 1982, as a consultant. He was also a member of the Consortium of Universities advising UPM and

Construction Administration Phase IV — 1975 to 1986

representing Cal Tech.

Dr. Abdullah Dabbagh, a bright young Saudi, then became director of the Research Institute. Later, in 1989, Dr. Dabbagh was elected to the board of directors of Saudi Aramco. This was another example of the "Saudi-ization" that was beginning to take place in all fields. Dr. Pickering always spoke highly of Dr. Dabbagh. He said that he was a very capable young man, and with more experience, he would be very good at the job. And so he was. When the first Arab astronaut, Saudi Prince Sultan bin Salman ibn Abdul Aziz, made the space shot with the Discovery Space Shuttle, Dr. Dabbagh headed the scientific team of 15 or 20 scientists (mostly from the university), who came to the States with Prince Sultan and helped arrange deployment of their experiments in space.

Now these young Saudis are the early heroes of the Saudi science field. I'm sure they will continue to accomplish much. The Kingdom exploited Prince Sultan's trip into space to the fullest. One of the main objectives was to inspire young Saudis to know that they could do these things. Here Prince Sultan was an astronaut, had gone into space, and successfully completed the mission. So, they were saying to all young Saudis, "You can do the same things. You can do great things."

The Research Institute was completed in December 1981, after four years of construction. It was very well equipped and soon began taking contract work from Aramco, government agencies, and other users, doing testing and scientific research work. They also began setting up a reference lab of standards for equipment and measurements.

Some of our most pleasant friendships and social relationships were with people from the Research Institute. They were very interesting, talented, and unusual people, or they would not have been there. Bill and Mary Tiedge came in about 1978, recruited by Dr. Pickering. Bill had worked with Dr. Pickering for about twenty-five years at JPL. He was a mechanical engineer and had just taken early retirement from JPL. He came to

Jebel Dhahran and the New Saudi Generation

the Research Institute as manager of technical services, and did an excellent job. Mary began working as secretary to Dr. Hall until he passed on. The Tiedges, the Pickerings, and others were, like ourselves, thoroughly enjoying their work and life at UPM. It was a challenge and a rewarding experience.

Some of those in the above category were: Fred and Irene LaViolette, Alex and Iby Vajda, Dan and Maryanne Fairbanks, Jack and Helen Doty, to name a few. Jack was a professor in the College of Industrial Management.

Before I left Houston in August 1975, Joe Thomas gave me a briefing, a rundown on the various key players in the project. One of them was a Mrs. Grace Kirkwood. He said, "Mrs. Kirkwood is a friend of CRS. Her husband is president of the American University in Beirut. He is also on the board of UPM. She is a landscape architect and designed the master plan for landscaping of the university. Anything she wants, you do. If she wants an airplane ticket to somewhere, you get it for her."

That being the case, we certainly thought she must be a key player. When we stopped in Beirut on our way to Dhahran, we thought we should meet Mrs. Kirkwood. And so we did. We went out to AUB and had a good visit with her and Dr. Kirkwood. She gave us a briefing on the university in Dhahran.

A few years later, Dr. Kirkwood had an unfortunate experience. During the civil war in Lebanon, in about 1978, two of the deans of AUB were shot and killed right on the doorstep of the campus by disgruntled students. The assailants were then looking for Dr. Kirkwood. He barricaded himself in his room and outwaited them. They never did get him. But it did shake him up considerably, and he resigned not too long after that. He and Mrs. Kirkwood then moved to New York in retirement.

Mrs. Kirkwood was a very unusual and talented lady. She revisited the university about six months after we arrived in Dhahran. Although she had no official capacity for CRS at that

The Saudi scientific team designed and analyzed space experiments carried on by Prince Sultan bin Salman during the Discovery Space Mission. Prince Bandar bin Sultan, Saudi Ambassador to the United States, is fifth from the left on the back row.

Jebel Dhahran and the New Saudi Generation

time, she had made the landscaping layout, and had witnessed most of the original planting, as she had planned it. She wanted to inspect the job, so she and I went over the entire campus. She wore me out and was always about six steps ahead of me. Up and down the hills. She could remember every plant that was supposed to be there. She would look at one place and say, "Where are my bougainvilleas?" Of course, I didn't have the vaguest idea.

She returned a year or so later when she was consulting on a job for Aramco. We went over everything again. She was reasonably happy then with the way the planting was turning out.

Charles Lawrence recalled: "Mrs. Kirkwood was into what grew naturally. She knew of plants in Lebanon and other places that would survive. And judicious placing of trees would help control the effects of the wind and sand that blow. Mrs. Kirkwood came in early, and everything was done under her guidance and direction, because Zaki Yamani had asked her if she would like to do that. She was delighted. She had done some landscaping for Yamani's home in Taif, and it worked out very well. There is a lot more landscaping and watering going on at UPM now than we had ever envisioned. I think it is absolutely beautiful."

One of the companies that ended up doing much of the landscaping on campus was a Lebanese company named Rabya. Its managing director was a young Lebanese by the name of Samir Kriedy. I remember that Mrs. Kirkwood very early had told me that if we could ever get him working on campus, we should do so. She had no idea what would develop later.

Samir told me that he had been a student of Mrs. Kirkwood's in landscaping back at the American University in Beirut. He then told me how he had helped to start the company, Rabya. It eventually expanded to doing more landscaping all over Saudi Arabia than any other company. Samir was a typical Lebanese, very personable, industrious, flexible, resilient, and able to bound back from any situation. He was very knowledgeable

Construction Administration Phase IV — 1975 to 1986

about his trade.

Samir told me how he had gotten a job to do some work in Saudi Arabia while he was still in school. He had gone to Mrs. Kirkwood for a recommendation. She wouldn't give it to him, although she said he was one of her best pupils. He was really shocked. She said, "No, you haven't done anything yet. I don't know what you can do. You are a good student." She wouldn't actually put her name down. Later, of course, she acknowledged his talent, but I guess she was going to make him prove it.

Landscaping was, indeed, one of the very important parts of the project. Lewis May was head of the landscaping department of CRS. He was responsible for the UPM work after Mrs. Kirkwood's initial work, and for all other CRS work in the Kingdom. He did an excellent job and became an authority on landscaping in Saudi Arabia and the Middle East, writing a book on the subject.

The sand and soil are quite fertile, not at all sterile, if they get water, sweet water. So, the secret is watering. For all the planting that we did there, we provided underground sprinkler systems. Aramco was a mass of green with the trees and planting that it had done over forty years. The university was more sophisticated and architecturally done in relation to the buildings than Aramco was. In five years, we began to see the results.

When we left in 1986, it was beginning to look beautiful. Pictures that we had taken when we arrived eleven years earlier as contrasted with the way it looked when we left, were amazing. In that time, the trees had grown big, and the flowering plants were picturesque. For much of the area, the concept was to leave it with a natural desert look. From the standpoint of economics, it would be too expensive to plant everything. Soil erosion and climate control were also important aspects of landscaping.

The last year we were there, Prince Mohammed, the son of King Fahd, became the Amir of the Eastern Province. He visited the university, and decided there wasn't enough landscaping.

Approach to Jebel - 1975

Approach to Jebel - 1991

Construction Administration Phase IV — 1975 to 1986

So, he authorized additional money for landscaping on the main approach road. I understand that some of the money was a personal contribution from the prince. That was done after we left. I have heard it is quite beautiful.

Postscript 1991:We were happy to be able to see the new landscaping on our visit to the university in October 1991. The new landscaping is truly beautiful and a great enhancement of the campus.

As I mentioned previously, this book deals primarily with the design of the campus and buildings for King Fahd University of Petroleum and Minerals in Dhahran.

After 1975 CRS began designing many other facilities around the Kingdom of Saudi Arabia unrelated to their work at KFUPM, including facilities for the F-15 and AWACS programs. Truitt Garrison was in charge of these projects overall for CRS in the Houston office.

There were many CRS architects and engineers involved in this work. Obviously I cannot mention all of them. However, there were two that I shall take note of here.

Perry King, an architect with much overseas experience in Thailand and other areas of the world, was located in Riyadh and he, along with E.C. Kobs, did much of the work in developing new business in Saudi Arabia and elsewhere in the Middle East. Perry King later went to Hong Kong and established an office there for CRS.

Bob Kirkham, a long-time architect with CRS, was construction manager for a large facility near Dammam, Saudi Arabia for the Halliburton Company.

These projects were vital to the development and well-being of Saudi Arabia.

While we at KFUPM did not work directly with these people, we sometimes did have occasion to interface with them.

Chapter 14

The Agony of Implementation

The Lebanese contractor, Express Contracting Company, who was building the 189 houses, had all kinds of difficulty from the start in 1975. That experience demonstrated to me the ability of the Saudis to manage things and the ability of the Lebanese to survive. The university, out of self-interest, through various means heiped to get the job finished.

When I arrived, excavation for the 189 houses was just beginning. As previously mentioned, there was a rather serious site problem, because of an error in the survey. There was much more dirt fill required than had been anticipated.

At that time, there were no ready-mix concrete plants where you could call up and order so much concrete. It all had to be mixed on the site by hand in two-cubic-meter mixers. You had to try to count the number of bags of cement to see that it was according to specifications. There were no testing labs.

That was my first real problem. I was not a structural engineer. I had not really been a field architect to the extent of having to do testing. In Houston, we just called the laboratory, which would send somebody out to do what was needed. All we did was to check the test results. We knew what the concrete strength was supposed to be, and that was all we had to do.

I found out in Dhahran that I actually had to do the testing. There was no one else. That presented quite a problem, because that wasn't my field. Not only that, there was no testing equipment. Most tests in the States are done by the cylinder method, and there were no cylinders. All we could do was put together some wooden cubes, which had different criteria, although the cube method is used somewhat in Europe. For six months I really struggled with that, and felt that it might be my demise, because we were getting such bad test results. We were not getting the strength of concrete we were supposed to have.

Jebel Dhahran and the New Saudi Generation

Now, this was not an uncommon problem in that area, because of the nature of the materials and the lack of expertise in this hand-mixing by the native workers. I remember one time in particular, I was watching a worker and counting the number of bags of cement. I said, "How many bags did you put in?" The worker told me and I said, "Are you sure?"

He replied, "Of course I am sure. I am a bedouin." The bedouins are noted for their mathematical ability. I've heard many very unusual tales about what they can do with mathematics. He was quite offended that I should think that he did not have the right number of bags.

We then took samples of the concrete in cubes and took them to the university civil engineering lab. There we had equipment for curing, crushing, and testing the concrete cubes to determine the strength. Our specifications usually called for a strength of 3,000 or 4,000 lbs./sq. in. in compression. The whole process was a specialized procedure. It was a problem, and we did get some bad test results. Fortunately, after about six months, CRS sent out Bob Cook to take over that aspect of the work. Not that we didn't have more problems, but he did bring an element of expertise, and I could concentrate on the architecture.

The contractor tried to improve his abilities by getting proper equipment. It was not possible just to go down to al-Khobar and order a batching plant, a ready-mix truck, or a concrete pump. So, he sent his project manager to Germany, where he purchased two ready-mix trucks, two concrete pumps, a batching plant, and other specialized equipment. Then the problem was getting it down there. The equipment from Germany had to come over land, through Turkey and Yugoslavia by truck.

For the next few months, after the project manager, a German-American named Carl Schou, returned and said that he had made the purchases, we waited day by day for their arrival. In about six months the equipment arrived. Things did improve considerably.

The Agony of Implementation

It was hard to realize that by the time we left, eleven years later, it was possible to go down to al-Khobar, buy such equipment, and have it almost immediately. All these things were a matter of development. It will never be the same again, because now the Saudis have all these facilities.

But in many ways, the agony of the early days of implementation provided a lot of excitement and interest, the uniqueness and challenge of the task. Also, I just couldn't believe that I was getting telexes and correspondence from all over the world. Not having been much of a world traveler before that, I was fascinated at being involved with such faraway places.

At the beginning of the 189 House Project it became apparent that there was an urgent need for a new master survey of the UPM property. Prior to this there had been numerous surveys made in bits and pieces by various contractors.

In 1975 CRS sent over a surveying consultant, Jim Griggs, from Houston, on a year's contract to consolidate and update all surveys, and coordinate them with available Aramco information. This was beneficial in avoiding pitfalls as had developed with the 189 Houses due to errors in the survey.

In 1982, construction documents for two hundred faculty houses were put out for bids. The low bidder was a large Saudi company. In reviewing the bids, Don Chambers did not feel that the Saudi bid was the best for the university. The reason that he felt that the low bidder was not the best, was that the price was too low. He recommended the second lowest bidder, a Korean company.

Every contractor bids according to the same plans and criteria. All have basically the same suppliers, so there is a reasonable difference that you can have. If a bid is unreasonably low, there is something wrong. If you give that contractor the job, you are usually going to have problems later on. Many contractors think that if they can just get the contract, then they can somehow finagle more money later on in the contract. It's a gamble.

The contract was awarded to the Saudi contractor. In the end, the company went bankrupt. It had many projects around the Kingdom.

The housing project actually was supposed to be handed over in November 1982, so it was already a year late in the fall of 1983. The project had gone from bad to worse. The contractor finally hired some British construction managers to organize the project and make an effort to finish it. Well, no matter how well organized you are, if there is no money, there is not much you can do about it. There was very little to operate the job with.

The project manager told me that sometimes at night he'd meet the contracting company's owner at his airplane at the airport, and he would hand him a bag of money. That was supposed to take care of the payroll for the week. The contracting company was fast coming to the end of its rope. The British construction managers that had been hired were capable, but it soon became evident to them that there was nothing that they could do to save this kind of a deal.

In January 1983, we were assigned an additional architect, Vance Creviston of Houston, for one year, who took charge of the housing project. He brought his twelve-year old son, Courtney, with him.

The contractor's project manager was an American. It was not readily apparent to me just what the situation was between the Saudi contractor and his manager.

We had regular meetings with the project manager and the university administration to try to resolve some of his construction problems, but they were primarily financial. It did appear that the problem was really out of the manager's hands, and yet he was held responsible.

The Agony of Implementation

The Saudi who owned the contracting company was a rather personable fellow with stories, jokes, and a disarming manner. He had been educated in England.

One evening, the project manager was arrested without warning at his home and taken to jail on unspecified charges. Rumors circulated for several weeks.

One day, the Saudi who owned the contracting company dropped by my office unexpectedly and chatted with Vance Creviston and me for a couple of hours, describing an alleged plot about his manager's siphoning off money from the project.

The project went on for some months with the contracting company owner becoming personally less and less in evidence.

The project came to a halt.

One year after his incarceration, the project manager was released and returned to the U.S.A. The allegation did not prove to be true. He was a bitter man.

Unfortunately, this was the type of "horror story" that circulated back in the U.S.

Reviewing this case with a young Saudi familiar with it, he acknowledged regretfully that it was true. However, he added, "Now tell about the Belgian contractor who did the same thing." He referred to a case (not at the university) where a Belgian contractor with a large defense contract skipped the country after receiving the advance payment and abandoned the project completely.

So, it was, in fact, "tit for tat." There were some bad Saudi contractors, but there were many bad Western contractors who unscrupulously tried to take advantage of the conditions that prevailed.

The university said that it had to have fifty of the houses by September 1983. It agreed to put up the money each month for the labor, food, and construction materials that were needed. It appointed one of the young Saudis on Mansour al-Saber's staff, Abdul Rahman al-Harthy, to supervise the accounting. All of it had to come through us, of course. However, there wasn't much that we could do except to verify that there wasn't any major discrepancy. Mostly, it was bills for food to feed the Filipino laborers.

At the end of 1983, the university did receive fifty of the houses. They weren't totally finished, but by compromising here and there, they were occupied. They turned out to be successful houses. Everyone liked them.

In 1984, even the British construction managers left. At the same time, the contracting company's owner just disappeared as far as the job was concerned. He left the job in the hands of a Lebanese architect, who had been project manager with three contractors at UPM —the Lebanese housing contractor, ECC, who got into trouble; the large Lebanese contractor, CCC, for Phases II, III, and IV; and now this Saudi. It wasn't long before he too was under the gun, and it actually looked as if he might be vulnerable.

About this time, it got so bad that the Filipinos were writing letters to me pleading for help. All their credit was exhausted in the market, and they didn't have any food. I took this problem to the university. The officials were somewhat skeptical. However, I convinced them of the seriousness of the situation. I was concerned that without any money, the Filipino workers might start robbing, rioting, or something. At that point the university decided to take over and started providing food and materials required to finish the fifty houses.

I had to appear before the communications committee, which is a select committee of all the top Saudis, the deans, and other officials. Dr. Bakhrebah was on sabbatical leave at this time. I explained to them exactly what had happened. I felt it was urgent to get the problem resolved, because I thought that we had a potential time bomb on our hands.

For the next year or so, the Lebanese project manager held the contract together. Then the Filipinos started trying to leave the country. They went to the Labor Board. I'll say this for the Saudi government. It has an effective and fair Labor Board.

The Agony of Implementation

These were expatriates who were taking their grievances against a Saudi contractor to the Saudi Labor Board. The Labor Board appeared to be a reasonably fair and just operating group. It often ruled in favor of the expatriates.

The project manager began to succeed in getting them out of the country, about ten at a time through the Labor Board Grievances Committee and with some remuneration. In the next two years, it dwindled to where there was none on the job except a handful of Filipinos, and no work was being done. They were stagnant. In the meantime the government appointed an adjudicator to resolve the company's debts. This went on for a couple of years. The 150 houses remained unfinished.

This was an example of taking the low bid, when the low bid wasn't credible. In a similar situation later during a Bids and Tenders Committee meeting when the committee wanted to take another low bid that didn't sound credible, Dr. Bakhrebah told his committee, "We got into trouble once; let's not do it again." In this case, the contract was awarded to the second lowest bidder.

The Saudis had a procedure for initiating a contract, which I think was the cause of many of the problems. It was the method of providing an advance payment. The purpose of the advance payment was to help the contractors mobilize and induce them to get out there and do work. The procedure had some merit and was reasonable in that it helped to get work started in that part of the world where it wasn't at all easy.

As soon as a contract was signed, the Saudis gave the contractor an advance payment equal to 20% of the value of the contract, and he provided a bank guarantee. This was repaid monthly as his income began to generate. This could amount to quite a bit of money. If a contractor had a $30 million job, right off the bat he got $6 million dollars without doing a lick of work. Now, the point was, he was supposed to use the money

Jebel Dhahran and the New Saudi Generation

to mobilize and get the job going. That was good for the owner, but there was no provision made to monitor where that money went, so that there was temptation goes without saying. The contractor could take the money and put it in a bank in Geneva or somewhere and draw interest.

Contractors didn't always use the money as they were supposed to. They would try to make the job run off the monthly cash-flow, but it's not possible to generate enough income that way to keep a job going the way it should. They would put in very little or none of their own capital. It often was a self-defeating thing for the owner. It was a great temptation to take the job just to get the advance payment, and then not really care what happened.

This was one of the negative experiences. With the volume of work going on, it was inevitable that some contractors would turn out that way.

One of the many problems we had, in the first few years, was the matter of shipping items such as parcels. In the early days, the organization for shipping and receiving at the airport was not thoroughly functioning. CRS would ship drawings and parcels, and we would have to pick them up at the airport. The volume of things that were shipped in was so great that they couldn't be processed. Everything was unloaded and left by the control tower on the runway. The big warehouse buildings couldn't hold everything. It was quite a problem just getting through customs and even locating anything. The university had customs people who would help do that, but often we had to do it on our own as best we could.

One time early in 1976, when the drawings came out for Phase IV, we had already invited the contractors to pick up plans. Then, for some reason the drawings didn't arrive. I went to the airport and couldn't find them, although CRS/Houston confirmed that they had been shipped. We had always asked

The Agony of Implementation

the Houston office to put big identifiable labels on them, because in the masses of boxes and crates that we saw, they were very difficult to identify. This particular time it was becoming very critical. The contractors were coming in to pick up plans, and we couldn't give them to them.

It was the time of Ramadan, which meant that everything operated about half-time. I had been out several times to the airport to try to find this one big crate of drawings that was supposed to be there. I couldn't locate it. Then it was a matter of having Houston send them again, which would take too long. I thought I would try one more time.

I got a young Saudi, Diej al-Dossary, in the UPM purchasing department, and we went there together. By chance, we located our crate. It had a very small quarter-inch high lettering, and we were just lucky to have identified it. Diej by-passed the authorized routine, got hold of a fork lift truck and operator, gave him some money, and had him barrel his way in there and get out with it. The British manager of the area was infuriated that we had done what we did.

In wandering through all these things that were sitting out there, I could imagine how many items were lost and never seen again by the owners. I came across one big crate that was opened, and out of it had spilled on the ground somebody's wedding albums and personal things that must have been highly prized. They would never see them again.

You read about these things in U.S. papers, and they always sounded so cynically critical of the Saudis. It was a very difficult situation that everyone was trying to cope with. Eventually it was overcome, and the process became quite orderly and well managed. They were just trying to do everything overnight. It reminded me of the beginning of World War II, when the U.S. Navy at Solomon's Island, Maryland, was trying to build and organize an amphibious training base, putting people and landing craft in there by the hundreds. It was a terrible mess trying to train them, house them, and feed them overnight.

Jebel Dhahran and the New Saudi Generation

Again, I am the Arab apologist. It wasn't because it was the Arabs or Saudis; it was the circumstances. They had a crisis, and they were trying to overcome it. They did as well as anyone would have done under the circumstances.

In 1980, at the beginning of the construction of the academic buildings for Phase IV, which Redec Daelim was going to build, there was considerable excavation that had to be done. The Koreans had an interesting starting procedure. Most of them were Buddhist, although some were Christian.

When they started a project, after most of the excavation work was done, they would have a ceremony. They had a table with all kinds of fruit on it. They would come up one at a time and kneel and bow.

This was intended to set the stage for the project by warding off any evil and invoking the blessing of their deity for safety. This event proceeded in a very colorful way. We had discovered some caverns underneath the area, and some of the Saudis were down inspecting them at that time. One of them came up and saw the Koreans kneeling and bowing. Excitedly he said, "What are they doing?" I replied, "Well, they are just praying for the blessing of their deity."

Later when the project was topped out, the Koreans put a tree on it. Then they had another ceremony, as contractors do in the United States. Most of the projects were safe, although on that project, there was one Korean killed. You can't build that many buildings or do that much construction without the possibility of something like that happening.

As the Koreans were excavating for the academic buildings, the top of the ground suddenly cracked open, and they discovered that they were sitting on top of the large underground cavern that I have referred to. This opened up all kinds of speculation. Harry Cretin, our structural engineer, was excited about the geological implications, but the construction implica-

The Agony of Implementation

tions were rather ominous. As they broke this open, they found they could go down inside, and there was a large cavern extending over a considerable length. It was as big as a normal sized room that you could walk into. On the inside it was white with crusty-like salt crystals.

The main structural implication was that we couldn't simply go ahead and put our footings where we wanted. The cavern that we could see was not the concern. The concern was that this implied that there might be more. The question was, "Where were they?" Test borings had been made before the project started. These caverns did not show up at all on the test borings, strangely enough.

A contract was then given to McLelland Engineers of Houston, who by this time, had developed a fairly good operation in Dhahran. They had to run resistivity tests, small borings to determine how solid it was all along the line of footings. This was time-consuming and cost additional money, but it was the only thing to do. We determined that there was a string of caverns all in one direction. These were known as "solution cavities." We finally concluded that there were no more, and that we could pour footings where we wanted them. We filled the one large cavern with concrete and proceeded.

This was a fascinating side-play to the project. We had hoped that when we arrived inside, we might find artifacts or something, but we didn't. Everyone was interested. The geology professors from the university wanted to see it. Reports were written about it. They said the caverns were formed from 20,000 to 2 million years ago. By coincidence, Aramco ran into caverns on a project of theirs some distance away at about the same time. We compared notes. They appeared to be continuations of the same line of cavities.

Earlier, I referred to my first meeting with Dr. Bakhrebah in the CRS office in Houston in which we had a rainstorm and

Korean Ceremony

Cavern Discvovery

The Agony of Implementation

the patio flooded. When we arrived in Saudi Arabia the weather was normal — hot and humid. Then, as usual in October, it began to cool off. In November, we had some very heavy rains. The rainy season generally is considered to be from about November to May. This being our first experience, we didn't know what to expect. In November, the first heavy rain came.

Immediately, there were reports of leaks in the buildings. I tried to point out to the UPM administration that leaks were not uncommon in buildings anywhere. I remembered dealing with that problem from the day I started practicing architecture in the office of Leon Chatelain in Washington, D.C. in 1946. Of course, that was not a good answer. The Saudis were inclined to be quite upset about it.

With these first rains, the major problem areas were identified. As is often the case, they were in the most sensitive locations. One problem location was over the top floor of the Administration Building, directly over the rector's office and the board room. This one persisted. As more rain subsequently came, I tried to identify the problem. The buildings were still under warranty to CCC. The solution was going to be difficult. Water can be very devious and subtle. I worked with CCC to find a solution.

The roof deck of this building was terrazzo tile, which is fairly common over there. There was membrane waterproofing under this, but obviously the water was going through the tile joints and the membrane. The question was to find out where. The contractor, in a delaying action, would determine where it leaked below. Then, he'd go up and take a few tiles off and try to repair that spot and it would leak in another. It was obvious that the problem was more widespread than that.

After many efforts to get him to do something of a more permanent nature, I finally threatened in writing to call his bank guarantee, which exists until the end of the warranty period. This did seem to cause some action, as well as some ill-will. He then got with it and removed the entire terrazzo tile roof deck.

Jebel Dhahran and the New Saudi Generation

We found that the membrane waterproofing was, in fact, defective. It was all broken up. I think it was recalled from the market later.

Then, it was a matter of what to use as replacement waterproofing. Materials weren't all that available. Fortunately, that day a British fellow stopped by our office, a salesman for a British product. He had some material in stock in al-Khobar. It was self-adhering and it seemed it would fill the bill. The contractor purchased a quantity of it and laid it all over the old membrane. He then applied new terrazzo tile. That was the end of the problem.

A major crisis occurred when he had all the tile off. The contractor didn't have the new membrane down yet, and that night we had one of the heaviest rains ever. It was also a severe electrical storm. Mildred and I were sitting in our little house. The lights were out and we had candles. I was wondering what was happening up on "Jebel Dhahran." I said to Mildred, "Maybe we'd better pack our bags tomorrow, because I don't know what is going to happen."

The next morning, I went to see the senior adviser, Dr. Hall. His office was across the corridor from the rector and adjacent to the board room. His office was flooded. Poor Dr. Hall had his pants rolled up, and he was trying to organize things. The whole suspended ceiling had caved in and water was all over everything. I thought I'd better "bite the bullet" and go across the corridor to see the condition of the rector's office. To my surprise, I found it was dry as a bone. The rector walked out of his office smiling. Everything was fine. There was no problem. I didn't know whether he knew what had happened to Dr. Hall's office, but I thought if ever there was a case of Divine Providence, this was it. Dr. Hall said later, "You sure were lucky it was my office and not his." Fortunately, the previous day, Dr. Hall had transferred all of his most sensitive files to another

The Agony of Implementation

location in the building.

It was a terrible electrical storm with high winds and torrents of rain. Of course, everyone had trouble. Aramco had 500 houses that leaked. We had, besides the administration building, the student affairs building, which developed leaks. There was also the recreation center, the library and many houses. Each of these was an individual problem which was hard to identify. For instance, in the student affairs building, as in the administration building, it was also a matter of waterproofing and flashing a concrete roof slab with a terrazzo deck.

By far the worst problem was the library, because of the potential damage to many valuable books. Again this condition was a flat roof with two inches of water standing, heavy north winds blowing it over the sides and running down right through the stained glass windows. The water would come down in sheets to the floor inside. The staff would have to move the book stacks from the wall to save them. This one was a real puzzle.

Everyone would ask, "Why don't you do something?" Well, I didn't know what to do. It was the old story. When it wasn't raining, you couldn't see the problem. When it was, you had a disaster. I climbed up and inspected the caulking around the windows while it was raining. The caulking was solid. These were leaded glass windows, and the leaded joints were not leaking. I finally decided, incredible as it might sound, that the water must be coming right through the glass. This was stained glass that had considerable fissuring. It was made in Mexico. I saw that, in fact, it was actually coming right through the glass face itself. These were very finely designed stained glass windows. They depicted Arabic motifs and were the "pièce de résistance" of the building.

The contractor had assigned to me a Jordanian fellow named Marwan. He was sincere and diligent. He and I scoured around and finally decided we would cover the windows with glass on

Jebel Dhahran and the New Saudi Generation

the outside. We didn't want any joints, so we found in the nearby town of Dammam some acrylic plastic sheets, cut them to the right shape and installed them in one piece over the glass on the outside. We would only have to caulk the perimeter, and that we certainly could do. We did that, and it solved the problem.

One of the main things I was concerned about was the architectural effect. At night the light shined from the inside out, and in the daytime from the outside in with a beautiful and colorful effect. Fortunately, this addition had no adverse effect at all on the design appearance of these beautiful windows. The only thing I was ever concerned about was that it might fade or discolor. Nine years later it was still in place and looking fine. The blowing sand had a slightly abrasive effect on the plastic. But it still was architecturally effective, and we had solved the problem.

Before we actually had the solution to this, every time it would rain, Marwan and I would rush up to the roof to see what we could do. These windows were on the corners. One idea was to "sandbag" the corners, providing a perimeter barrier, so that the water wouldn't run over the edge at the point where the windows were below. This was a dam, more or less, on each corner, L-shaped. Well, there was no such thing as a sandbag around. We went to Dammam and actually had some bags custom-made. We filled those with sand and placed them around the corners as sort of a sandbag dam.

The rainfall that year, 1975-76, was so heavy that it was said officially that the actual classification of the area was changed from arid to semi-arid. With that kind of rain, the desert does blossom. We would drive out over what was normally sand desert and there would be a light green fuzz of grass everywhere.

This experience brought home to me the initiative and independence that you were expected to exercise out there. I had

The Agony of Implementation

written to CRS and given to our project manager, Conrad Neal, in Houston, a rundown on these problems, and what I planned to do. I said, "If you have any comments or suggestions, please let me know." I didn't get a response, comment, suggestion or anything. I think the general policy was stated one time by Joe Thomas, "That's what you are there for. It's your problem. You solve it."

What you begin to realize in a situation like that is that there is the home office side, in the sense of being concerned about liability. Of course, liability is a big and legitimate concern. In retrospect, I can see that for Houston to have acknowledged this situation and discussed it with me in writing would possibly be acknowledging an error or omission, which it might be considered liable for. I'm sure the best attitude from its standpoint was "hands off, it's a field problem." Then there is no credibility established for a liability claim.

The contractor basically is responsible to provide a waterproof building. The architect designs and details. Sometimes you may find that the architect's details might have contributed to the problem. Most specifications are written in such a way that you can still throw the responsibility on the contractor. If some detail doesn't look as if it will work or do the job, the contractor is supposed to bring it to the architect's attention, discuss it, and do something about it.

Referring back to what I said about the British fellow popping into our office with the waterproofing material just at the right time, I would say that this was indicative of what began to develop after the first year or two that we were there. At first we had only an occasional salesman come by, and there was not the marketing setup for various materials as there is in the States.

Within a few years, it was almost like the States. Salesmen came calling constantly, just to drop in, as they would here. They were working out of their sales offices in Dammam or al-Khobar, representing products from all over the world. Many

Jebel Dhahran and the New Saudi Generation

of them had begun to stockpile materials in warehouses, so they usually had stocks available. This was part of the development which had begun. It was amazing to me how much had to be done, how it all got started and kept expanding in every direction.

I think no one can work in the Middle East for any period of time without running into some problems with the potential of being negative in one's experience. I can think of several which occurred vis-a-vis CRS for me.

The first one was the concrete problem which developed early. I found this difficult to cope with primarily because of my own lack of expertise in that area. That was resolved through actions we took to try to correct by structural additions what allegedly was poor concrete quality. That hurdle was passed.

Another incident occurred at the end of 1985 when the Saudi government became quite strict about people working in the Kingdom without a formal contract. CRS had one overall contract which it had been operating under. We found that we were operating without a current formal contract, since the projects that were originally involved under that contract were already completed. So, in fact, we were operating like the old oil operators on a "handshake basis."

The new projects which we were working on, by rights should have had new contracts. Nevertheless, we continued to work on them according to the original contract agreement not really knowing the implications of this, and there was nothing we at the site could do about it anyway. The university itself apparently didn't realize the implications of the law. Consequently, when it came to a head, we suddenly received communications from the legal department in Houston that CRS was considered to be in violation of the law. The case had now been referred from the Saudi Ministry's Engineering De-

The Agony of Implementation

partment to the Legal Department. CRS was going to be called on the carpet subject to a penalty.

I will say that Mansour al-Saber had only tried to keep everything going in the midst of an indeterminate procedure. When Dr. Bakhrebah got back after a year's absence, he contended that Mansour had acted above his authority. However, the only alternative would have been for us to leave, and we didn't see how we could do that. We then received a long telex from the CRS legal department in Houston and the CRS office in Riyadh saying that CRS was now up for a penalty and was going to have to appear in court. CRS lawyers in Riyadh were going to appear for the firm, and it was subject to a fine. If it happened again, somebody would go to jail. The question was, who would go? I was project manager there on the site.

As we worked along with it, I had quite a bit of communication with the legal people in Riyadh and provided them with the information they requested. Mansour and the university were as cooperative as they were able to be. They were on the spot, too. They were really responsible for the situation, but they were not inclined to put themselves in too vulnerable a position. But we did wrangle through and finally got it all sorted out. Every project got a contract. However, the government did impose a fine on CRS.

The CRS lawyers in Houston said that if it happened again and someone had to go to jail, it probably would be E.C. Kobs in Riyadh because he was technically in charge of CRS' entire operation in Saudi Arabia. This showed the incongruity of these situations, because E.C. had nothing to do with this particular problem. By the time I left, we had a contract for each man and project.

There was an incident in 1984 that I felt in some ways hurt my credibility temporarily with CRS. The last two years that we

Jebel Dhahran and the New Saudi Generation

were there, we started construction on the Energy Lab. It hadn't been going long before the university decided that it wanted to fill in two courtyard areas and use the space for a Laser Lab. This required some structural revisions. The original drawings had anticipated this to a certain extent and had allowed for some steel brackets to be cast into the concrete columns at these open bay areas. A new floor could then be added using the steel brackets for support. The incident occurred while Harry Cretin was on vacation, and I was looking after his work.

When the university decided that it wanted to add these floors, CRS began work on the design. We sent photographs of the interior to Houston. CRS noticed that the brackets weren't in place. I had, in fact, observed that the Koreans had failed to put them in. With all the things that were going on, I had not caught it until after the concrete was poured. Harry returned and said that he had discussed it with the Koreans, and they could not install them, as designed. The size of the bracket anchors and the reinforcing steel in the columns just would not fit together. I called the Korean manager in. With his back to the wall, he admitted that actually they had forgotten them, although there was some validity to Harry's claim that they would not fit.

I tried to decide how to reply to the CRS question of why the brackets weren't in place. I asked Harry, and he still maintained that they couldn't be installed, as designed. Admittedly, this was a lapse of judgment on my part, because I know that you never put any blame back on the home office. I asked Harry, "Are you sure that's a true statement?" He replied, "Positively yes, and I'll argue with them about it." I sent a telex. It went to the head structural engineer, and he would not accept that statement, contending that the brackets could have been installed as designed. After it was all over, it was difficult to prove whether they could or couldn't have been installed. I think the thing that damaged my credibility was that it looked as though we were trying to get off the hook by blaming the

The Agony of Implementation

home office for something — and perhaps we were.

CRS made a new type of detail, all the elements went in, and everything was fine.

There was one situation which had the potential for being a very serious problem. Initial geological surveys and borings come as close as they can to determining all the soil conditions. Of course, there is always a certain possibility of errors or omissions. This particular case was an addition to the Library, which we started in 1977. It was the first building that the Koreans built on campus. It was a rather quickly conceived project. In January 1977, the university advised CRS that it wanted to expand the Library. CRS sent out a programming team immediately and within two months it had the addition designed and drawings completed. We had the project under contract to the Korean firm, Redec Daelim, by July of 1977.

The Koreans are very careful, competent workers. In this particular situation, there was a combination of adverse circumstances. The original drawings showed that the outside footings for the existing Library were bearing on solid rock. They showed the addition going straight down from the existing footing, some 15 meters.

We started excavating and then realized when we saw the bottom of the existing footing that it really wasn't on what you would call "bedrock." Instead it was a stratified sandstone, a sort of compacted clay. If you put water to it, it would dissolve. We then stopped that portion of the work and raised a red flag back in Houston. Immediately CRS recognized the problem and began making some additional analysis. It sent a man out for a couple of weeks to do the additional design and drawings right on the spot. There wasn't much expertise around, but we got McClelland Engineers, who were new to the area. Dan Hannah, whom I had worked with on a serious foundation problem on the Rice University boiler house when I was with

Jebel Dhahran and the New Saudi Generation

Calhoun, Tungate, and Jackson, had begun to set up a complete foundation operation in Dhahran. He had some portable drillers to take soil samples and make test borings. Tom Turton was in charge of our work for McClelland.

By the time McClelland came on the scene, the Koreans had already excavated down too far, to a point that was precarious. It was all right as long as everything was stabilized as it was. This was in November just about the time for the rains to start, and it was indeed potentially dangerous. If the rain had come with that kind of exposure under these footings, the whole building could have been in trouble, because there was a great surcharge from the material under the existing building.

The Koreans worked ahead as fast as they could. CRS completed the drawings with the new design, which was to go down to the bottom level and build up a concrete retaining wall enclosure, compacting it with proper fill material all the way up these fifteen meters. This was a slow process. In the meantime, we were concerned that we might get a heavy rain. Sure enough, it did look as if it would rain, and the Koreans spent several days and nights working around the clock trying to beat the rainy season.

I spent a couple of nights with Mr. Jong Chi Kim watching the situation. At one point, when the weather was especially ominous, he looked at me and said in an agonized voice, "What are we going to do?" He was a Buddhist. I told him that I thought the only thing we could do was pray. Instinctively, I raised my eyes upward and said that "He" would take care of us if we listened to Him. We did get through that crisis. It didn't rain, although one time it looked very much as if it was going to come down, but it didn't. Everything was safe.

From then on, every time we had a problem, Mr. Kim would raise his eyes and look up, then look at me and smile. And it always worked.

The Agony of Implementation

Claims in international work almost become a way of life. At the university on our jobs, there were three major claims: the forty houses by Express in 1975, the 189 houses site fill problem, and the Heavy Equipment Lab built by Beta Company. Express Contracting Company, headed by Jack Seikaly, filed a claim for a considerable amount of money after the 189 houses were done. Don dealt with that one and went all the way through the various facets of English, Arabic, the Saudi Courts, etc. In the end, I don't think they were awarded very much.

Another claim had been filed by Express before I arrived in 1975. This shows how long these things go on and how tenacious the Lebanese are. These were forty houses that CRS was involved in. CRS didn't actually design them, but it took over construction supervision at a certain point. A local Saudi architect had designed them, and they had a lot of problems. The plans were incomplete. Back in those days before 1975, things were very loose compared to what they were later. Jack Seikaly was still pushing this claim in 1985. Don was now in Houston and it fell on me. I had to dig out all the old files. Then we had any number of meetings with the committee, which the university had appointed. Seikaly would come from Beirut, we would have meetings and then another subcommittee would be appointed.

They appointed a young Saudi, named Sagaf, as subchairman. He was a junior engineer on Mansour's staff, and he took the assignment seriously. We had all the files, so I helped him get it together. He was very conscientious. We worked together a long time, going through the various items, analyzing them, and coming up with some figures. Sagaf and I wrote an extensive report. Finally, the report was translated into Arabic, and Sagaf signed it.

There were a lot of young fellows like that. You certainly couldn't put down or belittle their efforts to do a job, under somewhat of a handicap.

Jebel Dhahran and the New Saudi Generation

One specialized project that we did is worth noting. In the Heavy Equipment Lab, which we completed in 1986, one part was what is known as a "reaction floor." This high-strength floor can be used to test materials under very high loads or force conditions. The concrete floor was about three feet thick, sitting on concrete walls below, so that it could withstand great impact with little or no vibration. At about three meters on center, there were holes through this floor with metal sleeves. These were used for fastening through to large steel beams on the surface, which then had very heavy loads applied. It is called a "reaction floor" because it can withstand and measure reactions to very high forces of about 50,000 pounds per square inch.

This was not spelled out in detail on the drawings. The main problem was that the tolerances required for this kind of work are extremely small, much smaller than the average construction work, approximately 1/2 mm. to 3 mm. horizontally and vertically. It is very difficult to build anything in concrete to that precision. The specifications indicated tolerances that were normal for typical concrete construction. This then became a contractual problem. The Turkish contractor contended that to achieve that result required a lot more cost than he had figured.

We finally came to the conclusion that although we could try to hold to the position that he had to do it, it was a rather untenable position. Normal construction isn't to that kind of precision.

Mansour al-Saber then visited the University of Texas, where there are several reaction floors. He found that they didn't even have the tolerances that we were after. We knew that one was being built at King Saud University in Riyadh. Mansour, Harry Cretin, and I made a trip there and visited with officials after it was already built. The tolerances were out of line and they were trying to decide what to do about it.

We were determined that our finished product was going to be what it should be, with the proper tolerances, even though

The Agony of Implementation

that meant that we were probably going to have to pay the contractor more money, which is always a problem. We learned that there were specialists who did nothing but build these kinds of floors. There was one that looked particularly good, a French company. We contacted the company in Europe and got preliminary information. Then the general contractor got a price from the company to see what it would cost for it to take over this work and make the sleeves to the required precision. It would supervise the installation and would be responsible for the end result's being as required. A change order would be necessary to cover this extra work.

Through a good bit of finesse we finally got this change order through the university with the Bids and Tenders Committee's approval. When it came time to do it, this delayed the project, but the university allowed an extension of time.

The French specialists were hired and achieved the required tolerances, which were checked many times and recorded. Now, the University of Petroleum and Minerals has a reaction floor which is built to tolerances as slight as half a millimeter. I dare say that is one of the few in Saudi Arabia and perhaps in the Middle East that is properly done.

Something that we take for granted here is the supply of electrical power. That became a problem there with all the development that was going on. The company which ultimately became responsible for that was the Saudi Consolidated Electrical Company (SCECO). When we first went to Saudi Arabia, there were frequent power outages, surges, and a general deficiency of electrical power. By the last four or five years we were there, SCECO had built power lines across the desert into remote parts. In the area where we were, it was running new main feeder lines everywhere. The problem then became to schedule the timing of the amounts that were to be required in the

Jebel Dhahran and the New Saudi Generation

various locations. The university had to plan for a building, and by the time it got to the point where it needed to turn the power on, it might be months before it was available. I felt that SCECO probably did as good a job as it could under the circumstances. The university would have to schedule its needs far ahead and pay considerable money in advance. Not many of our projects were delayed for a long period of time because of that, but it was always a problem, always an harassment.

Having mutually good relations with a contractor, if at all possible, has always been a working criterion of mine. An example of the value of this policy occurred during the construction of the Library addition. On the first floor plaza entrance, a small secondary lobby was designed.

The Koreans brought to my attention that the drawings showed a ceiling of a certain height, which seemed to them unnecessarily low, and they asked me for a confirmation. I looked at the detail they referred to and concluded, "that's the way it shows, that's the way they should build it." At that particular time, I was harassed with many demands and decisions to be made. So, admittedly, my decision might have been made without sufficient study and consideration. The Koreans then proceeded to build it the way it was shown on the detail.

The CRS designer of the project, Glen Bradford, was visiting the university later, and he saw the ceiling 85% complete. He commented that it didn't look the way that he had it in mind. On further rechecking the drawings, I was dismayed to find another detail, which showed it as he intended. This was another case of the fact that regardless of any discrepancy in the drawings, it was our job in the field to see that it turned out all right. I told Glen, "I'll take care of it, somehow."

After he had returned to Houston, I talked to J.C. Kim, the

The Agony of Implementation

project manager. We had established a good relationship on the job. He knew that if it was left as it was, it would look bad for me, and yet he had no obligation to change it. He finally said he would correct it at no extra cost to the owner (which we could not possibly ask the owner to pay for under the circumstances). He ripped it out and rebuilt it. I'm sure it cost some thousands of dollars. He did this so I could save face. It was this kind of thing that did make you feel warmly towards the Koreans.

When Glen visited some months later, he went straight to the Library to see what had happened. After looking at it, he said simply, "That looks fine."

To him, it was as simple as erasing it off a pencil drawing. The "agony of implementation" was no concern of his, and understandably so.

That was what we were there for.

PART V

PERSONAL ENCOUNTER — 1975 TO 1986

Chapter 15   Amenities

Chapter 16   Character, Culture, and Climate

Chapter 17   Anomalies

Chapter 18   Overtones — Religious and Political

Chapter 19   Visitors

Chapter 20   Extracurricular

Chapter 21   Arab Travels — In Kingdom and Out

"An honest tale speeds best, being plainly told."

William Shakespeare

Chapter 15

Amenities

I've always thought that the world is really tied together by Hilton, Sheraton, Hyatt, and Marriott Hotels. Fine hotels have always fascinated me. I loved to go to them around the world. We tried to stay in the most famous ones, like the Oriental in Bangkok, Raffles in Singapore, Georges V in Paris, Dorchester in London, Beau Rivage in Geneva, Bauer au Lac in Zurich, Mena House in Cairo, Shah Abass in Isfahan, Peninsula in Hong Kong, Grand in Taipei, New Otani in Tokyo, Etap Marmara in Istanbul, Saltee Oberoi in Kathmandu, Lanka Oberoi in Colombo Sri Lanka, Silla in Seoul, Kahala Hilton in Honolulu and Plaza in New York. In Saudi Arabia, one of the reasons the Saudis did not want many visitors, except as necessary to do the work, was the lack of these facilities. In Dhahran, Riyadh, and Jeddah, from the time we arrived to the time we left, there was construction going on for first-class new hotels - Marriott, Meridien, Hyatt, Ramada, Holiday Inn, and others.

The only really good hotel in Dhahran when we arrived was the al-Ghosaibi, a Saudi hotel. It would be booked up for weeks ahead. CRS would schedule trips for the various teams. It was up to us to find a place for them. We would go down to the al-Ghosaibi and practically beg for a reservation. It was a real fight to get a place several weeks ahead of the team's arrival.

There was a Saudi hotel, the International, at the airport, which was under construction the first five years that we were there. (Most of the news media during the Gulf War were headquartered at this hotel. CNN and other TV networks' broadcasts were usually made from the front or back of the hotel. Remember the blue domes? The university was in the background, but was never allowed to be shown for security reasons). When it finally opened, it was a very fine hotel. Mildred and I often ate there with our friends. Harry Cretin and I would

Jebel Dhahran and the New Saudi Generation

meet there every morning and have breakfast, read the paper, and discuss the days activities before going to work. As each new hotel would open, Mildred and I would be the first there for dinner. It would fascinate us for a while until a new one would open. In Dammam, the Oberoi was a fine hotel, operated by East Indians, of high quality. These hotels became oases in the desert.

We did have other things going for us. We had access generally to the Aramco dining hall, although it was really for Aramco employees.

As the number of people grew, understandably, Aramco had to try to limit the outsiders, so it added a pretty steep surcharge on the meals for non-Aramcons. We did a lot of complaining, as did all the university people, because we felt there should be an affinity between the university and Aramco. But Aramco didn't see it that way.

There was a U.S. military mission at the air base. This had been started back in the 1950s. There has been an advisory American military presence there all that time. The mission had a club which was primarily for military people. Active and retired military people were allowed in as members, those from Northrup, McDonnell Douglas, etc.

For ten years, we were not able to get in as members, although we often went as guests with friends. The last year, when many people were leaving, the club needed more members, and we were finally admitted. That helped to make the last year more pleasant, because we could go there and get a really good American meal in the evening in a very nice atmosphere. It became a pleasant place to socialize.

Transportation was very important. Our contract provided that the university should supply us with an automobile. When we arrived, however, there was a short supply. The university

Amenities

had a method by which a contractor, when awarded a contract, was obligated to furnish a certain number of cars to the university, depending on the size of the contract. Then the university would allocate these cars to various people. It provided CRS with its cars out of this supply. When we arrived there was only one good car. With the contract for the 189 houses, the Lebanese contractor was due to furnish one car. We finally received a Peugeot station wagon from him for our use, which we had for several years.

From then on the cars came to us through the various contracts, and we never lacked for good cars. The university furnished the gasoline, which was fifteen cents a gallon. It was later raised to thirty cents. Our maintenance work was done by the university for the first couple of years. When the larger contracts came into being, like the CCC and Redec Daelim contracts, these companies had good automotive departments for servicing their own vehicles. As an amenity to us, they would also take care of our cars. All of that worked very well.

Two weeks after we arrived, Mildred went to interview at the Dhahran Academy, the international school with an American curriculum located at the U.S. Consulate and she was hired as a teacher. The consulate is on the grounds originally granted to the university by royal decree of King Faisal. In the beginning, this school was under the auspices of the U.S. Consulate, but in later years, it was put under the Saudi Ministry of Education.

Thus, it became SAIS, Saudi Arabian International School. It was run by Americans, but there was a Saudi representative, who would check in whenever he wanted to. The curriculum, however, was never affected, except as it related to Muslims. When we first went there, no Muslims could go to the school. Then, the school allowed non-Arab Muslims, Indians, Pakistanis, etc. Saudis could not attend, by decree of the government.

Saudi Arabian International School
(Dhahran Academy)

School Bus

Teaching Children English

Amenities

The school had about 700 pupils and 100 teachers when we arrived. By the time we left, it had almost 2000 pupils and 300 teachers. It also expanded to include other areas besides Dhahran. There were schools at Jubail, Ras Tanura, and Udahliyah. On the west coast, there were Taif and Kamis Mushayt. These were all under the same American management.

The students received quality education. They could attend only through the ninth grade, however, and then they had to go outside the Kingdom. The Saudis did not allow any expatriates over the ninth grade to stay in the Kingdom to go to school. Their reasoning was that they felt the Western teenagers would be a bad influence on the Saudi teenagers. So, expats would send their teenage children away to school either in the U.S.A. or in Europe. The staying power for many expats was the fact that they could send their children to these fine schools, which they normally wouldn't be able to afford, since they were subsidized by their companies.

SAIS had 48 nationalities of students. (Aramco had its own schools, so SAIS didn't include "Aramcons.") Many SAIS students came there not knowing how to speak English. The academy had a program called TOEFL, "Teaching of English as a Foreign Language." The students would start that at the same time as starting classes. Before they were finished, they could not only speak English, but they could pass their exams — sometimes with honors. They were not only the children of professors at the university, but also children from all the companies around: Northrup, McDonnell Douglas, Halliburton, Schlumberger, etc. All the companies that were doing business in Dhahran could send their children to that school. They charged tuition, which the companies paid.

The school had some good administrators, and we got to know most of them socially. They were all people that had a little something extra on the ball, or they probably wouldn't have been there.

Jebel Dhahran and the New Saudi Generation

The Dhahran Academy, or the Saudi Arabian International School, was originally comprised of small temporary portable-type buildings. It later built several new buildings of a more permanent nature.

Once a year, there was an international conference of the Near East School Association, NESA. This was a conference of all the American schools in the Middle East, from Cairo, Athens, Turkey, Saudi Arabia, Iran, India and others. We went to several of these, and they were most enjoyable. I would take a week of my vacation time to go. The first year in 1976, we went to Isfahan, Iran. The next year we went to Rhodes, and in subsequent years to Turkey, Athens, and India. These conferences were primarily for getting the teachers together to exchange ideas and with some instructional educational elements involved. It was also a break and a chance for everyone to travel. Part of Mildred's way was paid, and that made it economically feasible.

We did not return to Houston for Christmas our first year in Saudi Arabia in 1975. In fact, we had decided to "tough it out" and not return for Christmas of 1976.

However, the rule of thumb in the Middle East is to "expect the unexpected." On December 20, 1976, Don Chambers received a call from Joe Thomas in Houston saying CRS wanted him to collect the outstanding bill at the university and have me bring it back to the Houston office so it would be in hand by December 31st. This amounted to a cool million dollars. Don immediately set about with Adnan Khayal, the comptroller of the university, to obtain a check for that amount. He also told me to get ready to go.

I immediately made application for exit visas for Mildred and myself. Thanks to cooperation from Dr. Bakhrebah and the UPM passport department, the visas came through in record time.

Amenities

I went to al-Khobar and checked for airline reservations. Of course, it couldn't have been a worse time. By a happy coincidence the airline was able to give us one confirmed reservation and one unconfirmed on a Pan Am flight from Bahrain on December 21st to New York, then on to Houston. After a last-minute hassle to "bump" one of us, we boarded the plane in Bahrain.

I felt like a diplomatic courier. Don and Adnan had come through with the check in good time, and we joked about whether I should tape it to my chest or lock it in my briefcase chained to my wrist.

We arrived in Houston in time for the CRS Christmas party. Conrad Neal said the rumor was going around that Walter and Mildred had disappeared and were last seen living in Switzerland.

That was my once-in-a-lifetime opportunity to have a million dollars in my hand — one of the serendipities of the assignment.

Our social life was one of the most pleasant things about the whole experience. We had friendly social relations with several Saudi families, visited in their homes, and had them in our home. We invited Dr. Bakhrebah, Dr. Nasser Rashid, Abdullah Mufti with their families as well as other Saudis to our house. I remember the first Christmas that we were there in 1975, we didn't go home to the States, so we invited Dr. Nasser Rashid and Dr. Bakhrebah and his family over. We had a Christmas tree and Dr. Bakhrebah's family even brought a little gift. I have received Christmas cards from some Saudis. Some are less conservative than others. It is a shame that there seems to be the separation of East and West, because I don't know that everyone wants it that way. A lot of it is only custom.

When we first went there, we were told by Joe Thomas that CRS was neither fish nor fowl, and we should maintain a "low profile." After all, we were really contractors or consultants.

Progressive dinner group, UPM

Christmas sing at Hensels - Aramco

Dick and Sharon Adam's library - Aramco

Jebel Dhahran and the New Saudi Generation

Thanks to Mildred, we never really adopted that attitude. That terminology wasn't in her vocabulary. We mixed right in with everyone, and no one to my knowledge ever really objected. I think we earned our way. Dr. Bakhrebah once said to me about Mildred, "You know, she is very well liked by the Saudi ladies." That was evidenced by the fact that twice she was elected president of the University Women's Club during the eleven years that we were there. And we weren't faculty or staff. The first time that she was elected, she was nominated by Afaf Bakhrebah.

The Women's Club was comprised of the wives of the faculty and staff. They had many activities which were of benefit to the university families. Mildred always tried to get the Saudi ladies involved in these activities. They seemed to want to become involved, but some didn't have the confidence to do so. I think that basic to her good relations with them was the fact that she liked them, and this feeling was reciprocated.

We also developed friends at Aramco through our church group. There were no churches officially allowed in Saudi Arabia other than the Islamic religion. However, at Aramco, the Saudis did tacitly allow them to function. In other words, they just closed their eyes to the fact that they existed. Occasionally, some groups would get into trouble by getting too ostentatious. Sometimes the Catholics or the Mormons couldn't resist having an Easter sunrise service or something out in the open, and they would have a problem. There was a large Catholic group, a Church of England group called The Canterbury Society, a Mormon group and a non-denominational Protestant group.

Then we started a small Christian Science group. At one time before 1960, there had been a fairly large and active Christian Science group, but it didn't exist when we arrived. Our group grew from four or five up to thirty or thirty-five at one time. It was low-key. We met at Aramco at various locations that were available. We developed a very friendly group, not

International Day at Dhahran Academy

Christmas Stories at UPM

Jebel Dhahran and the New Saudi Generation

only from a religious standpoint, but as a means of socializing. Some of our Aramco friends, other than those already mentioned, were Hillman and Mary Rose Phillips and three children; Sam and Pat Quincey and daughter; John and Hue Sommers and two daughters; Bob and Betty Sievert from McDonnell Douglas; and Kathy and Adel el-Messidi. Friendship was a valuable commodity.

Our first Christmas there, we were able to see the last Christmas pageant that Aramco staged. This was something that had been done previously every other year for a long time. It was held in the open on a crispy cold night about December 20, 1975. This was a pageant of the Nativity. There were live "angels," camels, and goats, as well as a choir singing Christmas music. A few Saudis attended, but most of those present were Westerners. After that year, it was canceled and was held no more. On our campus, we had a local musical group that would put on a show every month. There was a Christmas sing at various houses. This was all inside and private, of course.

The Saudi attitude, generally was that you could do what you wanted in private, as long as you didn't disturb anyone. In the case of people who liked to drink, there was no liquor sold publicly or legally. There was some smuggled in. Privately, a lot of people made their own, which was called "siddiqi." This means "friend" in Arabic. They made this out of various ingredients that they could purchase locally, such as grape juice, apple juice, yeast, etc. If the violation occurred in private homes, there was generally no problem. The cardinal offense would be giving it to Saudis. Or if they tried in any way to influence the Saudis in this direction. Then they really got in trouble, and they might spend some time in jail.

The people who got into trouble had no excuse, because they were well aware of the rules. You sometimes read of people who were caught in that sort of thing lamenting how unfair the Saudis were. When videocassette players came in at Aramco,

Amenities

some people got into trouble because they started renting videos as we do here. That would probably have caused no trouble, but soon they brought in pornographic ones. They were caught. They were out to make a pile of money, and they were violating the law. They came back to the States and told stories to the press about how badly they were treated by the Saudis and how unfair it was.

There were no public theaters in town. However, private performing groups developed. For instance, the university had a small entertainment group that performed musicals, and also there was a children's group. The British Aircraft Corporation at the air base had a good theater group, and there was another group that developed in one of the private compounds in al-Khobar. No matter where you are in the world, there is talent, and it will come out one way or another. Aramco put on some excellent productions. Nevertheless, most of our entertainment had to be just socializing with each other.

The local television programming was quite good. Aramco had a station which was in English. It had good news broadcasts and good programming of British and American serial programs and documentaries. There were at least six or seven stations that we could get besides Aramco — Dammam, Bahrain, Qatar, Dubai, Oman, Kuwait, and Abu Dhabi. Each of these had an Arabic and an English station. There was plenty of TV available. One of our projects on the university campus in about 1982 was the installation of a central antenna system, which allowed good reception in all the houses and also provided closed circuit capability.

The barriers of ignorance and misunderstanding are no match for the modern-day technology of television.

Our life-style changed considerably in many ways between our arrival and our departure eleven years later.

Jebel Dhahran and the New Saudi Generation

In al-Khobar there were a number of banks: the Dutch Bank, the French Bank, the British Bank, Riyadh Bank, the Saudi American Bank, and others. I was amazed to find out that I could go to the NCB at Aramco and open an account simply with a personal check drawn on the Texas Commerce Bank in Houston, and then immediately withdraw cash from it. Within several years, however, that simple trust disappeared. Apparently no one wrote bad checks there, but as foreigners came in, that problem came also. Soon after, a branch of the Riyadh Bank was opened at UPM. Then the NCB at Aramco was not interested in having accounts of university people, so I switched to the UPM Bank. In several years the bank built a nice little building on the periphery of the campus. It was designed locally, and Mansour saw that it got built. You could do anything there: transfer funds, get travelers checks, and cashier's checks.

Mildred's check from Dhahran Academy came from the Dutch Bank (al-Hollandi al-Saudi). It was a small downtown bank. You would go in there and literally see people (as in the stories you hear) with a suitcase full of money. When you deposited a check, it would go through a tortuous process from person to person. You would try to follow it around with your eyes to see where it was from one basket to the next until it finally came back to you and would be ready to cash.

The Arabs are good with figures. In spite of the fact that it seemed unlikely that a check could go through without getting lost, the tellers never seemed to lose anything, and they rarely made mistakes. Ultimately they had automatic counters and all the modern paraphernalia.

While you would still go through a certain involved process in cashing a check, everything was well organized, and a big improvement had taken place from when we first arrived. Lots of money changed hands. There were stories about the bedouin who came in regularly with a sack of money, maybe $300,000 or more, and would want to deposit it or do something with

Amenities

it. The stories weren't so far-fetched. It really happened. Now, there are Saudi travelers checks and possibly there will be a Saudi stock market. There are the latest electronic facilities, computers, everything.

Airline reservations were in the same category. At first, there were no computers. When we left, most ticket offices had them. I never really had any airline reservations around the world that didn't work out. However, hotel reservations weren't that good. Sometimes, I would make hotel reservations for various places around the world. When I got there, they had never heard of me.

To anyone over there, such as ourselves in Dhahran, the airport became a symbol of contact with home. It was somewhat reassuring every evening at 5:00 o'clock to see from our balcony the Pan Am 747 from New York set down on the runway at Dhahran Airport. I used to go out at noon just to have lunch and sit and watch the planes come in. Later when a new terminal was built, it wasn't possible to do that. We were constantly going out to meet the CRS people, and it became almost a form of recreation. The general exhilaration from the activity of coming and going was really something to see.

Most of the planes going to Europe would leave at night. The schedules were arranged in order to allow passengers to arrive at their destinations at the right time. For instance, if you left at night, you arrived in London, Paris, or Amsterdam the next morning on KLM, Lufthansa, British Airways, and later British Caledonian. Many flights to the Far East also departed at night. You would see the people getting ready to leave with great anticipation. Even though we enjoyed the work there, after we had worked very hard for nine months, we were ready to take a break. There was always the anticipation of leaving. Not only that, but you were usually going to interesting places. You would see people who were getting ready to go everywhere in the world, and there was great excitement.

The Korean Airlines and the Philippine Airlines would arrive

Jebel Dhahran and the New Saudi Generation

and depart at night. They would have hundreds of people at a time, workers coming and going in large groups. At certain times, there would be tremendous activity. The Middle East Airlines would fly in from Beirut constantly filled with Lebanese and Palestinian workers. No matter what the trouble was in Beirut, Middle East Airlines kept flying in. Only a couple of times was it totally suspended, when the runways at Beirut Airport were so damaged by bombs that planes could not land or depart.

It was exciting to think that this was a prime focal point in the world. I'm sure it has changed now and will never be that way again. Even if the oil situation eases up and there is money available, there will not be the need for these great numbers of workers. The infrastructure is built. Now, it is a specialized type of people that are needed for technical maintenance and operation, and not in such quantities.

One of the things that made me feel at home was the American Businessmen's Association in Dhahran. I don't know just when it started. I'm sure it wasn't there when we arrived. I joined in 1980. It had monthly meetings at the Meridien Hotel, with a buffet luncheon and then a guest speaker, sometimes a Saudi, sometimes an American or other Westerner. The idea was to get the American businessmen together. Just as in the case of such groups here, they would discuss common problems and get acquainted. It was a pleasant and useful thing to be a member.

The U.S. consul in Dhahran also had a meeting every two months for the American businessmen. It was probably the most informative thing around. The consul and his staff would give a briefing on everything — politics, business, and all kinds of problems. By attending you did learn quite a bit about what was going on and what the attitude was between the Saudis and the Americans. There were always a number of people in jail

Amenities

for various alleged offenses. There was a surveillance of that by the consul. He would tell how many people were in jail, but there was little that he could do in that kind of situation. If the violation was something like drugs or alcohol, obviously he couldn't intervene. You were pretty much on your own if you ended up in that situation.

The early social life on campus, as I heard it from Don Chambers and others, was certainly different than it was when we arrived. In the early days, there were gatherings at the rector's house with both men and ladies present, as well as students.

We did attend some social gatherings when we first arrived with both men and ladies present. Usually the men and ladies were together for a short while, then the men would retire to a room and play a card game called "Bilot," which they loved to play. The ladies stayed together and talked. At our first party the men didn't specifically ask me to join them, so I didn't. I didn't know how to play "Bilot" anyway. I sat with Mildred and the ladies and talked, which was rather unusual. Those kinds of parties definitely diminished very soon. The rector's wife had a party every year for the new professors' wives. Mildred was always invited. They were quite colorful and entertaining affairs, she said, with dancing and music.

At all the mixed functions, the men and ladies would eat separately. There would be one large table with all the food. The fare was always sumptuous. The ladies would get their food first and go into their room. Then the men would get theirs and go into their room. That was a semi-public thing, you might say. We were at many private affairs, however, where we just visited the two of us with the two or more of them. You could have your private Saudi friends and visit, men and ladies. You read accounts that say there was never any mixed fraternization. Generally, that was true, but it wasn't all that forbidden.

Jebel Dhahran and the New Saudi Generation

When we arrived in 1975, the university was just completing the *Recreation Center*. This was to be a welcome addition to the campus, with tennis courts and a bowling alley. Later, we made several additions to it with squash courts, racquetball courts, additional tennis courts, another swimming pool, additional group function and dining facilities. By the time that we left, it was a very complete recreation center. At first, there were mixed parties at the center. The manager, Pete Waddell, was British, a very capable and likable fellow who had managed some good clubs in England. There were parties with Saudis and Westerners present. There was entertainment, Saudi music and pageant-type shows. That sort of mixing didn't last very long except for some family-type functions put on by the Women's Club.

The University Women's Club included American, British, European, Oriental, and Saudi women. It had various functions throughout the year for the women. It had a few annual mixed functions, such as an "International Night," at which each nationality would set up booths and have food and exhibits of clothes and crafts from its native country, every country that you could imagine. Then there were always special occasions like Halloween. There was a library, pool tables, ping pong tables, a bridge club, and a music club. Several years later Pete Waddell was replaced by a Saudi. Pete then joined the physical education staff, being an outstanding athlete as well. This gradual "Saudi-ization" was typical throughout most of the departments. With the two swimming pools, the families could swim together while the bachelors swam separately.

The rector had, on his own, tacitly allowed women to drive on campus. They were already allowed to drive unofficially at Aramco, but they didn't at the university until about 1976. Then a number of the ladies took advantage of this. Mildred never wanted to even attempt it. It wasn't worth it, really. They

Amenities

couldn't go anywhere except on the campus. A lot of the ladies liked to do it just to show that they could. One of our secretaries, Jacqui Flint, a Britisher, drove her car to work every day, since she could come from her house the back way, which was rather obscure. June Brandie preferred to ride her bike. She wore a cap and clothes that gave her a "boyish" look. Driving a car was helpful to some of the ladies in going to the grocery store.

One of the forms of recreation provided at the university was a movie every Thursday night (equivalent to our Saturday night in the West) in the auditorium. There were packages of movies that were sent over from the United States by Aramco. The university took some of what Aramco had. About half of them were worth seeing. The Saudis were always concerned about corruptive influences. Many of the Saudis would come with their children, not knowing what the movies were about. They were generally of acceptable quality. They were screened by the recreation department as were Aramco's. There were never any R-rated films, but there were some pretty raunchy PGs occasionally.

One time a Western movie was shown that my brother, Robert, was in which was called "Shame, Shame on the Bixby Boys," in which he had a major role. It was more or less a "spoof" of the TV series, "Bonanza." I mentioned this to him later and he said, "That's funny, I didn't ever receive any royalty from its being shown overseas."

We had a friend at Aramco who censored the movies. Kissing was never allowed in a movie. You would see the man and woman come up within a foot of each other, and then suddenly they wouldn't be there any more. The kissing would be all over.

One bureau of the Saudi government was what was called the Government Office for Social Insurance (GOSI), which is similar to our Social Security. This had interest to us from the standpoint that, although I was not eligible for it, Mildred was. CRS did not originally qualify because there had to be fifty employees or more, and until later years in the Kingdom, CRS didn't have that. Eventually CRS did qualify, but it was too late for me.

From the day Mildred started at the Dhahran Academy, contributions were made to her account. This had a significance eleven years later, when because of her age when she started work there, when she terminated, and the number of years she had served with contributions made to her account, she actually was qualified for a lifetime pension from the Saudi government similar to our Social Security.

Before we left Saudi Arabia, we took the necessary steps of going to the GOSI office in Dammam and getting a copy of her account. We then made application six months later as required, in January of 1987.

One year later, she began receiving monthly payments from Citibank in New York, as well as retroactive payment to the time she left.

This was tangible evidence to us that the Saudi Government did honor even its minor obligations. It could easily have wiggled out of it. The interesting thing is that she probably is one of a handful of Western women that have ever been qualified to receive a lifetime pension from the Kingdom of Saudi Arabia. The only others would possibly be lady doctors, nurses, and teachers at Aramco, and there were few of those with that kind of tenure.

About 25 miles from the university, the Arabian Gulf penetrates into the desert to form what is known as Half Moon Bay. This is a beautiful tranquil bay with very good beaches. Aramco has a good segment of the beach there. There is a public beach, a university segment, and an Air Force Survival Training Station. The university built a recreational area with tables for

Scott Pendleton – Falconer

Cookout at Half Moon Bay

Jebel Dhahran and the New Saudi Generation

picnics, a snack bar, and toilets. They also had a place for boats and there was a lot of windsurfing and sailing. It was very pleasant. The students also had their own segment of the beach.

It was really a beautiful place to sit and try to realize where you were. I would always have to mentally picture a map to believe that I was really in the land of the Arabian Nights.

One time Mildred and I spent the night there using a tent we borrowed from Bob Cook. We managed to put the tent up. One of the Saudis that I knew at the university had pitched his tent with his family further up on a sand dune, a much larger tent. Mildred had already retired for the night. He came down and said, "Why don't you come up for a while and visit?" I replied, "No thanks, we'll see you in the morning."

The next morning, we were going about cooking our breakfast. At about 7:00 o'clock it began to blow. These heavy winds or "shamals" come up very quickly. I saw my friend going towards the restrooms with his little boy in the car. The next thing I knew, the wind was very strong. Mildred and I were frantically trying to take the tent down, and it was all that we could manage. We struggled for a good while, so I didn't really pay attention to what was going on around us. We finally got it down, and I looked to see where my friend was. His tent was there, but he was gone. Everybody was gone.

We headed back to the university. When the sand is blowing, it is like being in a fog. You can't see where you are going. We couldn't even see the road. But we did get back all right.

The next day, I saw my Saudi friend in the office and I said, "You know, Abdul, that's amazing how you got out of there yesterday. You Arabs really have a sixth sense about such things. That was quite a wind. How did you know to leave? How did you know what was coming?" To which he replied, "Oh, I heard it on the radio when I was taking my son to the restroom." So much for the Arabs' sixth sense. But at least he had sense enough to get out. He said, "We didn't worry about the tent. We just left it there to blow into the sea."

Amenities

That was Half Moon Bay. We always went out with the CRS people when they visited and with our friends from Aramco. It was one of the pluses. The Saudis loved it too. You could often see Dr. Bakhrebah in his wetsuit, windsurfing.

On a clear day or night, we could see Bahrain from our balcony. The atmosphere there can be crystal clear. We could also look out on a beautiful morning and see the rising sun glistening off the blue-green waters of the Persian Gulf.

Some people's comments and experiences notwithstanding, we don't think it's hard to understand why we felt we had a happy and fruitful experience in Saudi Arabia.

CHAPTER 16

CHARACTER, CULTURE, AND CLIMATE

The amazing accomplishments of the Saudis in the ten years of 1975 to 1985 might be called the "Golden Decade" of Saudi Arabia. This was a country that was mostly desert and very remote from the Western world. But the Arabs, per se, did have a glorious past. When Europe was in the Middle Ages, the Arab/Islamic world was thriving.

There has been enough written about the so-called cultural and personality differences of the Saudis. So, I don't intend to spend a lot of time on that, because, frankly, that is not what it is all about.

What is important is how these people took this opportunity which came to them, and what they did with these unlimited resources of money. They have not used it to anyone's detriment. They decided to build their country. Just the ambition and belief that they could do it are astonishing to me. The tremendous logistics and manpower problems alone would be discouraging. Also deciding priorities of what they should do.

Besides its material accomplishments, Saudi Arabia now is a prime political factor in the Arab world and the Middle East through the use of its money. When the Israelis invaded Lebanon in 1982, the Saudis were not unrealistic enough to think they could intervene militarily for the Lebanese and the Palestinians and come out on top. So their work was done behind the scenes, by use of their money and their ability to reason with the other Arab nations. They have been definitely a positive political influence. All of this was going on at the same time they were planning multitudes of new projects and executing them. Also, they were trying to control the tremendous social changes that were going on in the country as a result.

Something that many writers seem to take great pleasure in

Jebel Dhahran and the New Saudi Generation

elaborating on is what they see as the personality differences of the Saudis as contrasted with Westerners. Many Westerners went over there and expected the Saudi to fit into a preconceived stereotype. In our own country, you can find every type of personality there is. In Saudi Arabia, that is also true.

For instance, I knew Saudis that were gregarious and outgoing. I remember one fellow who became one of the department heads at UPM. He was short and heavyset, although later he lost a lot of weight. Many of them who were inclined to be heavy have rigorously lost weight. They can be quite disciplined in that regard. I could just imagine this fellow back in his college days as being the prankster, the "good-time Charlie" who kept things lively.

Then there were those who were quite withdrawn, and it was difficult to determine just how they felt about you. I think a lot of times that is the picture that many Westerners have of them as being devious. I don't think it is deviousness so much as it is that they just don't rush to display their feelings and emotions. They can stare you right in the eye, and you don't have the vaguest idea what they are thinking.

They sometimes get emotionally aroused among themselves in Arabic and they sound as if they are just ripping each other apart. Yet, when it is all over, they shake hands and there is nothing to it. So, it is just a matter of the way they express their feelings.

They are inclined to sit back, watch, observe and all the while they are determining what they think about you and how you act. To some this appears devious. They are quick to spot insincerity. I think many Westerners don't realize that when they come into the Kingdom with their glad handshake and think that's going to impress them. While perhaps it might sometimes, usually the Saudis can see through that, and they know whether you are saying things just to impress them or whether you are sincere.

I think that was one plus that I had, because I had shown that I was interested in the Saudis for many years past from the

Character, Culture, and Climate

things I had written at Rice as a student. They didn't necessarily accept that right off, however. I felt there might be some incredulity at first, as to whether that was genuine. But I think when they determined that it was, they felt that I was a friend who was there to help them and not just for personal and selfish reasons.

Sometimes they were overly suspicious. But then I think that I have tended to be that way all my life, too. They might go along until something doesn't click. When they see something that doesn't appear to be consistent, a red flag goes up and you have to overcome it, because there is then a suspicion that you are not really being straight with them.

Once you establish their confidence, it goes a long way. For instance, the help I gave them on the mosque and various other things I did, I felt resulted in a reciprocation of good will. They forgave me for a number of shortcomings after that.

One of the young engineers in Mansour's office was very able, energetic, had a long beard and was somewhat conservative in his beliefs. He was opposed to a number of things that were going on at the university. When we built the elementary school, he wouldn't send his children there because he didn't want them to associate only with the children of the Saudi professors on campus.

He was inclined to be hard, but at times he did have an element of compassion. I might tell him I was having a hard time doing something that I couldn't figure out. He would say, "Allah will help you." If I made a mistake, he became quite forgiving. "Well, everyone makes mistakes." He had some real "smarts." I remember Don Chambers saying, "He has a gleam in his eye."

There were a variety of young engineers on the staff of Mansour al-Saber, the Director General of Technical Affairs. There was Abdul Rahman al-Harthy, Abdul Malek Siddiqi, Abdul Karim Hadil, Redha Aytah, Saghir Ahmad, and Abdu Rashid Shaker. Secretaries were Noor Mohammed, Saif al-

Jebel Dhahran and the New Saudi Generation

Rahman Saif, Abdu Jabar, and Saghir Khan. Siddiqi, from Pakistan, was quite gregarious and outgoing. He was older and had a lot of experience. He was fairly able and intelligent. The others were young and inexperienced but seemed willing to learn.

They had the advantage of language over us. Others had the same advantage over them, however. For instance, the Koreans could use that advantage at meetings. If you were going along in English, and they wanted to say something in private, they would just switch to Korean, just as the Saudis would go into Arabic.

I never learned to speak Arabic well. I don't think they were sure just how much I could understand. In the long drawn-out meetings in Arabic, there are quite a few English words that don't have an Arabic equivalent. So, when it came to that, they would just throw in the English word. There are not a tremendous number of these, but there are enough so that with the Arabic that I might understand plus body language, very often I could tell the way a conversation was going.

I remember a number of times I would try my luck. It was always fun when something was totally in Arabic and I might get a glimpse of what I thought was going on. I would toss in a comment in English relative to that. If I was right, it would rather startle them, because they would think, "Well, he's been understanding us all along." If I was wrong, it didn't really make any difference, because I didn't know what they were talking about anyway.

I think that one of the hardest things for me was the attitude that developed among some of the Saudis that when they wanted something, they wanted it immediately. That has never been my nature. You just ask my wife. I began to feel that

Character, Culture, and Climate

innately I had a bedouin philosophy. I had heard that their philosophy was, "I'll do almost anything that I am asked to do, but very little that I am told to do." The attitude of the Saudis that I am referring to apparently arose from a sense of urgency stemming from the fact that they felt that they must develop their country as quickly as possible while conditions were favorable (later events have proved the wisdom of this attitude).

The Saudis were always very polite with me, however, and I never felt that I was being ordered around. But they did want something immediately when they wanted it. The trouble was that I found that many times I did do things much faster than I did before. So, having done it, they would say, "See, you did it." Then they would expect me to produce the next time in the same manner. In some ways, when I got used to that, it became a stimulation, although there was sometimes a little lack of reasonableness. They didn't always realize the time it took to do something.

I remember one instance when we were getting ready to build the minaret on the new residential campus mosque. The contractor was going up pretty quickly with the concrete forming. I had indicated that I thought that we should change a detail at the base of the minaret. A young Saudi from Mansour's office came into the office one day and wanted the detail right away. I said, "You seem to think that these design decisions are made suddenly, saying, 'This is it.' It takes study. Sometimes you have to study something in many ways for a day or two before you can determine what is the right thing to do." I studied it overnight and made a little sketch. It worked out fine.

They didn't always appreciate the design process. This attitude became a little problem for me. But, after we learned to work together, and after they began to appreciate what I could do, they would push as far as they thought they could, and they might just lay off completely.

Jebel Dhahran and the New Saudi Generation

One thing that was very important was the art of negotiation. I had never had much experience at that, and I never felt very adept at it. The assumption always is that the other fellow is trying to take advantage of you and so you try to "do him in" first. My problem was that I tended to think too much from the other person's standpoint. If I beat him down to the lowest price and I thought that would hurt him, I had a hard time doing it.

I think, more than that, I really didn't feel that was the way to get the best job. If there is something about his price or what he is going to do that is really out of line, of course you have to pare that down. You've got to be discerning enough to see that is this case. On the other hand, if you beat him down too low, you won't get a good job. He'll run into problems later, and then the problem is back with you.

My difficulty was that if I felt the Saudis were being unfair with the contractor, I was inclined to take the contractor's side. Now, this was really taboo as far as the university was concerned. We were there for them only, in their eyes. We weren't supposed to be standing up for the contractors. Sometimes that is misconstrued that you are in collusion with him. In the United States, the architect is contractually supposed to be more of an arbiter, although, in all honesty, most owners look on him as "their man." After all, they hired him in the first place.

After a while, the Saudis began to understand my attitude, and it was surprising how many times I heard Mansour al-Saber and Dr. Bakhrebah say, "Now, we want to be fair with the contractor." Dr. Bakhrebah explained, "I always had difficulty in educating one group after another of the Bids and Tenders Committee on this matter. The general impression among the Saudis was that expatriates were there only for money. They weren't there for our 'blue eyes'. Why should anyone leave his own environment for nothing. But were they doing it honestly, or not? That was what was important. We hire them, and we pay them. We have to get our money's worth from them. That came from dealing and co-operating with them on a basis of mutual trust."

Character, Culture, and Climate

One college that Dr. Bakr was instrumental in getting started in 1976-77 was the College of Industrial Management. We built a large building for it. I remember hearing Dr. Bakr expound on why he felt the Saudis should have that.

I recall in 1977 visiting with someone on the East coast of the United States. I mentioned that I thought the Saudis were good managers. This person, a top executive himself, said, "I can't imagine them being good managers." I replied, "That is what they are good at — that is what they like to do." His concept of them apparently was as camel drivers and bedouin types. They have always been good managers. They couldn't survive in the desert on the minimum that they had unless they managed what they did have well. That ability has carried on into the present when they have everything.

Many say that the Saudis don't like to do the nitty gritty, don't like to work. That may be true to a certain extent, but the fact is that they are good at organizing things. They love to have meetings. What sometimes seems to be ineptness could be the fact that they were developing so fast and with so many untrained people.

The College of Industrial Management turned out young men who knew enough about a particular field that they could be managers of whatever discipline it was. Of course, you can't have all "chiefs" and no "Indians", so they may have to learn more in the actual operations category. There were some who did. I knew a number of them in the various engineering disciplines who were "doers." They didn't just sit back and look.

Recognizing the need for technicians — mechanics, electricians, carpenters, etc., the government in about 1977 began a program for vocational training in the various trade categories. It began construction of about twenty-seven institutes around the country for this training. They were well designed for the purpose. Thinking that this would best be developed on a regional basis, they were built in all the remote areas of the Kingdom, not just in the cities. The local boys could receive

Jebel Dhahran and the New Saudi Generation

training in various skills and remain in their home areas, satisfying the needs of their own communities. This program was titled VOTRAKON and apparently had a degree of success.

Two characteristics of the Saudis that impressed me were dignity and pride. They never appeared to feel "inferior." This was interpreted by some as arrogance and was perhaps irritating to many Westerners.

When our daughter, Cheryl, was visiting us in 1977, the three of us drove to Riyadh. In the middle of the Dahna (the red desert), while driving along, we saw on the distant horizon a camel and two bedouin. We stopped and watched them approach slowly, gradually becoming more identifiable. It reminded me of when Lawrence of Arabia (Peter O'Toole) in the movie and his guide were at the well and Prince Ali (Omar Sharif) appeared as a distant spectre, soon becoming a close and ominous reality. When our two bedouin arrived, they said, "moya," which means "water" in Arabic. Cheryl then gave them a bottle of mineral water which we had.

I indicated that I would like to take their picture. One was on the camel, and one was standing on the ground. They were fairly ragged. The one on the ground straightened his clothes and stood erect at attention. There was no lack of dignity and pride in that young bedouin in the middle of the Arabian Desert, unaware of what the Western world generally considers to be necessary criteria for dignity and pride.

I was asked by the architecture department to sit on a jury to judge presentations of senior architectural projects. As is the case anywhere, there were "good," "average" and "poor" presentations. I was actually interested in some of the "poor" presentations. In spite of a lack of sufficient study and preparation, these students unflinchingly stood before the jury and made their presentations. Of course, the "good" ones were impressive, but there was something I found interesting in the

Bedouin on horizon

"Dignity and Pride"

Jebel Dhahran and the New Saudi Generation

"poor" ones, some of which had excellent ideas, just not fully developed.

I was visiting with Dr. Bakr some days later, and I commented on this. I said, "You know, even though there may not always be the pride of status and accomplishment, there is never an apparent sense of "inferiority." Until recently, in this country, you had very little of the world's goods. And yet, there was no sense of inferiority. In our country, if you are poor or uneducated, unfortunately, there probably is a sense of "inferiority."

Dr. Bakr was pensive for a few moments and then replied, "The difference is that here there was nothing to compare with. Nobody had anything — there was no "class" structure. Dignity and pride were from within, not dependent on outside material possessions and social status."

I thought of Shakespeare's line, "Comparisons are odorous."

My boyhood fascination with T.E. Lawrence and the Arabs was due for some disillusionment, when I learned more about Saudi Arabia, its geography, and its history.

Only a few weeks after arrival in August 1975, I was chatting with Dr. Bakhrebah and Abdullah Mufti in Dr. Bakhrebah's office about my long-standing interest in Saudi Arabia. Abdullah said, "Why do you think you were interested in the Arabs so long ago? Was it Lawrence of Arabia?" I had to admit that probably had something to do with it.

Abdullah said, and Dr. Bakhrebah seemed to concur, "You know, we don't give too much credit to Lawrence. He was too much 'show' and 'publicity'."

This was a blow to my boyhood hero's image. After learning more of the actual history and becoming familiar with the geography and politics of the Arabian Peninsula, I could understand his statement.

In World War I, the British assigned to Lawrence the task

Character, Culture, and Climate

of enlisting the support of the various Arab tribes in driving the Turks from the West coast of the Arabian Peninsula. Ibn Saud, by his own initiative, had begun eliminating the Turks from the Eastern coast. For his efforts against the Turks, the British agreed to recognize him as King of Central Arabia and the East coast — everywhere but the Hijaz area on the West coast. There his rival, Sharif Hussein, worked with Lawrence in driving out the Turks. Lawrence never even met Ibn Saud, who eventually vanquished Sharif Hussein to become the ruler of the greater part of the Arabian Peninsula. Hussein was the grandfather of the present King Hussein of Jordan, which nation was formed after World War I.

My boyhood "hero," T.E. Lawrence, was no hero to the Saudis I knew. They acknowledged him — that's about all. They gave more credit to my Arab "hero," Auda Abu Tayi, the Howeitat chieftain, without whom Lawrence could not have accomplished what he did.

I always felt the Saudis liked the Americans more than they did the British. There is something about British imperialists. Their world-wide empire is similar everywhere they have gone. They are good administrators, and the Saudis respect that, but they definitely are aloof and have a superior attitude towards the natives. This sometimes gives a feeling of inferiority, which the Saudis certainly don't like. They don't feel inferior. Even though they haven't had all the technology and scientific advantages, personally, they don't feel inferior. The Americans tend to come in and relate more on a one-to-one basis, on a personal basis. That perhaps doesn't make for the best colonialists, but the Saudis like that better.

One time, while talking to a young Saudi friend of mine, I mentioned something comparing the British and the Americans. He said, "Oh well, we don't hold the individual American responsible for what his government does. But the British we do." In other words, if the British government does something

Symonds' 1937 Sketch
(Adapted from portrait by Eric Kennington)

Character, Culture, and Climate

the Saudis don't like, they hold the individual Britisher responsible to a certain degree. I don't know how that logic stands up, but it was an intriguing theory.

Originally, we shopped in the open market, or "souq." Then a few small grocery stores appeared. When you bought things like frozen chicken, you had the feeling that it had been frozen and unfrozen several times. That all changed when the supermarkets like Safeway came in. As for clothes, you would usually try to get the basics back in the States when you were there. The Saudis finally developed some fine women's clothing stores, usually run by Lebanese, with Paris fashions, and very expensive.

Because of my size, I had a hard time finding clothes in town. The Saudi men generally are not that big. So, I would have to try to find what I needed when I was in the United States. I remember the first year, I was trying to get some khaki pants in al-Khobar. I needed a size 44 in the waist, and I looked everywhere. They had khaki pants, but they didn't have that size. I went into one store where there was a little Saudi with a twinkle in his eye. I said, "I need some khaki pants, size 44." He looked at me, sort of grinned and said, "I can give you two 22's." So, my shopping for clothes was limited.

Mildred did much better. As for toiletries and cosmetics, the stores had everything from Paris and all over Europe. There was no lack of those items. Mildred and the ladies had all they needed.

The popular image of the Saudi or the Arab, I think, is pretty heavy, but I found that quite a few had a good sense of humor. There was a lot of good-natured kidding, particular with those they liked. They used to kid me all the time about various things. Their personalities varied just as they do everywhere

Jebel Dhahran and the New Saudi Generation

else. There were very serious and studious types all the way to some real kidders and jovial types.

I remember one fellow that had been working at the university a long time. He was rather worldly and had been in and out of the Kingdom many times. We were in a meeting one morning and were having a difficult time about something. He was giving us a hard time and I finally said, "Look, Abdul, one of these days we're all going to be gone, and you're going to miss us." He replied quickly, "No, I'm not." I said, "Why not?" He said, "Because I'm not going to be here."

(Five years later Abdul Mohsin al-Juraib was killed in an automobile accident while driving from Riyadh to Dhahran.)

Generally, the Saudis love to come to the West, Europe or America. But they love their homeland, which is certainly normal. They love the desert, their sandals, and their native clothes, although when they go West, most of them shed them for stylish Western dress. I don't believe there are many who really want to move from Saudi Arabia permanently. Now that they have the amenities of the Western society, that makes it even better. They naturally feel more comfortable in their own environment.

With regard to dress, as many people now know, the typical native attire for men is the thobe, which is a long gown-like apparel. Then, there is the gutra, which is the scarf that is worn around the head. The thobe is usually white in the summer. The gutra might be solid white or red and white checked. The color originally denoted tribal connections. The agal is black and is a rope-like circular piece that fits on top of the gutra which is worn over a lacy skull cap on the head. Originally the agal was also used as a hobble for the camels. One could take it off and tie the camels legs so he couldn't get away.

It was surprising how clean the Saudis kept the white thobes. The little guys in the streets and markets might be a bit dirty

Character, Culture, and Climate

sometimes, but the men at the university, the administrators and professors, sometimes had thobes with embroidery and French cuffs with gold links, very handsome. In the winter, they would change to thobes made of English worsted. They even had pin-striped, brown, black or gray, really quite sharp. They often bought their Western clothes tailor-made in Paris or London. So, they liked the fine things as soon as they had access to them.

These clothes have a very practical connotation to the Saudis which some people don't realize. Because of the heat, the loose-fitting thobe is very practical. It doesn't fit tight on the skin, allowing the air to circulate inside. It protects the entire body. The gutra is a very practical thing, because one can wrap it around the face to protect one from the sun. At certain times of the year there are very heavy winds that continue for weeks on end. I found that was one of the few things that I really didn't like. I don't like wind blowing anyway, but this continual blowing was annoying. The Saudis would wrap the gutra over their faces so that nothing but their eyes were exposed. It became a filter that they could breath through. In the winter it would keep their faces warm.

Although they seemed strange to us, the native clothes were really very practical and will probably continue. If you look at Japan, however, you see that the original native costumes are now almost obsolete. I think probably the thobe and gutra, at least in Saudi Arabia, will continue on for a long time, even though the Saudis are used to wearing Western clothes when they come over here.

The women wear the black abhaya when they go out in public, with a veil that covers their faces. This is still the custom in Saudi Arabia, although not in all Arab countries. In Saudi Arabia you don't often see women in public without their faces veiled. This is something perhaps some of the women might prefer not to do. On the other hand, it is a protection in the sense that it is a great equalizer, because no matter whether a woman

Jebel Dhahran and the New Saudi Generation

is black or white, beautiful or ugly, they all look the same. So, maybe they don't mind it so much after all. Many of the things that we think they want to be liberated from, perhaps they don't mind at all.

Another apparel that the men wear sometimes is a cape which goes on top of the thobe and is called a "bisht." This, to a great extent, seemed to me to be a status symbol, or a formal business dress. Often when a Saudi from the university went to Riyadh and wanted to be prepared to look distinguished, he would take his bisht with him and it was rather classy looking. In the desert, the bedouin wore a sort of bisht, but a very heavy one, made out of wool and very warm. They had artistic embroidery and designs on them.

A Saudi friend of mine, that I did some personal work for, wanted to reward me in some way. He insisted on taking me downtown and buying me a thobe, gutra, agal, and sandals. It was a complete outfit — and a very good one with a tailor-made thobe.

The airport at Dhahran was a combination of military and civilian usage. The traffic was heavy, although there were never any major accidents that I knew of. The King Abdul Aziz Air Base for the Royal Saudi Air Force was there. There was an expansion of the international commercial facilities in a temporary manner, several years after we arrived. There is now a large new International Airport being built between Dhahran and Jubail, which will be a superport like the ones in Riyadh and Jeddah, which are quite beautiful. Those are the three focal points. When the new one is completed, the old one in Dhahran will become strictly military.

It is awesome that the country needed everything, and wanted everything on a grand scale. Around the Kingdom, the smaller airports were redone or newly built. The Saudis move all around the Kingdom now. You can get a plane going any-

Character, Culture, and Climate

where and it is full of men, women, and children going to visit relatives and friends. They make good use of their new-found freedom.

The first four or five years we were there, the military and commercial planes flew off the same runway. It was a matter of scheduling. At certain times of the day, you could see groups of US-made F-5's and British-made Lightnings, which were the two types of military planes there until the Saudis got the F-15's from the U.S. in about 1981, after a big hassle in Congress. When the F-15's came, some of the F-5's and Lightnings moved out to other parts of the Kingdom. It was a sight to see the new F-15's perform their maneuvers.

It was strange how some Westerners were so skeptical that the Saudis were really flying them. I know the Saudis did fly them. In fact, Abdullah Mufti's brother-in-law was one of the pilots who flew one of the F-15's over to Saudi Arabia.

The F-15's would perform on various occasions, as when dignitaries would come. From our balcony we could see the maneuvers, since we could see the air base. It was fascinating to see the shows. One of the princes, Mansour bin Bandar, loved to fly more than anything, so I was told. You could often see him maneuvering solo. I was at the air base one time with Truitt Garrison from CRS/Houston. I saw a photograph of two F-15's that had been taken from another plane while flying over the university. I expressed admiration for it and Prince Mansour said, "I'll get you one." He gave me the picture and I still have it.

A number of the princes became pilots. Prince Bandar, who now is Saudi Ambassador to the United States, was a jet pilot and wing commander in the Royal Saudi Air Force. Prince Sultan bin Salman, the first Arab astronaut, was not a military pilot, but he did have a lot of jet flying hours.

Abdul Aziz al-Moghrabi, Abdullah Mufti's brother-in-law, is a jet pilot and colonel in the Royal Saudi Air Force.

These young Saudis are rather daring types. They love to travel fast, surprisingly enough, considering that the culture,

F-15s flying over the university

Royal Saudi Air Force Photo

Character, Culture, and Climate

the people, and the modes of transportation in years past have been so slow. They can't seem to wait to get to where they are going. They have developed a substantial and effective air force with these young pilots, one generation away from the life of the desert.

Other planes, which we didn't see in Dhahran, since they were based in Riyadh, were the AWACS. These planes were leased from the United States and were flown primarily by Americans, since they were not owned by the Saudis. They are highly sophisticated, and had Saudi operators along with the Americans. Since then, the Saudis have begun operating AWACS wholly-owned and flown by the Saudis.

In reference to the impatience of the Saudis, a standard joke was the definition of a "microsecond" as the "length of time between the changing of a traffic light and the honking of the Saudi behind you."

The impression that you sometimes get when you read the things that people have written about Saudi Arabia is that rubble, dirt, and filth were everywhere. Of course, initially the Saudis didn't have all the utilities, so they didn't have the ability to keep things clean and orderly all the time. When construction started on such a massive scale, with hundreds of construction sites adjacent to each other, it was impossible to keep everything tidy. At the same time that they were digging up the streets in al-Khobar, they were laying underground sewers, water lines, power lines, etc. At the university, clean-up was a constant effort.

In other places, such as Riyadh and Jeddah, it was the same. I thought that Jeddah was particularly interesting, because the mayor of Jeddah, Dr. Mohammed Farsi, was an architect, and he was intent on making Jeddah a showplace. There were a number of things that he did. He decreed that all buildings should be painted white. The beige stucco look that most build-

Jebel Dhahran and the New Saudi Generation

ings had was rather dingy and dark. If you paint something white, it takes on an entirely different character. Observe the picturesque villages along the Mediterranean with their white buildings and red-tile roofs. There weren't many red-tiled roofs in Saudi Arabia. Typical construction was a flat roof with a parapet. The majority of buildings in Jeddah were painted white and it certainly did change the overall appearance.

In Riyadh and Jeddah there were multi-million dollar contracts to clean up the city in every way.

At the university this was also true. We had sometimes ten to fifteen contractors working on the campus. Control of them for access, along with 3500 students, was a tremendous problem from a safety standpoint, as well as the congestion and the rubble that developed. Every now and then we'd have to get after the contractors to clean up. They were supposed to take debris off the campus, but there was so much going on that it was very difficult to monitor everything completely. Suddenly, you'd see an area that was obviously being used as a dump. You couldn't see the dumping at the time it was being done, but in a little while it would look terrible.

In about 1981, the university actually contracted with CRS to come over for a site clean-up project. CRS surveyed the entire campus, not just for clean-up, but to provide miscellaneous amenities that it recommended be built, which would make clean-up and maintenance easier. It prepared plans and specifications. The project was awarded to a Saudi contractor, and tremendous amounts of rubble were removed from the campus, and the amenities were constructed. It was a big improvement. About five years later and after many more contracts, the condition began to repeat itself, so, the university was going to have to do it all over again. It was a constant effort under those circumstances.

When you read some of what has been written about such things, often there is no justification or reason given for the

Character, Culture, and Climate

conditions. The fact was that big efforts were being made to overcome such problems. Underlying, there was a basic desire among the Saudis for cleanliness and orderliness. This is something that people don't generally give them credit for.

Many people in the West are obsessed with the idea that the Saudis have harems with many wives. We associated more or less with the intelligentsia, many of them PhD's, but most had come from humble stock. There were a few princes that attended there, but for the majority, their fathers and mothers probably came from the desert or small towns, because a generation ago, there wasn't much else. They were very conscious of family, and they loved their children. There is probably less child and wife abuse there than anywhere else.

The Islamic law says that a man can have four wives, if they are treated equally. Of course, that would pose a problem many times. I knew one business man that we visited who had several wives. He brought one to a mixed social occasion that we attended. Perhaps he thought she could mix better with the Westerners. This fellow was not educated but was successful and wealthy.

I felt that most of the young Saudis that I knew didn't want more than one wife. They tend to have large families, with five or six children.

The university was not the highest paying place. A professor's salary was probably not on the scale of ours here. If a Saudi wanted to make a lot of money, he had to go out into business, and many of them did. They would have partners in business out in the community. I had the opportunity to work with some of them and help them.

The general Western view seems to be that the Arab women are mistreated. While there are no doubt cases where it does occur, just think what happens here. Generally, in the home, it appeared to me, the women rule the roost.

Saudi wedding

The bride and groom

The Mufti children: Mohanned, Majed, Gihan - 1986

With the Mufti Family - 1980

In Arab clothes

Planning with Abdullah Mufti

Character, Culture, and Climate

We visited overnight in Riyadh with a young Saudi friend of ours and his family. Next door to him there was a very fine villa being built. When we got up the next morning, he had visitors downstairs. It was the neighbor woman. She was actually a bedouin type wearing the bedouin mask. She and her husband were building this very expensive house. It was almost completed, and she had come over to see how our friend's house was furnished. She was in the process of buying furniture. She was very outspoken, all in Arabic, of course. We were introduced, but could not converse. A little while later, her husband came along. She was, without question, the boss of that house.

As far as the relationship of son to father or mother was concerned, the Saudis took good care of their parents. Mansour's mother and father both lived with him.

Mansour was very dutiful towards his father and mother. His father passed on several years after we arrived. His mother, as far as I know, is still living. His mother's grandmother was still living and reputed to be 125 years old. She visited the university and walked around the residential area by herself. Perhaps 125 was an exaggeration, but I feel sure that she was over a hundred.

The Arabic calendar is set up according to the phases of the moon, with twenty-nine or thirty days to each month. Mansour said that his mother could tell the date of the month by looking at the moon. Also she could predict the correct date for planting of crops and harvesting, by the position of the stars relative to the moon. He said this ability was common among the older Arabs, especially those with farming abilities.

He had three sons and four daughters. He talked of disciplining his sons and said sometimes he had to be a bit hard on them to get them to do their homework. Whenever his mother came in the room, with the boys, he said he got out. "I don't want to be around when she is there," he said. I think probably she stood up for the boys as grandmothers sometimes do.

Jebel Dhahran and the New Saudi Generation

Speaking of the mother's place in the home and status vis-a-vis the children, I read somewhere that the wife of King Abdul Aziz, the mother of the "Sudairi Seven," required that the seven princes have lunch with her once a week, at which time she would get a report on their weekly activities — and this until they were grown men.

The following concerns the "taboo" about Westerner's association with Saudi women. The rector asked me to remodel his house on campus several times. The last time, he just turned it over to his wife. He called me and told me to go meet with her myself. She had already done the ground work and had selected many of the materials she wanted to use. But they didn't know what they wanted to do in the way of remodeling.

It became clear to me pretty soon that she wanted something more elegant than they had. I agreed with this. I felt that the rector of the university, even as a president of a university here in the United States, should having something more commensurate with his position. This was not so much a matter of personal endowment, as it was the fact that he represented the university. He entertained kings, queens and princes. Yet he had a house that really wasn't much better than anyone else's.

When I met with her, she said, "Dr. Bakr's house should be more elegant. You tell him that." Of course, I didn't tell him that, but I did go talk to him. One of the ideas that I had was along the lines that she had in mind. He was not in favor of spending much money. I couldn't resist going ahead and making a sketch of this idea. When he saw the sketch, he liked it so well that he wanted to go ahead with it, and the whole thing began to develop.

His wife and I drove all over al-Khobar and Dammam looking at fixtures, selecting materials, fabrics, and so forth. There was never any problem. We would get out of the car, go into the shops together, and she would bargain with the storekeepers. Her driver was always with us. Dr. Bakr never worried about it, and I never worried about it. She knew what she wanted, and she had very good taste. When the work was finished, it was really very nice. It was, in my opinion and in hers, no more than a rector of a university should have. It was elegant and with a very definite Arabic character. I must say, I really enjoyed working on it.

One characteristic of many of the Saudis that we observed was their penchant for elegance. Perhaps this was because those we knew were the elite, educated abroad, and exposed to the West, but I don't think it was just that. We in the West always tend to attribute everything to ourselves. If anyone else has aspirations toward higher things, we think we are the source. Actually, these people had elegant culture in the Middle East long before the West was where it is today.

As soon as the money began to become available, the merchants went to Europe and England and bought the finest Royal Dalton and Wedgewood china, Gorham silverware, and the latest Paris fashions. Soon there were fine shops there, and the women dressed elegantly. They had an appreciation for fineness and elegance in their houses. When they were able, many had the finest furnishings, and in good taste.

For instance, one young Saudi that I knew went out into the business world from the university and did very well. He built a beautiful villa for himself. He hired an Egyptian architect who helped him with the design. Then I think he did much of the interior himself. We had lost social contact with him and his family the last few years, primarily because we were both so busy. I didn't want to leave Saudi Arabia without establishing that contact again.

We invited them over one night, his wife and him, and had a very nice evening together before we left. They then invited us to their new house, which was by this time completed and

Jebel Dhahran and the New Saudi Generation

furnished. It was truly elegant, interesting, and unusual. It had a large two-story atrium living area with a family room on the second level, overlooking the lower level. All the furniture was custom-made to his design. He had made several trips to Italy and the Philippines to have it made.

He mentioned that he might build a larger house. This aspect of their character always impressed me, these so-called "desert people."

The Saudi professors that lived on campus didn't own their homes there. All had tenure, so they treated them almost as their own, with their own furnishings and so forth. When we built new houses on campus, the Saudis were always the first to get them, of course. That was understandable. As a result, they constantly upgraded their situation. The houses that were provided by the university were furnished, but it was minimal. Most of the professors brought their own furniture and added their own touch.

Life and housing on the campus were obviously different from what they were in al-Khobar. While it was "compound living," it felt more "open", because there were no walls between houses. The individual houses were more as they would be in the United States, one beside the other with nothing but a hedge or fence separating them. There was much discussion about "privacy" each time CRS designed new houses.

The foreign companies in town all built compounds with a controlled entrance gate and a more or less "open" concept. Some had very fine housing such as you might find in the United States condominium types.

Some companies didn't have their employees in compounds, however. We had friends with Northrup, and they had a villa in al-Khobar. The outside didn't look like much, but there was a high wall around it for privacy. When you got inside the wall, it was entirely different. It was what you might find in New Orleans or Vienna, where you walk down the

Character, Culture, and Climate

street, and you can't see what's behind the walls. You go inside a courtyard and it's like another world. Each one has created his own environment.

When you come out onto the street, as in al-Khobar, there is not a lot of setback from the street. So, it tends to give a feeling of being somewhat congested. That is one thing that we can't appreciate enough in a city like Houston, the setbacks. In-town parking was a problem with everything so close. There was no such thing as zoning. Anyone could build anything anywhere, so it tended to create a hodge-podge.

The university houses all of the professors and senior staff personnel on campus. This amounted to about 1500 families. While we were there, we built over a thousand houses. You can imagine what this creates in terms of required logistics and ancillary facilities. I don't know of any American university that does that. Just from the standpoint of maintenance, you can see how much that would require.

Shortly before we left Dhahran, one of the Saudi ladies that Mildred worked with, whose husband was a professor of Islamic studies, wanted us to have dinner with them. She invited us to a fine restaurant in one of the big hotels with her husband and her. Now that was a Saudi and his wife and Mildred and I together in public, and the Saudi lady didn't wear a veil. We had dinner and a long evening talking, just as we would here in the States. We talked about everything and really enjoyed the evening. I'm not saying some of the restrictions you read about aren't true. But I am saying that it really depends on the persons, on the individual's attitude, and how he or she feels about you. I think they felt comfortable with us, even as we did with them.

I never really felt the antagonism that some people say is there. Incidentally, the Saudi we went out to dinner with that night at the hotel made a point of the fact that his name was

Jebel Dhahran and the New Saudi Generation

Issa, which is Arabic for Jesus. Many Arabs are named Mohammed, but here was one whose name was Jesus.

Perhaps many Westerners do not know that some commonly used biblical names have Arabic equivalents and are often used, such as:

Hebrew/English	*Arabic*
Aaron	Haroun
Abraham	Ibrahim
David	Daoud
Jacob	Yacoub
Jesus	Issa
Joseph	Yussef
Joshua	Yahya
Mary	Miriam
Moshe/Moses	Musa

The Saudi women are often the ones that have money in a family, through inheritance or otherwise. I knew one professor there who unashamedly acknowledged that his wife was the one with the money. In fact, she wanted to be in business. She would very much have liked to establish a business. She mentioned this once to me. Some of them did have businesses. Of course, it had to be under certain conditions. The banks began to open services for ladies only, helping with money management and investments.

There was one Saudi lady downtown who had developed a very nice art shop. It was in a residential area. If one walked by, it didn't look like a shop. You had to know it was there. She had to operate it discreetly, you might say. I think it was known generally by the authorities that she had it, but she didn't flaunt it. She had lived and travelled in the United States.

Character, Culture, and Climate

The holy month of Ramadan presented some inconveniences for the expatriate, in that you could not shop regular hours, and you couldn't go to restaurants for food until sundown. However, there were some compensating pleasantries involved. The breaking of the fast for the day at sunset is called "Iftar." This normally consists of light food — juices, dates, tea, sandwiches, cakes etc. The International Hotel at the airport provided beautiful tables of delicacies. So, we would often go to the hotel at 9:00 p.m. for "Iftar" during Ramadan.

One very prominent difference that you had to get accustomed to was the juxtaposition of the weekend. Friday is for the Muslims their weekly "day of rest" similar to our Sunday. Therefore their "Saturday" occurs on Thursday.

I think that one of the things that was difficult for us to realize was that our perception of things over there and our interest in the people were not shared by many of our friends back home. This was understandable in a sense. How would they know? They hadn't seen or known the people over there. They had misconceptions that they read about. There were a lot of stories that came back. Some of them true, some of them not — what we called "horror" stories over there.

When we were in Houston on several occasions, we made a point to associate with Saudis that might also be there. One was a young accountant named Abdul Aziz al-Auda, whom I had known at the university. He left in 1977 and took a job at a much better salary with a group that was coming to Houston to participate in a joint project with Shell, a petrochemical project in Jubail. The negotiations extended over several years. One summer when we were in Houston on vacation, I contacted him. We usually stayed with our friends, Bob and Ethel MacIntire. Bob was rather well placed in the Shell Company. One night we asked Abdul Aziz, his wife and two small children over for dinner. We had a barbecue in the back yard. We thought Bob and Ethel would be interested in meeting a Saudi family. It was a very pleasant evening for all. Our son, Richard, a local Houston attorney and our daughter Cheryl were also there, as well as my brother Bob, the actor.

On another occasion, the secretary general of UPM, Dr. Saleh Bakhrebah, was in Houston with his wife, Afaf, and three children. We had them over to the MacIntires and then went to dinner at the Inn-on-the-Park. Our son Richard was also there. It was a most enjoyable evening. Dr. Bakhrebah and his family seemed to enjoy being with our friends.

Entertaining al-Auda family at MacIntire's in Houston - 1979

Character, Culture, and Climate

Language is a very important part of the Saudi culture, very much the basis on which everything is done. Most decisions are arrived at by consensus. The university voted by majority rule, but in general, there was a method of consensus in which participants would sit and talk and talk. Soon all the facets of a problem would be out in the open. The positions would change individually until finally they would arrive at a consensus in which they all agreed. It is thus even in the Council of Ministers. It is government by consensus, and not so much somebody dictating something to someone else. It is all of them sitting around talking and finally coming to a majority decision or conclusion. The Ministry of Information refers to this as "Saudi Democracy."

That probably derives from the desert culture where the bedouin sat around the fire drinking coffee and telling stories. It is a trademark of the culture. The bedouin didn't do much writing, but they communicated by stories down through the ages, word-of-mouth. Thus, language became the central core of the culture. They developed great poets.

I sat through hours and hours of conversational meetings in Arabic, not knowing what the Saudis were saying. Traveling through the country with them, I never knew the agenda. I would think they were going to do this or that, and then after long conversations, before I knew what was going on, off we would go. I would just follow along. There wasn't much I could contribute to it.

The first few months we were there, we went over to Bahrain to get our work permit. We contacted an American there that had known a lady that we knew in Houston. She had given us his name and address before we left Houston. We called him and in deference to our mutual friend, I'm sure, he and his wife invited us to dinner one night on the roof of their house in Manama. It was really quite pleasant under the stars. He was with one of the oil companies there. He said that in Manama there were a Kiwanis Club, a Rotary Club, Lions

Jebel Dhahran and the New Saudi Generation

Club, and so forth. He was a member of the Kiwanis. He said the Arabs, the Bahrainis, were active members. They loved it. They liked to sit around and talk, so they made great Kiwanians and Rotarians. That was their way of working. However, such clubs do not exist in Saudi Arabia.

With regard to the various Arab groups, many people in the United States don't really understand the differences. I know I didn't clearly before I went over there. The Arabs in general comprise the largest segment of the population of the Middle East. The Arab nations are Syria, Jordan, Iraq, Kuwait, Bahrain, Qatar, United Arab Emirates, Yemen, Oman, Saudi Arabia, and Lebanon. The area which is now Israel was known as Palestine, which included the West Bank, the Golan Heights and Gaza Strip. The Arab countries of North Africa include Egypt, Sudan, Libya, Algeria, Tunisia, Morocco, and Western Sahara. These nations are of various ethnic backgrounds but speak Arabic and are predominantly Muslim, which qualifies them to be called Arab nations.

The Palestinians, Syrians, Jordanians, Iraqis, Lebanese, and most North African Arabs dress in Western clothes and look similar. The Syrians and Lebanese have a strong French influence and generally speak French as well as Arabic.

The Saudis, Kuwaitis, Bahrainis, Qataris, and those in the United Arab Emirates (which includes Sharja, Dubai, and Abu Dhabi) all dress in the typical thobe and gutra. The majority of the Saudis are Sunnis, and they are the strictest as far as their religious culture is concerned. There is an anomaly in the fact that the majority of Bahrainis and Iraqis are Shiites and yet the rulers are not Shiites.

The Yemeni look different from the Saudis. They don't wear the white thobe and gutra. They wear more of a turban-like head-dress. All the men wear daggers. Most men wear a skirt-like apparel, and the black abayas of the women are different.

In Oman the men wear a different headdress and slightly

Character, Culture, and Climate

different apparel. It is strange that there are such differences when the peoples are geographically so close together. While they all live in the desert, more or less, the Saudis are the ones who live in the big desert of the Arabian Peninsula.

As I mentioned in the theme I wrote in college fifty years ago, there is a desire for Arab nationalism, to all be under one umbrella, but it appears to be a long way off. The Arabs are very factional in their attitudes, and there is constant fighting and bickering among them. It is hard to see how the Pan-Arab Movement, as such, can really come to successful fulfillment any time soon.

Most of the Saudis at the university spoke very good English. Some spoke with very little accent. Mansour used to chide me all the time about not learning Arabic, after having been there ten years. Well, I'll have to admit that I should have done better. He would say, "We go to your country, and we learn English. Why don't you learn Arabic when you come to our country?" I replied, "You seem to require such perfection." I didn't mean to offend him, but one morning he chided me about it, and I said, "Mansour, you don't speak perfect English, but we don't care. When we try to speak Arabic, if we don't speak it perfectly, you criticize every little thing. We are intimidated, so most people don't bother."

The thing that was amazing to me was the language handicap that they had to live with. Imagine, if we had to deal with things for the first time beyond our normal experience and with such a language barrier. But they managed to do it. They operated in both Arabic and English, whereas we dealt only in English. It was an admirable effort on their part. When Arabic was required for certain things, we would hire a translator. Besides the language barrier, there were three other not so difficult handicaps that we had to deal with – weights, measurements, and currency. Weights were in kilos and grams, measurements were metric, and currency was in riyals.

Jebel Dhahran and the New Saudi Generation

The Saudis are in general a rather stoic and fatalistic people as far as disaster and death are concerned. Although the women often display grief, the men seldom do. The rector's father passed on, while I was helping the rector with some personal things. Mansour's father also passed on while he was living at the university. In both cases I sent them condolence cards, because that is our custom. They never mentioned them, so I didn't know if that was customary with them or not. On television, you saw considerable emotion and grief displayed by the women. In Beirut and other places in Palestine they always seemed to be grieving in soap operas and in real life — and understandably so. They usually had much to grieve about.

Dr. Hall passed on in May 1981 while we were there. We visited with Mrs. Hall at the time. Mildred and Mary Tiedge helped her close up and clean out the house after 25 years in the Middle East, seventeen years at the university. There were a number of Saudi ladies that came to visit her, all sitting around in black, grieving for Dr. Hall.

Not many of the Saudis that I knew had pets. Occasionally they might have a Suluki dog. That was the indigenous Saudi dog, very similar to a greyhound, a racing dog. Very often there was one of those in a family, especially the bedouins. One time we were driving to Hofuf, and we saw on the desert some bedouin families traveling with their camels and paraphernalia. At the end of the caravan there was a a little Toyota pickup with two Suluki dogs.

Some Westerners brought their cats and dogs with them. They were allowed in, if they had shots.

Most people think of Saudi Arabia as a burning hot desert, and so it is a good bit of the time in certain areas. The surprising thing is that there is just as much beautiful weather there as there is unpleasant weather. Where we were on the Persian Gulf, it

Character, Culture, and Climate

probably is better than some other places. We arrived on August 15th, and stepping off the plane was like stepping into a sauna bath. The humidity and temperature were both close to 100° F. Even at night that made for a rather unpleasant sensation.

In October it begins to break. You might get the first little break of cool breeze coming in from the northeast. From November through May rain is possible. The torrential rains and electrical storms that I mentioned previously were out of the ordinary. That doesn't happen every year. From November to April the temperature generally is no higher than the 70's during the day and as low as 40 degrees F. at night. It is very pleasant. You start wearing a jacket or sweater in November until about March — then sport shirts only after that. So, about half the year the weather is pleasant. In June, July and August temperatures can get up to 120 degrees.

The thing that I personally disliked the most were the sometimes heavy winds in June, July, and August. These winds are called "shamals." They blow generally from the northeast, but sometimes from the southwest, the desert. The sand would penetrate anything and everything. It seemed to blow right through the walls. That was one of the first problems I encountered with these new houses when I arrived. The sand infiltrated like water.

Of course, everyone complained. In our office, I got to where I didn't pay much attention. Our secretary, a Ukrainian lady, Slawa Olesniesky, couldn't understand it. She said, "Doesn't it bother you?" I said, "There isn't much I can do about it." We could tape around the joints and windows, which did help some. Sometimes the wind would blow without stopping for two weeks at 40 to 50 miles per hour. It got very annoying after a while.

I don't know that it had ever snowed in Dhahran. However, in Riyadh to the south and west of us, it was known to have snowed. In the Asir, in the southwest, it is an entirely different environment — like a different country. There are mountains

Jebel Dhahran and the New Saudi Generation

and trees, and the temperature never gets extremely hot. So, there is a wide variety of climates over the peninsula. Dhahran was probably as good as any in the overall picture.

During about three or four months of the year, the heat and humidity were uncomfortable. However, gradually everything was air conditioned and you forgot that you were, in fact, in the middle of a scorching desert. On occasions, however, the breakdown of a compressor or some other component part, destroyed the illusion and brought back reality. Generally, "down-time" was a couple of days in your house.

On the main campus, a breakdown did not occur very often. One notable exception was in 1976. The corrosive effect of the local water (even after treatment) on the tubes of the chillers, finally necessitated a major shutdown in the month of July, while a change was made from rotary to centrifugal type equipment. It happened that the main CRS design team was visiting at that time. Nevertheless, we sat in Building 10 auditorium and watched *"Gone With The Wind,"* which was being shown that week. The metal on the seat armrests was so hot that you could hardly touch it.

I think that I made my most noteworthy contribution to CRS at that time. Mildred had gone to London for the summer. Every night the CRSers, Charles Lawrence, Joe Thomas, Bruce Appling, Wallie Scott, and others would come to my house. I bought containers of chocolate ice cream and mixed up gallons of delicious chocolate milk shakes. I was credited with ensuring the survival of the CRS team that summer.

The first two years that we were there, we drove a Peugeot station wagon that was not air-conditioned. In spite of the heat, Mildred and I drove to Jubail, Hofuf, and all around on weekends. I think that was one of the few times that I really felt sorry for Mildred — perspiring in 120 degree heat and never complaining. I was satisfied that she was a survivor.

Character, Culture, and Climate

The overlapping of cultures, ancient and modern, was sometimes the source of an eerie feeling that you experienced, but could not perceive with the five senses.

The presence of goats on campus when we first arrived was not uncommon. I recall that I was amused when I began reading the correspondence in the CRS office in 1975, before leaving the United States. One memo from Bob Hendrickson to the CCC project manager said, "Dear Hassan, I have warned you many times that goats are not allowed on campus. We continue to see their unauthorized presence and again advise that this will not be tolerated."

This, in some ways, was a 'conditioner' for the new environment we were about to enter.

As late as August 1982, I received the following memo from Mansour al-Saber, "A small camel has been noticed in the academic site under the care of a laborer who works for Redec Daelim. The policy of UPM doesn't allow such animals to be owned by people inside the UPM perimeter. So, please instruct Redec Daelim to take away this camel and issue a circular to all contractors to this effect."

Something about this seemed incongruous. After all, this was Saudi Arabia, where camels were a prized possession and originally were a vital part of the economy. Now they were not wanted.

About a year after we arrived, I was sitting one afternoon at the crest of Jebel Dhahran on the plaza outside of Building 10, looking over the Persian Gulf. My mind's fantasy carried me back hundreds of years when a native Arab of Jazirat al-Arab may have been sitting there. I became aware of the sound of goats and an occasional strange human sound. I looked over the edge of the jebel and there a few yards away was a bedouin with his flock of a dozen or so goats sifting around for something

Jebel Dhahran and the New Saudi Generation

edible. The human sound was the call the bedouin made occasionally to the goats. The whole thing seemed to be almost an apparition — a time warp carrying me back. Here was a bedouin with his goats in the shadow of a modern university building —seemingly oblivious of the implications of the twentieth century.

The ancient and modern cultures were indeed overlapping.

CHAPTER 17

ANOMALIES

Our original visas to Saudi Arabia were good for ninety days. This meant that they would expire on about the first of November according to the Arabic calendar. I didn't even think of this until one day I received a phone call from the Passport Department advising me that we had to go to Bahrain immediately to get our visas renewed. It was all important.

We dropped everything and went to the airport to try to get a flight to Bahrain. This was a real hassle, but we managed and finally got over to Bahrain in record time. We didn't have a place to stay, and there weren't any rooms available. There weren't the hotels then that there were later. They were all under construction. The best one was the Gulf Hotel. We tried everywhere without success.

Finally, I called the CCC office in Bahrain and asked if it could help us. The office sent someone to us, but he wasn't much help, so we ended up back at the first hotel that we had looked at. We didn't want to stay in it because it was pretty bad. It was typical third world. But we had to take it. We had no choice.

The next day, we went to the Saudi Embassy to see about getting our visa renewed. The best it would do was to renew our visa for two weeks. For a work permit, which we needed, we were told that we had to have a letter from UPM and a copy of my Rice University diploma, which I hadn't anticipated. We returned to Dhahran the next day and were legitimized for at least two weeks.

I sent off immediately to James Morehead, registrar at Rice University, for a copy of my transcript and to H. R. Winslett, my ex-office partner and Rice roommate, for a copy of my diploma, which hung in my office in Houston. I got the letter from Dr. Bakhrebah and other credentials from the U.S. in record

Jebel Dhahran and the New Saudi Generation

time. In two weeks we were back in Bahrain. This time it was about the same as before. We had no reservations, but we did manage to get into the Delmon Hotel by just camping in front of the manager's desk and bugging him all afternoon. He never did say he would give us a room, but for hours would just say, "We'll see." Finally, he came through with a room. The Delmon was one of the old hotels which was fairly good. It had a good restaurant.

We started going to the Saudi Embassy every day. I got cross-wise with the Pakistani secretary that we talked to, and I thought that my attitude might have had something to do with the delay. We came back the next day, same thing. Came back the next day, same thing. We had been there about a week, and we were running out of money.

One day we were wandering around on foot, and we saw the American flag flying. It apparently was the American ambassador's residence. At that point, we felt as if, "I'm an American, and they'll take care of us." However, the ambassador's residence was not where we needed to go. We found out where the American consulate was and went there. We talked to the vice-consul and I said, "It seems strange doesn't it?" He replied with a bit of cynicism, "Not necessarily." He was a pleasant fellow, but there wasn't anything he could do. The fact that we even asked him showed a bit of naiveté on our part.

To try to get rid of our frustrations, we went down to the beach and walked along the sand. I thought I began to detect a little rebellion in Mildred as she walked along resolutely without looking at me, as much as to say, "What have you gotten me into half-way around the world from my home and family?" While I must admit to some frustration, I think I was more inclined to say, "Ain't this fun?"

We went back to the embassy every day for four or five days and sat, drinking tea all the time. The Saudi consul finally came in, a very tall, slender fellow. I made some comment inquiring

Anomalies

as to how visas were issued. The Haj to Mecca was coming up soon, and I asked if that had anything to do with the difficulty. Whatever the problem was, in about fifteen minutes he came out and said that we could have our work permit. At one point the consul had said, "Is your wife very angry?" To which I replied, "Of course not," as though that happened to us every day.

We enjoyed, to a certain extent, staying at the Delmon, eating good meals, and sight-seeing around Bahrain. Bahrain does have an interesting history, but after a while, we had had enough of that.

A lot of world traffic came into Bahrain. Bahrain is an island, a kingdom, a separate sheikdom about thirty miles off shore from Dhahran. A causeway has been built, which is an impressive engineering feat. Now you can drive to Bahrain in an automobile. Everyone was skeptical that Saudi Arabia would follow through on this, since alcohol and gambling are not allowed in Saudi Arabia. Bahrain does allow these things. There are so many incongruities in the Middle East. Bahrain is predominantly Shiite, as is Iran. In fact, Iran claims that Bahrain really belongs to it. Yet, with all the conservatism there, Bahrain does have liquor in the hotels, as well as casinos.

Many international flights must be caught in Bahrain rather than in Saudi Arabia.

The next day we returned to Saudi Arabia and were then set for at least two years.

We felt that we had passed the first big test of dealing with the incongruities that you had to learn to live with in the Middle East.

Because of the various stories that one heard, the thought of "jails" did stand in the background as somewhat of an ominous specter. I think the thing was that we were unfamiliar with the judicial system there and felt much less confident that, given the same set of circumstances, we would fare as well as we would in the U.S.

One thing about the "modus operandi," as far as the jail situation was concerned, was that whenever there was an apparent infraction of some kind, or violation, the normal routine was to get the manager of the project. This attitude apparently had a sociological background. Traditionally, when a member of a tribe commits a crime, the authorities contact and deal with the head of the tribe and hold him responsible.

Dr. Bakhrebah commented, "This is a modern version of that. Another thing is that, after all, this is a developing country. There are wonderful things that have been accomplished. But you can't just close your eyes on a Middle Ages country, then open them and find a twentieth century country. Things do take time to develop. And it does make sense to hold the manager responsible because he knows his workers and is the only one who knows where they are all living. This is true for the Saudis as well as expatriates. For example, if a Saudi defaults on a loan, the authorities contact his employer."

When we first arrived, the Lebanese contractor building the 189 houses had an American project manager and assistant manager. The assistant was new and he wasn't very aware of how he should conduct himself. On the job one day, he got mad at some workers and called them "dirty Arabs." They were Yemeni workers and they reported this to the police. The police came out looking for the American assistant manager, but he had managed to stash himself away somewhere. The project manager was out of the Kingdom at that time, so the police finally took the bookkeeper, a Lebanese fellow, and put him in jail, but soon released him. That was a typical situation. The offending assistant manager was promptly sent back to the U.S.A.

Don Chambers was very alert to such things. One time, in the early stages of Phase IV, the contractor had to do some

Anomalies

blasting in the rock. The people that were best at that were the Germans, so it was a German contractor that was doing the work. Explosives were highly monitored and restricted in the Kingdom. During the blasting, there was an accident. The contractors would drill holes in the limestone, place the charges, and detonate them. Sometimes, a charge wouldn't detonate in a particular hole. In that case the explosive was still there, and it was dangerous. A warning was always issued to the workers, who would come back, not to put their jackhammers down in the same holes again.

Sure enough, somebody would do it. One of the explosives went off, blasted a guy, and pretty well messed him up. It didn't kill him, but the first thing the police did was grab the German superintendent and put him in jail. Then the police came over to our office and said that they wanted to talk to Don. The Lebanese contractor brought them. Don managed to avoid them. He had learned that the best thing was to stay completely away from the police, if possible, and not get involved. You could never predict what was going to happen.

Automobiles were another cause of people landing in jail. It was often difficult to pin down responsibility in an accident.

One of our best friends, Warren Phillips, who was very experienced, had been in Iran with the U.S. Army as an adviser to the Shah. He and his wife, Carol, were in Saudi Arabia with Northrup, after retiring from the Army. He spoke Arabic. One day we heard that he had been in an automobile accident and was in jail. In this case, he was totally innocent. A truck had tried to pass around him and make an illegal turn. In doing so, the driver hit a pedestrian, an Indian, who was killed. The police not only arrested the driver of the truck causing the accident, but they took our friend as well. His car had been slightly damaged by this truck. He was put in jail.

Jebel Dhahran and the New Saudi Generation

Fortunately, he knew the Amir of the Eastern Province, Abdul Mohsin bin Jiluwi. Right away he was toid that he should claim an injury of some kind. That enabled him to be shipped to the hospital, which was better than the jail. After a few days, he received word that the Amir had heard of his case. Very soon after, he was released. But it was a very trying experience for him. He had helped many others in similar situations, but never believed that it would happen to him.

One of the main problems on campus was speed control of automobiles. As on many campuses in the States there were too many cars in the hands of students. There were about 3500 students and at least 1500 cars down by the dormitories every morning. The students would get into their cars, drive up to the main campus, park and then come back after classes. Many did walk, but they had to walk up a steep hill, often in very hot weather.

Nevertheless, the main problem was that each student wanted to have a car. We built several parking garages, but they were not available to the students. They were for faculty and administration, but they did release the surface parking for students.

The same was true in downtown al-Khobar. Some parking garages were built. In other words, the Saudis followed the path of any normal development in the United States, except that they were doing it in much more telescoped time frame.

When we first arrived, there were few police cars in the area. The university was considered an entity to itself, more or less sacrosanct. As years went by, however, in order to show that they had authority, the police began patrolling the campus regularly.

Anomalies

I was very grateful for having driven there for eleven years without a problem. We had a couple of near misses, but never a bad accident. The first year, I drove without a driver's license at all. Then, the police started tightening up, and we had to take an exam to get a license. Every three years it was renewed.

Everything began to move in all areas of control. First, the only police were in jeeps with no radios. Then a few motorcycle police, then police cars, modern and up-to-date, and lots of them. Motorcycles never really took hold.

The first year, we would often go to the old public beach at Half Moon Bay, before UPM opened its beach. One weekend, we said that we would take the six-year-old son of our Aramco friends, Audrey and Tom Benedikston, together with his friend out to the beach. We drove as close as we could up to the sand dunes that rise from the coast, and we parked.

Before we knew it, the boys had jumped out and said, "We'll run on up to the top of the hill." They got half-way up, and we thought we had better get up there where they were. We tried to follow them, but it was very slow going in deep sand. By the time we got to the top, they were nowhere in sight, had absolutely disappeared. Immediately, I had all kinds of visions of their heading off in the direction of the big desert. I couldn't see or know which dune they had gone over. I panicked. I started running across the top of the dune hollering for them. Mildred stayed back and said that she would look around there. I kept running and shouting. I think some Saudis who saw me thought that I had gone berserk. I was petrified.

Mildred finally found them. They had gone to the top of the dune, and instead of going in the direction that I thought they were going, they had circled back and come around below and back down to the water again.

That shook me up so that while driving back, I really knew what it was to feel disoriented. I couldn't think of where we had

Jebel Dhahran and the New Saudi Generation

been or where we were going. Things just didn't seem to come together right. We got back to Aramco, and the parents never knew anything about it.
I finally became reoriented.

Half Moon Bay - Overnight Campout   *author's sketch*

Chapter 18

Overtones — Religious and Political

I sometimes felt that some Saudis thought that I might be a potential convert to Islam, since I was interested in what they believed, and I obviously felt no antagonism toward their religion. Mansour al-Saber and I made a number of business trips together to Jeddah and Taif. We would sometimes talk over dinner at night at the hotel.

I remember on one trip he was particularly interested in talking to me about the Koran and such things. I think that he was trying to enlighten me. I was impressed with his sincerity, and I did appreciate his willingness to share his beliefs with me. What he told me would surprise many Westerners. He would recount stories in the Koran, many of which were the same stories that we have in the Bible. I couldn't resist telling him, "Why yes, I know that story. It is in the Bible."

The Koran is really a remarkable book. Mohammed didn't write anything, even as Jesus didn't. Most of the stories were verbal back in those days. It was apparently compiled and written in the seventh century A.D. There is a great lack of knowledge in the West about this. However, the Muslims can't blame the West for that entirely. They have kept themselves closed, preventing the communication that would promote understanding. They have not let anyone try to understand, so there is an antipathy that has developed, probably from the time of the Crusades, between East and West. And leaders like the Ayatollah Khomeini do not present a good image to the West.

One time Mansour and I were in Jeddah. We were going to Taif, so we went over to the market to find a taxi. It's always fascinating to watch the Saudis bargain. You just sit back and listen to them negotiate in Arabic. It might take an hour to agree on the right price and the right driver.

Jebel Dhahran and the New Saudi Generation

We were going to drive up the escarpment, which rises from sea level up to about 8000 feet, where Taif is located. There is a road that winds up the mountain, which was built about twenty-five years ago. It is an engineering masterpiece. We finally got our taxi. We sat in the back seat and talked all the way. Mansour was very talkative. We talked about politics, religion, and culture.

Finally, we came to the point at which you turn to go to Mecca. It is about five miles from that point. Non-Muslims cannot go in there. You continue along the road to go to Taif. If you divert there, you will end up in Mecca. Before we arrived there, Mansour said, "You have always said that you would like to see Mecca. Now is your opportunity."

In other words, if I had said the right things at that time, in his presence, I would have allegedly been converted to Islam and could have gone to Mecca. I said, "Well, no thank you," and indicated that I was happy with my religion as it was, my desire to see Mecca notwithstanding. I don't know how serious he was, but if I had done that, I don't think he would have objected.

We arrived in Taif in several hours. We were going to visit the rector's family place there. He had a sort of recreational building with a long porch, which overlooked the hills around Taif over his extensive vineyards. The servants brought out all kinds of food. It was quite idyllic.

Again we sat, looked over the hills and talked. At one point Mansour said more or less to himself, "This man is very deep." I think what he meant was that he felt I was a religious man. I never talked much about it, but my habits were more in line with his. There were some similarities he could understand. I believe that is what he was thinking. There was something he respected and related to.

Something that many Westerners don't realize is that Muslims accept the Old Testament of the Bible as being the Word of God to man, basically. When I say that they accept it, I mean

Overtones — Religious and Political

that they acknowledge the authenticity of many of the stories in the Bible. The Bible, per se, is not allowed in Saudi Arabia, so you can't say that they really accept it in that sense. They believe that the Koran and the Bible are both from God, but that the Koran supersedes the Bible, chronologically.

They believe that they are the descendants of Ishmael, who was the son of Abraham and Hagar, the Egyptian bondmaid whom Abraham had to send away at Sarah's request. She wandered down the coast of the Red Sea, and they believe that it was at Mecca, where the Kabah is, that she found the water that saved them. It is called the Well of Zam Zam and is within the confines of the Grand Mosque. When people talk about the Jews being Semitic, they need to realize that the Arabs are also Semitic. They all came from the same roots.

Another thing is that the Muslims accept Jesus as a prophet, but not the Son of God. They do not deny Jesus, as the Jews do. They say that Jesus was a legitimate prophet. During our discussion Mansour said that they believe in the immaculate conception, or virgin birth, of Jesus. They believe that Jesus was taken up into heaven, in other words, the ascension, but they don't believe that he died and came back to life again. They believe that someone else actually was crucified in his place. They believe that he will someday return to earth.

Some of the writings that I have read say that Muslims consider Christians to be infidels. The definitions that I got from them was that an infidel was anyone who doesn't believe in one God. We were careful not to enter into any religious debates. Our company had told us that we shouldn't do that. In my association with Muslims and having worked on and been in many mosques with Mansour, we did have some discussions.

I never really felt any antagonism towards Islam. Any conflicts I might have felt, I never attributed to that. It was usually just personality. In my particular case, I don't like to be pushed, and they are pretty good pushers. As a matter of fact, it is probably good for me to have somebody push me a little.

Jebel Dhahran and the New Saudi Generation

There are a wide variety of Muslims, from the very strict fundamentalists to the more tolerant. The Saudis that I knew were mostly religious. They faithfully broke for prayer when they were in meetings. They were obviously dedicated Muslims, but they never flaunted it to me. They never offended me with it at all.

Of course, I had to conform to some extent. I didn't have much sympathy for the Westerners that came into the Kingdom and got all upset because they had to adjust to prayer times and so forth. After all, we went there voluntarily, and if that was the law of the land, that is what we had to accept. The ones that went there and complained and were very unhappy about it were those who, in my opinion, were usually not tolerant themselves. They were not considerate of the fact that they had voluntarily entered someone else's culture and should abide by it.

We can certainly think back in our own country to times when we had (and still have) extremists. These people have been more or less isolated for thousands of years, and we seem to think they should be just like us. I never had much trouble with that. I just set it aside and adjusted.

There were converts to Islam among the expats, but not many Westerners. They were mostly Orientals. Periodically the names of converts would be published, and they would usually be Korean, Malaysian, or Filipino.

Most Christians are not aware of the common ground that they share with Muslims. It would be helpful if they were.

The word "Islam" means "submission to God, or Allah," which name is interchangeable among the Muslims. "Allah" means "The Powerful One" or "The Exalted One."

All three religions, — Judaism, Christianity, and Islam — regard this one God as all-powerful, all-knowing, all-present and all-compassionate. All three affirm that He created the heavens and the earth, that he made man good, but man has fallen from his original state of perfection, and that prophets have been sent by God to call man to repentance. All three warn

Overtones — Religious and Political

of the coming of a great day of judgement and offer the hope of a final resurrection from the dead.

I wish to quote here from an article in the Winter 1988 issue of the Principia College Alumni Magazine entitled "The Bible and the Koran" by Archibald Carey, Jr., PhD, Professor Emeritus of Philosophy at Principia College in St. Louis, Missouri:

> "Mohammed transformed a small group of warring tribes in one of the most desolate areas of the world into the foundation of a great empire that at its height controlled more area than that of the Roman Empire and that founded great universities which kept the arts and sciences alive when Europe floundered in medieval barbarism.
>
> "Mohammed is in accord with what most of us would agree are some of the finest spiritual insights in the Bible. He calls for mercy, for kindness, for charity, for brotherly love, for justice, for greater social equality, for the acceptance of all races as the creation of God, and for the worship of one God as the God of all mankind.
>
> "Perhaps one of the most important similarities between the Bible and the Koran is that both scriptures speak out to the most godlike aspects of humanity, and as we respond we may yet transform ourselves and our world community for the better."

The Palestinians were throughout the Middle East. Again, the image that they have in the eyes of the West, is really different from what they are. They are a highly intelligent people, very educated. The main reason, I see, that the problem has developed as it has with America, Israel, and the Palestinians is that the Palestinians, when they were unjustly evicted from their lands, did not fall down and roll over. They resisted and stood up for their legitimate rights. The reason Israel and

Jebel Dhahran and the New Saudi Generation

the United States don't want to talk to the PLO is that they are the only ones who are organized to do anything for the Palestinians in general. There are many Palestinians in Saudi Arabia. They are mostly administrators, money people. I never met a Palestinian who didn't feel that the PLO was his or her legitimate representative.

It was some time before I realized that many people who you thought were Lebanese were really Palestinian. Most of the main people of CCC, the large Lebanese contractor that came to do the Phases II, III, and IV work, including the project managers on site — Fawzi Germanus, Raymond Ghannoum, and Mohammed Saudi — were really Palestinian. I remember one time I made a comment that I thought Israel had taken over in Palestine, and there wasn't much that could be done about it. It seemed that way to me at that time. The reply I received showed that in their mind, they were never going to accept that. They said, "Of course, there is something that can be done." Well, that was over fifteen years ago, and it has gotten worse. The fact is that they do not see it as an impossible correction to make. They never will give up trying.

We became good friends with some of the Palestinians and their wives at the university. When you talked to them, you found that they were born in places like Jaffa, Bethlehem, and Nazareth. That was their home. Imagine to yourself if you were suddenly thrown out of Texas and you were born in Waco, Dallas, Houston, San Antonio, or Austin and you couldn't go back. If you did manage to return, you would be going to your home, which was now occupied and under the control of a foreign country. How would you feel?

There were many young Palestinians with the contractors, Palestinians who were born outside of Israel or Palestine. Their fathers had been dispossessed. Some had lost hundreds of acres of land, just driven out. It's not hard to see why they felt the way they did.

Overtones — Religious and Political

Often Americans came over and felt that they should adopt an anti-Jewish stance. One American engineer in our office in particular, had the most rabid anti-Jewish philosophy of anybody I knew. He was so rabid that it turned you off. I was inclined to be pro-Arab, feeling that the Arabs had a lot of justice on their side. He was so anti-Jewish, that he almost made you feel pro-Jewish, because of the inclination to help the underdog or the person being attacked. However, he was just as rabid about blacks, indicating an obvious prejudice, a deep-seated bias in his thinking. I remember Mansour al-Saber saying one time, "We don't want you to be necessarily 'pro-Arab.' What we want is fairness. We want you to see both sides of the matter."

The Saudis didn't feel good if you would spout off against the Jews. In the first place, they weren't at all sure you weren't just saying that to win their favor. In the second place, in centuries past, the Jews and Arabs have lived together peacefully. So, their attitude was not just anti-Jewish, although it was anti-Zionist. They felt that a great injustice had been done to the Arabs.

Dr. Bakhrebah once commented, "As far as I am concerned, I am not anti-Jewish per se. I think through our history as Arab people, we have shown this, although we are strongly anti-Zionist. That is a political statement that I am making, rather than a religious one. I am not anti-Jewish. I am not anti-Buddhist. I am not anti-Christian. I am not anti-Hindu or whatever religion."

It is recorded history that when President Roosevelt went over and met with King Abdul Aziz, there were promises made that were not fulfilled because of Roosevelt's death. Prior to that, the British role in Palestine was one which has commonly been called a "betrayal." In 1948, when the Israeli state was founded, the Saudis saw this as a great injustice, and there has been no concerted effort made to correct it, until recently. You can read dissertations on both sides, of course.

Perhaps the Palestinian problem did become a "cause célèbre" with the Saudis, but it was nonetheless indicative to them of an overall injustice towards the Arabs.

CHAPTER 19

VISITORS

During the first seven or eight years we were at the university, it was really the showplace of the Kingdom. There was nothing else in Saudi Arabia that could compare with it. Whenever dignitaries would visit the Kingdom, most would first go to Riyadh, which was where the King resided. Then they would be scheduled to go to Dhahran to see the university. While we were there, there were visits by Queen Elizabeth (she addressed the faculty and students) and Prince Philip of England, the King and Queen of Spain, the President of France, the Queen of Denmark, the King and Queen of Malaysia, and others. The highest-ranking Americans that visited that I knew of were the Secretary of Defense, the Secretary of State and Vice-President George Bush. The Saudis were proud to show it off.

The last four or five years, however, they had many other completed projects in the Kingdom to show. But I think the university remains one of the best things that has been done. It is still a showplace.

About three months after we arrived at the university in November 1975, an international conference on solar energy had been scheduled to convene. This seemed a rather ambitious undertaking for the university, which was in the early stages of development.

This created an interesting opportunity to put the facilities to use and to observe what the Saudis could do with them. I was imbued with the sense of responsibility that we were there to see that it came off properly, since much of Phases II and III had just been completed. For instance, the 800-seat auditorium with its simultaneous interpretation facilities had never been used.

Jebel Dhahran and the New Saudi Generation

The main concern that we had was the sound system and the simultaneous interpretation. Neither Don nor I was an electronics expert, and the system as we tested it had operational difficulties. There were no real experts there. There was a fellow in charge of electronics for the university, a Pakistani, Brahim, who tried valiantly. All I can remember is his incessant "testing 1, 2, 3, 4 — testing 1, 2, 3, 4 — testing 1, 2, 3, 4." But he didn't really know much about it.

The night before the conference, we were in the interpretation booths trying to make the system work, unsuccessfully. The next day we again tested it unsuccessfully. Zaki Yamani was to open the conference, and when he first spoke we really didn't know whether it was going to work or not. To our surprise, it did, and everything went fine.

The Saudis didn't have people that could interpret simultaneously, so what they did was to have a prepared text in front of them, and as the speaker would speak in English, the translation was made in the booths by the interpreters from the English text into Arabic and French. This gave a fairly good simulation of simultaneous interpretation.

The solar energy conference went very well, and there were many technical papers presented by engineers and scientists from all over the world. The idea of having the conference was to show that the Saudis had an interest in all forms of energy and that Saudi Arabia is not totally hung up on oil. The Saudis recognize that there are other vital sources of energy that would and should be developed. Solar energy should be as much of a resource in Saudi Arabia as oil. That was the main thrust of the conference. There were several professors at the university who were particularly interested in solar energy. We remodeled one of the existing buildings to install solar collectors, to provide research data, and to perform tests on solar energy.

Queen Elizabeth and Prince Philip visit UPM - 1979

Jebel Dhahran and the New Saudi Generation

In January of 1977, our daughter Cheryl went on a trip to Africa with her college group from Principia College in St. Louis. She spent several weeks in Kenya, and we thought that it was an opportunity for her to visit us in Saudi Arabia. So I managed to get her an entry visa.

The plan, according to the college people, was that when they got ready to leave Kenya, she would go with them to Cairo, and then take the plane from there to Dhahran. That just didn't set well with me. I had been to Cairo by myself the summer before and it was the most confusing airport I had seen. I couldn't imagine a 19 year-old girl, never having traveled in the Middle East, negotiating that transfer.

I said that she should get a flight from Nairobi to Jeddah, and I would meet her in Jeddah. The idea was that somebody would be with her in Nairobi when she got on the plane. I could call if she didn't arrive on schedule and see what happened. If need be I could go down to Nairobi to meet her. Mainly I would be able to communicate, and she would be with her friends. So that was what we finally settled on.

The college group left Nairobi for London at night and Cheryl's plane to Jeddah didn't leave till the next morning. There was a British lady, Lady Erskine, a plantation owner's wife, who was well known to the Principia group. She took care of her that night and got her on the plane the next day.

I flew to Jeddah to meet her at the designated flight of Pakistani Airlines. It didn't arrive on time. It was very hot and humid. I went back and forth between the place where you had to meet the planes and where you had to find out arrival information. This was the old airport in Jeddah. Finally the plane came in about four or five hours late. It was one of those airports where you can't see who is coming until the person walks out the door. Finally down this long corridor I saw her coming. She had on her prescribed long flowing dress carrying big African baskets over her shoulder.

Visitors

We had reservations on a plane for Dhahran late that night. I was staying in the Khandara Palace Hotel. Jeddah was the same as Riyadh and Dhahran. There were not many good hotels at that time. The Khandara Palace was probably the best. It was interesting because you had the feeling you were back in time, with Egyptian waiters dressed in their long galabias and turbans. That evening before our flight we visited an exhibit in the hotel where a French company was selling gold, diamonds, and all kinds of highly priced jewelry. All the world was trying to get its hands on some of the oil money that was floating around. We then left Jeddah and flew to Dhahran.

We came into our house about midnight, and Mildred was anxiously waiting for us. Cheryl spent about seven weeks with us there and was able to get a job substitute-teaching at Mildred's school. She was taking education courses, but she had never taught. It was good experience, and the school insisted on paying her. During the seven weeks there she made money to take home. Part of her college course was writing a report of this trip, a sort of written presentation with slides. She had put that together and was able to try it out on our friends. It turned out very well. She had some great pictures and a very good presentation.

An interesting incident occurred in 1979. I received a telex from Conrad Neal in the CRS office in Houston saying that a friend of CRS's, a well-known columnist from the Houston Post, Lynn Ashby, was coming to Dhahran, arriving on a certain KLM flight. I was to meet him at the airport and show him around. I met him as requested and got him checked in at the Marriott Hotel.

I had organized an agenda of things for him to do. I took him to the U.S. consulate to interview people. We had a party for him one night with some American university professors there. Being a journalist, he was always mentally or physically

Lynn Ashby at Hofuf - 1979

Lunch in Hofuf Oasis - 1976
Bill and Aileen Caudill, Mildred, Warren and Carol Phillips

Visitors

taking notes and gathering information that was useful. One time we took him to visit a Saudi friend of ours, so he got to see a very fine young Saudi family and talk to them. We took him out to Hofuf, the old town west of Dhahran. He took pictures and visited the camel market. We did just about everything we knew to do with him.

When he got back to Houston, he wrote a series of articles with pictures in the Post about his visit. Now, in retrospect, I realize this was a very risky thing to do as far as I was concerned, because he didn't really enter Saudi Arabia as an approved journalist. He entered as a "communications expert," so-called, and he came on an invitational "inaugural flight" of KLM. He probably got as many pictures and as much information as anyone ever did in that short a time. His articles were very well done. There was really nothing offensive in them that I could see. In fact they were complimentary to Saudi Arabia.

Just to show how quickly such things are observed, however, he quoted in one of his articles something one of the guests at our party had said and even mentioned the professor's name. The professor told me later that about a week afterwards his Saudi chairman called him in and handed him the article and said, "How about this?" But there really was nothing offensive in his articles, so I never heard any objections. In fact, I think they were well received, because the Saudis got some publicity that was not unfavorable, which wasn't easy for them to come by in those days.

Several months after we arrived, the university announced there was to be a talk by the United States ambassador to Saudi Arabia, who was just at the point of terminating. His name was James Akins. He was going to give a talk in the auditorium, and Zaki Yamani was going to introduce him. The talk was in English, and it was attended mostly by the faculty.

Jebel Dhahran and the New Saudi Generation

Zaki Yamani introduced him in glowing and affectionate terms. The Saudis really thought a lot of him. They thought of him as a friend, and they hated to see him retire as the ambassador. I think this was because he seemed to be understanding and sympathetic to their cause. In his talk he made no bones about the fact that he had gotten cross-wise with Henry Kissinger, probably for the above reason, so he was relieved.

He told about how the oil embargo came about and the price of oil had shot up. He told about the early days after World War II when Coca-Cola was more expensive than oil. There was a great inequity that existed as far as the Saudis and their oil were concerned. They were being exploited.

Akins said that he was held responsible by the U.S. government for the Saudis getting the idea of the oil embargo and raising the prices. He denied that this was true. He said, "After all, they had the same slide rules that I did. They could figure it out. It didn't take a genius to see what would happen if the price of oil came up to what was proper." In the early days, it was something like one dollar per barrel.

He blamed the Saudis, however, for not doing a better public relations job. To this day, of course, there are reasons why they can't seem to do a good public relations job in the States. James Akins became a private consultant, because he had a great knowledge of oil and the Middle East.

The strange thing to me is that many of the ex-ambassadors and ex-diplomats to the Middle East come back to the U.S.A., and they obviously have a correct understanding of the Middle East and its problems. They bring this knowledge back but nobody listens or wants to listen.

The general attitude of the Saudis at that time seemed to be, "Why should we finance the extravagance of the West?" America with a population of five percent of the world uses twenty-five percent of its oil and gas. There was obviously a great inequity existing. Why should the U.S. consume most of the resources? Obviously the U.S. was using more than it needed in compari-

Don Chambers, "Muff" and Charles Lawrence

Mildred with Charles Lawrence

Jebel Dhahran and the New Saudi Generation

son to the rest of the world. So the Saudi attitude was, "Why should we finance that with unreasonably low oil prices?"

Another distinguished visitor who came to the university and spoke in 1978 was Senator William Fulbright. I was unaware until that time that Fulbright was sympathetic to the Arab cause. He was very knowledgeable about the area and felt that there were adjustments that needed to be made. Apparently, that was the reason he was defeated by the Jewish lobby. Like Akins, he had a lot of interesting things to say.

In the spring of 1976 the university decided to start a department of architecture. Bill Caudill, chairman of CRS was asked by the rector to come over and help set it up. He made a presentation of a possible organization and curriculum. The university did get the department started the next fall. It took a couple of years to get fully into an architectural program. King Faisal University already had an architectural design program, so this was supposed to be more in the nature of architectural engineering. However, it developed in several years into a full-fledged architectural design curriculum.

While Bill Caudill and his wife, Aileen, were there, we took them out to Hofuf and showed them the old town and the old souq. We went to the potter and the caves. They had a great time, and it was enjoyable to have them there.

In 1984, Tom Bullock, then chairman of CRS, expressed the thought in Houston that it would be appropriate if Charles Lawrence could visit some of the buildings he had so successfully designed in Saudi Arabia but had never seen. Lawrence had retired in 1981 and his ability was appreciated and respected at UPM.

A visit was arranged for him and his wife, "Muff," who had never been to Saudi Arabia. Dr. Bakhrebah enthusiastically arranged for this visit to take place. Unfortunately, when Charles and "Muff" arrived, Dr. Bakr and Dr. Bakhrebah were both out of the country on business. However, Charles did get to see the fruits of his original conceptions, and I'm sure it must have been gratifying.

He participated in a seminar with the Saudi architectural students in a beautiful new building he designed on the campus which twenty years earlier, on his first visit, was the barren Jebel Dhahran — the geological outcropping which Fred Davies of SOCAL had looked at longingly from Bahrain fifty years before. By no stretch of the wildest imagination, could Davies have imagined the amazing changes that would take place there.

CHAPTER 20

EXTRACURRICULAR — 1975 TO 1986

One thing that made the experience more satisfying to me professionally — and probably was an important part of my good relations with the Saudis —was "extracurricular" architectural work that I did, besides performing construction administration duties on the buildings that CRS designed. My contract with CRS stated that I should not get involved in any enterprise that constituted a conflict of interest with my work at UPM. Since all of this work was UPM-related, I felt that I could rationalize that it was in accordance with these guidelines, on the assumption that it didn't interfere with my official work.

Within a year or two, there were some extracurricular projects on campus that needed to be done. I took them on and soon was working on a variety of such projects. I would work on them at home at night. It was diversionary for me and in a sense was a form of recreation. They turned out to be some very interesting projects, because they allowed me to do some design-work and work outside of the normal CRS/UPM format.

The CRS attitude towards this sort of thing was not necessarily negative. I discussed it several times with Joe Thomas. His attitude was, "If everything goes all right and it creates good relations with the client, fine. If you get into trouble, you're on your own."

As far as the extra things which I did for the university were concerned, many of them were too small for CRS to be bothered with. It would be too expensive. CRS was getting to the point where it had to charge for everything. It couldn't afford to do a lot of free work. If the university wanted CRS to do something, there had to be a fee proposal. If I did it, and it came off all right, the university was happy. None of my extracurricular work involved large projects, but a number of them were unique.

Jebel Dhahran and the New Saudi Generation

One very interesting extracurricular project was the installation of the first seismic monitoring station in Saudi Arabia, one that could record earthquakes around the world. This was done at the instigation of Dr. Adnan Niazy, who was instrumental in promoting it. He was chairman of the geology department and a fine scientist.

We had never heard or read anything about earthquakes in Saudi Arabia. However, Dr. Daboussi, who was instrumental in establishing the new Energy Lab, became interested in the subject of earthquakes. Our buildings were not designed to earthquake criteria since that area is not classified as an earthquake zone. Harry Cretin talked with some of the university faculty on the subject. He wrote to Don Chambers suggesting that we should give it consideration.

For my own enlightenment, I wrote to a geologist friend of mine in Houston. He sent me maps which showed continental plates colliding just east of the Persian Gulf. The collision zone formed the Zagros Mountains in Iran and is the source of severe earthquakes in that country. The maps also showed earthquakes had occurred in the Red Sea and in Yemen. In 1982, there was a severe earthquake in North Yemen, which probably generated the impetus for consideration and study of earthquakes in our area.

The following is a generalized summary of seismicity associated with the Arabian continental plate according to my friend in Houston:

"Most of the country of Saudi Arabia has a history of being seismically inactive, and for a very good reason. The country occupies the central portion of the Arabian continental plate. The edges of this tectonic plate are seismically active but only the western boundary of the country is coincident with an edge of the Arabian plate, and today the seismic activity along the western edge of the plate is minimal. The remainder of the seismically active boundary of the plate is well separated from Saudi

Extracurricular - 1975 to 1986

Arabia by several countries: Jordan, Syria, Iraq on the north; Iran on the east; Oman and Yemen on the south. Hence most of Saudi Arabia ends up being located on a relatively stable piece of the Arabian continental plate. Seismic activity in the countries mentioned above range from mild to severe with highly destructive activity concentrated along a line marked by the Zagros Mountains which run from the northern tip of Iraq southeasterly through Iran to the Gulf of Oman.

"It would not be surprising for someone in Dhahran to feel a tremor originating from an especially strong crustal movement along the Zagros line. To what degree the tremor would be felt, would of course, be dependent upon several factors (type of soil upon which one is standing, location of the epicenter, etc.)"

And so it happened one day in 1984. June Brandie and I were standing at the file cabinets when suddenly everything seemed to roll and the floor under us felt that it was moving. Our first instinct was to run for the door, but in a few seconds it stopped. Then our reaction was, "Did you feel that? Did it really happen?" At first we thought it might be the effects of blasting, which often occurred, but this felt different. Then the thought of an earthquake occurred to us – but that seemed out of the question. In the *Arab News* the next day, there was a report that others had felt it also, and it was thought to have been an earthquake. So, we began to think that the idea of earthquake studies for Dhahran was not so farfetched after all.

Another project of note was a unique sundial that was designed by one of the Egyptian-American professors, Dr. Nagib Daniel. He originally made it with his students out of concrete. When Phase IV was being built, Dr. Bakhrebah said, "We'll make it a monument." It was in the form of a crescent, the

Jebel Dhahran and the New Saudi Generation

Arabic symbol, and according to Dr. Daniel, it was one of a kind. The crescent was set at precisely the right angle to the sun. All the calculations were done by Dr. Daniel. There was an aluminum pencil rod that was suspended through the center of it. It would record the time of day according to the sun, in Arabic and English, year round with certain corrections. Certainly, I had not seen anything like it before. The new version that we were going to build, had to be done appropriately, not out of concrete. It was to be a change order to CCC's contract.

We decided to make it out of granite. Dr. Bakhrebah wanted to use Saudi granite, produced over in the Taif area. But there was no one in the area who could put it together. The Italians are really the best marble and granite workers. So, CCC had to buy the rough blocks of granite from a company in Jeddah and ship them to Torino, Italy. Then, I worked through correspondence with the people there who were going to make it. Dr. Daniel was on leave that year in Florida, so I had to communicate with him there. This thing was so technical, so precise, that if it was made wrong, it would be of no use. Through elaborate shop drawings prepared by the Italians, I was able to satisfy myself that it was accurate and precise enough. The Italian company constructed it and shipped it to Dhahran.

Dr. Bakhrebah and I then had to decide where to locate it. It was monumental and needed a proper setting, where it would be available but not subject to damage. We went to the top of the Administration Building, looked down on the Medan, and agreed on a spot. Finally, it was installed under the supervision of an Italian, who was sent down from Torino. It turned out to be a handsome piece of sculpture and a useful monument.

An extracurricular assignment of a different nature occurred in 1981. The rector's brother was deputy mayor of Taif. Taif is the summer capital, you might say, for the government. The climate is very pleasant in the hot summer months. There are

Extracurricular - 1975 to 1986

many palaces there, so it's a very important area. The municipal government was reorganizing its public works office for building permits and various controls. The rector sent over a team from UPM for advice and consultation, and he appointed me to it. My area was supposed to be "beautification." I went with the team and consulted with the Taif officials on the various aspects of city beautification.

A young Saudi professor of architecture, Farouk Konash, and I were a team. He had done his undergraduate work at UPM and received his architecture degree from the University of Arizona, and he was very talented. I wrote a report while there on the beautification of Taif. I don't know what was done with it. Farouk translated it into Arabic, and I assume it was useful.

A master plan for Taif had been prepared by a German firm which, to my mind, was totally unimplementable. I pointed this out in a diplomatic way in my report. Something had to be done, but it would have to be a little here and a little there, according to an overall concept. The German firm was superimposing a new city over an old city. I was sure that it couldn't be done.

Another extracurricular project, through Mansour al-Saber, was for Prince Abdul Aziz bin Salman. The prince's father was governor of Riyadh, and his brother was Prince Sultan, the first Arab astronaut. Prince Abdul Aziz had graduated from UPM, where Mansour had known him.

The prince's father had a palace in al-Khobar and Prince Abdul Aziz was going to live in it, since he was soon going to be married. Apparently the prince had asked Mansour to remodel this palace.

Mansour had an insatiable desire to work. He wanted to learn about everything, and he would tackle any job. As opposed to Dr. Bakhrebah, he'd get in with the nitty gritty to implement things. Dr. Bakhrebah was very good on broad concepts and high-level administration. Mansour would take it and get it done.

Jebel Dhahran and the New Saudi Generation

One day, Mansour asked me to come meet him at the palace. At first, it was just little things. He didn't like this light fixture here, or he wanted to do something over there. I'd give an opinion, and many times it turned out well.

The family palace had originally been done by a Lebanese. The interior was not really "elegant." It was "lavish" in a Lebanese style. The prince wanted to gut it completely and redo it. He had another architect on that. Finally, I agreed to help Mansour on the exterior design. I made a little perspective. A perspective with color usually goes over big. Whether we could implement it exactly as shown was the question, and apparently it was going to have some problems. The design was used to a certain extent.

It was quite nice when it was finished. Mansour deserved much of the credit. I met with Prince Abdul Aziz a number of times. He was a very pleasant fellow and bore a strong resemblance to his grandfather, the great King Abdul Aziz, when he was a young man.

One time we were sitting and talking. I said something about the theme that I wrote back in college to let him know I was not just recently interested in the Arabs.

He said, "Well, now that you have been here for ten years, what do you think of us?"

His question was direct and really put me on the spot. I said I thought the Saudis were a people with great talent, a tremendous potential, and that they had a great opportunity. I felt that they had made the most of it, but I thought it would take the future to tell the extent of their success.

Sometime in 1977, Dr. Bakhrebah told Don Chambers that two dilapidated brick piers just north of the U.S. consulate were of historical significance and should be preserved. Express Contracting Company had been using them to mark the entrance to the site of the 189 houses project. With all the trucks

Original brick piers

King Abdul Aziz Monument

Residental Mosque

Sundial on Medan Plaza

and vehicles passing through them, it was surprising that they were still standing.

We then put a fence around them for protection. Dr. Bakhrebah said that he wanted them made into some sort of monument. That assignment fell to me.

The significance of these piers was that they were erected by Aramco back in 1939 to mark the entrance to the campsite for King Abdul Aziz, when he came to inaugurate the flow of oil to the world from the newly discovered oil wells in the Eastern Province of Saudi Arabia.

I wrote to Floyd Ohliger, who was living in retirement in Pennsylvania, to confirm the authenticity of the piers and their original purpose. He had been the manager of Aramco's operations during its earlier days in the 1930s.

He replied (Appendix III) and confirmed that the piers were, indeed, authentic, and he described the purpose for which they were built — to mark the entrance to the King's campsite. There were no roads, at that time, so some identification was necessary.

When we received the assignment from Dr. Bakhrebah, CCC was working in the area, so we gave CCC the job of building the monument as a change order to its contract. We restored the piers to their original appearance in a permanent way and created a circular platform around them. I designed a wall behind them containing a large granite (from Taif quarries) plaque with an Arabic inscription prepared by Dr. Bakhrebah (Appendix IV). To be able to read the inscription, the visitor would have to walk through the very location where King Abdul Aziz had walked over fifty years before.

When Crown Prince Fahd visited in 1981, he asked Dr. Bakr where we got the history. Dr. Bakr told him that we had researched it from Aramco records. Prince Fahd seemed impressed and pleased. He had a great affection for his father.

Saudi Arabia does not have many monuments to individuals. This is one of the few, I'm sure. On the granite plaque was

Jebel Dhahran and the New Saudi Generation

engraved the likeness of King Abdul Aziz. The carving and inscription were done by a noted Egyptian sculptor who was doing work for the new conference center at that time.

Another project occurred in 1978. After the contract was awarded to CCC for Phase IV, the largest phase of the university project, I noticed the name of the electrical contractor. I knew that a classmate of mine at Rice University was chairman of that company, Fisk Electric Company.

The next thing I knew, my classmate, Lloyd Davis, appeared on the scene, and we renewed our friendship of almost forty years. From then on he would come to al-Khobar about every six months or so, and we would visit. We knew each other at Rice (then called Rice Institute) in 1940. My first professional job in the summer of 1941 was in Galveston with the Corps of Engineers, and Lloyd also worked there that summer. So, we went way back, and here we were almost forty years later 10,000 miles from home working on the same project.

In 1978, on one of his trips to Saudi Arabia, Lloyd asked to meet with me. Mildred and I went down to al-Khobar where his project manager, Jimmy Willamet, and his wife had a villa. Lloyd then asked me if I would design a villa and an office building for him. His Saudi partner was one of the big families in Saudi Arabia, the al-Qahtani's. Their joint company was called Qahtani-Fisk. I hated to pass up the opportunity. Of course, this sort of thing might be questionable as far as CRS was concerned, since there might appear to be a conflict of interest. But there wasn't. I wouldn't allow it to be.

It took a year to develop the design and the drawings. Construction began in 1979. Jimmy Willamet, who was from New Orleans, and I worked closely for a year. Lloyd wasn't there most of the time, of course, but he arranged for most of the furnishings. He was quite a connoisseur of art with an

Extracurricular - 1975 to 1986

uncanny knack for stumbling across valuable objects. Once rummaging through an old shop in Jeddah, he came upon a vase that his instinct told him was not just any old vase. He bought it for a low price. Having it appraised later in London, he confirmed it to be a Chinese vase from an ancient dynasty.

The design that I did was influenced as much as anything by the work that I had done with MacKie and Kamrath in Houston, whose architectural style was inevitably along the lines of Frank Lloyd Wright, which would be an innovation in Saudi Arabia. It took about a year to build the project, and then Lloyd brought over all of his furnishings. The building was finished in May of 1980.

Lloyd was chairman of the board of Fisk Electric and Telephone Company overall. The president of the telephone company was James Lovell, the astronaut of Apollo 8 and 13, the mission that got in trouble and ended up going around the moon and coming back safely with a disabled craft. Another good friend of ours, Scott Pendleton, a young man who had graduated from Texas A&M University in journalism, was working in al-Khobar for the *Arab News*. His father had known Lloyd when they were both in the Young Presidents Organization in Houston.

The villa was designed mainly for entertaining. It had a large living area two stories high, where Lloyd could entertain about 100 people. He could have parties and invite all the Aramco people that he was interested in. The first party was in May 1980. Lovell, Lloyd, and Scott were there, and it was a great party. Most of Fisk's workers were Filipinos. In order to make them happy, Jimmy had bought a lot of musical instruments to enable them to have a band. They are very good musicians and could put on a good performance. Lloyd was back in the days when I had my dance band at Rice — when we played Glenn Miller's "Moonlight Serenade" and that sort of thing. The villa had a cantilevered balcony projecting over

Jebel Dhahran and the New Saudi Generation

the living area below. Suddenly the sounds of "Moonlight Serenade" wafted from the balcony. Lloyd had put all the Filipino musicians up on the balcony. It was a great touch, but I told Lloyd later that the balcony really wasn't designed for that kind of load. But, nothing happened.

From then on until we left in 1986, Fisk had parties several times a year. Sometimes, even Qahtani came. When Jimmy Willamet left, a young man named Clark Battle, also from New Orleans, became project manager for Fisk. We became good friends.

The villa really served its purpose well. I was keeping my fingers crossed, however, about the fact that I had done this work. I eventually told Don Chambers. Here I had done all this work without his knowing it, which wasn't exactly "kosher" (if you will pardon the expression). Don said, "It's strange you didn't tell me anything about this." I said, "If I had told you about it, it never would have worked."

All of these things were enjoyable, although they took a lot of work. In a way, work was recreation — diversionary work, that is. Fisk eventually sold it's half of the company to a British firm, which later sold it to Qahtani. Now the entire company is owned by the Saudis.

(Post Script 1991 — The last Iraqi Scud missile, which destroyed the Army barracks and killed 28 U.S. soldiers at the end of the Gulf War, hit about four blocks from the Qahtani-Fisk building.)

An extracurricular project on campus which was especially gratifying to me was a mosque. UPM wanted to build a small one in the residential area and apparently didn't ask CRS to do it.

The Saudis had hired a local firm that had a British designer. He had designed the mosque, and they were getting ready to build it. One day Mansour called and asked me to come over to a meeting. He didn't tell me what it was about.

Extracurricular - 1975 to 1986

When I arrived at the meeting, there were the contractor and the architect for the mosque. They were discussing details. I feigned disinterest, because I didn't see how I had time to get involved in it. I told him I couldn't be involved. Several weeks later, I thought I had divested myself of it, but he called me again and said, "You've got to help us with this mosque." He had gotten cross-wise with the architects and had fired everybody. Now, he wanted to build it and needed help. At that point, I saw no choice but to help him get it done. The basic design was there. But the implementation, the detail, the finesse, you might say, was still to be done. Piece by piece, I helped him put it together with some revisions. The basic structure didn't change. Mainly, I helped with the development of the aesthetics of it.

The minaret was pretty much a replica of the minarets on the Grand Mosque in Mecca. It had a large globular element on top with the "hilal", which is the spire or crescent that is usually on top. It looked totally inappropriate to me, because the mosque had a certain contemporary look about it. I told Mansour, "I know you probably like that minaret. I hope you'll not be offended, if I tell you that I think you'll be criticized if you put it up this way, certainly by the UPM architecture department."

I made some alternative sketches and showed them to him. He did what I recommended to the top of the minaret. Then we put an interesting hilal on top, which was made in Damascus. It turned out well. I helped him with every detail: light fixtures, landscaping, etc. However, I felt later that he gave me more credit than I deserved. He always referred to that as being a little "jewel" of a mosque. And it truly was.

I learned a lot from that. I told some friends in the States of that experience, and they seemed to think that I must have converted to being a Muslim. They thought that nobody could work on or go into a mosque who was not a Muslim. Well, that isn't true. Mansour and I went all over Saudi Arabia looking at mosques. He would take me in to show me the various designs, because he wanted me to see them. There was never any question. Everybody knew that I was a Christian. I had to take off my shoes, of course. There really are a lot of misconceptions about many of these things. In this residential mosque, there was a balcony for the ladies to pray. Mansour said a mosque in the old days was almost a community center. He remembered studying in the Grand Mosque in Mecca. There was an extensive library there used by students and others.

From September 1983 to September 1984, Dr. Bakhrebah was on a year's sabbatical leave in the States. Sometime in March 1984, I got a call at home at lunchtime. I used to go home for lunch and sit and take a nap for a half hour. It was Dr. Bakhrebah's Indian secretary, Karimullah. He said Dr. Bakhrebah was in town and wanted me to come up to his office at once. When I arrived, Dr. Bakhrebah told me that UPM wanted to build an elementary school. He wanted me to take the afternoon off and lay out a schematic design. He showed me the area that he was thinking of using, which was where the Koreans had their working camp, but they were soon due to move. He wanted me to make a master plan layout for a Saudi school — a kindergarten, a boys' elementary and a girls' elementary. He wanted it by 7:00 o'clock that night. He then called in one of the Saudi professors, Dr. Abdul Aziz Almana, to give me a briefing as to size, the number of students, etc. I had performed pretty rapidly for Dr. Bakhrebah on previous occasions, so he seemed to feel that I could do it.

This school idea had been kicking around for a long time. The Muslim children, the children of the Saudi professors, were having to be bussed off the campus to school some distance away. There was a desire to set up a school on campus, so they wouldn't have to do that.

Dr. Bakhrebah had returned from the U.S. to Dhahran to celebrate the birth of his first son, Abdullah. He already had

Extracurricular - 1975 to 1986

four lovely daughters and as with all Saudi fathers, he was anxiously hoping this time for a son. While there, he learned of the efforts to get the school started. So, he grabbed the ball. That was his "prime forte," getting things moving. He didn't believe in standing around and talking about it forever. After a certain length of time he wanted to get something done. I dare say, if he hadn't returned at that time and done what he did, the school might not be there today.

I dropped everything and went home. I began laying out a master plan in this area for the buildings that they wanted to build. That night at 7:00 o'clock, I met at Dr. Bakhrebah's house. Dr. Dabbagh was also present. They had comments and revisions, and we came up with a tentative plan.

There was going to be a small party for someone that evening given by the rector. It was for the ex-chief of police of al-Khobar. I was invited, so I went, even though I was going to have to work all night to have this thing done for Dr. Bakhrebah by 7:00 o'clock the next morning. I had a good Arabic meal, which was the main thing I was interested in, and I sat while everybody talked in Arabic. Finally, I went home and worked the rest of the night on this revised layout.

I came in at 7:00 o'clock and showed him what I had done. He wanted to present it at 8:00 o'clock to the communications committee. This was a forum where the deans and administration officials discussed things and decisions were made. We presented this to the committee. They discussed it and before we were through, Dr. Bakhrebah had gotten approval from the rector and the committee to proceed. He wanted to get started right away.

He then called the Koreans into his office and asked them to give him a price. They were rather taken aback and wanted to call their head office. They didn't know just what to do. Dr. Bakhrebah said he had two million riyals. The Koreans didn't know whether they could do it for that or not. In the end he got a tentative commitment from them.

Jebel Dhahran and the New Saudi Generation

In twenty-four hours, he had gotten preliminary plans and the Koreans' commitment to go ahead with it. He then said, "Gentlemen, I have to catch a plane at twelve o'clock (this was about 10:00 o'clock.) I'll be back in about six months, and I hope to see a school." With that he left.

It's not hard to see why Dr. Bakhrebah was secretary-general.

Then Mansour al-Saber took over, and we started to build the school. By October it was basically done. The criteria given to us were that it had to be inexpensive and it had to be built fast, so that was the basis on which it was done. It was on a sloping site, which made it rather difficult. One of the requirements was that we had to have walls around high enough not to see over, between the boys and the girls. The urgent thing seemed to be the kindergarten, so that was started first. It was sometime the next year before the boy's school and the girl's school were started. Then some landscaping was done.

By the fall of 1985, the school was functioning, and the students were all there. They had their own local teachers — Saudi and expat ladies on campus. Later several buildings, designed by the young Saudi architect, Farouk Konash, were added. That was in 1986, not too long before I left. Now, there is a complete mini-campus with temporary buildings. The plan was eventually to build a permanent school, but the way things were going, I would guess this temporary school will last a long time. Dr. Bakhrebah was talking about five years, but I'm sure it will be longer than that. It's always wise when building "temporary" buildings that they have some "permanent" qualities.

Dr. Hall had his office directly across the corridor from Dr. Bakr's. His official title was "senior adviser." He did much for the university as its adviser. Across from him and behind Dr. Bakr, an office was set aside for the chairman of the board of the university, Sheikh Zaki Yamani. To my knowledge, he never

Extracurricular - 1975 to 1986

used the office, but it remained there as long as the administration offices were in that building. When we built the new administration building, there was no office for him there. By this time, UPM was no longer under the Ministry of Petroleum and Minerals, Hisham Nazer was on the board, and Zaki Yamani was not.

In 1979, Dr. Hall was told that he was going to be moved down to the first floor to a rather small office. His retirement time was coming soon.

Dr. Hall made big contributions to the university, and the Saudis acknowledged it. Several commented to me that they respected him greatly. They appreciated what he had done. He made many comprehensive organizational studies and projections. He was also instrumental in hiring some of the top people around the world, because he was an internationally known educator.

In spite of this move downstairs, he wasn't willing to give up right away. One day he called me and said that he had gotten the approval of the rector to implement an idea that he had. This new space that was given him was susceptible to expansion, without any detriment to the building. Dr. Bakhrebah told me to look into it, and if it could, in fact, be done without compromising the building in any way, he would see about it.

I did this, and then went to the Koreans to see about building it with a minimum of time and money. It could be done very well. Dr. Bakhrebah gave the OK to go ahead. Dr. Hall ended up with better space than he had upstairs, although he was removed four floors from the rector. He remained happily there until he passed away in 1981. I often took visitors by to see him, because he was so interesting to talk to. He would tell about the early days of the university.

Dr. Bakhrebah had a very creative mind and dreamed up a number of extracurricular projects, some of which were

Jebel Dhahran and the New Saudi Generation

unique. One became known as the VIP Train Project. The many dignitaries that visited the university were always given a tour of the campus. Sometimes these were large groups, and it was quite a walk, at least an hour or two, often in the hot sun. Dr. Bakhrebah came up with the idea that they should have a passenger train like Disneyland. Visitors could ride around and see everything in comfort.

CRS in Houston made a study for routing with the modifications that would be required to the campus. The problem was that there were a number of places where there were steps. These had to be converted into ramps to allow a train to pass acceptably. A 6-7% slope is the most you can have satisfactorily. Dr. Bakhrebah came back from his sabbatical, and he wanted to get the project going. It was a project that he could grab hold of and get into the swing of things again after a year's absence. He got the Koreans and the Turks to submit prices.

The Koreans had the best price, as well as the boldness to enter into such a project. It required some design engineering on their part, since we didn't have any structural drawings. Some of it was a little tenuous, so we worked closely with them. In the meantime, the university had let a contract for the personnel vehicles according to CRS specifications. When the modifications were completed, there was one trial run. While it navigated all right, it apparently wasn't too successful, because it was never used again, to my knowledge. I think if loaded up with people, even with acceptable ramps, it still had a little scary feeling. There wasn't confidence that it was altogether safe. Nevertheless, the added ramps were useful on the campus for handicapped people and maintenance reasons. It was just one of those good ideas that didn't work out as planned.

Extracurricular - 1975 to 1986

In May of 1977, we received a communication from a *Christian Science Monitor* representative in London saying that he had been assigned to come to the Middle East to see about beginning distribution of the *Monitor* in that area. He wanted to know if we could give any idea of who a possible distributor might be in Saudi Arabia. I replied that it appeared to me that the best distributor in al-Khobar was an establishment called al-Khasindar. I then talked to the nephew of al-Khasindar and gave him the contact, Tony Periton, in London. Tony replied that actually he had already been considering him, and it did look as if he was probably the best one.

Tony and his wife, Jill, were coming down to Jeddah from London to visit with the U.S. vice-consul, John Owen. He was not going to get over to Dhahran. For something different, we decided to fly over to Jeddah to meet them. We were going to stay at the Khandara Palace Hotel.

We planned to leave Dhahran for Jeddah on a Wednesday evening. At about 9:00 o'clock in the morning of the Wednesday that we were going to leave, Dr. Bakhrebah called me and said that he wanted me to design a monumental arch. On the spur of the moment, King Khaled had announced that he was coming to the Eastern Province. They had been anticipating this, but they never could get the definite word on his visit. Finally the word came, and it was rather sudden. It was the first time he had officially visited the Eastern Province since becoming King after King Faisal was assassinated in March 1975. Immediately, everybody all over town went into frenzied activity to erect monumental royal arches.

Dr. Bakhrebah wanted one for the university. He wanted something impressive and indicative of the university. He had been allowed a space on the old road to the airport, and he wanted me to design something by noon. This was 9:00 o'clock in the morning. I had learned always to say, "OK, I'll try it" to Dr. Bakhrebah. Rarely ever did I say, "No, I can't do it." I sat down at my desk and started sketching. By noon, I had come up with what I thought would be an appropriate idea, monumental and reasonably simple to build, and indicative of the university.

First, I had to rush out to the road and see what the width was. I had to determine whether trucks could pass under it, what the height should be and so forth. Dr. Bakhrebah's man, Abbas, came to my office exactly at 12:00 o'clock wanting to know where the sketch was. I said, "You are going to have to give me until 2:00 o'clock." He left and returned exactly at 2:00 o'clock. By then, I had a finished sketch, in which I had the design pretty well established with some controlling dimensions on it and designation of materials and general construction method. He took that and rushed off.

That night, Mildred and I left for Jeddah. We visited there with the *Monitor* representative on Thursday and Friday. On Friday we returned to Dhahran about midnight. The King was supposed to arrive on Sunday. As we drove from the airport, we passed the location where the arch was supposed to be. Nothing. I thought, "Aha! They didn't do it after all."

The next morning, I called Abbas, who was in charge of it for Dr. Bakhrebah. I said, "What happened to the arch?" He replied, "We are working on it." I said, "What do you mean? I went by there at 12:00 o'clock last night, and there was nothing there." He said triumphantly, "We started on it about 1:00 o'clock this morning."

They worked all Friday night, all day Saturday, and Saturday night. Sunday morning it was ready for the King. So, he rode under the ceremonial arch erected by UPM. The design had two pylons on either side, indicative of the UPM water tower. Then it had an arch across the road with Arabic messages provided by Dr. Bakhrebah, flags and pictures of the King with lights at night. I must say, in all modesty, it was the most impressive arch in town.

Royal Arch for King Khaled's visit - 1977

Royal Guard

Jebel Dhahran and the New Saudi Generation

The university officials thought that they were going to leave it up for a while, because it was a fitting entrance from the airport. It stayed up about six weeks. Then they took it down, because it wasn't meant to be permanent. The basic structure was made of steel angles on a concrete foundation. This solid construction proved to be fortunate, because strong winds came up that night, and many arches around town were blown down. It was covered with plywood and painted. That was the kind of extracurricular assignment that really made the job interesting for me.

Shortly after that, the *Monitor* appeared in al-Khasindar's store. He would usually have about two dozen copies. I would check on them every week to see how they were moving. There didn't seem to be much movement.

This went on a few months, and then distribution stopped altogether. I went into the store one day and asked, "What happened to the *Monitor*?" The manager replied, "We didn't sell any." I said, "Give it a little time." Soon it reappeared. Within the next year the distribution improved. I'm sure some additional efforts were made from London to keep it going. It was then sold in the airport, in al-Khasindar's, and in at least three of the hotels. It was also eventually sold in the university book store.

Saudis that I knew appreciated this paper. When I was first interviewed by Dr. Bakhrebah in Houston in 1975, he said he read the *Monitor* regularly when he was in college in the United States. He commented, "It is a very good newspaper." I think that the Saudis appreciated what appeared to them as a rational, fair approach to things. They respected that.

John Cooley and Joseph Harsch's articles, as well as others, were often reprinted in the *Saudi Gazette*, an English-language Arab newspaper.

Extracurricular - 1975 to 1986
_____

There were many other extracurricular projects, but the above-mentioned were probably the most unique and interesting. They really gave me a more intimate view and association with the "New Generation of Saudis" than some of the official CRS work. I was happy that I had that opportunity.

SYMONDS' TRAVELS

CHAPTER 21

ARAB TRAVELS —
IN KINGDOM AND OUT

One of the fringe benefits of working in Saudi Arabia for most expatriates, including ourselves, was the opportunity that we had to travel. Situated halfway around the world from the United States, we could go almost anywhere on our way home. Every year, it was a matter of saying, "Where shall we go this time?"

The company would pay our way back to our home each year, in our case to Houston, a direct flight from Saudi Arabia to Houston and back. We could actually get a round-the-world ticket cheaper than we could get a direct round trip economy flight. So, we actually saved the company money by going around the world. Being loyal employees, we were quite willing to make that "sacrifice" for the company. We went around the world five times. Very often we came home at Christmas also, which the company didn't pay for. Sometimes we would get a cheap fare to London and then fly "standby" to Houston from London.

We visited 43 countries and came round trip to the U.S. at least 15 or 16 times. We flew on about 40 airlines for a total of about 300,000 miles. My boyhood dream of traveling around the world to exotic places became a reality.

Within months of our arrival in Dhahran in 1975, several of the professors, our friends and neighbors, Ed and Charlene Peattie, Clarence and Lois Beauchamp, Marie and Lewis Hatch decided that we would go to Jubail for a picnic. Jubail is about 75 miles north of Dhahran. By this time we had our Peugeot station wagon.

Jebel Dhahran and the New Saudi Generation

The contrast of Jubail then as opposed to what it became ten years later is unbelievable. It was still a sleepy little coastal village, although somewhat more than it was when the geologists first arrived from Bahrain to explore for oil 43 years before. It had a customs office, a market, and a few houses. Dredging had begun for the new harbor. There was a little island out there, which was later filled in and connected to the mainland. We went out to have our picnic on this little island.

One of the things about this trip, which became a conversation piece, was a wood door that I acquired there. This became famous with the CRS people. E.C. Kobs said that if anything happened to me, he wanted that door.

We were walking along near the water, and we came upon a free-standing concrete block wall. For what purpose it was built, was not apparent. It had a double door at one point, with very interesting wood motifs, not carving but appliqué, on it. One leaf was lying on the ground. The other was still hanging on the hinges. I was fascinated with it.

One of our neighbor ladies, who had been in Saudi Arabia a couple of years and had learned a little Arabic, was walking with me. The others had gone on ahead. I said, "I sure would love to have that door." She said, "Let's go ask for it." Around the corner was the customs house and a guard was standing there. We went over to him and she, with a little bit of Arabic that she knew, said something about "bab," which means "door." We convinced ourselves that he said it was all right to have it. I seriously doubt that he did say that. When we left to go home several hours later, we went around the corner to where the door was. We picked it up, put it on top of the station wagon, and headed for home.

We had it in our house standing in the corner, and it became "famous." I began to be concerned, however, that we had taken something that we shouldn't have, although due to our naiveté. It was just lying on the sand, and there didn't seem to be any reason why we shouldn't take it. That was how we rationalized.

Arab Travels — In Kingdom and Out

We didn't do anything to it but brush off the sand and set it in the corner. It was picturesque and remained in our house for eleven years. When we returned to the United States, we didn't know if anything was going to happen about it in customs or not. The Filipino moving company packed it up and shipped it. No problem.

The curious thing was that everybody admired it and would like to have had it. The next year, a teacher friend of Mildred's, a Russian-American, and her husband went to Jubail, and the other half of the door was still hanging there. They went to the guard and asked if they could have it. He said, "No." They said, "Well, some friends of ours were here last year, and they got a door." He replied, "If it's lying on the ground, it's o.k. If it's hanging on the wall, it's not o.k."

A short trip that we sometimes took close to us on the way to Jubail was a place called Tarut Island. This was twenty miles north of Dhahran. Access to it was by means of a causeway built across from the mainland. Its main activity was agricultural. This whole area was in what was called the Qatif oasis. The thing about Tarut was that historically it went back to the time when Bahrain was the ancient place called Dilmun. The artifacts there indicate history going back thousands of years. The inhabitants lived to themselves for centuries. They are fishermen as well as farmers. They go out into the Gulf to fish in the ancient boats they call "dhows." There are many natural springs that bubble up in the Gulf at that point.

An excursion that we often took was west of Dhahran about a hundred miles to the ancient town of Hofuf. This was in the al-Hasa oasis and claimed to be one of the oldest continuously inhabited towns in the world. I have seen pictures of Hofuf back in the early days of Aramco, and it hadn't changed a lot, the main street, bazaar, and the souq. It is changing now, however. There has been a lot of building, but

Jebel Dhahran and the New Saudi Generation

the arched souq remains and is still identifiable. The smell of spices with the native men and women squatting there selling everything: grain, spices, pots, rugs, daggers, and thobes — everything you could think of.

I mentioned earlier that we took Lynn Ashby of the Houston Post out there. He bought thobes for himself, his wife, and his children. Later, he wrote an article about the thobes in the Houston Post. Afterwards, I had requests from Rice classmates, Bill Ballew and Hugh Gragg, to bring some for them, which I did on our next return trip. I also brought for each of them a tape of Arabic music, which is a little weird to the unaccustomed Western ear. There are almost twice the number of notes as in traditional Western music.

On the approach to Hofuf, there are very unusual outcroppings of hills and rocks hundreds of thousands of years old. You could see where tremendous boulders had broken off and rolled down. The camel market in Hofuf was something that everyone wanted to see. Every weekend, the bedouin brought camels in for trading along with goats and cattle. This was the Saudi Arabia of hundreds of years ago, except for the Toyota and Nissan pick-up trucks. You almost hoped that it would never change. I don't imagine it will for a while, even though the encroachments of modernization are appearing.

About ten miles west of Hofuf beyond the al-Hasa oasis, there were some large caverns formed by the erosion of the sandstone over hundreds of thousands of years. All of this presented a geological history that the early pioneer geologists of Aramco analyzed. It was fascinating to walk down the old streets in Hofuf. Back in the corners you might see a marking on a wall, "Testhole No. 2," made by the geologists in their early surveys.

On the way to the caves, there was a corner where a native sat with his turning wheel making clay pottery. Everybody stopped there. We purchased several pots from him. These were turned out of clay on a wheel which he pedalled with his feet.

Hofuf camel and sheep market

Hofuf potter at work

Hofuf street

Arab Travels — In Kingdom and Out

When we first went there in 1975, he was just a little guy with his wheel back in the cave. Ten years later, when we visited, he had built a complex. He had a showroom and his own residence there. He had prospered and expanded. He had learned about marketing.

The al-Hasa oasis was the home of the bin Jiluwi tribe, who were related to the al-Saud Family. Abdullah bin Jiluwi fought alongside Abdul Aziz when he defeated the Rashids at al-Musmak Fortress in Riyadh. Abdul Aziz gained the support of the people in al-Hasa. The tribe of bin Jiluwi remained strong supporters of the al-Sauds. Abdul Mohsin bin Jiluwi was governor of the Eastern Province until 1985 when he retired and Prince Mohammed, the son of King Fahd, became governor. Al-Hasa has always been an important landmark, or area, in the Arabian Peninsula. It was a stronghold of the Turks during the period of their occupation. The main campus of King Faisal University is now located there.

In December of 1975, we had been in Saudi Arabia just four months. We had been out of the Kingdom to Bahrain a couple of times getting our work permits. That was all. So, we felt like having a little break. That year the Id al-Adha, or Haj, holiday came at about the same time as the Christmas holiday. This doesn't happen very often because of the fact that Ramadan and the Haj move back about eleven days every year on the Gregorian (solar) calendar, because of the difference with the lunar calendar, which the Muslims use. If it is May 11th this year, it will be May 1st next year, and so on. During the holiday, we decided to make our first trip to Riyadh.

Back in my youthful days in high school, I had read that Riyadh, Saudi Arabia, and Lhasa, Tibet, were two places that Westerners were not allowed to go under severe penalty. My youthful adventurous ambition was to go to Riyadh and Lhasa.

Jebel Dhahran and the New Saudi Generation

I only got within 400 miles of Lhasa, but I did get to Riyadh. When I got there, it was hard to believe that it ever had been considered to be a forbidden city.

We decided that we would take the train, which runs from Dammam to Riyadh. We drove to the airport and left our car, because we intended to fly back. We hired a taxi to take us to Dammam to get the train. When we arrived there, we found that we couldn't get tickets that day. We would have to get them a day ahead. We decided that we didn't want to wait, but we still wanted to go. We asked our taxi driver how much he would charge to drive us to Riyadh. Many of the things that we did when we first arrived, we wouldn't have had the nerve to do later. Maybe it was ignorance. Or we were more adventurous then.

He told us how much it would be. It was not a large amount compared to what it might have cost later. We said, "OK." We had satisfied ourselves that he was a fairly good driver while driving from the airport to Dammam. We then had to go back to the airport to get some kind of passes that he would need along with our passports to clear certain checkpoints along the road. We finally got all that taken care of.

Then we said, "Drive us down to the grocery store." We loaded up with crackers, cheese, dips, and all kinds of things to eat. We sat watching the scenery and eating cheese and crackers, while he drove about 75 miles per hour. We just couldn't worry about that. We knew that Allah had to be taking care of us. I was reading an article recently that said that the road between Riyadh and Dhahran at that time was almost impassable. But that wasn't true. It wasn't the best road in the world, but if you can drive 75 miles an hour, it can't be the worst.

We arrived in Riyadh without reservations, and the town was rather dead, because many Westerners had gone home for Christmas, and many Arabs had gone to Mecca. We had it all

Arab Travels — In Kingdom and Out

to ourselves, figuratively speaking. We went to the Intercontinental Hotel and got a good room without any hassle. The Intercontinental was one of the first really fine hotels in Saudi Arabia, built and owned by the Saudi Government. It is beautiful, very elegant.

From there we took various trips around. We saw the town of Diriyah, which is the old town that the al-Saud family first ruled several hundred years ago. Now it is all ruins, but it was fascinating to walk around. It had not been restored at that time. Since then, the Saudis have become interested in history, archaeology, and restoring things. To me, it was much more interesting unrestored. It was left just as it had been for hundreds of years. There is a beautiful oasis right along side of it, where a new village has been built.

We went out to the street where many of the royal palaces are, past King Faisal's green-roofed palace and King Khaled's palace, where a new impressive entrance gate was being built. Our driver could not speak much English, but he managed to communicate, pointing out the various palaces.

We saw al-Musmak Fortress in the center of Riyadh. It was there that the historic battle occurred between Abdul Aziz and the Rashid governor of Riyadh, Ibn Ajlan, who was killed. The doors to the fortress still hold the head of the spear thrown by Abdullah bin Jiluwi, Abdul Aziz's cousin. Standing across the street from the door, I made a sketch of it. We later went to the souq several blocks away. A Saudi came up to me and wanted to see what I had done. I showed him the sketch and he said, "Good." Unbeknownst to me, he had watched me make the sketch.

One of the most interesting sites was the old palace of King Saud, the son of King Abdul Aziz, who inherited his throne but later abdicated in favor of Crown Prince Faisal. His palace was down in an oasis called Nasiriyah. We parked in front of it, and no one was around. We walked up to it and looked through the *al-Musmak Fortress – Riyadh*   *author's sketch*

glass in the front door. There in the main entrance hall was a large staircase. Hanging on the wall was the Saudi emblem and other artifacts. Actually, it looked as if somebody had just walked out of it, closed the door, and that was it. If you came that close several years later, you probably would have been arrested.

We saw many fascinating sites in Riyadh, but it was quite a contrast to the Riyadh that we saw ten years later with all the modern buildings and highways.

When we returned to the hotel, we were eating in the coffee shop when I heard someone behind me who sounded like an American. Something that he said caught my attention. I turned around and recognized Harwood Taylor, an architect that I knew from Houston. That evening we saw Harwood and Vic Neuhouse, his partner, in the lobby waiting for one of the princes that they knew, and we visited with them for a little while.

You had the sense of being in a faraway place, and seeing someone you knew was rather exciting. Neuhouse and Taylor were big architects in Houston. Their firm was known as 3D International. They did quite a bit of work in Saudi Arabia, although I don't think they fared as well as CRS.

The next day, we took the plane back to Dhahran, and that was the end of our first trip to Riyadh.

In 1978 during Mildred's "spring break," we decided to go to Jordan and Syria. We flew to Amman, Jordan and stayed at the Intercontinental Hotel, where we found a travel agent in the hotel to work out our excursions for us. We hired a driver to take us down to the Dead Sea the first afternoon. It was hard to realize that we were at the famous Dead Sea of Bible history, in the very area where Jesus and the Disciples may have traveled.

The next day, we hired a driver to take us to Damascus. At that particular time, there was no problem. We arrived at the Syrian border, and he managed to negotiate our visas for us.

Jebel Dhahran and the New Saudi Generation

This was at the time that the Israelis were invading southern Lebanon and pushing up to the Litani River. So, there was a war going on, but it hadn't been going on long enough to make a difference.

We arrived at Damascus without any problem and stayed at the Meridien Hotel. We saw in the lobby an advertisement about the next day, Easter Sunday. They were going to have a big celebration. They had chickens, rabbits, and Easter eggs in the lobby. We bought tickets for the occasion. The next day, we had a designated table in the ballroom, which was all decked out for an Easter celebration. It was a family affair, and all the children danced and sang to a live orchestra. It gave me a warm feeling for the Syrians, contrary to the popular image we have of them in the United States as being pretty heavy people. Many of them are Christian, although the majority are Muslim.

We took a tour of the city, to Paul's Gate, to the famous Umayyad Mosque, and to the "Street called Straight" of Bible renown. We also went to the house where Ananias is said to have lived, where Paul was taken when he was converted after being made blind on the road to Damascus. History abounds in this ancient city.

The next day, we drove back to Amman, after visiting the souq and buying some Damascus silk tablecloths and ties. In Jordan, we stopped at Jerash, which is the site of some of the largest Roman ruins, arriving back in Amman late at night.

We learned a few days later that the border to Syria had been closed, and Americans could no longer get visas at the border. It was necessary to apply ahead of time. When we left the USA three years earlier, Syria was listed by the State Department as one of the countries that Americans should avoid. We didn't follow that advice. I think there was some kind of problem on the road to Damascus right after we were there, and that is why it was closed.

The next day, we hired another driver to take us down to

Arab Travels — In Kingdom and Out

Aqaba. We knew of Aqaba from "Lawrence of Arabia." We had a very good Palestinian driver and guide. We stopped at Petra on the way from Amman. This is the site of the Nabatean ruins similar to those at Madain Saleh in Saudi Arabia. These people were totally hidden from outsiders. Entry was only through narrow passages. In order to have water, they drilled wells outside on higher ground, creating aqueducts carved in the rock to carry the water down to the central living area. We then drove on to Aqaba and stayed at the new Holiday Inn there. It appeared that the local residents were getting ready for an increase in tourist activity in Aqaba with several large hotels under construction. There were a number of tour groups from Europe there at that time.

Aqaba is a beautiful port village. It seemed to me that it should become one of the fine resort areas of the Middle East after the demise of Beirut. Across from Aqaba, we could see Elat, the Israeli town. This is the point at which Israel and Jordan converge, separated only by the narrow portion of the Red Sea. We drove down a few miles from Aqaba and could see the northwestern entrance into Saudi Arabia. We stayed in Aqaba two nights. One night, we flipped on the television and were surprised to see my brother Robert in an episode of "Love Boat." Oddly enough, we caught him on various shows a number of times throughout our world travels.

We then told our driver that we wanted to see the country where Lawrence of Arabia had been. On our way back from Aqaba to Amman, he took us deep into the desert. We had the feeling that we were a long way from nowhere. We saw a railroad that Lawrence had blown up and a burned-out locomotive. We finally ended up at a Jordanian police station way into the Wadi Rum, as the area is called. We entered into a large bedouin tent, Mildred and I and our driver, Musa. All the men were sitting around the fire drinking coffee. One had his six-year-old son, who was the center of attention. Mildred had on a long dress and a scarf over her head. Although it was obvious

Wadi Rum - His father rode with Lawrence

With Palestinian guide, Musa, in Wadi Rum

"Lawrence of Arabia" Targets

Damascus - Medina Railroad

Burned-out locomotive

Rub al-Khali - "Empty Quarter"

Medain Saleh - Nabatean Carvings

Jebel Dhahran and the New Saudi Generation

that she was a woman, they didn't pay much attention.

We sat down by the fire, and they all kept talking in Arabic. They gave us tea and coffee. We sat and listened. We noticed our driver, Musa, who was middle-aged, talking animatedly to one of the soldiers. It turned out that they discovered that eleven years earlier Musa had driven this fellow from Beirut down to Mecca to perform the Haj. When they realized that, they had quite a conversation.

There was an old man there, a bedouin-type fellow. I said to Musa, "Ask him if he was here when Lawrence was here." When Musa asked him, the old man became very animated in Arabic. He said, "Yes, I was only ten-years-old, and my father rode with Lawrence." He said that when Lawrence and company were preparing for their final ride to Damascus, they bivouacked right near this place where we were. That made it doubly interesting for us. Here we were in the very place where Lawrence of Arabia had been sixty years before. When we saw the movie again after returning to the States, I recognized the place as being the area in the Wadi Rum where Auda Abu Tayi (Anthony Quinn) had camped.

As we were approaching this police station earlier, we passed some outcroppings, some hills, and I said to Musa, "That looks like the place in the movie where Lawrence first donned his Arab clothes and met Auda Abu Tayi." He replied, "That is right. Back when that was filmed, I used to drive the company, the actors, and staff all up and down this area." He was employed by them as a driver during the filming.

We then continued on towards Amman. On the way, we stopped at a place called Karak, which is an old castle fort built by the Crusaders. It was the general route through which the Children of Israel traveled and is mentioned in the Bible. We went on to Mount Nebo, from which Moses is said to have viewed the Promised Land, but never got to enter.

From Amman, we returned to Saudi Arabia. Another of my youthful ambitions had been fulfilled.

Arab Travels — In Kingdom and Out

In 1979, a group got together from the university to take a trip down to an old Portuguese sea port on the Gulf about 75 miles south of Hofuf. Our group leader was an American professor of English, Virgil Miller, who had made the trip before. We had a caravan of about fifteen cars and drove along a fairly good road along the coast. We arrived at a place called Uqayr, which had been a port used in the old days by Hofuf and the vicinity.

It was fascinating to come to places like this where it seemed that time had stood still for so long. Here were these ruins quietly sitting there. It was a compound-like fort with a large central building and a grandiose staircase approaching it. Living quarters were around a central parade area. Higher up on a hill were the ruins of a watchtower. Everyone had brought his lunch, so we sat around on the beach and did our exploring as we wished. We returned to Dhahran that evening after an excursion several hundred years into the past.

The Rub al-Khali, known as "The Empty Quarter," in the south of the Arabian Peninsula is the largest sand desert in the world and lies just north of Yemen and Oman. Not many people who have been in Saudi Arabia have had the opportunity to see it. We were fortunate in getting to do so. I made three trips down there. This area has been written of by famous Arabists such as Wilfred Thesiger and St. John Philby. It is the size and complete stark bareness that are so impressive. The area nowadays is the known source of great quantities of oil which have not yet been tapped. Aramco has done considerable exploration there, but doesn't need to tap that oil yet. When the time comes to do so, it will be very expensive to put into production because of the isolated location. But it can and will be done.

We had a friend, Paul Christensen, who was a pilot for Aramco. He had been raised at Aramco, where his father was a ship pilot. He went to school in the States after the ninth grade.

Jebel Dhahran and the New Saudi Generation

After graduating from college, he took up flying. He was a bush pilot in Alaska for a while.

The second year that we were there, in 1977, we heard from a friend of ours, Jack Wilson, who was chief pilot for Champion Paper Company in the United States, that he had met Paul's parents at a dinner party in California. Jack told Paul's parents about our being in Dhahran, where they had lived. When Paul and his wife, Cindy, came to Dhahran, he called us and we became good friends until we left. They had two babies while they were there, and we saw them grow to be young girls five or six years old, a third generation of Aramcons.

Paul flew Zaki Yamani and others all around Europe many times. He made regular flights to the Rub al-Khali to take supplies to the seismographic teams that were there. He flew a Fokker F27, from which most of the seats were removed, leaving perhaps a dozen seats for passengers. One day Paul said, "How would you like to fly down to the Empty Quarter with me tomorrow?" We replied, "There is nothing that we would like better."

"Meet me at the Aramco terminal at 7:00 a.m."

This was our first glimpse of this great red sand desert. It was awe-inspiring, indeed. Paul also took Cindy and their six-month old baby. We had lunch at the camp with the workers in air-conditioned trailers. They lived pretty well while they were there, with Filipino cooks who prepared excellent food. These fellows would stay at the site for two weeks at a time.

The workers had a baby gazelle which they had found in the middle of the desert. It is still a mystery to me how it could have survived like that. It was their mascot, of course. These fellows are typical of the ones that I mentioned earlier, the American roughnecks who live under these conditions. They were straight-forward, hardworking, and the Saudis liked them.

Arab Travels — In Kingdom and Out

Many tours were conducted by Aramco groups. One such group was called DOGS, Dhahran Outing Group. It conducted tours all over the Far East and many within the Kingdom. Others conducted tours in the Kingdom through the airlines and hotels.

One tour that we particularly enjoyed was organized by the Aramco Historical and Cultural Society. We had always wanted to go to a place called Madain Saleh, which is north of Medina and is the site of some very interesting historic and ancient ruins.

We flew to Medina and stayed at the Sheraton Medina Hotel. Non-Muslims are not allowed to go into Medina, so the Saudis built a hotel just outside the city limits, and this allows Westerners, non-Muslims, to stay very near Medina. It was operated by the Sheraton Hotels. From that hotel there were tours organized to go to Madain Saleh. This is an area that is at least 2000 years old or more. It is similar to and built by the same people who built Petra in Jordan, the Nabateans. These were ancient people that secluded themselves among these sandstone outcroppings in which they carved tombs and housing. They did not have, however, the natural security that the people at Petra did.

An interesting thing about them is that the carvings reflect classical motifs, indicating that they had been exposed to Roman culture. They had pediments, columns, and adapted details similar to what the Romans built. At Petra the Romans actually came in later and added to the designs and carvings of the structures. Madain Saleh is quite spectacular, but the Romans were never there. Lawrence of Arabia, who began his career as an archaeologist, was fascinated with both Madain Saleh and Petra to the north.

East of Medina there is another place called Hanakiyah, where there are 4,000-year-old carvings made by primitive people long before the Nabateans. These are crude and nothing like those at Madain Saleh. On the way to Hanakiyah from

Jebel Dhahran and the New Saudi Generation

Medina was an interesting sight — a long horizontal line of what appeared to be volcanic rock. On checking later, I found that geological maps show this as an area of ancient volcanic activity. Outcrops of the ancient volcanics are found throughout a large area of west central Saudi Arabia-north and east of Jeddah.

We managed to visit all the Arab countries except Iraq, Kuwait, South Yemen, Oman, and the North African Arab countries. In the fall of 1983, we came back early from summer vacation. By September, we thought that we would take one more short vacation before school started, so we joined an Aramco tour going to Dubai, one of the city states in the United Arab Emirates, the UAE. The seven sheikhdoms constituting the UAE (formerly called the Trucial States) elect their president. The confederation is then ruled by him with a council.

We flew to Dubai, stayed at the Hilton Hotel, and then we took tours around Dubai. Dubai has an estuary or waterway backing up through it from the Gulf. Everything revolves around that, giving it a unique character, and a picturesqueness that other Arab cities do not have. There are many canal-type boats. We visited most of the new modern hotels -- the Hyatt, which has an ice skating rink, the Sheraton, and others. The idea of an ice skating rink in that part of the world sounds anomalous at first, but the people take to it quickly. CRS planned a large rink for Aramco, but it was never authorized. There are contrasts, such as the old souq and the modern new and fashionable shopping centers. The city is really quite modern. The British are the predominant presence there. It is so different that there are public fashion shows in the hotels, and mixed alcoholic drinks. The natives dress the same as the Saudis, but they have a somewhat different mental outlook, being less restricted.

We visited various areas around Dubai, including one long

Arab Travels — In Kingdom and Out

trip for a full day by bus to al-Ain in Abu Dhabi, almost to the border of Oman. This is the heart of the agricultural area for the United Arab Emirates. Again there was a fine Hilton Hotel there, where we had another sumptuous buffet lunch. In the afternoon we visited the camel markets, which did bring us back to the realization of where we were, emphasizing the great contrast between the old and the new. We visited some inscriptive ruins that were over a thousand years old.

The most outstanding thing is how the agriculture has been developed. It is luxuriant. We then drove to Sharjah, another city-state nearby, which boasts an elaborate and unique new covered bazaar. A considerable amount of manufactured material that we began to use in Saudi Arabia was made in Sharjah.

In March of 1984, during the spring break, we decided to take a trip to North Yemen. The wife of one of the university professors, a German lady, was organizing a trip down there, having been there previously. Friends of ours at Aramco, Nancy and Bruce Hensel, had a guest, Mary Vance Trent, visiting that month from Washington D.C. She had been a long-time career person with the Foreign Service of the State Department and had been all over the world in various diplomatic posts. When she heard about our proposed trip to Yemen, she got all excited about going, so we managed to include her on the tour, and we all flew down to Sanaa, North Yemen. We stayed at the Taj Sheba, a hotel operated by East Indians, although there is a Sheraton hotel there which we thought was much better. From there we took various trips into the country side.

The Yemenis are quite different from the Saudis. People that live in high climates and altitudes like Yemen are often different from those who live down in the valley, the desert, or sea level. This is true in Mexico. The Yemenis are Arabs, but they dress differently and in some ways a little more colorfully than the Saudis. The men all wear daggers in their belts. They have a different history from the northern part of the peninsula. Although it is under one rule, the various towns are more or less provinces, individual city states. You have to have permission to enter a particular city.

Most of the towns are built up on tops of the hills in a very skillful way. The buildings are built of solid masonry, six to eight stories high. They have a design about them that is quite original, using many colored glass windows with white stucco or plaster-of-paris decorations. I'm sure the towns that we visited must have been the same as they were over a thousand years ago.

The people were pleasant, especially the children, outgoing and friendly. The only unpleasant thing was a habit that they have of chewing on a curd sort of weed called "gat." It is a leaf which is some sort of stimulant. They start about noon and chew it all afternoon. Their cheeks will bulge way out with a wad of it inside. The trouble is, it takes up so much of their agriculture space to grow this stuff, it really doesn't do their economy any good.

The fabulous Queen of Sheba and her Kingdom of Saba were further to the west in Yemen. We wanted to visit it, but we would have had to take a four-wheel drive jeep to get there. We couldn't take the time to do that. I was told that presumably Job, the Bible character, was buried there.

Yemen is generally ruled by tribes, and their tribal wars go on all the time outside of government jurisdiction.

There were many Russians and Chinese working in North Yemen. It was surprising to see how many Russians there were in North Yemen. They were apparently military advisers.

Mary Vance Trent and I went out to the United States Embassy just to see what it was like. Being a former State Department officer, she managed to get the attention of the staff and a tour by a Marine. The embassy was in a compound, with one of the picturesque old Yemeni houses as headquarters. CRSS is now designing and building a beautiful new embassy

Arab Travels — In Kingdom and Out

for the United States, which I understand is right next to the Russian compound. Apparently, Sanaa is one of the few places in the world where you can see U.S. F-15s and Russian MIGs lined up on opposite sides of the runway at the airport.

(From March 1987 to March 1990, Don Chambers was in Sanaa, North Yemen, in charge of building the United States Embassy, which CRSS designed.)

When I took over from Don Chambers in June 1982, I began to perform the various functions included in that position. One of these was accompanying the Bids and Tenders Committee on its visits to various contractor's works around the Kingdom. The committee was composed of about seven or eight Saudis from among the faculty and senior staff members, chaired by Dr. Bakhrebah. This allowed me to see parts of the Arabian Peninsula that I would never have managed to see otherwise.

One of the most interesting trips that we made was to al-Jawf and Sakaka in North Central Arabia. This area abounds in history. It is said to have been the home of the Midianites, the ancient traders who were located on the trade route from Persia to the Holy Land. They were the people who rescued Joseph from the pit where he had been cast by his brothers. They took him captive and sold him later to the Egyptians.

The Muslims are fascinated with the story of Joseph because of his complete submission to the will of God. One chapter of the Koran tells of his deeds.

Al-Jawf and Sakaka are about fifteen kilometers apart. At al-Jawf there is a fortress named Qasr Marid (also known as Qasr al-Ukaider), the foundations of which are believed to date to 300 B.C. There is also a mosque built by Umar, the second caliph (634-644 A.D.), that is still being used.

The oasis at al-Jawf has one of the earliest recorded settlements in North Arabia, the ancient name of which was "Dumah."

Jebel Dhahran and the New Saudi Generation

According to The New Westminister Dictionary of the Bible, Dumah was a tribe descended from Ishmael (Gen. 25:14; I Chronicles 1:30), Dumah being one of Ishmael's twelve sons. It's territory was probably the region called "Doumaitha" by Ptolemy and "Domata" by Pliny on the confines of the Syrian and Arabian deserts. It was later known as "Domat al-Jandl" ("Domat of the Stones"). It is present-day al-Jawf.

Something that aroused my curiosity was that at a short distance from the oasis, there lies a huge mound of stones (apparently igneous or volcanic). We drove all around this. It appears in the photograph which I have included herein. I was not able to verify its likely origin or content, but would assume the name "Domat of Stones" might derive from this phenomenon.

At Sakaka there is an old fort named Qasr Zabal at the top of a hill near an oasis. This had doubtless been the scene of many battles. Mansour al-Saber and I, with a British fellow, climbed as high as we could. We didn't get into the fort, but there it was sitting as it had for at least two hundred years. Around the outside on the oasis side, I found what appeared to be musket balls imbedded in the sandstone. It was fascinating.

Many of these sites were not open to everyone, and you really were not supposed to be there without permission. In this case, we went without asking. In the oasis at al-Jawf we met a young man whose family were the owners of the land. He took us through the orchards of grapes, pomegranates, and dates. It was a luxuriant area. By their standards, they would be considered to be wealthy. He did not dress in typical Saudi clothes, but wore trousers and a sport shirt.

He then invited us into his house for tea and coffee. We all sat around on the floor and, of course, the conversation was in Arabic. An old man with a story-book look of an Arab soon joined us. It was his father. He was asked about the fort at Sakaka. He confirmed that it was the scene of many fierce battles and referred to "rivers of blood" that were said to have flowed. This would have been tribal warfare that involved

Qasr Marid Fortress and Oasis at al-Jawf (Ancient "Dumah") — Saudi Ministry of Education

With Bids and Tenders Committee

Sightseeing ancient ruins at al-Jawf

Qasr Zabal at Sakaka

contests for dominance of the area. The histories of these areas have been written, but in Arabic.

When I returned to Houston several years later, my excitement about "musket balls" imbedded in the sandstone fort at Sakaka was tempered somewhat when I showed them to my geologist friend. He explained that these "balls" were small round concretions in sandstone, a common geological occurrence in some regions. In geological terms, a concretion is an inclusion in sedimentary rock, usually rounded, which results from the formation of successive layers of mineral matter being deposited around some nucleus such as a grain of sand in the sedimentary rock.

In spite of such scientific analysis, the little round concretions still serve to bring to mind a picture of musket balls flying through the air as ancient battles raged around the old fort.

The committee and I drove all around the Sakaka area in a Ford Suburban — sightseeing. At one place, we were surprised to come upon a Saudi Boy Scout camp. It apparently is affiliated with the International Organization of the Boy Scouts.

Actually, my Saudi companions were as excited as I was, because it was the first time that they had been to that part of Saudi Arabia. They were raised in different parts of the Kingdom and had not travelled to these areas before.

In 1986 when Halley's Comet was due to rendezvous with our planet, a group of us went out in the desert about fifty miles west of Dhahran to be a part of the historic occasion and get a glimpse of it. We had seven or eight cars in a caravan. Someone had scouted out the area and determined a good place to go. Fortunately, there were people around, professors and others, who were always doing things like that. We took our car and were prepared to spend the night. It was March and was quite cold.

We followed each other to the designated location, and then

Jebel Dhahran and the New Saudi Generation

we tried to decide if it was all right to drive in there without getting stuck. A couple of cars did get stuck, but everybody finally got out. It was a part of the desert where there was vegetation. We camped around wagon style. Everyone built his own fire and had his supper. About four o'clock in the morning was the time that had been determined would be the best to see the comet. This area was near a mound or a small hill, where we could have a clear view. The idea of being out there was that there would be no lights around, although there still was a little glow on the horizon from al-Khobar.

We slept in our car. About four o'clock in the morning Mildred shook me. Someone was going around waking everyone up, because the time was right. Someone had a telescope, but we just looked through our binoculars. These people knew exactly in which direction to look. It couldn't be seen with the naked eye. So, if you didn't know in which direction to look, you would never see it. We had it pretty well pinpointed, and sure enough it was really there. It was a thrill to see. We could definitely see the tail.

That is how we saw Halley's Comet on a cold night in 1986 from the middle of the Arabian desert. The last time it had passed our planet, it had looked down on a vast desert of nomads and tribes of the descendants of Ishmael and Abraham without a hint of what the next century would do to this isolated peninsula.

When Halley's Comet next passes by, what will it see?

In February of 1986, knowing that we were going to be leaving in a few months, we decided to take one last look at Saudi Arabia. We went with some friends to Riyadh, Sharon and Dick Adams, Armogene Paulk, and Barbara Howke, all from Aramco. We also wanted to ride the Dammam-Riyadh train, that we had always talked about doing but had never gotten around to. We flew to Riyadh and stayed at the beautiful

Arab Travels — In Kingdom and Out

new Marriott Hotel in downtown Riyadh. From there we planned various sight-seeing trips. I had arranged with Rasheed, the long-time Pakistani executive secretary in charge of the CRSS office in Riyadh, to provide us with a driver and someone to take us around and show us the sights. He made available to us a very helpful Pakistani driver and guide, Salam, who took us to see the new American Embassy designed by CRSS. He also gave us a tour of the King Saud University, which is a fabulous group of buildings. CRSS was associated with Hellmuth Obata and Kassabaum of St. Louis on this project in a group known as HOK+4.

The University of Petroleum and Minerals in Dhahran is without question one of the finest projects in the Kingdom, but the sheer size of King Saud University as well as the architecture and detail is very impressive. It was designed for 20,000 students.

In my opinion, it is overbuilt, whereas UPM is just the right size for the number of students. It is designed for 4,000 students and that is about what it has. It is a very efficient operation, whereas King Saud University will be difficult to manage and operate.

The new U.S. Embassy in Riyadh designed by Bill Caudill, is impressive. I think it must have been about the last project that he did. It is certainly one of the finest of our embassies around the world. Salam then took us out to the old town of Diriyah again. It was about the fourth time that we had been there, but some of our friends had never seen it. We drove to the souq and Kings Row, where many palaces are located. All in all, it was a great trip, but the startling thing was remembering and comparing to it our first trip ten years before in December 1975. Instead of the low mud or stucco type buildings, there were glass and marble skyscrapers, beautifully designed. It truly was amazing what could be done in ten years by people who had the ambition, the will, and the money.

For our return trip by train to Dhahran, we had all agreed to meet at the railroad station at 3:00 o'clock on Friday, after

Jebel Dhahran and the New Saudi Generation

our separate shopping sorties to the Riyadh souq. Salam had promised to see to it that all six of us were at the station on time.

I then had my first encounter with the problem of taking pictures. The Saudis warn you plenty of times that you can't take pictures around airports. And there are other prohibited areas such as military installations. But it never occurred to me that the railroad station was in that category. In retrospect, I can see that it might be so. When we arrived, I had everyone line up in front of the station to take a picture. The next thing I knew a policeman appeared and wanted my camera. I suddenly realized that I had goofed. He took my camera, and I followed him to the station office to see what would happen. Soon he brought it out again. Actually, I hadn't taken any pictures yet. I tried to tell him that it was an empty roll. Of course, he would be unsure of that, so he took the film out and gave my camera back to me, without any further problem. That was my one and only problem with a camera in Saudi Arabia.

(One time Don Chambers was on campus taking some pictures that CRS in Houston had asked him for. Suddenly the police drove up in a jeep, took his camera, and were going to take him to jail in Hofuf without further ado. Don said he wouldn't go until he had been able to talk to someone in authority at the university. About that time, one of the Saudi vice-rectors walked by. Don explained the problem. After an animated Arabic conversation that lasted about fifteen minutes, the vice-rector was able to convince the police that Don was O.K., and they left. It proved to be a weird coincidence. The next day, one of the heads of state was to visit the campus, so the police were conducting a preliminary security check. Seeing Don taking pictures, they assumed that he must be up to no good. You soon learned to expect the unexpected.)

Our train was a streamlined one similar to the Burlington and Santa Fe that used to run from Houston up to Chicago and Des Moines. It had about eight cars. We boarded and found some comfortable seats in a car with a snack bar. Soon we were on our way. Each car was divided in two, and each half had two televisions facing each way. Before long the entertainment started. The trip was about six hours long. Half of the time Tom and Jerry cartoons were shown and the rest of the time wrestling. After a while, the "entertainment" was not entertaining, so we read, slept, or watched the scenery, which did prove to be of interest.

We left Riyadh about 3 o'clock in the afternoon, so it was daylight for several hours. We could see across the Dhana, or the central desert, which is red sand. It is very picturesque and awe-inspiring. Outside of Riyadh, we passed through other oasis areas, including Hofuf in al-Hasa. We were amazed to see the agricultural development. This has been one of many major efforts and accomplishments. With proper watering, the Saudis can grow wheat or whatever they need, and they have done so.

We arrived back in Dammam about 10:00 o'clock at night, where Garland Paulk was anxiously waiting for Armogene. He had not been able to go with us. We were happy that we had made the trip by train. When we first went to Saudi Arabia, our friends from Northrup, Carol and Warren Phillips, told us of having made the trip on a hot summer day, and it was not easy. They said it was all right to do once only. Conditions had improved considerably, however, and our trip was comfortable and enjoyable, and we really couldn't complain, especially if you liked Tom and Jerry cartoons and professional wrestling.

In March, a few weeks later, which was the spring holiday, we decided to take another trip to an area where we hadn't been. We flew to Abha in South Arabia. This is dramatically different from the Eastern Province. It is not sand and desert but has mountains and much vegetation. We had a little difficulty in breathing, because we had been used to living at sea

Jebel Dhahran and the New Saudi Generation

level for so long. It was about 10,000 feet elevation near the hotel, the highest in Saudi Arabia.

We stayed at the Intercontinental, which is another of the fabulous new hotels around the Kingdom. As I understood it, it was originally built as a sort of palace for royalty. A portion of it is still reserved for and occasionally used by the Royal Family, and is not open to the public. The hotel is in beautiful Arabic design. There were not many people there, so it was rather empty looking. We arrived in Abha on Thursday. By Friday and Saturday, there were tours that had filled up the hotel. All the hotels have sumptuous buffet dinners on Friday. I think that was one of the most enjoyable things about traveling around the world, the wonderful food that we ate.

We signed up for some of the tours that were being offered. It was by coincidence that we saw the name of the Indian fellow who had conducted our tour out of the Medina Sheraton to Madain Saleh four years before. We asked about him and everyone said, "Oh yes, he is the director of marketing. Do you know him?" The next day, the staff made sure that we saw him. He then insisted on providing us with a special tour with an Indian tour guide.

In Abha, we were very near Kamis Mushayt, which was built mainly as an air base. It is an Arabic town, but there were quite a number of Americans there for the F-15 and other air projects. The international school that Mildred was with had a branch there. Some of our friends had gone to Kamis to work. It was such an entirely different environment, it was hard to believe that we were in Saudi Arabia. When we were up in the hills, we thought it looked a lot like the hill country of Texas. There were fir trees and cedars and rolling rocky hills.

We went to a museum that had been completed. It is very well done, and although it was closed that day, our driver managed to get us in through someone that he knew. It looks out over the escarpment and the valley that goes down to the Red Sea coast. It is spectacular scenery. We told our friend at

Arab Travels — In Kingdom and Out

the Intercontinental that we were going to the Intercontinental in Taif, and he told us whom to contact there. Someone that he knew very well was in charge of the activities and tours there.

We flew to Taif and checked in at the Massarah Intercontinental Hotel. Again, there weren't many people around at that particular time. Every weekend, tours would come in, so these places weren't sparsely populated all the time. I am sure that they relied a lot on expatriates. As those numbers diminish in the Kingdom, it will no doubt have an effect on the number of people that go sightseeing. I think, however, the number of Saudis who travel to see their own country will increase.

(In earlier chapters, I have mentioned Dr. Nasser al-Rashid, who was the CRSS partner and the first Saudi that I met in Austin in July 1975. I also mentioned the fact that he now has become one of the truly big entrepreneurs in Saudi Arabia. He started his own engineering and development firm in 1975. As is the case anywhere, those who really succeed and become "big," usually have something extra "on the ball," so to speak. Sometime after 1975, there was to be an international conference of foreign ministers in Taif. This was the first occasion of its kind to be held in Saudi Arabia, and there were no adequate facilities of the quality needed in Taif at that time. Nasser Rashid contracted to build a luxury hotel comparable to the best in the world in nine months time. He joined with a French company, Oger, to accomplish this task. In less than nine months there was a beautiful Intercontinental Hotel, equal to any in Europe, ready for the conference. This is indicative of the qualities in the Saudis that the Western world should take note of and appreciate for future reference.)

At the Intercontinental, we contacted the friend of the Indian fellow that we had seen in Abha. He said he was from Sri Lanka (old Ceylon). He didn't look Sri Lankan, so I asked him about it. He said that he was Malaysian. He was born in Malaysia, but his family went to Sri Lanka when he was small, so he was raised there. People like him from the Far East with

Intercontinental Hotel - Taif

King Saud University - Riyadh

Arab Travels — In Kingdom and Out

ability came to Saudi Arabia to work. He ended up as marketing director of this large hotel.

There weren't many tours at that time, so he insisted on personally taking us on one. He drove us into the mountains. The landscape and geography were entirely different from what we were used to in Dhahran. It was similar to Abha. We had been to Taif before, so we knew what to expect. He showed where King Fahd's palace is in the mountains. Then we went to downtown Taif to the souq, which was one of the most interesting that we had seen. We saw a number of Afghan refugees on the streets. Taif was an important town back in Mohammed's time.

From Taif we flew to Jeddah, where we had reservations at the Red Sea Palace Hotel. I had always heard about it, and I was anxious to see what it was like. We found that it was Swiss-operated, which automatically gave it a certain credibility. It was located facing the Red Sea but set back on a little lagoon. It was near the old buildings that provide a lot of the fascination that Jeddah has architecturally, with its "mashrabiyas," the wooden projections on the windows, which serve as sunshades and screens. The character is unique.

We found an Indian driver, who drove us all around the town, new and old. He took us out on the corniche, which is the road around the waterfront that has been so beautifully developed. The city has commissioned sculptors and artists over the past ten years to create this very unique art work, some humorous and amusing, but all very impressive. We passed a Holiday Inn, which was of eye-catching Arabic design. Inside it was quite exotic such as you might see in the movies, with somewhat of a Mogul Indian character, double-curved arches, etc.

We then went to a museum that Mildred had read about in the newspaper. It was owned by a Saudi, Abdul Raouf Hasan Khalil, who had been raised in Jeddah, but his father had sent him to school in Cairo. He was interested from early years in

Jebel Dhahran and the New Saudi Generation

collecting things, art objects, European as well as Middle Eastern. He had designed and built this unusual mixture of buildings, all Middle Eastern in character, and he had filled them with his collections. It must have been worth 20 or 30 million dollars. It was open to the public. This was a project that he had launched on his own, which was in itself unique. There are not many things like that in Saudi Arabia. I imagine over time it will become more well known. I mentioned this to some Saudi friends back in Dhahran. Some had heard of it, but none had seen it. It was truly an accomplishment worthy of note.

Our next stop by air was Yenbo. We had always heard about Yenbo, which figured importantly in Lawrence's campaign. It is on the Red Sea and is the geographical equivalent now of Jubail on the Arabian Gulf. The towns are connected by oil pipelines. The idea is that the Saudis did not want everything concentrated on the Arabian Gulf, so they built Yenbo as a refining and petrochemical center, which then connected the two sides of the peninsula. You might say it was an effort to avoid putting all their eggs in one basket.

It was a very ambitious project. CRS had done some big housing projects there. When the Saudis build a housing project like that, they practically build a city. There was a Hyatt Hotel. We stayed at the Holiday Inn, which had a good Arabic character.

The whole area was different from Dhahran and Aramco, that had been in place for forty years. Old Yenbo had been there from the last century, but the industrial city had just developed and been built in the last five to ten years. Otherwise, it was a rather bare desert-type port village.

We boarded our plane in Yenbo for our flight back to Dhahran with a short stop in Riyadh and a last look at the fabulous King Khaled International Airport. As we looked down on this vast desert in the land of the Arabian Nights, my mind

Artwork on Corniche – Jeddah

Jebel Dhahran and the New Saudi Generation

tried to tell me, "You will be back." My instinct told me I was seeing it for the last time (see postscript 1991). While the friendships we had made were genuine on both sides -- and I am determined to believe it; and equally as determined not to feel like an "old shoe" being cast off -- it did begin to appear that we would have to admit that we had accomplished the purpose for which the Saudis had allowed us to come there.

To quote again from my Rice Institute theme of half century ago:

> "In choosing the subject for my theme, I was led solely by my interest. I chose to write on the struggle of the Arab people for independence from foreign aggression because I am interested profoundly in the Arab people. It is my ambition to travel someday in their land. In writing about them I have been able to learn much, and I sincerely hope to be able to impart perhaps a small bit of my familiarization with the subject to someone else. Contrary to the belief of many persons, the Arabs are not a backward and intellectually inferior race. It is true that they are not as far advanced as other peoples in the scientific world today, but the history of the Arabs for the past five centuries has been one of suppression and aggression by foreign nations, which stifled all incentive for progress. If I have shown by my writing that the Arabs have possibilities of once again (provided they are released from the hindrance of foreign meddlers) becoming the great people that they once were, of producing men such as Mohammed, the Prophet, and of building such glamorous cities as the Baghdad of old, then my purpose is fulfilled."

Postscript 1991
I am happy to say my "instinct" was wrong. In October 1991, the Saudis invited Mildred and I back for a visit to Saudi Arabia.

PART VI

EPILOGUE

Epilogue

Postscript No. 1
Postscript No. 2

Appendix No. I	1938 Rice Institute Theme
Appendix No. II	Dr. Saleh A. Bakhrebah Letter
Appendix No. III	Mr. F. W. Ohliger Letter
Appendix No. IV	King Abdul Aziz Monument Inscription
Appendix No. V	Student Yearbook 1968-69

Bibliography

Index

"All men dream, but not equally."

"We did what we set out to do, and have the satisfaction of that knowledge."

T. E. Lawrence
Seven Pillars of Wisdom
1926

EPILOGUE

Within a few years after the twenty-first century dawns, Saudi Arabia will be observing its seventy-fifth anniversary. It will have come in that short time from a vast peninsula of desert inhabited by uneducated bedouin, merchants, and live stock herders ruled by tribal sheiks and sometimes dominated by foreign powers, to a unified nation with modern cities, highways, seaports, airports, universities, elementary and secondary schools, manufacturing plants, industrial complexes, hospitals, and a modern army, navy, and air force. All in seventy-five years! Thousands of young men with advanced university degrees will be contributing to the well-being of their nation. Saudi Arabia also will be the focal point for almost a billion human beings who hold to the religious beliefs of Islam with its center in Mecca.

What will the future hold in store? One can say with reasonable credibility that the four major determining factors will be:

1. Government
2. Economy
3. Military
4. Religion

Government: Saudi Arabia is an absolute monarchy. But it is a monarchy unlike any that has existed before in history. The base of power for the Saud Royal Family is broader than any present or previous monarchies, and it has proved itself to have an exceptional ability to govern. The extent to which the Saud Family keeps the welfare and individual hopes and aspirations of the non-royal citizens foremost in mind will determine its success or failure.

Epilogue

Economy: The economic well-being of Saudi Arabia presently depends on the abundant supply of the natural resource of crude oil, the presence of which was not even known to exist at the time of its founding in 1932. Diligent efforts are being made to expand the economic resources to other areas.

Oil can be relied on for perhaps a hundred years with the demand and resultant income varying and possibly being obviated altogether by other energy sources.

Military: In the past twenty-five years Saudi Arabia has developed a modern army, navy and air force, with the latest equipment and training facilities.

Emphasis is on defense, and it is unlikely that the Saudis will ever have forces capable of aggressive or expansionist actions, and their manpower is limited. Basically, they are not a warlike people, contrary to popular perception.

Religion: This is the single most emphatic feature of Saudi Arabia's character (aside from oil) and will continue to focus the eyes of one billion Muslims around the world on Mecca. It will continue to absorb much of the time and energy of the nation in providing and caretaking these facilities for the world.

This responsibility also presents a somewhat negative aspect, as witnessed in past disturbances involving so-called "Pilgrims" with political motivations rather than religious. The Saudi government has demonstrated its resolve and ability to cope with this aspect in recent years.

The question of indigenous conflicts arising from Fundamentalist Muslim factions, while disturbing, appears to be a manageable threat, because of the overwhelming predominance of moderate Muslims in Saudi Arabia.

Saudi Arabia is blessed with many young men who have proved an outstanding capacity for accomplishment. Having experienced the freedom of intellect, their world now extends far beyond "the distant horizon." They are truly Saudi Arabia's most valuable "resource."

Epilogue

Drawing again from my Rice Institute theme of fifty years ago:

"There is undoubtedly a new generation rising out of the gangrene mass of the old, a young Arab generation, healthy and strong and dynamic, educated along modern lines, fired with new ideals, social and political, and joining in the struggle of the nationalists everywhere in the Arab world.

"So, perhaps the Arab people, having thrown off their yoke of bondage, will once again contribute to the world of literature and art and will rise again to the remarkable cultural and intellectual greatness that was once theirs."

Two weeks before I left Saudi Arabia permanently on July 9, 1986, I had dinner one evening at one of the local restaurants (Mildred had already gone to London). When I came out of the restaurant, I ran into a young Saudi professor of architecture at UPM, Farouk Konash. He was the one that I went to Taif with as part of Dr. Bakr's team to analyze the needs of the Taif city government. We greeted each other, and then just stood for a few moments without speaking. He finally said, "You are leaving?"

I was feeling the anticipation of vacation that I usually felt after nine months of hard work. I replied happily, "Yes, in about two weeks." My pleasure was obvious. He looked at me quizzically. I don't think another word was spoken. We parted without a "Massalama" or a "Fi aman Allah."

During the next two weeks, I felt that several of the young Saudis seemed to be trying to determine if I was sad or happy to leave. One said, "You'll be back in a year."

I can say, in all sincerity, I was sad to leave, although I knew that it was time.

Epilogue

On December 31, 1988, CRSS closed its office at the university in Dhahran, having completed all work under contract. The files covering the work of twenty-four years were shipped in a container back to Houston.

As Wiley Walker, the final CRSS project manager in the Houston office said, "There are only three people in the world who know what are in those files — Don Chambers, now in North Yemen, Keith Babb, now in England, and you, now in Houston. Guess who's elected."

At the request of CRSS in April 1989, I spent a number of nostalgic weeks at the CRSS office in Houston sorting out the records of over 50 separate projects, 700 change orders, and payment certificates for a billion dollars worth of construction.

By a sad coincidence, on April 8, 1989, Wallie Scott passed on in Houston after retiring from CRSS, the last surviving name partner of Caudill, Rowlett, and Scott.

On March 4, 1989, Dr. Bakr Abdullah bin Bakr, the continuing rector of King Fahd University of Petroleum and Minerals, wrote to Tom Bullock, the CRSS chairman:

"We certainly enjoyed our long and fruitful association with CRSS. During the past quarter of a century our university has considerably expanded in all respects, including the physical facilities. While we are proud of these achievements, we are pleased to acknowledge the contribution of CRSS in helping us give shape to our dreams. CRSS and its contributions will always be remembered."

King Fahd University of Petroleum and Minerals was the kind of project that every architect dreams of. Bill Caudill often wrote what he called "TIBs" for "This I Believe." One of the TIBs was: "UPM is the CRS team's most significant project and its greatest contribution to architectural advancement."

And the buildings have become famous all over the world, symbolizing a modern Saudi Arabia in control of its own destiny.

Epilogue

In 1983, CRS had bought Sirrine Company in South Carolina and adopted the logo "CRSS."

On October 26, 1989, Tom Bullock retired and Bruce Wilkinson was elected chairman and chief executive officer of CRSS, Inc.

With the writing of this book, I must reluctantly admit that the "Personal Encounter," which began for me over fifty years ago at Rice Institute, is now a pleasant memory.

Jebel Dhahran and King Fahd University of Petroleum and Minerals stand as an impressive symbol of the "tangible" and "intellectual" resources of Saudi Arabia and of those many young Saudis of the "New Generation" who, I am confident, will continue to make their "dreams" become "realities."

POSTSCRIPT No. 1

بكى صَاحِبي لَمّا رأى الدَربَ دُونَهُ   وَأيْقَنَ أنّا لاحِقَانِ بِقَيْصَرا
فَقُلْتُ لَهُ لاتَبْكِ عَيْنُكَ إنَّما   نُحَاوِلُ مُلْكَاً أوْ نَمُوتَ فَنُعْذَرا

(امرؤ القيس)

"My friend wept as he saw the way which lay ahead, and realized at last that we were bound for Caesar. I said, 'Do not weep, for we are attempting to gain a kingdom and none will blame us if we perish in the attempt.'"
Imrou al-Qayse

On July 29, 1990, Mildred and I had dinner at the Doubletree Hotel in Houston with Dr. Saleh Bakhrebah and his wife, Afaf, and Don Chambers and his wife, Pat. Don and Pat had just returned to Houston after three years in Sanaa, North Yemen where he was CRSS project director for building the new United States Embassy there. Dr. Bakhrebah and his wife had come to Texas from Saudi Arabia for a few weeks to enroll two of their daughters in college.

This was the first time that we had been together in over four years after spending eleven years working together in Dhahran, Saudi Arabia building the King Fahd University of Petroleum and Minerals. It was a time of nostalgia and reminiscing about this unique and constructive experience.

Dr. Bakhrebah is still at the university as dean of engineering sciences, having retired from his position as secretary general after ten years.

It was pleasant that night to reflect on this great university and speculate on the influence and impact it may have on the future of the Kingdom of Saudi Arabia and its young citizens.

Four days after our evening together, we were startled to hear that Iraq had invaded Kuwait, and the perception prevailed that it was threatening Saudi Arabia. During the next several weeks, the status quo of the region changed dramatically to an extent that none of us could have imagined. It is at

Postscript No. 1

this time impossible to visualize what the long-term effects of these events will be on Saudi Arabia. Regardless of how the Iraq problem is resolved, Saudi Arabia will never be the same. The massive U.S. military presence there will require the greatest skill and sensitivity to disengage successfully, leaving the Kingdom with post-surgical scars.

Hopefully, the university will continue to provide maximum opportunities for many young Saudis who now have "broadened their horizons beyond the rolling dunes of sand."

W. S. S. Jr.
Sept. 3, 1990

POSTSCRIPT No. 2

In January 1991 we watched with morbid fascination in Houston as CNN displayed on our TV screens Scud missiles flying from Iraq over Dhahran and Riyadh. We saw the Patriot missiles launched by the U.S. military intercepting and destroying the Scuds before they could hit the ground.

If not intercepted, the Scuds might have hit any number of locations with devastating effect -- the U.S. Consulate and the International School, the Dhahran International Hotel, the Saudi Air Base, the University of Petroleum and Minerals, hundreds of residences (including the one we had lived in), several shopping centers and highways -- or right in the middle of Aramco itself.

In Dhahran and al-Khobar, all Scuds were intercepted but one, which hit a temporary Army barracks, killing 28 U.S. soldiers not far from the Saudi Air Base. This was a tragic happenstance and not the result of skillful targeting. A few hundred yards in another direction and it would have landed in an open field. Those Scuds that were intercepted were not totally harmless, however. The hundreds of pieces of shrapnel from the Scuds and the Patriots caused some residual damage.

As we watched this awesome spectacle on TV, we wondered how Saudi Arabia would recover from this interruption of its daily life style, which in general is rather relaxed and slow-moving. We speculated with some apprehension that Saudi Arabia might never be the same after this ugly interlude.

In October, less than nine months after these events, my wife and I had the opportunity to visit Saudi Arabia again.

During the war, hundreds of people had left Dhahran for the west coast, and the King Fahd University of Petroleum and Minerals had closed down. During our visit, we were happy to see a resumption of normal living patterns. The hotels and restaurants were the same, and people were about their business as before the war.

Postscript No. 2

The enrollment at the King Fahd University of Petroleum and Minerals is as high as it has ever been. Aramco is beginning to rehire personnel aimed at reactivating operations previously closed down.

We spent several days in Riyadh, and the same picture and appraisal were apparent as in Dhahran. One block from the Sheraton Hotel, where we stayed, a Scud missile had directly hit a school and demolished it. Fortunately, the school was closed, and there were no casualties. King Fahd ordered that it be rebuilt as soon as possible. Less than nine months later, a beautiful new school, larger and better than before, was in operation. This is indicative of Saudi resolve and ability to overcome adversity.

The future is still bright for the Saudis. They are fast acquiring a high degree of education for their people – men and women. They are a rational people with great ability and a disinclination towards rash and ill-considered actions. They are honest and trustworthy allies, and it is in the best interests of the United States to maintain that relationship and try to better understand their culture.

W.S.S. Jr.
May 13, 1992

Appendix I

Research Paper written in 1938 while a student at Rice Institute

THE
ARAB NATIONALIST MOVEMENT

by
WALTER S. SYMONDS, JR.

RICE INSTITUTE, HOUSTON, TEXAS
MAY 10, 1938

A clear and interesting report— The order is especially clear and logical. It was a pleasure to read this paper. My only suggestion is that various details of custom and life should be included to add interest.

2+

Appendix I - Rice Research Paper

Preface

In choosing the subject for my theme, I was led solely by my interest. I chose to write on the struggle of the Arab people for independence from foreign agression because I am interested profoundly in the Arab people. It is my ambition to travel someday in their land. In writing about them I have been able to learn much, and I sincerely hope to be able to impart perhaps a small bit of my familiarization with the subject to someone else.

Contrary to the belief of many persons, the Arabs are not a backward and intellectually inferior race. It is true that they are not as far advanced as other peoples in the scientific world today, but the history of the Arabs for the past five centuries has been one of suppression and agression by foreign nations, which stifled all incentive for progress. If I have shown by my writing that the Arabs have possibilities of once again (provided they are released from the hindrance of foreign meddlers), becoming the great people that they once were, of producing men such as Mohammed, the Prophet, and of building such glamorous cities as the Baghdad of old, then my purpose is fulfilled.

Walter S. Symonds, Jr.
May 10, 1938

Appendix I - Rice Research Paper

The Arab Nationalist Movement

I. Conditions of the Arabs prior to the World War were anything but favorable.
    A. The Turks ruled the Arabs with bloody tyranny.
    B. Secret societies for Arab independence were formed by Arab officers in the Turkish army.
    C. The rulers of the northern Arabs and those of the desert Arabs attempted to establish relations.

II. Great Britain made a pledge to the Arab people.
    A. She promised "a confederation of Arab States or one Independent Arab State, conditioned upon an Arab revolt against the Turks."
        1. Sir Henry McMahon, High Commissioner for Egypt, wrote a letter to this effect to Hussein, Sherif of Mecca.
        2. This was the first recognition by a European power of a pan-Arab movement.
    B. Great Britain then recognized Hussein as King of Hedjaz rather than King of Arabia.
        1. She concluded the Sykes-Picot treaty several months later with France, dividing Palestine, Iraq, and Syria between them.
        2. This constituted the much-discussed betrayal of the Arabs and was a distinct blow to the pan-Arab movement.

Appendix I - Rice Research Paper

III. Ibn Saud, meanwhile, was pursuing his own course of conquest in the heart of the peninsula.
    A. He ousted the Turks from Hasa and ended the rule of the Rashids in central Arabia.
    B. In 1926 he was recognized as King of Hedjaz, Nejd, and its Dependencies.
    C. He has put King Hussein out of the picture and is now recognized as King of Saudi Arabia.
    D. He has succeeded in opening the eyes of the Arabs to many things.
        1. He has shown them the wonders of modern science:
            a. Through the wireless and telephone.
            b. Through the automobile.
        2. He has made them realize the valuable resources of their land.
        3. He has established a real brotherhood among all the tribes.
        4. He has made them realize the superiority of the rural life over nomadism.
        5. Above all, he has taught them that Allah himself has entrusted him with the task of unifying Arabia.
IV. The present Zionist situation in Palestine presents a difficult problem.
    A. The Zionists claim that Palestine should not be included in the United Arab Kingdom because of clauses in Mc Mahon's pledge and the Sykes-Picot treaty which excludes Palestine.

Appendix I - Rice Research Paper

B. Great Britain has proposed a partition of Palestine between the Arabs and the Jews.
   1. If the scheme carries through, Amir Abdullah will proba ly be ruler of Arab Palestine.
   2. In the partition the colonies south of Jaffa and a section in the Safed region should be under Arab government,, and the Jerusalem corridor should be admi:istrated by the mandatory power.

V. Possibilities of the uniting of Arabia are hopeful.
   A. Internal factors aid.
      1. The desert Bedouins are now united rather than at war as in former times.
      2. The reaction of the population against foreign corporations and the mercenary spirit of foreign educational and benevolent institutions also aid.
   B. External factors aid.
      1. The presence of Turks in Alexandretta and the French in Mt. Lebanon help to agitate the Arabs.
      2. The British partitioning policy in Palestine agitates the Arabs of Saudi Arabia.
   C. Ibn Saud is on good terms with all European powers.

Appendix I - Rice Research Paper

The Arab Nationalist Movement

Many empires and nations in the past have risen and fallen; many races of people have struggled to free themselves from bondage imposed upon them by more powerful races; and many races have struggled for their so-called nationalism. This struggle is an old story, which has often been repeated. Today in Arabia this story is again being repeated.

Before discussing the subject of Arab nationalism, it is necessary to realize just what the word means. Lothrop Stoddard defines nationalism as a state of mind. He says that " nationalism is a belief, held by a fairly large number of individuals, that they constitute a ' Nationality '; it is a sense of belonging together as a ' Nation.'" It is this desire to "belong

---
1 Lothrop Stoddard, The New World of Islam (New York, 1922), pp. 157-158.
---

together as a 'nation'" which has inspired the leaders of the Arabs during the past several decades to lead their people in asserting their integrity and freedom from foreign rule.

The geography of Arabia is in itself enough to discourage an attempt to unify the Arabs. A vast peninsula of desert, it is bounded on the North by Turkey; on the West by the Red Sea, the Egyptian frontier, and the Mediterranean Sea; on the South by the Arabian Sea; and on the East by Persia and the Persian

Appendix I - Rice Research Paper

Gulf. The peninsula is split into numerous states and tribes ruled by their respective Amirs and chiefs. There are vast expanses of desert between these tribes, thus making it difficult to communicate and to create singularity of thought, which is essential to a unified state. In spite of these very unfavorable conditions there has been for hundreds of years, since the Prophet and the first four Caliphs, a distinct desire by the Arabs for a unified and independent Arab State.[2] Recently this dream

[2] Ameen Rihani, "The Pan-Arab Dream," Asia, XXXVIII, 44.

has been growing in intensity and appears to be approaching its realization.

For four hundred years prior to the World War the Arabs suffered continuously under the Ottoman rule of the Turks. All hopes of an Arab nationalist movement were completely crushed, and the Arabs lived in constant suppression. The civilization of the Arabs suffered a severe decline. The Arabs whose lands were once fertile, whose ancestors contributed valuably to the world literature, science, and art, and whose city of Baghdad was one of the wonders of the world had definitely vanished.[3] Besides

[3] Sir Stanley Maude, "The Proclamation of Baghad," The King of Hedjaz and Arab Independence, p. 13.

exerting their power on the Arabs with extreme cruelty, the Turks disregarded all respect for the one thing which is foremost in an Arab's mind--his religion.[4]

[4] Ibid., p. 10.

Appendix I - Rice Research Paper

The first indications of the contemporary nationalist movement of the Arabs appeared in the first decade of the present century. The rulers of the states of Nejd, Yemen, and Asir succeeded in driving the Turks from their respective territories.

5 Rihani, op. cit., p. 44.

Although this was not actually the nationalist movement, it was the rejuvenation of the Arab spirit. In 1908 during the Turkish revolution several young Arab officers in the Turkish army met in Constantinople to form a secret movement for the liberating of the Arabs from the Turkish rule. Another conference was held in Paris in 1913. At the outbreak of the World War Ibn Saud,

6 Ibid.

then Amir of Nejd, proposed a meeting of all the Arab rulers for the purpose of an independence movement. Because of the antagonistic attitude towards Ibn Saud of two rulers, Ibn ur-Rashid and the Sherif Hussein, the meeting never took place.

7 Ibid.

Soon after the event of the World War the pan-Arab movement received its first recognition by a foreign power. This was in the form of a pledge from the British to the Arabs. It was a letter from Sir Henry McMahon, High Commissioner for Egypt, to Hussein, Sherif of Mecca, pledging aid in the establishing of "a Confederation of Arab States, or one United Arab State, conditioned upon an Arab revolt against the Turks." The Arabs

Appendix I - Rice Research Paper

8 M. W. Weisgal, The Claims of the Arabs and the Answer of the Jews, p. 8.

revolted and succeeded in driving the Turks from Arabia. They had successfully carried out their part of the agreement with Great Britain. Now they thought that they would receive aid from Great Britain in establishing an empire, "independent in its internal and foreign affairs, bounded on the East by the Persian Gulf, on the West by the Red Sea, the Egyptian frontier and the Mediterranean, and on the North by the boundary line of the two vilayets of Aleppo and Mosul, and down to the Persian Gulf"--so they thought. 9/ But evidently Great Britain and France were pur-

9 Rihani, op. cit., p. 44.

suing policies of their own, irrespective of pledges; for a few months after the conclusion of the agreement with Hussein, England and France negotiated the Sykes-Picot Treaty, which divided Palestine, Syria, and Iraq as spheres of influence between them. England recognized Hussein not as King of Arabia, but only as King of Hedjaz, a province in Western Arabia which occupies a little less than 150,000 square miles. 10/ The Arabs had been be-

10 "Proclamation of the Sherif of Mecca", The King of Hedjaz and Arab Independence, (London, 1917), p. 4.

trayed. England had failed to carry out fully her agreement. This was a severe blow to the nationalist movement, which under Hussein had made considerable progress. During the short reign of King Feisal, Hussein's son, hope was again renewed but term-

Appendix I - Rice Research Paper

iated with his death. [11]

---

11 Rihani, op. cit., p. 45.

Once again the movement is gaining a foothold. This time under a man of superior leadership, "bent upon leading his people to assert their national integrity and to modify ancient national cultures as a means of withstanding the ever-rising pressure of the modern world." [12] The man is Ibn Saud, formerly the Amir of

---

12 Henry Filmer, "Modern Iran", Asia, XXXVIII, 23.

Nejd. The Arab world and the British Foreign Office began to take notice of him after he had put the Turks out of Hasa and ended the rule of the Rashids in Central Arabia. [13] He has succeeded in

---

13 Rihani, op. cit., p. 45.

---

putting all other rulers out of the picture, and he is now recognized by Great Britain as King of Saudi Arabia, which includes Hedjaz, Nejd, and its Dependencies. [14]

---

14 Ibid.,

Ameen Rihani says that Ibn Saud "never flatters or minces words. He is forthright and free, with an engaging breeziness at times, whether he is expressing an opinion of meting out praise or condemnation." [15] He is as quick to condemn the Arabs as any-

---

15 Ibid.

---

one, and he believes that the plight of the Arabs is of their own making. "Let them unite today," says Ibn Saud, "and there will be

422

Appendix I - Rice Research Paper

no foreigners to give them a headache tomorrow." 16/ Being more

---
16 <u>Ibid</u>.

---

a man of action then of words, he has opened the eyes of the Arabs to things which to them had never before existed. He has shown them the wonders of modern science. He has made the vast distances of the desert recede to the might of the wheel and engine. He has filled them with awe by the wonders of the telephone and telegraph. Through him the Arabs have learned that continual tribal warfare is unprofitable and that domestic life is much superior to their habitual nomadic life. They have seen by the production of oil and the mining of gold that their land is not as barren as they once thought it to be. But above all, he has taught them that Allah himself has bestowed Ibn Saud with the "task of unifying the power and preserving the integrity of Arabia." 17/

---
17 <u>Ibid</u>.

The nationalist policy of the Arabs in Palestine presents a slightly different problem. The presence and attitude of the Jews lends difficulty to the movement there. Because of certain clauses in the Sykes-Picot Treaty the Zionists claim that Palestine should not be included in any scheme for the national unification of the Arabs. 18/ There is at present a proposal by Great Britain to

---
18 M. W. Weisgal, <u>op. cit</u>., p.9.

---

form a partition of Palestine between the Arabs and Jews with a British Mandate containing the cities of Jerusalem and Bethlehem. 19/

Appendix I - Rice Research Paper

19 Jackson Fleming,"A Visit to Amir Abdullah", Asia, XXXVIII, p. 64.

In case of such a partition it is generally assumed that Amir Abdullah, the present ruler of Transjordania, will become ruler also of Arab Palestine. 20/ The ultimate success of this nationalist

20 Ibid, p. 63.

movement depends largely on the solution of the problem in Palestine.

Few people had heard of Arab nationalism in 1900. In 1926 it was still regarded as being of rather doubtful strength and vitality. 21/ Today it is regarded as a distinct probability.

21 Hans Kohn, "The Restless Near East", Asia, XXXVIII, p. 20.

The principle responsibility lies upon the shoulders of Ibn Saud. His task is not at all easy. He must continually address at the same time the Arab world, the tribes, the world of Islam, the powers of the Near East, and the European powers. For each he must use a different word and different gesture for every circumstance.

22 Rihani, op. cit., p. 45.

There are many favorable and unfavorable factors concerning the realization of the Arab independence. The favorable factors appear at present to predominate. About two years ago a treaty of Arab Brotherhood and Alliance was concluded between Saudi Arabia and Iraq. The State of Yemen has recently adhered to this Treaty;

Appendix I - Rice Research Paper

and the Arab principalities of the Persian Gulf are likely to follow eventually. 23/ The Prime Minister of the Syrian Republic,

---
23 Rihani, op. cit., pp. 45-46.

Jamil Mardam Bey, recently declared that a democratic government in Syria is being established, whose utmost goal is Arab unity. He stated that "in exerting every effort to attain this goal, his government would first remove all customs barriers between Syria and other Arab states, would abolish passports and would recommend the adoption of a uniform program of education." 24/ The Foreign

---
24 Ibid.

Ministers of both countries signed the Protocol at Riyadh in November, 1936, which abolished visas for the necessary free movement of the border tribes. 25/ In Nejd before the days of Ibn Saud

---
25 Ibid.

---

the Bedouin tribes fought and killed each other continuously. They now live domestically and in peace.with a feeling of brotherhood. The Bedouins of Northern Arabia are divided by the mandatory powers into the territories of Syria, Transjordania, and Iraq. This causes an unnatural and inharmonious separation. When there is a drought in one territory, the Arabs cannot cross the border into another in order to get water for themselves and their animals. This causes the illiterate Bedouins, who cannot be reached by propaganda, to awaken to the evils of foreign rules and restrictions. The mercenary spirit of foreign institutions also stirs up dislike

Appendix I - Rice Research Paper

by the Arabs for foreign occupation of their land. The colonial policies of foreign powers is another aggravating factor. Ameen Rihani writes that "the presence of the Turks in Alexandretta, the French in Mount Lebanon, the British and Jews in Palestine, together with the intended separation and independence of these countries from Arabia, is producing storms of resentment throughout the Arab world." [26] All of these conditions have a very

---
26 Ibid.

---

definite effect on the Arabs, causing them to combine with a common interest--the independence of Arabia from all foreign encroachments.

Up to the present time Ibn Saud has had very friendly relations with Great Britain. This friendship is based on a treaty made by his grandfather, Amir Feisal, with the British representative, Colonel Pelly in 1865. [27] This friendship has endured many

---
27 Ibid, p. 46.

---

difficulties in the past, but it faces its most severe crisis today. As yet Ibn Saud has not overrun Yemen. However, it is doubtless that he will, sooner or later. When he does he will be at the border of the Aden Protectorate, whose tribes are bound closely to Great Britain by treaties. He will then have desires to extend his control into the Aden Hinterland. Hence the probable difficulty. [28]

---
28 Leonard Handley, "In the Aden Hinterland", Asia, XXXVIII, p. 49

Ibn Saud is on friendly terms with all European powers, many of

Appendix I - Rice Research Paper

whom are the rivals of Great Britain. Recently there have been obvious attempts by Mussolini and his Fascists to gain the favor of the Arabs and to alienate their affection for the British. There have been many anti-British broadcasts from Bari. This Fascist propaganda has had its effect. However, "the Arabs do not believe everything they hear in the loud speaker." [29]

---

29 R. G. Woolbert, "Mussolini Flirts With Islam", Asia, XXXVIII, p. 32.

The question at present is "Who is going to be the friend of the new Arabia?" [30] It is obvious that the Arabs would prefer

---

30 Ibid., p. 34.

Great Britain, if the Palestine situation could be settled. Whether this can be settled to the satisfaction of both parties remains to be seen. One fact, however, is certain: "There is undoubtedly a new generation rising out of the gangrened mass of the old, a young Arab generation, healthy and strong and dynamic, educated along modern lines, fired with new ideals, social and political, and joining in the struggle of the nationalists everywhere in the Arab world". [31] And from all outward indications it is obvious that

---

31 Ameen Rihani, "The New Syrian Republic", Asia, XXXVIII, p. 51.

---

with this new generation of Arabs there will spring forth a new Arabia, united and independent. "The center of gravity of the Muslim faith will return to Arabia, its birthplace". [32]

Appendix I - Rice Research Paper

32 Leonard Handley, op. cit., p. 49.

So perhaps the Arab people, after having thrown off their yoke of bondage, will once again contribute to the world of literature and art and will rise again to the remarkable cultural and intellectual greatness that was once theirs.

Appendix I - Rice Research Paper

Bibliography

Filmer, Henry. "Modern Iran", <u>Asia</u>, XXXVIII, pp. 23-28.

Fleming, Jackson. "A Visit to Amir Abdullah", <u>Asia</u>, XXXVIII, pp. 63-65.

Handley, Leonard. "In The Aden Hinterland", <u>Asia</u>, XXXVIII, pp. 49-50.

Kohn, Hans. "The Restless Near East", <u>Asia</u>, XXXVIII, pp. 17-20.

Maude, Sir Stanley. "Proclamation of Baghdad", <u>The King of Hedjaz and Arab Independence</u>, London, 1917, pp. 12-15.

"Proclamation of the Sherif of Mecca", <u>The King of Hedjaz and Arab Independence</u>, London, 1917, pp. 6-11.

Rihani, Ameen. "The New Syrian Republic", <u>Asia</u>, XXXVIII, pp. 51-54.

Rihani, Ameen. "The Pan-Arab Dream", <u>Asia</u>, XXXVIII, pp. 44-46.

Stoddard, Lothrop. <u>The New World of Islam</u>. New York, 1922, pp. 157-238.

Weisgal, Meyer W. <u>The Claims of the Arabs and the Answer of the Jews</u>, I, New York.

Woolbert, Robert G. "Mussolini Flirts With Islam", <u>Asia</u>, XXXVIII, pp.32

Appendix II

Letter from Dr. Saleh A. Bakhrebah

BTA/100/426/77

1 NOVEMBER 1977

Mr. Walter S. Symonds
CRS

Dear Mr. Symonds

I would like to thank you for your valuable assistance in helping us to prepare for the inauguration ceremony when the cornerstone for Phase 4 Construction was unveiled.

As you know this ceremony marked a very important step in the continued expansion of the University and was honoured by the presence of His Majesty King Khalid Ibn Abdul Aziz. Many other distinguished guests were present and we were very pleased to have been able to arrange such a successful celebration for this occasion.

The dignified and impressive design which you prepared for the backdrop to the festivities was much admired by all our guests. Your rapid response and major effort to achieve this result in a very short time was very much appreciated.

Again my deepest thanks for helping us so effectively to celebrate this joyous occasion.

With warm personal regards.

Sincerely yours,

DR. SALEH A. BAKHREBAH
DEAN OF BUSINESS &
TECHNICAL AFFAIRS

Appendix III

Letter from Mr. F.W. Ohliger concerning brick pillars

FLOYD W. OHLIGER
BUCKS COUNTY
PINEVILLE, PENNSYLVANIA 18946

15 August 1980

Mr. Walter S. Symonds, Jr.
Resident Architect
University of Petroleum and Minerals
Dhahran, Saudi Arabia

Dear Mr. Symonds:

At last we have confirmation, if confirmation is necessary at this stage. The brick pillars on the site of your park are indeed the remnants of the arch which formed the entrance to King Abdulaziz' camp when he visited the area 28 April - 1 May. The occasion was the ceremony of opening the valve to start the flow of Saudi crude oil to the ports of the world. The actual date was 1 May 1939. Bill Palmer who participated in erecting the pillars provided the confirmation.

The pillars, including the pipe extensions, were wrapped in cloth - white trimmed in green. The headboard across the top - probably about a meter wide - had the same covering. On the headboard was the Saudi Royal emblem - crossed swords with palm tree. The creed of King Abdulaziz and his country could have been there also but I'm not sure.

So far we have not come up with photos of the arch in question but we will continue, particularly Palmer, to see if we can find some. There is a good chance that none were taken since all hands at the time were kept very busy on other things during the entire visit. We had planned for the King and his retinue to stay up in our compound but there were so many who had joined up with the procession that on arrival there the King chose to move down to the site in question in order to be with the well-wishers. On the late side of the day all of our men heaved to to build a small city with running water, electricity and the necessary comforts. It was quite an operation.

I hope this information reaches you in time to be useful. I will send you copies of photos if we find them.

My best wishes,

Floyd Ohliger

Appendix IV

INSCRIPTION
KING ABDUL AZIZ MONUMENT

A Royal Camp was erected in this area for the man who united the Arabian Provinces and was protector of its modern prosperity, His Majesty King Abdul Aziz bin Abdul Rahman al-Faisal al-Saud, during the period 28th of April 1939 to 10th of May 1939.

His Majesty, God Help His Soul, came to this area to celebrate the opening of the oil pipeline valve that would begin the flow from the Kingdom, declaring the opening of the doors of generosity to his loyal countrymen, through the help and protection of God.

The Royal Camp held 2700 people and His Majesty was accompanied by the Royal Princes, Ministers, Highest Government Officials, and important personalities of the Eastern Province. His Majesty received also His Highness Sheik Sulman bin Khalifa, the Prince of Bahrain.

These two pillars defined the Camp Entrance and have been restored in their original shape and location.

The oil wealth, a diminishing resource, was found in this place, which was later chosen to be the location for the University of Petroleum and Minerals, as a means to develop human power which has an immortal source.

It was a very wise decision by our benevolent government to promote the role of the University by -

Education, to produce the necessary human resources:

Scientific Research, to broaden the horizons of knowledge and to solve problems:

General Services, to offer the services of the University to the largest section of citizens.

The location chosen for the University of Petroleum and Minerals links the tangible resource of power with the permanent intellectual resources, and is a symbol of the continuation of the sunny present to a prosperous future, with the help of God.

Appendix V

Appendix V is a partial reproduction of "THE YEARBOOK OF THE STUDENTS OF THE COLLEGE OF PETROLEUM & MINERALS DHAHRAN, SAUDI ARABIA FOR THE YEAR 1968 - 1969".

This was the second yearbook that was published by the students and includes the first graduating class. In a sense, these students and others like them are the pioneers of the New Saudi Generation. A few of these students now have sons who are students, a second generation at the university.

Quoting from the letter from the Editor-in-Chief, Moujahed Husseini, in the yearbook:

" . . . we hope to give those persons who are not familiar with the College an idea of who we are, what we do, how we do it, and what we aim for the future."

This is also my purpose over twenty years later in including this as an appendix, as well as giving credit to the early founders of the university, acknowledging their accomplishment.

Appendix V - College of Petroleum & Minerals Student Yearbook

الكليه
الكتاب السنوي
لطلبة كلية البترول والمعادن
الظهران - المملكه العربيه السعوديه
١٣٨٨ - ١٣٨٩

AL-KULLIYAH
THE YEAR BOOK OF THE STUDENTS OF
THE COLLEGE OF PETROLEUM & MINERALS
DHAHRAN, SAUDI ARABIA
1968 - 1969

Appendix V - College of Petroleum & Minerals Student Yearbook

الاهــــداء

الى صاحب القلب الكبير
الى عظيم متواضع قل نظيره
الى حامي الدين وناشر العلم
الى باعث النهضة الجبارة في اطراف بلاده المترامية
الى جلالة مليكنا المفدى فيصل بن عبد العزيز آل سعود المعظم
الى جلالته نتقدم بكتابنا المتواضع هذا دليل شكر وولاءً لرعايته كليتنا وطلابها ، وتقديراً لكل ما يبذله جلالته في سبيل العلم وطلابه ، وعهداً علينا بان نكون كما ارادنا : بناة مملكة المستقبل .

DEDICATION

To His Majesty King Faisal, Sponsor of our Educational and Cultural advancement, we humbly and respectfully dedicate this yearbook as a sign of our gratitude for the support and kindness with which he has cherished our College and encouraged its rapid growth over the past few years, and as a mark of our appreciation for his love of knowledge and interest in education of all forms in the Kingdom of Saudi Arabia.

Appendix V - College of Petroleum & Minerals Student Yearbook

حضرة صاحب الجلالة الملك فيصل بن عبد العزيز آل سعود المعظم

HIS MAJESTY KING FAISAL BIN ABD-AL-AZIZ AL-SAUD

Appendix V - College of Petroleum & Minerals Student Yearbook

صاحب السمو الملكي الأمير فهد بن عبد العزيز النائب الثاني لرئيس مجلس الوزراء ووزير الداخلية ورئيس لجنة السياسة العليا للتعليم بالمملكة

PRINCE FAHAD BIN ABDUL-AZIZ
Second Deputy Prime Minister, Minister of Interior,
Chairman Higher Education Council

Appendix V - College of Petroleum & Minerals Student Yearbook

عــميد الكــليه
DEAN OF THE COLLEGE
1963-1969

Dr. Saleh Ambah

عــميد الكــليّــة
DEAN OF THE COLLEGE
1971

Dr. Bakr Abdullah Bin Bakr

Appendix V - College of Petroleum & Minerals Student Yearbook

أعضاء مجلس الإدارة
THE MEMBERS OF THE BOARD OF TRUSTEES

سعادة الدكتور فاضل خيري القباني
وكيل وزارة البترول للثروة المعدنيه

Dr. Fadhil Kabbani
Deputy Minister of Mineral Resources

صَاحِبُ المَعَالِي الشَّيخ أحمَد زَكي يَمَاني وَزير البَترُول وَالثَروة المَعدِنيَّه

His Excellency Sheikh
Ahmad Zaki Yamani
Minister of Petroleum and Mineral Resources

سعادة الدكتور عبد العزيز الخويطر
مدير جامعة الرياض بالنيابه

Dr. Abdul-Aziz Khowaiter
Vice Rector of Riyadh University

سعادة الدكتور عبد الهادي طاهر
محافظ المؤسسة العامة للبترول والمعادن (بترومين)

Dr. Abdul Hadi Taher
Governor, General Petroleum and Mineral Organization (PETROMIN)

Appendix V - College of Petroleum & Minerals Student Yearbook

BOARD OF TRUSTEES

الدكتور هارولد هيزن
عميد متقاعد للدراسات العليا بمعهد ماساتشوستس للتكنولوجيا

Dr. Harold Hazen
Dean Emeritus, Graduate School of M.I.T.

سعادة الأستاذ عبد الوهاب عبد الواسع
وكيل وزارة المعارف

Mr. Abdul Wahab Abdul Wasi'
Deputy Minister of Education

المسيو جـان فافر
مدير العلاقات الخارجية لمعهد البترول الفرنسي

Mr. Jean Favre
Directeur des Relations Etrangeres,
Institut Francais du Petrole

الدكتور صموئيل كيركوود
رئيس الجامعة الأمريكية ببيروت

Dr. Samuel B. Kirkwood
President, American University of Beirut

Appendix V - College of Petroleum & Minerals Student Yearbook

BOARD OF TRUSTEES

سعادة الأستاذ محمد صالح جوخدار
وكيل وزارة البترول والثروة المعدنية بالنيابه
Mr. Mohammad Joukhdar
Acting Deputy Minister of Petroleum and Mineral Resources

سعادة الأستاذ فهد الدغيثر
مدير عام معهد الادارة العامه
Mr. Fahd Al-Dughaither
Director General, Institute of Public Administration

أعضاء مجلس الاداره يناقشون مناهج كلية الهندسه مع بعض الاداريين.

Members of the Board of Trustees meet with some of the administrators to discuss the Engineering curriculum

Appendix V - College of Petroleum & Minerals Student Yearbook

COLLEGE ADMINISTRATION

الدكتور روبرت كنج هول
كبير مستشاري الكليه
Dr. Robert King Hall
Senior Advisor

سعادة الدكتور ناصر ابراهيم الرشيد
عميد الشؤون الفنية والادارية
Dr. Nasser Ibrahim Al-Rashid
Dean of Business

الدكتور رونالد سكوت
عميد الهندسه
Dr. Ronald Scott
Dean of Engineering

الدكتور هاري سنايدر
عميد العلوم والخدمات التعليميه
Dr. Harry Snyder
Dean of Science & Educational Services

Appendix V - College of Petroleum & Minerals Student Yearbook

COLLEGE ADMINISTRATION

الأستاذ رضا ناظر
مساعد العميد للشؤون الاداريه
Mr. Rida Nazer
Asst. Dean for Business Affairs

السيد عدنان خيال
مدير قسم المحاسبة والماليه
Mr. Adnan Khayal
Director of Accounting and Finance

لسيد عبد المحسن الجريب
مدير الاسكان والخدمات
Mr. Abdul Mohsin Juraib
Director of Housing & Services

السيد أميديو بورو
مدير قسم الصيانة والخدمات
Mr. Amedeo Poro
Director of Maintenance and Services

Appendix V - College of Petroleum & Minerals Student Yearbook

ي مناقشة مع بعض أعضاء هيئة التدريس...
In discussion with faculty members ...

ثلاثة من مختلف نشاطات سعادة العميد
THREE ASPECTS OF THE DEAN'S WORK

... ومــع الطــلاب ...
... with the students

...وأخيرا مع صاحب المعالي الشيخ أحمد زكي يماني .
... and finally with His Excellency Sheikh Ahmad Zaki Yamani

Appendix V - College of Petroleum & Minerals Student Yearbook

أول عضو فخري في رابطة الطلاب

كان لرابطة الطلاب عظيم الشرف عندما حظت في ٢٤ ذي القعدة ١٣٨٨ بتكرم صاحب السمو الملكي الأمير سلطان بن عبد العزيز وزير الدفاع والطيران بالانتساب إليها كأول عضو شرف فيها .

THE FIRST HONORARY MEMBER OF THE STUDENT UNION

On the 10th of February, 1969, the Student Union was honored by HRH Prince Sultan becoming the first honorary member of the Union.

حضرة صاحب السمو الملكي الأمير سلطان بن عبد العزيز يبدي انطباعاته عن الرابطة للدكتور صالح أمبه بينما يعلو السرور محيا منصور ناظر رئيس الرابطة الأسبق .

HRH Prince Sultan discusses the merits of the Student Union with the Dean, Dr. Ambah, while M. Nazer, ex-president looks on.

سمو الأمير سلطان يرد على تحية الطلاب له عندما أظهروا شعورهم بالتقدير والشكر لبادرة سموه بالتبرع بمبلغ (٥٠٠٠) ريال سعودي لمشاريع رابطة الطلاب .

HRH Prince Sultan salutes the students as they applaud his generous contribution of 5000 S.R. to the Union.

Appendix V - College of Petroleum & Minerals Student Yearbook

رابطـــة الطــــلاب

عند التحاقه بالكلية يصبح كل طالب عضوا في رابطة الطلاب . وتعنى هذه الرابطة بمختلف نشاطات الطلاب باشراف من ادارة الكليه ، والغرض منها تنمية روح المسؤولية والتعاون بين الطلاب . وينتخب مجلس الرابطة من الطلاب مرة كل فصل دراسي .

STUDENT UNION

All students at CPM automatically become members in the Student Union upon entrance. The Union is an organization which helps the students develop a sense of cooperation and responsibility. Members of the Union Board are selected once every semester by the students.

عضاء مجلس الرابطه :
جلوسا من اليسار : محمد جخدار ، أمين الصندوق – حمزه قرطلي ، رئيس اللجنة الرياضيه – جاسم الأنصاري، رئيس الرابطه –
سعيد الشامسي ، رئيس لجنة حي السكن – طارق البسام ، رئيس اللجنة العلميه –
قوفــا : منير شعراوي ، رئيس لجنة الأنديه – ابراهيم الأهدل ، نائب الرئيس – مجاهد الحسيني ، رئيس اللجنة الثقافيه.

Seated (L to R); M. Joukhdar, Treasurer; H. Geretli, Chairman of the Sport's Committee; J. Ansari, President; S. Shamsi, Representative of the House activities; T. Bassam, Chairman of the Science Club.
Standing: M. Sha'rawi, Representative of the Clubs; 1. Ahdal, Vice President; M Husseini, Chairman of the Cultural Committee.

Appendix V - College of Petroleum & Minerals Student Yearbook

لجـنة رؤسـاء البيوت
HOUSE CAPTAINS COMMITTEE

يهتم أعضاء هذه اللجنة بتنظيم الرحلات والحفلات والنشاطات المختلفة لبيوتهم في حي السكن .

The House Captains Committee is responsible for organizing activities and trips within each house in the Student Compound.

اللجنة الثقـافيّـه
CULTURAL COMMITTEE

تقوم اللجنة الثقافيه باصدار صحيفة « الصحراء » مرة كل فصل دراسي و « طوربيد لصحراء » مرتين شهريا لتغطية أخبار الكلية والطلاب . كما تقيم الندوات الثقافية وتحيي المحاضرات ينبثق عنها لجنة الكتاب السنوي .

The Cultural Committee promotes the exchange of Cultural ideas through a periodical newspaper Al-Satura TORPEDO.

Appendix V - College of Petroleum & Minerals Student Yearbook

اللجنة الرياضية
SPORTS COMMITTEE

تقوم هذه اللجنه باعداد برامج المباريات الرياضية بين البيوت ومع الفرق الخارجية بمساعدة قسم الرياضة البدنية في الكليه .

The Sports Committee arranges interhouse and interscholastic matches with the guidance of the Physical Education Dept .

لجنة النشاط العام
GENERAL ACTIVITIES COMMITTEE

نعتبر هذه اللجنه مسؤولة عن تنظيم حفلات الرابطة السنويه .

The General Activities Committee is responsible for the necessary preparations of the Student Union Parties.

Appendix V - College of Petroleum & Minerals Student Yearbook

النّادي الفَني
ART CLUB

بعض اعضاء النادي مع رئيسه فاروق كونش
Members of the Art Club with F. Konash, Chairman.

نادي التصوير
PHOTOGRAPHY CLUB

أعضاء نادي التصوير مع رئيسه يوسف الكوهجي .
Photography Club with Y. Kohegi, Chairman.

Appendix V - College of Petroleum & Minerals Student Yearbook

نَادي الموسيقى

MUSIC CLUB

يعطي الأستاذ محمد عقيل الجناحي أعضاء النادي دروسا في الموسيقى مرتين في الأسبوع .

Mr. Muhamad Agil Janahi, the music instructor, gives the members of the Music Club lessons twice a week.

أعضاء نادي الموسيقى مع رئيسه محمد شوكت حسن .

The Music Club members with their President, Muhammad S. Hassen.

الرِّيَاضَه
Sports

Appendix V - College of Petroleum & Minerals Student Yearbook

عند اقترابهم من سكن الأساتذة الجنوبي،
كان ز. شاهين في الطليعة يتبعه المِيداني ..

After circling the new faculty compound Z. Shaheen takes the lead while K. Maidani follows at a close distance.

... الذي ما لبث ان تخطاه محتلا المركز الأول .
وحل القناص ثانيا و ز. شاهين في المرتبة
الثالثه .

... but eventually dashes to take the first place. K. Gannas took second and Z. Shaheen came in third. Victory was for Al-Razi House.

Appendix V - College of Petroleum & Minerals Student Yearbook

أعضاء الفريق :
من اليسار : باغبره ، شمس ، بحارنه ، ميدني ، الغانم ، بكر (الكابتن) ، العوضي ، الغامدي ، با عبدالله ، شقدار ، المطلق ، غالب

The Football Varsity: (L to R) M. Baghabrah, A. Shams, N. Baharnah, M. Badyah, K. Maidani, M. Ghanem, A. Bakr (captain), M. Awadi, U. Ghamdi, M. Ba-Abdullah, 1. Shugdar, K. Al-Mutlag, H. Ghalib.

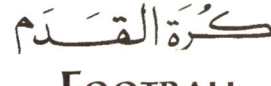

FOOTBALL

كرة ضعيفة من فريقنا يقطعها دفاع فريق مطار الظهران .
CPM players crowd in a bit too late to score a goal.

Appendix V - College of Petroleum & Minerals Student Yearbook

كُرَة السَّله

BASKETBALL

أعضاء الفريق : الآرنؤوط ، غالب ، شبيب ، م. حسيني ، جخدار ، روس ، هـ. حسيني (الكابتن) .
الجالسون : مازن بدر ، ز. شاهين ، ماهر بدر ، البسام .

Basketball Varsity Team; (Top, L to R) A. Arnaout, H. Ghalib, S. Shabib, M. Husseini, M. Joukhdar, Mr. Ross, H. Husseini (captain). (lower row) Mazin Badr, Z. Shaheen, Maher Badr, A. Bassam.

Down from a lost rebound... ... and up for a well blocked shot.

Appendix V - College of Petroleum & Minerals Student Yearbook

كُرة الطَّائِرَه

VOLLEYBALL

عضاء الفريق :
ن اليسار : جفري ، هـ. شاهين ، حديثي ، بروكتر ، بدير ، شرف ، غالب (الكابتن) .
لجالسون : بكر ، قرطلي ، حكمي . لم يتصور : أبو التين .

Volleyball Varsity Team: (Top L to R) A. Jifri, H. Shaheen, S. Hudaithi, Mr. Proctor, M. Budair, A. Sharaf, H. Ghalib (captain)
(Lower row) A Bakr, H> Geretli, A. Hekami; not photographed: R. Abuttin

شاهين يرسل كرة سريعة ومضمونه

Henry sends a fast sure serve.

أبو التين يتخلص بمهارة من كرة غير مواتيه

Abuttin cleverly handles a ball that he couldn't smash.

Appendix V - College of Petroleum & Minerals Student Yearbook

رحْلةُ الطلابِ الى تُركيَّا

STUDENTS TRIP TO TURKEY

... وغادرنا مطار الظهران الدولي ...
... and we left Dhahran International Airport...

... وبعد ساعات ثمان ، حطت بنا « ابن فرناس » على أرض المطار في تركيا ...
...and after eight hours we were in the Land of the Bosphorous.

457

Appendix V - College of Petroleum & Minerals Student Yearbook

STUDENTS TRIP TO TURKEY

... ثم مسجد السلطان أحمد المعروف بالمسجد الأزرق (١٦١٦م) ...

Next, we visited The Mosque of Sultan Ahmad, known as The Blue Mosque, which was built in 1616.

... وانتهى بنا مطاف ذلك اليوم الى قلعة (روميلي حصار» (١٤٥٢) على البوسفور .

Our last visit in Istanbul was to the Castle of Rumali Hisar (1452) on the Bosphorous.

458

Appendix V - College of Petroleum & Minerals Student Yearbook

رسـالة مِنَ المحـرر

أما وقد اقتربنا من الغلاف الأخير ، فيجدر بنا الوقوف قليلا لنعبر عن شعورنا نحو الذين ساهموا في اظهار هذا الكتاب الى حيز الوجود .

فسعادة عميد الكلية ، الدكتور صالح أمبه ، شمل ويشمل كل نشاط طلابي مثمر برعايته وتشجيعه ومساهمته . وكان للاهتمام الكبير والاقتراحات المفيدة التي أبداها عميد شؤون الطلاب ، الأستاذ عبد المنان الترجمان ، أثرها الفعال في عملنا . كما كان لاندفاع السيد فؤاد أبو حمدان وخدماته دورها في تسهيل بعض مشاكلنا . أما مطابع المطوع فقد أبدت لنا كل تشجيع وتسهيل لمشروعنا . فاليهم جميعا تقديرنا وشكرنا .

كما يجدر بنا أن ننوه بأن الكتاب السنوي كان فكرة بدأها الطالب عبد الله المقرن بالكلية في ربيع العام الماضي .. وها هو الكتاب الثاني بين أيديكم وقد أصدرته هذا العام اللجنة الثقافية في رابطة الطلاب بمساعدة نادي التصويـــر .

ولا يفوتني هنا أن أذكر بدور حضرات المعلنين الكرام الذين شاركوا بدعم الكتاب ماديا بالاعلان عن مؤسساتهم فيه . فباسم الطلاب والرابطة ، أتقدم اليهم بأعمق الشكر .

ولن تساءل من طلابنا عن هدف الكتاب السنوي أقول : « هو كتاب تحتفظ به لوقت طويل يذكرك بنفسك ، بكليتك ، بطلابها ، بأساتذتها ، بادارتها ، بمرافقها ، بملاعبها ، بنشاطاتها ، يذكرك بسنة كاملة من عمرك فضمه الى مكتبة ذكرياتك لترتفع قيمته لديك كلما مرت الأعوام » .

ولكل من لا يعرف الكلية ، يعطي هذا الكتاب فكرة عنا : من نحن ، بماذا نهتم ، من يهتم بنا ، ماذا نعمل ، كيف نؤدي أعمالنا ، كيف نقوم بنشاطاتنا ، وما هو المستقبل الذي نصبو اليه .

رئيس التحرير
مجاهد الحسيني

LETTER FROM THE EDITOR

As we approach the end of the book, we should stop for a moment to express our gratitude to those who helped us make this book a success.

We would like to thank Dr. Saleh Ambah, Dean of the College, for his continuous encouragement in this project and every other project initiated by the students, and Mr. Abdul-Mannan Tourjouman, Dean of Student Affairs, for his interest and precious advice to us. We would also like to thank Mr. Fouad Abou-Hamdan for his assistance on some of our problems, and the Al-Mutawa Press for their encouragement and consideration.

Our first yearbook was published last year, under the Editorship of Abdullah Mugairin who initiated the idea at the College. This book which you hold in your hands is our second edition edited this year by the Cultural Committee of the Student Union with the help of the Photography Club.

In the name of all the students, we would like to thank all those who generously supported us by advertising in this book. They are responsible in making this book financially possible.

The purpose of this book is to give the student something to save by which he can always remember his College, classmates, faculty, administration, facilities, and activities.

At the same time we hope to give those persons who are not familiar with the College an idea of who we are, what we do, how we do it, and what we aim for the future.

Editor in Chief
Moujahed Husseini

Appendix V - College of Petroleum & Minerals Student Yearbook

لجنة الكتاب السَّنَوي
THE YEAR BOOK COMMITTEE

من اليمين : شعراوي – شاهين ، محرر القسم العربي – حسيني ، محرر القسم الانجليزي – كوهجي ، رئيس نادي التصوير سمير شبيب – نور الدين عباس .

(R to L): Sha'rawi; Shaheen, Arabic Editor; Husseini, English editor; Kohaji, Chairman of the Photo Club; Samir Shabib; Nuruddin Abbas.

EDITORIAL BOARD

Editor In Chief:	Moujahed Al-Husseni
Manager Editor:	Henry Shaheen
Photography Editor:	Yousef Kohaji
Staff:	Nourreddin Abbas, Mounir Sha'rawi Mazin Badr, Faik Hafedh Hani Ghalib, Said Shamsi
Photographers:	Samir Shabib, Abdullah Sadat Samir Abdul-Jawad, Ibrahim Ghamdi

AL-KULLIYAH is published annually by the Student Union of the College of Petroleum and Minerals, and edited by the Cultural Committee. Photographs are supplied by the Photography Club (with the exception of Student Portraits) and the book is printed by the Al-Mutawa Press.

Appendix V - College of Petroleum & Minerals Student Yearbook

... والاهتمام بالطالب يتجاوز كثيراً مجرد الاهتمام بدراسته المرسومة أو باختيار الفرع الذي سيتخصص بدراسته . فاذا أردنا للطالب في كلية البترول والمعادن أن يكون عضواً نافعاً قائداً في المجتمع ، وجب علينا أن نزوده بأكثر من مجرد مجموعة من الدراسات المرسومة و بدرجة علمية في أحد ميادين التخصص لأن الدراسة المجردة والدرجة العلمية التي تقتصر على انها شهادة للطالب بأنه نجح في الدروس المقررة لا تؤهلان الخريج للقيام بالمسؤوليات التي نتنظر منه أن يقوم بها . والواقع أنه يحتاج الى شخصية متكاملة تقوم على سمو الخلق حسن التصرف والحماس للعمل بقدر ما تقوم على التحصيل العلمي ...
من كلمة العميد في فلسفة التعليم التكنولوجي

الظهران ٢٨ جمادى الثانية ١٣٨٥
الموافق ٢٣ أكتوبر ١٩٦٥

...The College of Petroleum and Minerals, in its own small field of influence, has chosen to demonstrate that we are capable of successful competition in science, in engineering, and in the technical fields of petroleum and minerals, in precisely those areas where the technological world has excelled. We intend to turn out of our College young men who will know their profession, and will know that they know it, and never again need feel insecure or inadequate. We intend to provide our Country with the human resources on which our Government can confidently base any policy of development...
From Dean's "The Role of The College of Petroleum and Minerals in the Industrialization of Saudi Arabia."
Conference on Science and Technology in Developing Countries.

Beirut - A.U.B. 7 November 1967

BIBLIOGRAPHY

Ali, Abdullah Yusif, *The Holy Qur'an Text*, Translation and Commentary, American International Printing Co. ,1946.

Almana, Mohammed, *Arabia Unified. A Portrait of Ibn Saud*, Hutchinson Benham, London. 1980.

Aramco and Its World edited by Ismail I. Nawwab, Peter C. Speer, and Paul Hoye, Washington, D.C. - Arabian American Oil Co., 1980.

Aramco, Facts and Figures, Dhahran, Saudi Arabia. 1983.

Berger, Morroe, *The Arab World Today* Doubleday and Co., Inc., Garden City, New York. 1962.

Butler, Grant C., *Kings and Camels*, The Devin-Adair Company, New York. 1960.

Carter, Jimmy, *The Blood of Abraham*, Houghton Mifflin Co., Boston. 1985.

Bantam/Britannica Books, *The Arabs, People and Power*, 1978.

Farah, Caesar E., *Islam, Beliefs and Observances* Barrons Educational Series, Inc. 1968.

Findley, Paul, *They Dare to Speak Out*, Lawrence Hill & Co., Westport, Connecticut. 1985.

BIBLIOGRAPHY

Fry, C. George and James Roy King, *The Middle East: Crossroads of Civilization* Charles E. Merril Publishing Co., Columbus, Ohio. 1973.

Holden, David and Richard Johns, *The House of Saud: The Rise and Rule of the Most Powerful Dynasty in the Arab World,* Holt, Rinehart and Winston, New York. 1981.

Howarth, D.A., *The Desert King: A Life of Ibn Saud*, Collins, London, McGraw-Hill, New York. 1964.

King Fahd University of Petroleum and Minerals, *Partners For Progress,* Fourth Edition, KFUPM Press, Dhahran Saudi Arabia. 1985.

Lamb, David, *The Arabs, Journey Beyond The Mirage,* Random House, New York. 1987.

Lawrence, T. E., *Seven Pillars of Wisdom,* Penguin Books, Inc. 1976.

Lawrence, T. E., *Revolt in the Desert,* George H. Doran Company, New York. 1927.

Lewis, Bernard, *The Arab's History,* Harper & Row, New York. 1960.

Ministry of Education, Department of Antiquities and Museums, *An Introduction to Saudi Arabian Antiquities,* Kingdom of Saudi Arabia, Riyadh, Dr. Abdulaziz Al-Khowaiter, Minister of Education. 1975.

Nazer, Hisham Mohaddin, *Achievements of the Development Plans (1970 to 1987)*, Ministry of Planning.

BIBLIOGRAPHY

Patai, Raphael, *The Arab Mind*, Charles Scribner's Sons, New York. 1976.

Rashid, Nasser I. and Esber I. Shaheen, *King Fahd and Saudi Arabia's Great Evolution*, International Institute of Technology, Inc., Joplin, Missouri. 1987.

Saudi Arabia, A Country Study, edited by Richard F. Nyrop, The American University. 1984.

Sheean, Vincent, *Faisal, the King and His Kingdom*, University Press of Arabia, England. 1975.

Shipler, David K., *Arab and Jew, Wounded Spirits in a Promised Land*, Penguin Books, New York, 1987.

Stegner, Wallace, *Discovery, The Search for Arabian Oil*, Middle East Export Press, Inc., Beirut. 1971.

Thomas, Lowell, *With Lawrence in Arabia*, Garden City Publishing Co., Garden City, New York. 1924.

Thesiger, Wilfred, *Arabian Sands*, Dutton, New York. 1959.

Winder, R. Bayly, *Saudi Arabia in the Nineteenth Century*, St. Martin's Press, New York. 1965.

INDEX

A

al-Abbas, Abu Mansour 11
Abbasid Caliphs of Baghdad 12
Abbasid Empire 14
Abdo, Bob 162
Abdul Aziz 19, 21-24, 341-42, 345-46, 350, 367, 369
Abdullah, Crown Prince 55
Abha 393-95, 397
Abraham 3, 8-9
Abraham's journey x
Abu Al-Hammayel, Mohammad 82
Abu Dhabi 21, 257, 302
Academic Buildings with Parking Garages 192
academic program 130, 132, 135
Accreditation Board for Engineering and Technology 130
Aden 4, 9, 15, 23
Administration Building 192, 227, 340
Administration of the University — 1985 138
adult education 41
advance payment 219, 221-22
Africa 8-9, 11-13, 328
al-Ageel, Abdul Rahman 158
agricultural development 393
Agriculture 40, 43, 45-46
Ahmed, Maqbool 173-74, 176
al-Ain in Abu Dhabi 383
Air Force 264, 403-4
Airport shipping and receiving 222
Akbar the Great 14
Akins, James 331, 332
Algeria 73, 82, 91
Alhambra in Spain 11, 13, 93, 98
Ali, son of Sharif Hussein 24
Almana, Abdul Aziz 350
Ambah, Saleh 62, 73-4, 76-8, 80, 83-6, 88-9, 95, 98, 100-05
American Businessmen's Association in Dhahran 260
American Declaration of Independence 19
American Embassy 391
American legation 33
American schools in the Middle East 250
American University in Beirut 137, 208, 210
Amir Faisal, Saudi Foreign Minister 29
Amirates, Fourteen 52
Amman, Jordan 371-73, 378
Andalusia 11
Anglo-Saudi treaty of 1915 22
antenna system, central 263
Appling, Bruce 306
Aqaba 373
Arab League 35
Arab nationalism 303
Arab nations 302
Arab News ii, 347, 358
Arab-Israeli conflict 3, 48
Arabia Petrae 8
Arabian Democracy 53
Arabian Gulf viii, 14, 15, 24, 129, 133, 136, 195, 264, 398
Arabian Peninsula 3-4, 13-14, 17, 20, 28-29, 33, 35, 47, 278-79, 303, 367, 379, 385
Arabian-Japanese Oil Company 81
Arabic calendar 293, 309
Arafat, Yasser 167
Aramco (Arabian American Oil Co.) ix, 30, 35, 59-70, 73-74, 76, 80-81, 83, 85-87, 92, 94-95, 100, 107, 110-11, 156, 159, 180, 202, 204, 206-207, 210-11, 225, 229, 246, 249, 254, 256-58, 262-64, 267, 315-16, 345, 347, 363-64, 379-83, 390, 398, 411-12
"Aramco And Its World" magazine 35
Aramco Historical and Cultural Society 381
Aramco soccer field 69

467

INDEX

Aramco-last Christmas pageant 256
Aramco's Local Industrial Developments Depart. 85
Arches, monumental royal 355, 358
Art of negotiation 274
Ashby, Lynn
   of the *Houston Post* ii, 329, 364
Asia 8, 14
"Asia" (Magazine) viii
Asia Minor 4
Asir 52, 305
Ataturk, Mustafa Kemal 14
Athens 164, 250
Athletic Stadium ix
al-Auda, Abdul Aziz 299
Auda Abu Tayi, Howeitat Chieftain (Anthony Quinn) 279, 378
AWACS 287

B

Baalbek in the Beka valley 162
Babb, Keith 171-172, 406
Baghdad 11-12, 14, 400
Bahrain 27-30, 32, 82, 129, 251, 257, 267, 301-302, 309-11, 335, 362-63, 367
Bakhrebah, Saleh A. i, viii, 61, 70, 103, 151, 157-58, 160, 172, 174, 177-79, 181, 189, 191, 205, 220-21, 233, 250-51, 254, 267, 274, 278, 300, 309, 312, 323, 334-35, 339-42, 345, 350-56, 358, 385, 409
Bakr, Abu 10
Bakr, Bakr Abdullah bin 66, 69, 73, 76-77, 82-83, 86, 132, 137-38, 158, 165, 172, 179-81, 206, 275, 278, 294-95, 335, 345, 352, 405-06
Balfour Declaration 16
Bangladesh 175-76
Banking 40, 258, 298
Battle, Clark 348

Bedouin 22, 24, 216, 258, 275-76, 284, 293, 301, 304, 307-08, philosophy 273
Begin, Menachim 16
Beirut 147, 152, 154, 161-65, 167, 170, 206, 208, 210, 237, 260, 304, 373, 378, (See Nightclub)
Beta Company 237
British and French "betrayal" of Arabs 23
Bible 317-19, 321
   New Testament 3
   Old Testament 3-4, 318
Biblical names 298
Bids and Tenders Committee 160, 221, 239, 274, 385
Boards
   Accreditation Board for Engineering and Technology 130
   Board of Directors of Saudi Aramco 207
   Board of the University _1985 137
   Civil Service Board 54
   Investigative and Control Board 54
   Saudi Labor Board 221
Bradford, Glen 240
Brailas, Alex 152, 156
Brandie, June 174, 263
Brandie, Keith 174
brick piers, two 348
British 22, 218, 220, 223, 228, 231, 257, 262, 278-79, 285
   British Aircraft Corporation 257
   British Airways 259
   British Bank 258
   British Caledonian 259
   typical British expatriate 154
   British football (American soccer) 155
   British High Commissioner, in Iraq, Sir Percy Cox 27
   British role in Palestine 323
Bronze Age 4
Bruce, Bob 169

INDEX

Buddhist 224, 236, 323
Buildings
  454 Housing Units 192
  Academic Buildings with Parking Garages 192
  Administration Building 192, 228, 340, Old 74
  Athletic Stadium vii
  Building for Highly Volatile Chemicals 190
  Building No. 11, the Gymnasium 189
  Conference Center 164, 192
  Data Processing Center 136
  Energy Research Laboratory 180, 195, 198, 201
  English Language Center 136, 141
  Faculty Housing 195
  Heavy Equipment Laboratory 238, 243-44
  Library 135-36, addition 241
  Press Building 190
  Recreation Center 230, 268
  UPM Computer Center 81
Bulaihid, Abdul Aziz 158
Bullock, Tom ii, 93, 106, 149, 334, 406, 407
Bush, Vice President George 325
Byzantine Empire North of the Mediterranean 13
Byzantines 10

C

Cairo University 73
Cal Tech 207
California Arabian Standard Oil Co. (see CASOC) 30
California Institute of Technology (Cal Tech)130
Caliph (or Imam), First, Second, Third and Fourth 10
Camp David Accords 16
Canterbury Society 254

"Caravans to Mecca" 8, 17
CASOC 30, 32-33
Caudill, Bill 93, 103, 106, 114, 149, 334, 391
cavern 224-25
Central Najd 33
Central Research Workshop 136
Chairmen of the Academic Departments 140
Chambers, Don 154, 157, 169, 170, 217, 250, 261, 271, 312, 342, 348, 385, 392, 406, 409
Choi, J.K. 194
Christian Christianity x, 3-4, 9, 11, 224, 319-20, 323, 350, 372
Christian reconquest of Spain 12
Christian Science Monitor 355-6, 358
Christmas 361, 367-68
Churchill, Winston 16
CIA 64
Civil Aviation Department 89
Civil Service Board 54
Civil Service Bureau 53
Civil war in Lebanon 161, 208
Clinic 180, 195
CNN 245, 411
College of Industrial Management 275
College of Petroleum and Minerals ix, 59-60, 132
Colorado School of Mines 130
Columbia University 92
Commodore Hotel 162
Commitees
  Bids and Tenders Committee 160, 218, 222, 240
  Communications Committee 221
  Visitation committee from the United States 130
Communications 40, 43
Competitive bidding 103
Conference Center 164, 192
Consolidated Construction Co. (CCC) 164, 171, 175, 181, 186, 189-190, 192, 206, 220, 227, 247, 307, 309, 322, 340, 345-46

INDEX

Consortium of American Universities 130
Converts to Islam 320
Cook, Bob 170-71, 216, 266
Cordoba 11, 13
Councils
 "Majlis Al Shura", (Consultative Council) 53
 Council of Deans _ 1985 138
 Council of Ministers 35-36, 50, 52-53, 91, 132
Court of Grievances 54
CPM 61-63, 67, 73-74, 76-78, 81-82, 84-86, 88-89, 93-94, 98, 100, 102, 104-106, 110
Crane, Charles, American philanthropist 28
Cretin, Harry 171-72, 176, 224, 234, 238, 245
Creviston, Vance 219
Crown Prince,
 Fahd bin Abdul Aziz 53, 186, 345
 Faisal bin Abdul Aziz 50, 91, 161, 369
 Saud bin Abdul Aziz 35
CRS (Caudill, Rowlett, and Scott) viii, ix, 61, 63-67, 69, 88, 93-95, 98-107, 110-11, 114, 147, 149, 150-52, 154-56, 160-62, 164-65, 169-72, 176-77, 180-81, 186, 189, 195, 198, 208, 210-11, 216, 222, 231-37, 240, 245, 247, 250-51, 259, 264, 267, 285, 288, 296, 306-307, 329, 334, 337, 346, 348, 354, 359, 362, 371, 382, 391-92, 398, 406-407
CRS Christmas party 251
CRS landscaping department 211
CRS lawyers in Riyadh 233
CRS legal department, Houston 232
CRS office in Beirut 154, 162
 in Dhahran 173, 175
 in Houston 225, in Riyadh 233

CRS, system of design and programming, "squatters" 198
CRS team 95, 98-100, 102-103, 107, 114, 306, 406
CRSS 63, 384-385, 391, 395, 406, 409
Crusaders 13, 317, 378
Custodian of the Two Holy Mosques, King Fahd 47

D

Dabbagh, Abdullah 207, 351
Daboussi, Osama 198, 201
Dahna (red desert) 30, 276
Dahna in Central Arabia 30
Damascus 11, 22, 349, 371, 372, 378
Dammam 73, 76, 157, 230-31, 246, 257, 264, 294
Dammam, the Oberoi Hotel 246
Dammam Well No. 1 32
Dammam Well No. 7 32, 70
Dammam-Riyadh train 390
Daniel, Nagib 339
Dantziguian, Gabis 165, 167
Data Processing Center 136
Davies, Fred 28, 30, 335
Davis, Lloyd 346
Day of rest 299
Dead Sea 371
Decker, Wendell vii
Delmon Hotel 310
Developments
 Industrial Development 40, 44
 First and Second Development Plans (1970-1980) 45
 Third Development Plan (1980-1985) 46
 Fourth Development Plan (1985-1990) 46
Dhahran Academy 247, 250, 258, 264
Dhahran International Airport 104, 259, 284
Dhahran International Hotel 411

INDEX

Dhahran Outing Group (DOGS) 381
Dhahran rim 110
Dhahran-Aramco complex 66
Dhahran-Dammam highway 100
Dhana, or the central desert 393
"dhows" 363
"dignity and pride" 276
Dilmun 363
al-Din, Salah (Saladin) 13
Director General of Technical Affairs 205, 271
Director of the Energy Lab 201
Director of the Research Institute 207
Diriyah 19, 20, 369, 391
Discovery Space Shuttle 207
Doctoral programs 135
Dodgson, Trevor 170
"Domat Al-Jandl" 386
"Domat of the Stones" 386
"Domata" by Pliny 386
Dormitories 160, 190, 195, 198, 202
"Doumaitha" by Ptolemy 386
Dubai 21, 257, 302, 382
Dumah 385, 386

E

earthquake 338-39
Eastern Gulf Oil Company 28
Eastern Province viii, 9, 27-28, 30, 53, 59-61, 98, 104, 107, 190, 211, 314, 345, 355, 367, 393
Education 39-42, 45 (see also American Schools in the Middle East; Elementary Schools; Ford Foundation, Educational Facilities Laboratory; Girl's education; Girl's schools; Madras Thagher School; Near East School Assoc. (NESA); Saudi Arabian International School (SAIS) (Dhahran Academy); Saudi Ministry of Education; Secondary Schools.)
"Education for the New Japan" 92

Egypt 8, 12-13, 15-16, 20-21, 23, 35, 328, 397
Egyptian Mamluks 13
El Mareb, Sabah 164
Elat, the Israeli town 373
Electricity 40, 44-45
Elegance 295
Elementary schools 41, 350
eleven million riyals from Aramco 86
Energy Research Laboratory 180, 195, 198, 201, 234
English Language Center 136, 141
Escarpment 318, 394
European Renaissance 12
Express Contracting Company 162, 215, 237, 342

F

F-15's 285, 385
F-5's, U.S. made 285
faculty 131-33, 136, 141, 145
faculty housing 195
family 251, 289, 293, 295-96, 298, 300, 304, 310, 318
Family of the Prophet 10
Farsi, Mohammed 287
Fatamid Dynasty 12, 13
ibn Faysal, Abdul Rahman 20
Fertile Crescent 4
Filipino 220-21, 320, 347
Filipino cooks 380
Finlay, Ed ii, 61, 67, 85, 94, 99, 103, 114
First and Second Development Plans (1970-1980) 45
Fisk Electric and Telephone Company 346, 347
Fitts, Grant vii
Ford Foundation, Educational Facilities Laboratory 93
454 Housing Units 192
Fourth Development Plan (1985-1990) 46
Fulbright, Senator William 334

471

INDEX

G

General Audit Bureau 54
General Petroleum and Minerals Organization 54
Germany 15, 33
Ghengis Khan 14
al-Ghosaibi Hotel 245
Girls' education 45
Girls' schools 41
Golden Age of Islam 12
"Golden Decade" of Saudi Arabia 269
Government Office for Social Insurance (GOSI) 263
Granada 11, 13
Grand Mosque in Mecca 319, 349-50
Grandsons of Abdul Aziz 55-56
Great Britain 15-16, 24
"Green Line" 167
Gregorian (solar) calendar 367
al-Gureishi, Abdul Aziz 73
Gwaiz, Abdul Aziz 159

H

Hadhramaut, an area of Yemen 9, 179
Hagar 8
Hail 21, 23, 52
Haj 175, 311, 367, 378
Half Moon Bay 110, 133, 264, 267, 315
Hall, Mrs. Margaret ii, 79, 84-87, 92, 304
Hall, Robert King 67, 84-87, 91-93, 95, 98-99, 102, 104, 160, 204-206, 208, 228, 304, 352-53
Halley's Comet 389-90
Halliburton, Richard 161, 246
Hamilton, Lloyd, SOCAL's chief negotiator 29
Harems 289
al-Harthy, Abdul Rahman 219, 271
Harvard Law School, Cambridge, MA 91-92
al-Hasa, Eastern Province of Arabia 14, 22, 27

al-Hasa oasis 363-64, 367
Hashemites 22
Health Care and Welfare 40, 42
Heavy Equipment Laboratory 237-38
Heavy winds or "shamals" 266, 283, 305
Hellmuth Obata and Kassabaum of St. Louis HOK+4 391
Hendrickson, Bob 307
Herzl, Theodor 15
Hester, Keith; registrar 87
Hijaz 13, 22-23, 129
Hill country of Texas 394
Hofuf 22, 27, 331, 334, 363-64, 379, 392-93
Holiday Inn 245, 373, 397-98
  Revolving restaurant atop - Beruit 161
Holmes, Major Frank 27
Holy Koran and Sunna 47
Holzman, Philip 81
Hong Kong 171, 175
Hotels (see Dhahran International Hotel; al-Ghosaibi Hotel; Holiday Inn; Hyatt; Intercontinental; International; Khandara Palace; Marriott; Massarah Intercontinnenal - Taif; Meredien; Ramada; Red Sea Palace; Royal Gardens; Sheraton; Taj Sheba - Sanaa)
House of Rashid 21-23
House of Saud 19-21, 50-51, 54
Houston Post 329, 364
al-Hudud, Ash Shamaliyah (Northern Frontier) 52
Hughes Tool Co., in Houston 111
Husseini, Moujahed 434
Hyatt Hotel 245, 382, 398

I

IBM 1130 computer 131
IBM 360-50 system 80
IBM and Kodak equipment 136
IBM-1301 80

Index

Ibn Ajlan, Riyadh Governor 369
Ibn Saud 19, 21-23, 29, 279
Id Al-Adha 367
Iftar 299
"ijma" (consensus) 53
Ikhwan "Brethren" 22
Ikhwan warriors 56
India 11-12, 14, 91, 176, 192, 250
Industrial Development 40, 44
Inferiority 278, 279
Institut Francais du Petrol (IFP) of Paris, France 137
Intellectual Resources 57, 90, 433
Intercontinental Hotel 369, 371, 395
International Committee of the YMCA 85
International conference on solar energy 325
International Hotel 245, 299
International Organization of the Boy Scouts 389
International School 394, 411
Invasion by Israel 167
Investigative and Control Board 54
Iran 27, 154, 157, 250
Iraq 4, 8, 11, 15, 17, 21, 23-24, 27, 29, 33, 35, 82, 382, 409, 411
Iraqi Scud missile 348
Ishmael 8-9, 319, 386, 390
Islam x, 3, 4, 9-11, 12, 14, 17, 19-20, 22, 47, 48, 51, 53
Islamic congress in Mecca 24
Islamic dynasties, Syria, Iraq, and Spain 17
Islamic Spain 12
Israel 16, 269, 302, 321, 322, 323 372
Istanbul 245

J

"jails" 311-312
al-Jalal, Ibrahim 158
al-Jawf 23, 52
Jazirat Al-Arab 3, 4, 33

Jebel Dhahran 28, 30, 32-33, 61, 63, 74, 93, 95, 98, 104, 129, 142, 156, 173, 192, 228, 307, 335, 407
Jeddah, Saudi Arabia 23, 24, 28, 29, 76, 179, 245, 284, 287, 288, 317, 328, 329, 340, 347, 355, 356, 397
Jerash, Jordan 372
Jerusalem 4, 13
Jesus 3, 9, 298, 317, 319
  Jesus and the Disciples 371
Jet Propulsion Laboratory in Pasadena, California 206
Jewish lobby 334
The Jewish State 16
bin Jiluwi, Abdul Mohsin 314, 367
bin Jiluwi, Abdullah 367, 369
al-Jiluwi 54
Jizan 53
Jordan 4, 8, 16, 17, 21, 60, 371-373, 381
Joseph 385
Jubail 22, 30, 249, 284, 299, 306, 361-363, 398
Judaism x, 3, 4
al-Juraib, Abdul Mohsin 282

K

Kabah 9, 319
Kamis Mushayt 249, 394
Karak, old castle fort 378
Karimullah, Indian secretary 350
Kazma Palace 29
Kennedy, John F. vii
Kenya 328
Kerr, Dick 30
KFUPM ii, v, 59, 133, 136, 142
bin Khalifa, Sheik Sulman 433
al-Khalifas in Bahrain 21
Khalil, Abdul Raouf Hasan 397
Khandara Palace Hotel 329, 355
al-Khasindar 355, 358

INDEX

Khayal, Adnan 106, 250
Khaybar 9, 23
al-Khobar 30, 156, 202, 204, 216-17, 228, 231, 251, 257-58, 281, 287, 294, 296-97, 314, 341, 346-47, 351, 355, 390, 411
Khomeini, Ayatollah 317
Khorasan 11
Kim, Jong Chi 236, 241
King Abdul Aziz viii, ix, 27-29, 32-33, 35-36, 40, 42, 47, 50-51, 91-92, 173, 192, 294, 323, 342, 345-46, 369, 433
King Abdul Aziz Air Base for Royal Saudi Air Force 284
King Abdul Aziz City for Science and Tech. (KACST) 142
King Abdul Aziz Monument, Inscription 433
King Abdul Aziz's 1939 encampment in Dhahran 90
King and Queen of Malaysia 180, 325
King and Queen of Spain 180, 325
King Fahd bin Abdul Aziz 40, 46-48, 55, 367, 397, 412
King Fahd University
of Petroleum and Minerals i, iii, v, ix, 30, 42, 76, 129, 131, 137, 145, 406-7, 411-12
King Faisal ix, 50, 53, 73, 80-82, 91, 149, 161, 175, 204, 247, 355, 369
King Faisal University 42, 334, 367
King Ferdinand and Queen Isabella 13
King Khaled 50, 53, 170, 186, 355, 369
King Khaled International Airport 398
King of Central Arabia and the East coast 279
King of Hijaz 24
King of Saudi Arabia 180
King Saud 50, 59-60, 369

King Saud University 42, 238, 391
King-Crane Commission 16
Kingdom of Saba 8, 384
Kirkwood, Mrs. Grace 157, 208, 210, 211
Kissinger, Henry 331-32
Kobs, E.C. 233, 362
al-Koheji, Yousef 82, 158
Konash, Farouk 341, 352, 405
Koran 3, 9-10, 19, 36, 317, 319, 321, 385
Korean 173, 175, 184, 192, 217, 224, 234, 235, 236, 240, 241, 272, 320
Korean Airlines 259
Kriedy, Samir 210
Kuwait 21, 154, 170, 257, 302, 382, 409

L

Labor Board 220-21
Lady Erskine, British lady 328
Lake Forest College, Illinois 92
language 249, 272, 301, 303
Laser Laboratory 201, 234
Lasprogato, Victor 169, 170
"Lawrence of Arabia" i, 23, 161, 276, 278-79, 378, 373, 378, 381
Lawrence, Charles ii, 64-67, 85-86, 93-95, 98-103, 107, 110, 114-15, 180, 210, 306, 334, 373, 378, 398
Lawyer, Frank 162, 180
League of Nations 15
Lebanese 154, 161-67, 184, 210, 215, 220, 237, 247, 260, 269, 281, 302, 312-13, 322
Lebanon 15, 21, 35, 60, 82, 88, 269, 302, 372
Lhasa 367, 368
Library 135-36
Library addition 230

INDEX

Library Infor. Retrieval Services
  1. Lockheed's "DIALOG" 136
  2. Systems Development
     Corporation's ORBIT 136
Life and housing on the campus 296
London 152, 171, 328, 347,
  355, 358, 361, 405
L'Orangerie, a fine French restaurant
  167
Lord Balfour
  British Foreign Secretary 16
Lovell, James (astronaut) 347

M

Madain Saleh, Saudi Arabia
  8, 373, 381, 394
al-Madinah 52
Madras Thagher School 179
Majlis 51, 53
"Majlis Al Shura", (Consultative
  Council) 53
Makkah 52
Malaysia 12, 325, 395
Malaysian 320
Manama 301
Marriott Hotel 245, 329, 391
Marxism 48
Mashrabiyas 397
al-Musmak Fortress 21, 367, 369
Massachusetts Institute of Technology
  130, 137
Massarah Intercontinental Hotel, Taif
  395
May, Lewis 211
McClelland, Bram 104
McClelland Engineers
  Houston 111, 225, 235
Mecca, Saudi Arabia ix, 8-9, 14, 17,
  19-20, 24, 27, 91, 129, 158, 175,
  311, 318-19, 349-50, 368, 378,
  403-404
Medan Plaza 192, 340
Medina 8-10, 14, 17, 19-20, 22,
  24, 381, 394

Meridien Hotel 245, 260, 372
Mesopotamia 8, 11, 23
Michigan,
  The University of 130
Middle East viii, 3, 8, 11, 12, 15,
  27-29, 33, 132, 136, 149, 152,
  154-55, 161-62, 164, 171, 192,
  201, 206, 211, 232, 239, 250,
  260, 269, 295, 302, 304, 311,
  321, 355
Middle East Airlines 88, 152, 164
Midianites 385
Milwaukee School of Engineering 130
Minister of Higher Education 136-37
Minister of Petroleum and Mineral
  Resources 91
Minister of Petroleum and Minerals
  59-60, 66, 136
Minister of Planning 39
Ministry of Defense 73, 105-106
Ministry of Higher Education
  61, 74, 89, 131, 138
Ministry of Justice 50
Ministry of Petroleum
Ministry of Petroleum and Minerals
  61, 74, 76, 88, 105, 173, 353
Ministry of Petroleum building,
  Riyadh 98
al-Moghrabi, Abdul Aziz 285
Mogul India 14
Mohammed, the Prophet 3, 9-11,
  14, 17, 47-48, 317, 321, 400
Mongols 14
Moorish architecture 98
Mormons 254
Moses 378
Mount Hira 9
Mount Nebo 378
Movies 263
Mufti, Abdullah i, ii, 50, 59, 77-79,
  82-84, 89, 98, 152, 158, 179, 251,
  278, 285
Muhammad Ali, Governor,
  Ottoman Province of Egypt 20

Index

Musa, driver 373, 378
Music club 83
Musket balls 386
Muslim 9-11, 13-15, 247, 299, 318-20, 349-50, 367, 381, 385, 404
al-Muwahidun 19

N

Nabateans 8, 373, 381
Nafud desert 129
Nairobi 328
Najd 19-22, 24
Najran 8-9, 53
Nasir, Nadim ii, 80
Nasiriyah oasis 369
National Guard 55
Natural resource of crude oil 404
Navy 403-4
Nazer, Hisham Mohaddin 39, 45, 91
Nazer, Reda 74
Neal, Conrad 151, 179, 231, 251, 329
Near East School Assoc. (NESA) 250
Neolithic Age 4
NESA Conference 164
New Administration Building 192
New generation of Saudis 359, 405, 407
New Westminister Dictionary of the Bible 386
New York University 91
News media during Gulf War 245
Nightclub, Beirut 162
Nile river 4
1984 Olympics 190
Noah's son, Shem (Sem) 4
Noble, George 104-6, 169
North African Arab countries 382
North Compound 76, 78
North Yemen 383-85, 406, 409
Northrup 249, 296, 313
Northwestern University, Chicago vii
Nye, Ed 104

O

Office boys 175-76
Ohliger, Floyd ix, 30, 32, 345
Oil embargo 149, 332
Oil pipeline valve opening 432-3
Old Administration Building 74
Oman 13, 20-21, 257, 302, 379, 382-83
Omar 10, 385
189 Faculty Houses project 154, 162, 215, 237, 247, 312, 342
OPEC 74, 91
Orchards of grapes, pomegranates, and dates 386
Organ. for Public Services and Discipline 54
Oriental Hotel, Bangkok 166
Ottoman Confederation 14
Ottoman Empire 14-15, 20, 22-23
al-Owaid, Mohammed 179
Owen, John, U.S. Vice-Consul 355

P

Pakistan 173, 175-76, 192, 326
Paleolithic (Stone Age) 4
Palestine 8, 12, 15-16, 23, 87, 269, 302, 304, 321-23
   British "betrayal" 323
   "national home" for the Jewish people 16
Palestine Liberation Organ. (PLO) 322
Palmyra 8
Pan-Arab Movement 303
Paris fashions 281, 295
Parthenon, Athens 95
Partners for Progress 129, 133, 142
Paseur, Herb 94, 100, 106, 149
Pasha, Ibrihim 20
Patriot missiles 411
Patterson, Frank 66
Paul's Gate 372
Pena, Willie 99, 114

INDEX

Pendleton, Scott 265, 347
Perry, Bill 106-7
Persia 10, 14, 129
Persian (Arabian) Gulf viii, 4, 8, 23, 129, 267, 304, 307
Personal History by Vincent Sheean 161
Petra 8, 373, 381
Pharoan, Gaith 192
Phase I 104, 110, 169-70
Phases II and III 104, 110, 154, 156, 189, 325
Phase IV 114, 170-71, 179, 181, 186, 189-92, 222, 224, 312, 339, 346
  Phase IV-B Revisions 191, 192
Philby, Harry St. John 28-29, 379
Philippine Airlines 259
Philippines 12
Physical Education Depart. 131, 136, 141
Pickering, William 206-7
Pilgrimage to Mecca 17, 175
Pilkington Company of England 192
Pioneer geologists of Aramco 364
Pioneers of the New Saudi Generation 434
Pipeline through Syria, Jordan, and Lebanon 60
Planetarium 202
Porro, Amedeo ii, 73-74, 76, 87, 91
Pre-qualification, Two-tier System 189
Press Building 190
Princes
  Abdullah, Crown Prince 55
  Abdul Aziz bin Salman 341
  Bandar, bin Sultan (Saudi Ambassador to USA) 285
  Mansour bin Bandar 285
  Mohammed bin Fahd, Amir of Eastern Province 211, 367
  Sultan bin Salman (astronaut) 207, 209, 341
  Saud al-Faisal, Saudi Foreign Minister 201

Prince Philip of England 180, 184, 325
Princeton University 130
Professor Whiting viii
Prog. for vocational training (VOTRAKON) 275
Programs of study 134
Protector of the Holy Cities 24
Pseudo-colonialism 70
Public theaters 257

Q

al-Qahtani 346, 348
Qahtani-Fisk 346, 348
Qasim area 22
Qasr Al-Ukaider 385
Qasr Marid 385
Qatar 21, 33, 257, 302
Qatif 9, 22, 363
Queen Elizabeth 180, 184, 325
Queen of Denmark 180, 325
Queen of Sheba 8, 384
"Quest For Excellence" 73, 145
Quraysh tribe 9
al-Qurayyat 52

R

Rabya Landscaping Company 210
Rainy season 227, 236
Ramada Hotel 245
Ramadan 83, 223, 299, 367
Rangeley, Colorado Junior College 93
Ras Tanura 32, 33, 87, 249
Rasheed, Pakistani secretary 391
al-Rashid, Harun 12
al-Rashid, Nasser 74, 88-9, 151, 251, 395
Rashids 21, 22, 23, 367
Reaction floor 238-39
Ready-mix concrete plants 215
Recreation Center 229, 262
Rector 132, 138, 141
Red Sea viii, 4, 12, 14, 15, 23-4, 319, 373, 394, 397-98

Index

Red Sea Palace Hotel 397
Redec Daelim 160, 176, 184, 190, 192, 195, 224, 235, 247, 307
Reformist Movement of Abdul Wahhab 19
Religious Facilities (including Haj Facilities) 40
Research Institute 136, 138, 141-42, 180, 201, 206-8
Residential mosque 350
Revolving restaurant atop the Holiday Inn 161
Rhodes 164, 250
Rice Institute, Houston viii, 150, 236, 309, 346, 400, 405, 407
"rivers of blood" 386
Riyadh 19-21, 24, 27, 32-3, 76, 88, 91-2, 98, 106, 161, 175, 177, 233, 238, 245, 258, 276, 282, 284, 287-88, 293, 305, 325, 329, 341, 367-69, 371, 390-93, 398, 411-12
Riyadh University 61
Rochester, University of 130
Rocheville, Charley 30
Roman culture 381
Roman Empire 8-9, 321
Roosevelt, President 35, 92, 323
Rowlett, John 94, 149
Roy, Paul 156
Royal Charter of the Institution 129
Royal Court or Diwan 51
Royal decree of King Faisal 204
Royal Gardens Hotel 166
Rub Al-Khali 24, 29, 379-80
Rupp, George President of Rice University ii
Russia 11
Russian compound 385
Russian MIGs 385

S

al-Sabah family 21
al-Saber, Mansour ii, 158, 172, 174, 177-78, 191, 205, 219, 233, 238, 271, 274, 307, 317, 323, 341, 352, 386
Safavid Persia 14
Safeway store 157, 281
Sagaf 237
Sakaka 385
Sakaka fort 386, 389
Salam, Pakistani driver and guide 391-92
Salt Water Conversion Commission 89
Sanaa, North Yemen 383, 385, 409
Sanitary Systems, Municipal 40
al-Saud 20-21
al-Saud Family 51, 54, 367, 369
al-Saud, Abdul Aziz ibn Abdul Rahman Al-Faysal 17, 21
ibn Saud, Muhammad 19
Saud Al Kabir 54
Saud dynasty 24
Saud Royal Family 47, 403
Saudi Arabia, home of Islam 17
  pesonality differences 269-270
  prime political factor in Arab world 269
  Seventy-fifth anniversary 403
  typical native attire 282
Saudi Arabian International School (SAIS) (Dhahran Academy) v, 247, 249
Saudi attitude 256
Saudi Boy Scout camp 389
Saudi Business magazine ii
Saudi camp 61-2
Saudi Consolidated Electrical Co. (SCECO) 239-40
Saudi Democracy 301
Saudi Gazette 358
Saudi government 220, 232, 263-64
Saudi granite 340

INDEX

Saudi Labor Board 221
Saudi legation 33
Saudi Ministry
 Engineering Department 232
Saudi Ministry of Education 247
Saudi Monetary Agency (SAMA) 54
Saudi resolve 412
Saudi scientists 198
Saudi stock market 259
Saudi teenagers 249
Saudi travelers checks 259
Saudi-ization 207, 262
Schoenberger, John 172
Schou, Carl
 German-American project manager 216
Scott, Wallie viii, 149, 306, 406
Scripture of Islam 9
Scud missiles 411
Second Crusade 13
Secondary schools 41
Secretaries 173-74, 176, 263
Seikaly, Jack 162-64, 237
Seikaly, Richard 162
Seljuks 12-13
Semitic 4, 8, 319
Senator William Fulbright 334
Seven Pillars of Wisdom i
Seville, Spain 11, 13
Shah Abbas the Great 14
Shamir, Yitzhak 16
Sharia, fundamental law of Islam
 19, 36, 47, 51
Sharif Hussein 22-3, 279
Sharif of Mecca 17
Sharifs of Mecca and Medina 14
Sharjah 21, 383
Sheean, Vincent *"Faisal, the King and His Kingdom"* 161
al-Sheikh family 50
Shell (petrochemical project), Jubail 299
Sheraton Hotel 381-83, 412
Shiite Fundamentalist Movement 162
Shiite regime in Iran 48

Shiites 10, 12, 302
Shilstone, Jim 110-11
 CRS consultant for concrete 110
Sinai 8, 13
Sirrine Co., South Carolina 407
Smittipong, Suthipan 180
Snyder, Harry 66-7, 85, 91-2
Soccer 69, 155, 189-90
Social life 251, 261
Social Security 264
South America 85, 92
Soviet Union 17, 48
Spain 11-13, 17
Squatters 198
Stanbaugh, John
 CRS bus. consultant, Tulsa, OK 106
Standard Oil Company of California
 (SOCAL) 28-30, 32, 335
Stanford University 73, 180
State of Israel 16
Steineke, Max ix, 32
al-Sudairi, Hassa Bint Ahmad 55
Sudairi Seven 55
Suez Canal 15, 23
Sulaiman, Sheikh Abdullah 29
Suleiman the Magnificent (1520-1566) 14
Sultan of Najd 24
sundial 339
Sunna (Sayings of the Prophet) 19, 36
Sunni state 12
Sunnis 10, 302
SUPPORTING SERVICES 1985
 136, 139
SWCC general manager, Mr. Jamjoom 89
Syndicate, London 27, 29
Syria 4, 8, 10-12, 15, 17, 21,
 23, 35, 60, 82, 371, 372

T

Table of construction at KFUPM 125
Tabuk, Saudi Arabia 9, 52
Taif 23, 249, 317, 318, 340,
 341, 345, 395, 397, 405

INDEX

Taisei Construction Company of Tokyo 110
Taj Sheba, Sanaa 383
Talmud 3
Tariki, Abdullah 59
Tarut Island 63, 363
Tarut island 9
Tayma 23
telephone system 169
Television, British and American programming 257
"Dallas" 167
10,000-seat Stadium 189
Tengler, Terry 111
Texas A&M University 347
al-Thanis in Qatar 21
"The Arab Nationalist Movement" _ Rice Inst. Theme viii
Thesiger, Wilfred 379
Third Development Plan (1980-1985) 46
Thomas, Joe ii, 67-9, 88, 98, 102, 104-7, 110-11, 114, 150-52, 170, 172, 179, 208, 231, 250-51, 306, 337
Thomas, Lowell 161
al-Thunayyan 54
"TIBs" 406
TOEFL, "Teaching of English as a Foreign Language" 249
Tooker, Harry 170-71
Torino, Italy 340
train from Dammam to Riyadh 368, 390-93
Train-Wreck Scheme 99
Transjordan 15, 35
Transportation 40, 43
Tripoli, North of Beirut 165
Trucial States 382
Tunisia 15, 73, 91
Turkey 14, 167, 216, 250
Turks 22, 23, 129
Turki ibn Abdullah, Saudi Ruler (1823-1834) 20
Twitchell, Karl 28, 29

U

U.S. ambassador 177, 331
U.S. consul in Dhahran 260
U.S. consulate 87, 247, 329, 342, 411
U.S. Embassy in Riyadh 391
U.S. Geological Survey 81
U.S. military mission 246
U.S. State Department 67, 372, 383-85
Udahliyah 249
Ulema, religious scholars 48
Umayyad Dynasty 11
Umayyad Mosque, Damascus 372
Umayyad prince, Abdul Rahman ibn Muawiyah Al-Dakhil 11
Unitarians 19
United Arab Emirates (UAE) 33, 382-83
United Nations 16, 35
Univ. of California at Los Angeles (UCLA) 39
Univ. of Petroleum and Minerals (CPM) (UPM) ix, 60-1, 68-9, 76, 89-0, 92-5, 98-107, 110-11, 114, 149-54, 162, 170, 173, 191, 201-11, 223, 229-30, 250, 263, 334, 337, 341, 348-50, 353, 356, 391, 405-6, 433
Universities in Saudi Arabia 42
University of Arizona 341
University of Chicago 92
University of Colorado 179
University of Houston 80-81
University of Illinois 179
University of Michigan 92
University of Riyadh 98
University of Southern California 73, 180
University of Texas 88, 151, 180, 238
University sponsored research 142
University Women's Club 254, 262
UPM Computer Center 81
al-Uqayr 22, 379
al-Uyaynah 19

INDEX

V

VIP Train Project 354
Visitation committee from the United States 130
Von Weiss, Howard 171-72
VOTRAKON 276

W

Wade, The Honorable Robert H. B. ii
Wadi Rum 373, 378
ibn Abdul Wahhab, Muhammad 19, 50, 54
Wahhabi Reform Movement 17, 19
Walker, Wiley 406
Washington, D.C. ii, 29, 33, 383
Water Desalination 40, 44
Well
  No. 2-6 32
  No. 7 viii, 39, 204
Well of Zam Zam 319
Wentworth Institute 130
West Beirut 163, 165
Wheaton College
  Norton, Massachusetts 92
Wheeler, Margaret 92
Wilkinson, Bruce of CRS ii, 407
Willamet, Jimmy 346, 348
Wilson, President Woodrow 28
Wines, Don ii, 66, 94, 98-9, 101, 114, 237, 250-51, 313, 326, 348, 392, 409
World War I 14-15, 22-23, 27, 279
World War II 33, 35, 91-92, 223, 332

Y

Yamama Establishment 191
Yamama International Hotel, Riyadh 88
Yamani, Ahmed Zaki 60, 91
Yamani, Hashim 201
Yamani, Zaki 60-3, 73-4, 76, 81, 84, 86, 88-91, 179, 210, 326, 331-32, 352-53, 380
Yearbook of the Students 434 (see appendix V)
Yemen 8-9, 12, 14, 20, 23, 179, 379, 382-85, 406, 409
Yemeni 302, 312
Yenbo 398
Young Arab generation 405, yoke of bondage broken 405

Z

Zionism 15
Zionist Movement 23
Zionist, Militant 16